'An impressively researche[...] [...] is a penetrating psychological [...] an important contribution to t[...] [...]graph

'A wonderfully rounded portrait of the philandering king . . . Fraser has evoked a world by exercising the gifts that make her one of the most brilliant biographers of our time: her scholarship and her great humanity. Precise details bring the past to life' *Daily Telegraph*

'Enthralling . . . her prose veers between the authoritative and the racy and makes excellent use of contemporary sources, creating the most enjoyable domestic biography of Louis since Nancy Mitford's *The Sun King*, 40 years ago' *Daily Mail*

'As she demonstrated in previous biographies of Charles II and Marie Antoinette, for esoteric detail, for marrying moments of grace and wit, no other historian is Fraser's equal'
Independent on Sunday

'With warmth, humour and not a little gossipy relish, she draws us intimately into the psyche and mores of many ladies who moved, motivated and occasionally mastered the alpha male' *Tribune*

'No one writes about historical women as well as she does'
Daily Express

'All the scandal and brilliance and bling of Louis and his ladies is shown in context – social, dynastic, political, religious – but depicted so deftly and vividly that you're there . . . This is an intriguing insight into the shifting roles of aristocratic women in 17th-century France' *Tatler*

'Antonia Fraser is the queen of historical writing' *Sunday Herald*

In *Love and Louis XIV*, Antonia Fraser's expertise on women in history shines through, bringing a sympathetic warmth to her depiction of the Sun King's many love affairs, his vast sexual appetite and the sheer variety of female personalities in his intimate circle' *Irish Times*

'A scintillating new book . . . ambitious and original in approach'
Mail on Sunday

'Fraser's narrative is balanced, wise and entertaining. This is clearly the book she was born to write' *Literary Review*

'Her delightful book supports the contemporary observation that "court life provides the funniest scenes imaginable", but the scintillating narrative is underpinned by a serious theme, arising from the conflict between the king's sex drive and his search for salvation' *New Statesman*

'This lively, compelling book . . . This book is pitch-perfect and should have a wide appeal. Fully alert to developments within the growing subject of court studies, Antonia Fraser draws on a wide range of sources and has an assured sense of context. The result is a balanced, insightful and plausible exploration of the Sun King and his women' *Tablet*

'Antonia Fraser's enthralling new biography . . . Her prose veers between the authoritative and the racy and makes excellent use of contemporary sources, creating the most enjoyable domestic biography of Louis since Nancy Mitford's *The Sun King* 40 years ago' *Daily Irish Mail*

'To her task of recounting and analysing emotions at court, Antonia Fraser brings vast reading, the knowledge of the seventeenth century already shown in her lives of Oliver Cromwell and Charles II and her account of the Gunpowder Plot, and knowledge of the human heart' *Times Literary Supplement*

'Entrancing' *New Statesman*

'This is Louis XIV with the boring bits left out'
                                                            BBC History Magazine

'Fraser brilliantly reconstructs the politics and religion of a lost time. Her generosity and sympathy bring the Sun King and his court vividly to life' Ruth Scurr, Book of the Year, *The Times*

Since 1969, Antonia Fraser has written many acclaimed historical works which have been international bestsellers. These include the biographies *Mary Queen of Scots* (James Tait Black Memorial Prize), *Cromwell: Our Chief of Men* and *King Charles II, and The Gunpowder Plot: Terror and Faith in 1605* (St Louis Literary Award; CWA Non-Fiction Gold Dagger). Four highly praised books focus on women in history: *The Weaker Vessel: Woman's Lot in Seventeenth-Century England* (Wolfson Award for History, 1984), *The Warrior Queens: Boadicea's Chariot* (1988), *The Six Wives of Henry VIII* (1992) and *Marie Antoinette: The Journey* (Enid McLeod Literary Prize, Franco-British Society, 2001). Antonia Fraser is the editor of the series *Kings and Queens of England* (Weidenfeld & Nicolson), and wrote the volume *King James VI of Scotland, I of England.* Her latest book, *Love and Louis XIV: The Women in the Life of the Sun King* (2006), is published by Weidenfeld & Nicolson.

By Antonia Fraser

Mary Queen of Scots

Cromwell: Our Chief of Men

James VI of Scotland, I of England
(Kings and Queens series)

King Charles II

The Weaker Vessel: Woman's Lot
in Seventeenth-Century England

The Warrior Queens: Boadicea's Chariot

The Six Wives of Henry VIII

The Gunpowder Plot: Terror and Faith in 1605

Marie Antoinette: The Journey

Love and Louis XIV: The Women in the Life
of the Sun King

LOVE AND LOUIS XIV

The Women in the Life of the Sun King

Antonia Fraser

The Sun, by the light which it shines on those
other stars which surround it like a court, is most
assuredly the most vigorous and the most
splendid image of a great monarch.

Louis XIV, *Memoirs for the Instruction
of the Dauphin*, 1662

PHOENIX

A PHOENIX PAPERBACK

First published in Great Britain in 2006
by Weidenfeld & Nicolson
This paperback edition published in 2007
by Phoenix,
an imprint of Orion Books Ltd,
Orion House, 5 Upper St Martin's Lane,
London WC2H 9EA
An Hachette Livre UK company

1 3 5 7 9 10 8 6 4 2

A CIP catalogue record for this book
is available from the British Library.

ISBN 978-0-7538-2293-7

Typeset by Input Data Services Ltd, Frome

Printed and bound in Great Britain by Clays Ltd, St Ives plc

The Orion Publishing Group's policy is to use papers that
are natural, renewable and recyclable products and made
from wood grown in sustainable forests. The logging
and manufacturing processes are expected to conform to
the environmental regulations of the country of origin.

www.orionbooks.co.uk

FOR HAROLD

nobilis et Nobelius

CONTENTS

LIST OF ILLUSTRATIONS

xi

Louis XIV Retreating with his Seraglio, 1693, anonymous engraving. *The Trustees of the British Museum, Department of Prints & Drawings.*

Louise de La Vallière, date unknown, by Jean Nocret. *Châteaux de Versailles et de Trianon (© Photo RMN/ Gérard Blot).*

Louise de La Vallière as a huntress, 1667, after Claude Lefebvre. *Châteaux de Versailles et de Trianon (© Photo RMN/ Gérard Blot).*

Athénaïs de Rochechouart de Mortemart, Marquise de Montespan, date unknown, by Louis Elle Ferdinand II. *Collection: Author.*

Athénaïs reclining in front of the gallery of her château at Clagny, date unknown, by Henri Gascard. *Private Collection (photo: Giraudon/ Bridgeman Art Library).*

Portrait of Athénaïs, date unknown, attributed to Pierre Mignard. *Musée du Berry, Bourges (photo: Giraudon/ Bridgeman Art Library).*

The Appartement des Bains at Versailles depicted on a fan, *c.*1680. *Victoria & Albert Musuem, London (photo. © V & A Images).*

*Spottallegorie auf Ludwig XIV, c.*1670, by Joseph Werner *(photo: courtesy of Schweizerisches Institut für Kunstwissenschaft, Zürich).*

Marie-Angélique d'Escorailles de Rousille, Duchesse de Fontanges, 1687, engraving by Nicolas de Larmessin III. *Châteaux de Versailles et de Trianon (© Photo RMN/ Gérard Blot).*

Madame de Maintenon, date and artist unknown. *Château de Chambord (photo: The Art Archive/ Dagli Orti).*

Madame de Maintenon with the Duc du Maine and the Comte de Vexin, date and artist unknown. *Château de Maintenon (photo: The Art Archive/ Dagli Orti).*

Frontispiece to *Scarron aparu à Madame de Maintenon et les reproches qu'il lui fait sur ses amours avec Louis le Grand,* 1664, by Paul Scarron *(courtesy of The British Library).*

Madame de Maintenon with her niece Françoise-Charlotte, *c.*1688, by Louis Elle Ferdinand II. *Châteaux de Versailles et de Trianon (© Photo RMN/ Gérard Blot).*

The 'Secret Notebooks' of Madame de Maintenon. *Bibliothèque municipale de Versailles.*

Madame de Maintenon as St Frances of Rome, *c.*1694, by Pierre Mignard. *Châteaux de Versailles et de Trianon (photo: Giraudon/ Bridgeman Art Library).*

*King David Playing the Harp, c.*1619-20, by Domenicho Zampieri.

School. *Châteaux de Versailles et de Trianon (photo: Giraudon/Bridgeman Art Library).*

Marie-Anne de Bourbon, Princesse de Conti, 1690-1, by François de Troy. *Musée des Augustins, Toulouse (photo: Bernard Delorme).*

Françoise-Marie de Bourbon and Louise-Françoise de Bourbon, date unknown, by Claude-François Vignon. *Châteaux de Versailles et de Trianon (© Photo: RMN/Gérard Blot).*

Louise-Bénédicte de Bourbon, Duchesse du Maine, c.1690-1700, by Henri Bonnart. *Musée de l'Île de France, Sceaux (photo: Pascal Lemaître).*

Mary of Modena, c.1680, by Simon Peeterz Verelst. *Yale Center for British Art, Paul Mellon Fund (photo: Bridgeman Art Library).*

Miniature painting of Mary of Modena, c.1677, by Peter Cross. *Fitzwilliam Museum, University of Cambridge (photo: Bridgeman Art Library).*

The Family of James VII and II, 1694, by Pierre Mignard. *The Royal Collection © 2006 Her Majesty Queen Elizabeth II.*

Sèvres vase depicting a party given by Louis XIV in 1689 at the Château of Saint-Germain-en-Laye. *Musée Conde, Chantilly (photo: Giraudon/Bridgeman Art Library).*

Letter from Adelaide Duchesse de Bourgogne to her grandmother. *State Archives of Turin.*

Adelaide Duchesse de Bourgogne, 17th century French School. *Galleria Sabauda, Turin (photo: Alinari/Bridgeman Art Library).*

Adelaide Duchesse de Bourgogne, in hunting-costume, 1704, by Pierre Gobert. *Châteaux de Versailles et de Trianon (© Photo RMN/Daniel Arnaudet & Gérard Blot).*

The Marriage of Adelaide of Savoy and Louis, Duc de Bourgogne, 1697, by Antoine Dieu. *Châteaux de Versailles et de Trianon (© Photo RMN/Daniel Arnaudet & Gérard Blot).*

Perspective View of the Château, Gardens and Park of Versailles seen from the Avenue de Paris, 1668, by Pierre Patel. *Châteaux de Versailles et de Trianon (photo: Giraudon/Bridgeman Art Library).*

Construction of the Château of Versailles, c.1679, after Adam Frans van der Meulen. *The Royal Collection © 2006 Her Majesty Queen Elizabeth II.*

Le Bassin d'Encelade, c.1730, by Jacques Rigaud. *Châteaux de Versailles et de Trianon (©Photo RMN/Gérard Blot).*

Louis XIV Welcomes the Elector of Saxony to Fontainebleau, 1714, by Louis de Silvestre. *Châteaux de Versailles et de Trianon (photo: Bridgeman Art Library)*.

View of the Château and Orangerie at Versailles, c.1699, by Étienne Allegrain. *Châteaux de Versailles et de Trianon (photo: Giraudon/ Bridgeman Art Library)*.

Bonne, Nonne et Ponne, date unknown, by François Desportes. *Musée du Louvre, Paris (© Photo RMN/ Daniel Arnaudet)*.

Detail of wood-carving round the windows of the King's chamber at Versailles *(© Photo RMN/ Christian Jean & Jean Schormans)*.

Quatrième chambre des appartements, 1696, etching and dry-point by Antoine Trouvain. *Bibliothèque nationale de France, Department of Prints & Photographs*.

La Charmante Tabagie, late 17th century, engraving by Nicolas Bonnart. *Bibliothèque nationale de France, Department of Prints & Photographs*.

The Cascade at Marly, from *Gardens of Marly*, early 18th century French School. *Centre Historique des Archives Nationales, Paris (photo: Archives Charmet/ Bridgeman Art Library)*.

Louis XIV, 1701, by Hyacinthe Rigaud. *Musée du Louvre, Paris (© Photo RMN/ Gérard Blot)*.

AUTHOR'S NOTE

'Magnificence and gallantry were the soul of this court': in writing about Louis XIV and his women, this is the contemporary verdict that I have borne in mind. Certainly I have hoped to convey magnificence in this book. How else could one write about the man who created Versailles in the early part of his personal rule and made it his official seat in 1682? There is extravagance inside and out; feasts to which only the King with his Gargantuan appetite could do justice, huge flower beds with every plant changed daily, multitudinous orange trees – the King's favourites – in silver pots, terraces where the court was driven indoors at night by the dominant perfume of a thousand tuberoses, money flowing forth like the fountains the King was so fond of commissioning, so that ornamental water itself became a symbol of power ... There are wildly obsequious courtiers such as the Duc d'Antin, who cut down his own avenue overnight because it impeded the view from the visiting monarch's bedroom, or the Abbé Melchior de Polignac, thoroughly drenched in his court costume, who assured the King that the rain at Marly did not wet.

And I have certainly depicted gallantry in all the many contemporary senses of the word, from friendship shading to love, the subtle art of courtship, the more frivolous and even dangerous pursuit of flirtation, down to sensual libertinage ending in sex. It is easy to understand why seventeenth-century France was popularly supposed to be a paradise for its women, who enjoyed 'a thousand freedoms, a thousand pleasures'. But if gallantry – or sex – is one of my themes, then religion is another. It is in the connection between the two that I believe the fascination of Louis XIV's relationships with his mistresses properly lies. This was the century in which penitent Magdalen was the favourite saint in France: symbolically his mistresses were painted, loose hair flowing, as

Magdalen in their prime, while flouting the rules of the Church in the most flagrant manner possible; their attempts to incarnate the saint's own penitence would come later. Thus the Catholic Church's struggles for the salvation of the King's soul strike a sombre note in the celebratory music of Versailles from the King's youth onwards and cannot be silenced. Lully is there with his graceful allegorical Court Ballets in which the King (and his ladies) danced; but he is also there with his themes of lamentation for the King to mourn.

My study is not however entirely limited to the mistresses of Louis XIV: possibly Marie Mancini, principally Louise de La Vallière and Athénaïs de Montespan as well as the enigmatic, puritanical Madame de Maintenon, whose precise status was doubtful. I had once intended this before my researches led me on to the richer story of his relationships with women in general. These include his mother Anne of Austria, his two sisters-in-law, Henriette-Anne and Liselotte, who were Duchesses d'Orléans in succession, his wayward illegitimate daughters, and lastly Adelaide, the beloved child-wife of his grandson. Inevitably, therefore, the story also reflects something of the condition of women of a certain sort in seventeenth-century France. What were their choices and how far were they, mistresses and wives, mothers and daughters, in control of their own destinies?

A portrait will, I trust, emerge of Louis XIV himself, the Sun King and like the sun the centre of his universe. But as the title and subtitle indicate, this is not a full study of the reign, so fruitfully dealt with elsewhere, in studies both ancient and modern, to all of which I acknowledge my deep gratitude. It was Voltaire, in the first brilliant study of 'le grand siècle', published twenty-odd years after the King's death, who wrote: 'It must not be expected to meet here with a minute detail of the wars carried on in this age. Everything that happens is not worthy of the record.' This is a sentiment which one can only humbly echo.

Let the King's sister-in-law Liselotte, Duchesse d'Orléans, have the last word, the copious correspondent whose outspoken comments cannot help making her my favourite among the abundant female sources of the period, despite the presence of the incomparable letter-writer Madame de Sévigné. 'I believe that the histories which will be written about this court after we are all gone,' she wrote, 'will be better and more entertaining than any novel, and I am afraid that those who come after us will not be able to believe them and will think that they are just fairy tales.' I have hoped to present the 'fairy tale' in such a way that it can be believed.

There are many people whose help was invaluable during the five years I spent researching and writing this book. First of all, I must thank Alan Palmer for his Chronological Political Summary. Professor Felipe Fernandez-Armesto also read the book at an early stage, as did my eagle-eyed daughter Rebecca Fraser Fitzgerald. Dr Mark Bryant allowed me to read his (2001) thesis on Madame de Maintenon in advance of his own published work on the subject; Professor Edward Corp drew my attention to important references; Alastair Macaulay advised me on the art he loves; Col. Jean-Joseph Milhiet gave me information concerning the remains of Madame de Maintenon; the late Professor Bruno Neveu was an inspiration; Sabine de La Rochefoucauld arranged illuminating visits to both Versailles and the Louvre; M. Jean Raindre was an enlightening and generous host at the Château de Maintenon, as were Cristina and Patrice de Vogüé at Vaux-le-Vicomte; Dr Blythe Alice Raviola, University of Turin, crucially assisted me over manuscripts, as did M. Thierry Sarmant, at the Archives Historiques de la Guerre, Vincennes. Niall MacKenzie provided translations of Gaelic poetry as well as advice; Renata Propper interpreted Liselotte's often ribald German; Lord (Hugh) Thomas of Swynnerton translated from the Spanish for the Mexican memorial service of Louis XIV, the text of which was kindly acquired for me by my daughter-in-law Paloma Porraz de Fraser.

I also thank wholeheartedly the following: Mrs H. E. Alexander, the Fan Museum, Greenwich, and Mrs Pamela Cowen; Neil Bartlett, late of the Lyric Theatre, Hammersmith, for his translation of Molière's *Don Juan*; Sue Bradbury, the Folio Society; Barbara Bray; M. Bernard Clergeot, Mairie de Bergerac; M. Michel Déon; Father Francis Edwards, SJ; Peter Eyre; Gila Falkus; Charlie

Garnett; '*ma fille française*', Laure de Gramont; Liz Greene, *Equinox*; Ivor Guest; Lisa Hilton; Diane Johnson; the late Professor Douglas Johnson; Laurence Kelly; Emmajane Lawrence at the Wallace Collection; M. Pierre Leroy; Sylvain Lévy-Alban; Cynthia Liebow; Frédéric Malle for his photograph of the blocked marriage door of Louis XIV; M. Bernard Minoret for allowing me yet again to borrow from his precious library; Graham Norton for information about the history of the West Indies; Dr Robert Oresko, especially for help in Turin; Dr David Parrott for Rantzau discussions; Judy Price for information about Cotignac; Professor Munro Price for a felicitous shared visit to the birthplace of Louis XIV; Professor John Rogister, the Vicomte de Rohan, President of the Société des Amis de Versailles, and Madame Anémone de Truchis, also of Versailles; Mme Jean Sainteny (Claude Dulong); Mme Dominique Simon-Hiernard, Musées de Poitiers; Chantal Thomas; Hugo Vickers; Dr Humphrey Wise, the National Gallery, London; Anthony Wright; Francis Wyndham; the staff of the Archives Nationales and Bibliothèque Nationale in Paris, the British Library, the London Library and Kensington Public Library in London.

My editors on both sides of the Atlantic, Nan Talese of Doubleday and Alan Samson of Weidenfeld & Nicolson, were enormously supportive. I thank Steve Cox and Helen Smith for the copy-editing and Index respectively. My PA Linda Peskin, who put the book on disk, must at times have felt like an extra lady-in-waiting at the court of the Sun King. My French family, the four Cavassonis, made visits to Paris an extra pleasure. Lastly, this book is justly dedicated to my husband, as ever the first reader.

Antonia Fraser
Feast of St Catherine, 2004–Lady Day, 2006

Note There are three perennial problems writing historical narrative for this period, to which I have offered the following solutions. First, names and titles, so often very similar, can be extremely confusing. For the reader's sake, I have tried to be clear rather than consistent; the list of Principal Characters, awarding one (slightly different) name to each person, is intended as a guide. Second, dates in England, Old Style (OS), lagged behind those on the Continent until 1752; I have used the French New Style (NS) unless otherwise indicated. Third, where money is concerned, I have included rough comparisons to the present day, again for the reader's sake, although these can never be more than approximate.

CHRONOLOGICAL POLITICAL SUMMARY

1610   Accession of nine-year-old Louis XIII as King of France following the assassination of his father, Henri IV. Regency of his mother, Marie de Médicis.

1615   Double royal marriage: Louis XIII weds Anne of Austria, daughter of Philip III of Spain; his sister, Elisabeth, weds Anne's brother, who accedes as Philip IV of Spain in 1621.

1617   Louis XIII assumes power, after countenancing murder of his mother's unpopular favourite, Concini.

1618   Thirty Years War begins in Prague with a Protestant revolt against the anti-national Catholic policy of the Habsburg Emperor in Vienna. In 1621 the war spreads to the Rhineland Palatinate and gradually involves all Europe.

1624   Cardinal Richelieu becomes King's chief minister. Over the next eighteen years his ruthless policies impose the autocratic authority of a centralised monarchy, destroying the last fortified strongholds of the French Protestant Huguenots and curbing the rights of the nobility. In foreign affairs he challenges Habsburg hegemony on France's eastern and southern frontiers.

1625   Charles I ascends the English throne; marries Louis XIII's sister Henrietta Maria.

1626   Richelieu subsidises Protestant Sweden's entry into Thirty Years War against the Emperor and Spain. He authorises the Company of the Hundred Associates to control New France and develop trade along the St Lawrence valley and regions explored by Champlain (who founded Quebec in 1608).

1635   France enters the Thirty Years War, grouped with Sweden, Savoy and the Dutch against the Spanish and Austrians.

1638 Birth of Dauphin Louis, future Louis XIV.

1640 Birth of his brother Philippe, to be known as Monsieur.

1642 Richelieu dies: the Italian-born Cardinal Mazarin, a favourite of Anne of Austria, succeeds him as chief minister. Start of English Civil War.

1643 Death of Louis XIII: accession of Louis XIV under Regency of Anne of Austria. French, led by future Prince de Condé (aged 22), defeat Spanish at Rocroi.

1648 Peace of Westphalia ends Thirty Years War: France gains southern Alsace and eastern frontier fortresses including Verdun, Toul and Metz but remains at war with Spain. The first Fronde: mob rioters (*frondeurs* = stone slingers) support protest of the Parlement de Paris (supreme court) against taxation and force royal family and Mazarin to flee Paris for eight months.

1649 Execution of Charles I; accession of Charles II (in exile). Second Fronde begins in Paris, primarily a conflict between rival nobles.

1650 Condé, his brother the Prince de Conti and brother-in-law Duc de Longueville, leading Frondeur nobles, arrested by Mazarin.

1651 Under threat of mob revolt in Paris, Anne of Austria releases Frondeur princes. Mazarin goes into temporary exile at Cologne. Louis XIV comes of age officially but Anne of Austria remains his chief counsellor. Condé leads Frondeur army in two years of civil war; opposed by Marshal Turenne, loyal to Louis.

1653 Mazarin returns. End of Fronde; Condé flees to Spanish Netherlands (pardoned by Louis XIV in 1659 and commands armies in later campaigns). Fouquet becomes finance minister; building up a fortune through peculation. Cromwellian Protectorate in England.

1658 Alliance between France and Cromwell's England; joint armies defeat Spanish at battle of the Dunes (June). Cromwell acquires Dunkirk but dies (September).

1659 Peace of Pyrenees ends war between France and Spain. France gains foothold on border of Spanish Netherlands and in Roussillon, on the eastern Pyrenees.

1660   Louis XIV marries Marie-Thérèse, daughter of Philip IV of Spain and his first cousin. Restoration of Charles II in England.

1661   Mazarin dies. Louis XIV takes power, never again appointing a chief minister. The corrupt Fouquet is replaced by Colbert, who reforms the financial system and undertakes a vigorous public works programme, later also becoming Minister of Marine and creating a navy. Marriage of Monsieur to Charles II's sister, Henriette-Anne.

1662   French defensive alliance with the Dutch, promising support if they are attacked by another country. Charles II sells Dunkirk to France.

1663   Colbert organises New France as a crown colony, with Quebec as capital.

1664   Colbert promotes trade by abolishing internal tariff duties.

1665   Philip IV of Spain dies; succeeded by Carlos II, son by his second marriage (to Maria Anna of Austria), half-brother to Queen Marie-Thérèse.

1666   Louis XIV declares war on England in support of the Dutch but no fighting ensues. Louvois appointed Minister of War. Anne of Austria dies.

1667   War of Devolution. Louis XIV claims that legally Spanish Netherlands 'devolved' on Marie-Thérèse at Philip IV's death; he sends Turenne's army into Flanders to enforce his claim.

1668   (January) English, Dutch and Swedes make alliance to compel Louis to end War of Devolution; peace comes in May with Treaty of Aix-la-Chapelle giving France twelve towns in Flanders and Artois, including Lille, but Louis does not withdraw claim to Spanish Netherlands.

1669   Colbert encourages founding of first French trading port in India.

1670   Secret Treaty of Dover made by Charles II and his sister Henriette-Anne: Louis XIV promises Charles subsidies: Charles agrees to declare himself a Catholic at a suitable moment and to support France if Louis attacks Holland.

Henriette-Anne dies thirty-nine days after making the treaty.

1671 Widowed Monsieur marries Liselotte, possible heiress to the Palatinate.

1672 England and France declare war on the Dutch. Louis invades Holland but meets strong resistance from newly elected Dutch Stadtholder William of Orange, son of Charles II's sister Mary. Frontenac begins ten-year term as Governor of New France establishing forts as far south as Lake Ontario.

1673–5 Successful campaigns by Louis's armies in the Palatinate and Flanders.

1677 William of Orange marries his cousin Mary, daughter of James, Duke of York and second in line of succession to English and Scottish crown.

1678 Peace of Nijmegen ends French war with Dutch and Spanish. Louis XIV gains fourteen towns in Spanish Netherlands, enabling Vauban to build fortresses eventually running from Dunkirk on the coast to Dinant on the river Meuse.

1679 Louis XIV sets up a Chambre Ardente ('Burning Chamber'), a special commission to investigate accusations of murder, witchcraft and Black Masses in the 'Affair of the Poisons'. Several leading personages in the kingdom implicated. In next three years Chambre conducts more than 200 interrogations: at least twenty-four executed; several more die under torture; others sent to the galleys or imprisoned.

1680 Highest council of Paris Parlement formally gives Louis XIV title of 'the Great'. 'Chambers of Reunion' set up in which jurists support Louis XIV's claims to Upper and Lower Alsace. Olympe, Comtesse de Soissons, Mistress of the Robes, flees France to avoid summons to Chambre Ardente. Her son, Prince Eugene of Savoy, refused military commission by Louis XIV, offers his services to Emperor Leopold I.

1681 Dragonnades, soldiers billeted by Louvois in Huguenot

communities to enforce conversions to Catholicism. Mass migration of Huguenot craftsmen begins. Canal du Midi completed, enabling barges to convey goods from Bay of Biscay to the Mediterranean.

1682 (April) Louis XIV abruptly closes Chambre Ardente with 100 cases still pending. (May) He moves the Court and government to Versailles. La Salle leads expedition down Mississippi, claims the region for France and names it Louisiana.

1683 Marie-Thérèse and Colbert die. Emperor Leopold I and Carlos II join Dutch and Swedes in anti-French coalition. Vienna besieged by Turks.

1684 Turkish threat induces Emperor to conclude Truce of Ratisbon with Louis XIV allowing France to retain all towns assigned by Chambers of Reunion.

1685 Charles II dies, succeeded by Catholic brother, James (II) Duke of York. Louis XIV revokes Edict of Nantes, finally denying Huguenots religious and civil rights guaranteed them by Henri IV. Dragonnades brutally enforce conversion to Catholicism. Several hundred Huguenot officers join the migration and enlist in Protestant armies abroad.

1686 Emperor Leopold and rulers of Spain, Sweden, Saxony, the Palatinate and Brandenburg form League of Augsburg, an alliance to check further French expansion.

1687 Fort Niagara built to prevent English colonists encroaching on New France.

1688 War of League of Augsburg begins: Louis XIV invades Palatinate supporting claim of Liselotte as successor to her brother, opposed by League alliance, now joined by Duke of Saxony. William of Orange accepts invitation from Whig lords to save English Protestantism, lands in Torbay and marches on London; James II escapes to France on Christmas Day.

1689 William of Orange and his wife proclaimed joint rulers as William III and Mary II in London. Mary Beatrice, wife of James II, settles at St Germain with her son

James Edward (born June 1688). England and Holland join League of Augsburg, now known as the Grand Alliance. France declares war on England. James II crosses to Ireland to rally Catholics against William and Mary.

1690　Battle of the Boyne: William III defeats James, who returns to St Germain.

1691　Many Irish Catholics flee to France and enter Louis XIV's army.

1692　English naval victory at La Hogue removes threat of French invasion.

1693　Louis XIV fails to capture Liège and never again joins his troops in the field.

1694　Mary II dies, leaving William III as sole ruler. French invade Spain.

1695　William III captures Namur.

1696　Treaty of Turin: Duke of Savoy abandons Grand Alliance and changes sides in the war; his daughter Adelaide betrothed to the Duc de Bourgogne, Louis's grandson.

1697　Peace of Ryswick ends War of the League of Augsburg. Louis XIV implicitly recognises William III as king in England, Scotland and Ireland, with his niece Anne as heiress presumptive. Mutual restoraton of all conquests since Peace of Nijmegen (1678), France surrendering right bank of the Rhine and Lorraine. Louis agrees that Dutch shall garrison chief fortresses in Spanish Netherlands.

1698　English, French and Dutch diplomats meet in London to discuss partition of Spain, seeking to prevent war when Carlos II dies.

1699　English and Dutch sign partition treaty with France but it is subsequently rejected by Emperor in Vienna and by Carlos II.

1700　Carlos II dies, having declared Duc d'Anjou (Louis's grandson and third in line of succession to French throne) as his heir; he accedes as Philip V.

1701　War of Spanish Succession begins: French troops enter Spanish Netherlands on behalf of Philip V. England,

Holland and Empire (fearing future dual kingdom of France and Spain) form Grand Alliance against Louis, recognising Austrian archduke as Charles III of Spain. James II dies; Louis XIV acknowledges his son James Edward ('Old Pretender') as James III.

New France: Antoine Cadillac founds Fort Pontchartrain du Détroit on the straits of Lake Erie.

1702   William III dies; Anne, daughter of James II, accedes; England and Holland cease to have common ruler.

1703   Savoy and Portugal join Grand Alliance against France.

1704   Duke of Marlborough leads army 250 miles from lower Rhine to upper Danube, linking up with Emperor's troops under Prince Eugene to win major victory over French and Bavarians at Blenheim in Bavaria.

1705   English navy takes Barcelona and Austrian 'Charles III' is recognised as King in Catalonia and Aragon.

1706   Marlborough defeats French at Ramillies and occupies Brussels and Antwerp. Eugene defeats French outside Turin and drives them from northern Italy.

1707   Act of Union unites England and Scotland as Great Britain.

1708   Marlborough and Eugene jointly defeat French at Oudenarde under Vendôme and capture Ghent and Bruges. Winter of 1708–9 is coldest on record in France.

1709   Malplaquet: final joint victory of Marlborough and Eugene but with heavy casualties: 24,000 dead or wounded, twice as many as French.

1711   Emperor Joseph I dies; succeeded in Vienna by his brother 'Charles III' who becomes Emperor Charles VI.

1713   Peace of Utrecht ends War of Spanish Succession: Spain and France never to be united under one ruler. Philip V recognised as King of Spain. Louis XIV accepts Protestant Succession in Britain and requires Pretender James Edward to leave France. French make concessions in North America, ceding Newfoundland and Nova Scotia. Holland occupies Spanish Netherlands, which are to be ceded to Emperor once Dutch have established barrier fortresses to prevent a French return.

1714   Queen Anne dies: succeeded by her cousin George I, Elector of Hanover. Peace of Rastatt concludes Utrecht negotiations, finally ends conflict with France, taking possession from the Dutch of Austrian Netherlands.

1715   Louis XIV dies. Accession of his five-year-old great-grandson as Louis XV, under the regency of his nephew Philippe, Duc d'Orléans, son of Monsieur and Liselotte.

PRINCIPAL CHARACTERS

Listed according to the name(s) used in the text

ADELAIDE: Marie-Adelaide, daughter of Victor Amadeus of Savoy and Anne-Marie d'Orléans, wife of the Duc de Bourgogne, grandson of Louis XIV

ANGÉLIQUE: Mademoiselle de Fontanges, later Duchesse de Fontanges, mistress of Louis XIV

ANJOU, Louis Duc d': Third son of the Duc and Duchesse de Bourgogne; later Louis XV

ANJOU, Philippe Duc d': *see* Philip V

ANNE Queen of France: Anne of Austria, daughter of Philip III of Spain, wife of Louis XIII of France

ANNE-MARIE Duchess of Savoy: Daughter of Monsieur and his first wife Henriette-Anne, wife of Victor Amadeus II of Savoy

ANNE-MARIE-LOUISE: *see* the Grande Mademoiselle

ATHÉNAÏS: Françoise-Athénaïs de Rochechouart-Mortemart, Marquise de Montespan

BÉNÉDICTE Duchesse du Maine: Anne-Louise-Bénédicte de Bourbon-Condé, daughter of the Prince de Condé, wife of the Duc du Maine

BERRY, Duc de: Third son of the Dauphin and Marianne-Victoire, grandson of Louis XIV, married Marie-Élisabeth d'Orléans

BOURBON, Mademoiselle de: Daughter of the Duc de Bourbon and Madame la Duchesse (Louise-Françoise, daughter of Louis XIV and Athénaïs)

BOURGOGNE, Duc de: Eldest son of the Dauphin and Marianne-Victoire of Bavaria, grandson of Louis XIV, husband of Adelaide

CARLOS II King of Spain: Son of Philip IV of Spain and his second wife Maria Anna, half-brother of Marie-Thérèse, Queen of France

CHARLES II King of England: Eldest son of Charles I and
Henrietta Maria of France, brother of Henriette-Anne
d'Orléans

CHARTRES, Louis Duc de: Only son of Philippe Duc d'Orléans
and Françoise-Marie

CHARTRES, Philippe Duc de: *see* Philippe Duc d'Orléans

CHRISTINE Duchess of Savoy: Princess of France, sister of Louis
XIII, wife of Victor Amadeus I, Duke of Savoy

DAUPHIN: Louis de France, only surviving child of Louis XIV
and Queen Marie-Thérèse, also known as 'Monseigneur'

DAUPHINE: *see* Marianne-Victoire

ÉLISABETH-CHARLOTTE: Daughter of Monsieur by his second
marriage to Liselotte, wife of the Duke of Lorraine

FRANÇOISE: Françoise d'Aubigné, wife of Paul Scarron, later
Madame (and Marquise) de Maintenon

FRANÇOISE-CHARLOTTE d'Aubigné: Niece of Madame de
Maintenon, wife of Duc de Noailles

FRANÇOISE-MARIE Duchesse de Chartres then Duchesse
d'Orléans: Mademoiselle de Blois II, illegitimate daughter of
Louis XIV and Athénaïs, wife of Philippe Duc de Chartres,
then Duc d'Orléans

GASTON Duc d'Orléans: Only brother of Louis XIII, uncle of
Louis XIV, father of the Grande Mademoiselle

GRANDE MADEMOISELLE: Anne-Marie-Louise de Montpensier,
daughter of Gaston Duc d'Orléans by his first marriage, first
cousin of Louis XIV

HENRIETTA MARIA Queen of England: Princess of France, wife
of Charles I, mother of Charles II and Henriette-Anne

HENRIETTE-ANNE Duchesse d'Orléans: Daughter of Charles I
and Henrietta Maria of France, first wife of Monsieur, known
as 'Madame'

JAMES: Duke of York, brother of Charles II, later King James II

JAMES EDWARD: Son of James II and Mary Beatrice, Prince of
Wales, later 'the Pretender' to the British throne/James III

LISELOTTE Duchesse d'Orléans: Élisabeth-Charlotte, Princess of
the Palatine, second wife of Monsieur, known as 'Madame'

LOUIS: King Louis XIV

LOUISA MARIA: Daughter of James II and his second wife Mary Beatrice

LOUISE: Louise de La Vallière, later Duchesse de La Vallière

LOUISE-FRANÇOISE: Daughter of Athénaïs and Louis XIV, wife of the Duc de Bourbon, *see* Madame la Duchesse

LOUISON: *see* Maria Luisa

MADAME: *see* Henriette-Anne and Liselotte

MADAME LA DUCHESSE: Louise-Françoise, Mademoiselle de Nantes, daughter of Louise XIV and Athénaïs, wife of the Duc de Bourbon known as 'Monsieur le Duc'

MADAME ROYALE: Jeanne-Baptiste de Savoie-Nemours. Duchess of Savoy, second wife of Charles Emmanuel, Duke of Savoy, mother of Victor Amadeus of Savoy, grandmother of Adelaide

MAINE, Duc du: Son of Louis XIV and Athénaïs, married Bénédicte de Bourbon-Condé

MAINTENON, Madame de: *see* Françoise

MANCINI, Marie: Niece of Cardinal Mazarin, early love of Louis XIV, wife of Prince Colonna

MARGARITA TERESA: Half-sister of Marie-Thérèse, daughter of Philip IV by his second marriage, wife of the Emperor Leopold I

MARGUERITE de Caylus: Marthe-Marguerite de Villette, cousin of Madame de Maintenon, wife of the Comte de Caylus

MARGUERITE-LOUISE: Daughter of Gaston d'Orléans by his second marriage, later Duchess of Tuscany

MARGUERITE-YOLANDE: Princess of Savoy, daughter of Christine de France and the Duke of Savoy

MARIA ANNA Queen of Spain: Daughter of the Duke of Neubourg. Second wife of Carlos II

MARIA LUISA Queen of Spain: Daughter of Victor Amadeus of Savoy, nickname Louison, sister of Adelaide, wife of Philip V of Spain

MARIA TERESA Infanta of Spain: *see* Marie-Thérèse

MARIANNA Queen of Spain: Daughter of the Emperor Charles X, second wife of Philippe IV, mother of Carlos II

MARIANNE-VICTOIRE, Dauphine: Princess of Bavaria, wife of the Dauphin

MARIE-ANNE Princesse de Conti: Mademoiselle de Blois I,
    illegitimate daughter of Louis XIV and Louise de La Vallière,
    wife, then widow, of the Prince de Conti

MARIE-ÉLISABETH Duchesse de Berry: Marie-Louise-Élisabeth,
    daughter of Philippe Duc d'Orléans and Françoise-Marie,
    wife of the Duc de Berry

MARIE-LOUISE Queen of Spain: Daughter of Monsieur and his
    first wife, Henriette-Anne of England, wife of Carlos II of
    Spain

MARIE-THÉRÈSE Queen of France: Daughter of Philip III and
    Élisabeth de France, wife of Louis XIV

MARY BEATRICE Queen of England: Wife of James II, daughter
    of the Duke of Modena and Laura Martinozzi

MONSIEUR: Philippe Duc d'Orléans, only brother of Louis XIV,
    married first Henriette-Anne, secondly Liselotte.

PETITE MADAME: Marie-Thérèse, infant daughter of Louis XIV
    and Queen Marie-Thérèse, died young

PHILIP V King of Spain: Formerly Philippe Duc d'Anjou, second
    son of the Dauphin, grandson of Louis XIV

PHILIPPE Duc d'Orléans: Duc de Chartres then Duc d'Orléans,
    only son of Monsieur and Liselotte, husband of Françoise-
    Marie, later Regent

SOPHIA: Electress of Hanover, mother of George I, aunt of
    Liselotte

VICTOR AMADEUS Duke of Savoy: Victor Amadeus II, Duke of
    Savoy, son of Charles Emmanuel and Jeanne-Baptiste, father
    of Adelaide and Maria Luisa

The Sun, by the light which it shines on
those other stars which surround it like
a court, is most assuredly the most
vigorous and the most splendid image
of a great monarch.

Louis XIV, *Memoirs for the Instruction
of the Dauphin,* 1662

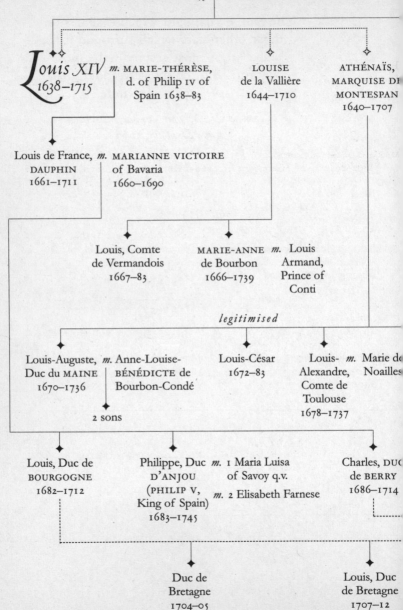

LOUIS XIII 1601–43 *m.* ANNE OF AUSTRIA 1601–66

*L*ouis XIV
1638–1715
m. MARIE-THÉRÈSE,
d. of Philip IV of
Spain 1638–83

LOUISE
de la Vallière
1644–1710

ATHÉNAÏS,
MARQUISE DE
MONTESPAN
1640–1707

Louis de France, *m.* MARIANNE VICTOIRE
DAUPHIN
1661–1711
of Bavaria
1660–1690

Louis, Comte
de Vermandois
1667–83

MARIE-ANNE *m.* Louis
de Bourbon
1666–1739
Armand,
Prince of
Conti

legitimised

Louis-Auguste, *m.* Anne-Louise-
Duc du MAINE
1670–1736
BÉNÉDICTE de
Bourbon-Condé

2 sons

Louis-César
1672–83

Louis- *m.* Marie de
Alexandre, Noailles
Comte de
Toulouse
1678–1737

Louis, Duc de
BOURGOGNE
1682–1712

Philippe, Duc *m.* 1 Maria Luisa
D'ANJOU
(PHILIP V,
King of Spain)
1683–1745
of Savoy q.v.

m. 2 Elisabeth Farnese

Charles, DUC
de BERRY
1686–1714

Duc de
Bretagne
1704–05

Louis, Duc
de Bretagne
1707–12

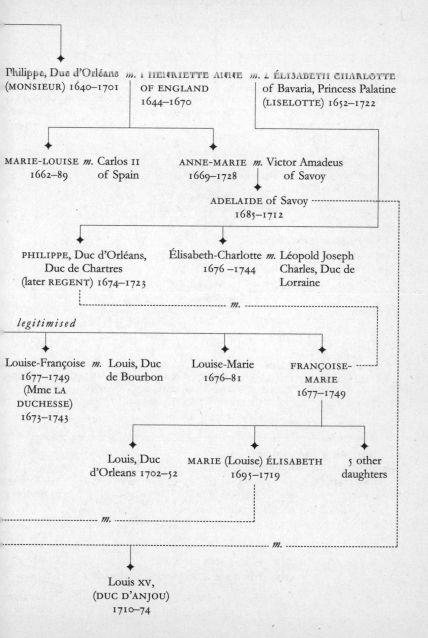

Philippe, Duc d'Orléans *m.* 1 HENRIETTE ANNE *m.* 2 ÉLISABETH CHARLOTTE
(MONSIEUR) 1640–1701   OF ENGLAND   of Bavaria, Princess Palatine
                              1644–1670   (LISELOTTE) 1652–1722

MARIE-LOUISE *m.* Carlos II   ANNE-MARIE *m.* Victor Amadeus
1662–89   of Spain   1669–1728   of Savoy

ADELAIDE of Savoy
1685–1712

PHILIPPE, Duc d'Orléans,   Élisabeth-Charlotte *m.* Léopold Joseph
Duc de Chartres   1676 –1744   Charles, Duc de
(later REGENT) 1674–1723   Lorraine

m.

legitimised

Louise-Françoise *m.* Louis, Duc   Louise-Marie   FRANÇOISE-
1677–1749   de Bourbon   1676–81   MARIE
(Mme LA   1677–1749
DUCHESSE)
1673–1743

Louis, Duc   MARIE (Louise) ÉLISABETH   5 other
d'Orleans 1702–52   1695–1719   daughters

m.

m.

Louis XV,
(DUC D'ANJOU)
1710–74

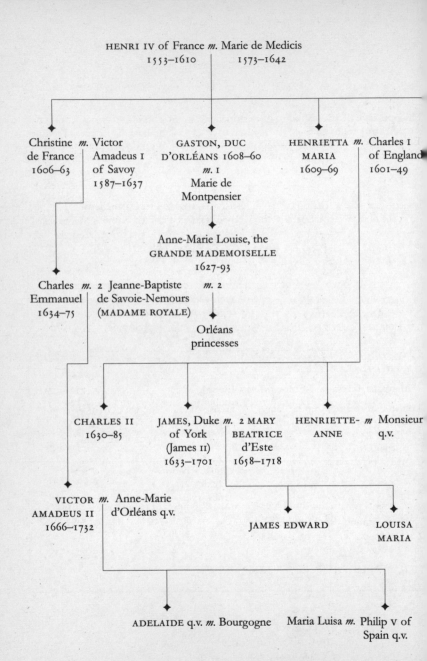

HENRI IV of France *m.* Marie de Medicis
1553–1610   1573–1642

Christine *m.* Victor
de France   Amadeus I
1606–63   of Savoy
             1587–1637

GASTON, DUC
D'ORLÉANS 1608–60
m. I
Marie de
Montpensier

HENRIETTA *m.* Charles I
MARIA   of England
1609–69   1601–49

Anne-Marie Louise, the
GRANDE MADEMOISELLE
1627-93

Charles *m.* 2 Jeanne-Baptiste   *m.* 2
Emmanuel   de Savoie-Nemours
1634–75   (MADAME ROYALE)

Orléans
princesses

CHARLES II
1630–85

JAMES, Duke *m.* 2 MARY
of York   BEATRICE
(James II)   d'Este
1633–1701   1658–1718

HENRIETTE- *m* Monsieur
ANNE   q.v.

VICTOR *m.* Anne-Marie
AMADEUS II   d'Orléans q.v.
1666–1732

JAMES EDWARD

LOUISA
MARIA

ADELAIDE q.v. *m.* Bourgogne

Maria Luisa *m.* Philip V of
Spain q.v.

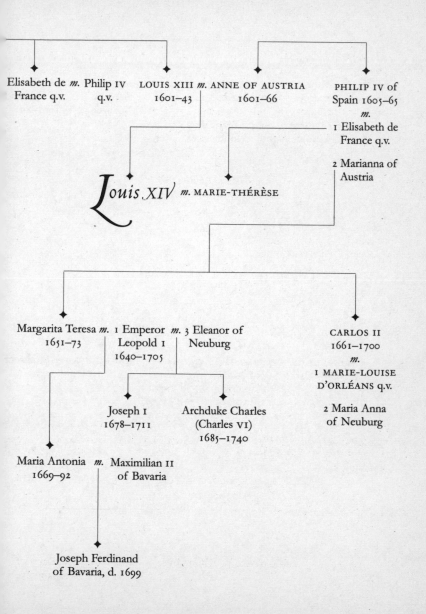

Elisabeth de *m.* Philip IV
France q.v.   q.v.

LOUIS XIII *m.* ANNE OF AUSTRIA
1601–43   1601–66

PHILIP IV of
Spain 1605–65
m.
1 Elisabeth de
France q.v.

2 Marianna of
Austria

Louis XIV *m.* MARIE-THÉRÈSE

Margarita Teresa *m.* 1 Emperor *m.* 3 Eleanor of
1651–73   Leopold 1   Neuburg
                     1640–1705

CARLOS II
1661–1700
m.
1 MARIE-LOUISE
D'ORLÉANS q.v.

2 Maria Anna
of Neuburg

Joseph 1
1678–1711

Archduke Charles
(Charles VI)
1685–1740

Maria Antonia *m.* Maximilian II
1669–92   of Bavaria

Joseph Ferdinand
of Bavaria, d. 1699

PART ONE

Spring

CHAPTER I

Gift from Heaven

They saw in the arms of this princess whom they had
watched suffer great persecutions with so much staunchness,
their child-King, like a gift given by Heaven in answer to
their prayers.

— Madame de Motteville, *Mémoires*

The first woman in the life of Louis XIV – and probably
the most important – was his mother, Anne of Austria.
When Louis, her first child, was born on 5 September 1638
the Spanish-born Queen of France was just short of her
thirty-seventh birthday.* This was an age at which a royal
princess might well expect to be a grandmother (Anne
herself had been married at fourteen). The Queen had on
the contrary endured twenty-two years of childless union.
Anne, as she told a confidante, had even feared the annulment of her marriage, since childlessness was one possible
ground for repudiation according to the Catholic Church.[1]
In which case the former Spanish Princess, daughter of
Philip III, would either have been returned to her native
country or possibly dispatched to govern the so-called
'Spanish' Netherlands (approximately modern Belgium), as
other princesses of her royal house had done, most recently
her pious aunt, Isabella Clara Eugenia.

The birth of a child, and that child a son – females could

---

* The name history has given her – Anne of Austria – is misleading since
Anne never visited the country. It marks the fact that her father was one of
the Spanish line of the (Habsburg) House of Austria.

3

not inherit in France under the fourteenth-century Salic Law – meant that the whole position of his royal mother was transformed. It was not only the obvious delight of a woman confronted with 'a marvel when it was least expected', as the official newspaper *Gazette de France* put it.[2] It was also the traditionally strong position of any Queen of France who had produced a Dauphin, an interesting paradox in the land of the Salic Law. This strength derived from the claim of such a Queen to act as Regent should her husband die during the minority of her son; a rule which had applied to Louis XIII's mother when Henri IV had died, and the dominating Catherine de Médicis in the previous century.

It was a situation that had already been envisaged at the time of Anne of Austria's betrothal in 1612. In poetical language the future Queen was described as the moon to her husband's sun: 'Just as the moon borrows its light from the sun ...' the monarch's death means that 'the setting sun gives way to the moon and confers on it the power of shedding light' in its absence'.[3] (The potential bride and bridegroom were then both ten years old.) A quarter of a century later, the reality was less poetical. Louis XIII was not in good health and a Regency in the next thirteen years – the age at which a French King reached his majority – was more likely than not. How long would it be before Anne, like Catherine de Médicis, was promoting herself as an image of revered maternality at the heart of government?

Furthermore the dynastic map of Europe was transformed. The heir presumptive to the throne of France, the King's younger brother Gaston Duc d'Orléans, on being shown 'physical proofs' of the baby's masculinity, had to accept that his rising hopes of accession had been fatally dashed.[4] But Gaston himself had only daughters. Next in line were the French Princes of the Blood, notably the Prince de Condé and his two sons the Duc d'Enghien and the Prince de Conti; their hopes were similarly blighted.

On the other hand the birth of a prince not only cut off hopes but also instigated ambitious thoughts of his eventual marriage to a princess. Gaston's daughter by his first marriage, Anne-Marie-Louise de Montpensier, was the richest heiress in France from the fortune of her mother who had died at her birth. She did not allow an eleven-year gap in age to prevent her dallying with thoughts of the Dauphin as 'my little husband'. Even more significant for the future was another equally august birth in Spain. Five days after the ecstatic Queen Anne gave birth to Louis, her sister-in-law, wife of Philip IV, gave birth to a princess.

These two high-born babies were in fact double first cousins (with identical grandparents), since a brother and a sister of France had married a brother and a sister of Spain. Unlike France, however, Spain allowed females to succeed: Anne of Austria had had to renounce her own rights on her marriage. There was at least a theoretical possibility that the Infanta Maria Teresa would one day succeed to the throne of Spain – or her children would. Another theoretical possibility, always present in the mind of Queen Anne, was that Maria Teresa might one day make a bride for Louis.

Under the circumstances, it is easy to understand how the infant Louis was described as 'Dieudonné' or 'Deodatus': Godgiven. And even as the years passed, the apparently miraculous nature of his conception and birth was never forgotten. One German diplomat would refer to the King's 'quite extraordinary birth' over forty years after the event.[5]

How miraculous was this birth, so unexpected and so awe-inspiring for the mother? Certainly a great deal of prayer had been applied to the subject as the years passed. There were pilgrimages to shrines, as befitted a Queen who throughout her life liked nothing so much as to visit convents and holy places. Saint Leonard was invoked against sterility; a hermit who was believed to have founded a monastery near Limoges in the sixth century, his intercession was held responsible for many miracles.[6] (He was otherwise the patron saint of prisoners – and after all the Queen was in the prison of her infertility.)

The Queen was fast approaching the age at which child-bearing itself was felt to be unlikely. This was a period when women were generally held to age faster than men, losing their bloom early – 'no woman is beautiful after twenty-two' was a popular saying – going further downhill after thirty.[7] Certainly, by the time of the Queen's thirty-sixth birthday on 22 September 1637 – and thirty-five was often seen as a cut-off point – her relationship with her husband, and also with her adopted country of France, had already had a long and troubled history.

The marriage of the two royal teenagers took place on the feast of St Catherine – 25 November – 1615. It was, it seems, consummated immediately, and after that there was a gap of more than three years. The twenty-fifth of January 1619 was the auspicious date on which the further completion of the royal union was announced in the gazette *Mercure Français* (it was after all a matter of state, just as the marriage had been). There were certainly rumours of royal pregnancies throughout the 1620s, and Louis XIII himself told the Venetian Ambassador later that his Queen had had four 'wretched miscarriages'.[8]

If the marriage was not egregiously unhappy by royal standards – notoriously low – it was certainly unhappy enough. Anne was an extremely attractive, even beautiful woman with her full, voluptuous figure, her thick bright chestnut hair, her luminous pale skin and her dark eyes with the green glints which gave them a special sparkle. She had her share of feminine vanity and was especially proud of her much-admired white hands, which seemed made 'to hold a sceptre'. As for her character, that was made up of contradictions. Anne was certainly pleasure-loving – she adored the theatre and gambling – but at the same time she was extremely pious.

Her piety did not stop Queen Anne from being a romantic, and it was not difficult for men to fall in love with her: 'her smile won a thousand hearts,' wrote Madame de Motteville, her lady-in-waiting. She was also *galante* in the crucial French term of the time which shimmers with different meanings throughout this period. In the case of the Queen, it meant flirtatious in the courtly, essentially innocent manner of the well-chaperoned Spanish Infanta she had once been. When the handsome Duke of Buckingham, who was gallant in every sense of the word, had 'the audacity' to court her in a famous scene in a garden, the Queen recoiled in horror. Nevertheless, in the opinion of Madame de Motteville, an important source for Anne's intimate feelings because she understood the Spanish world, 'if a respectable woman could love a man other than her husband, it would have been Buckingham who appealed to her'. The Princesse de Conti had a more cynical view: she would vouch for the Queen's virtue from the waist down, but not from the waist up.[9]

The sexuality of the husband of this romantic and unfulfilled woman was what would now be called troubled. Louis XIII formed lugubrious attachments to both men and women: late in his life, the Marquis de Cinq-Mars became his favourite. But at one point Louis fell yearningly in love with Marie d'Hautefort (his conjugal visits to Anne were said to have increased in consequence). However, when his friend the Duc de Saint-Simon* offered to act as a go-between, the King was shocked: 'the more my rank as king gives me the facility to satisfy myself,' he said, 'the more I must guard against sin and scandal.'[10] Low-spirited and

---

* Father of the famous memorialist the Duc de Saint-Simon and an important source for his son's information about the preceding reign.

willingly dominated by his great minister Cardinal Richelieu, Louis XIII was one half of an incompatible pair.

Furthermore, if the marriage did not provide a Bourbon–Habsburg heir, it did not bring about peace between Bourbon and Habsburg kingdoms either. Not long after Anne came to France, the slow strangulation of Europe in that long and complicated conflict known later as the Thirty Years War began. In this conflict, at the instigation of Cardinal Richelieu, the French and Spanish found themselves on different sides. Anne rejected the idea that she remained at heart a Spanish princess. Her tastes might be Spanish, from a predilection for late hours to a yearning for Spanish iced drinks and Spanish chocolate, but she prided herself on having become a Frenchwoman. Louis XIII on the other hand was pervaded with suspicions of his wife's disloyalty and over the course of their marriage remained convinced that she 'had a great passion for the interests of Spain'.[11]

It was a situation which perennially threatened the daughters of great monarchs married off abroad to further their country's interests. One can therefore appreciate the wise comment of Erasmus on the subject in the sixteenth century. In his *Education of a Christian Prince*, he pointed out the incongruity of such matches, which never actually did lead to international peace, and advised kings and princes to marry one of their own subjects instead.[12]

Various opposition movements in the country tended to implicate the King's brother – and of course heir presumptive for many years – Gaston d'Orléans. Anne was also suspected of joining with him, and in the ultimate alleged conspiracy before her fortunate transformation into the mother of a son, she was accused of plotting to marry Gaston after the King's death. And for all her French heart, she still wielded a Spanish pen, corresponding with her brother Philip IV, King of Spain. This was a matter which, when discovered, led to her disgrace in the summer of 1637. In due course her enemy Cardinal Richelieu secured from Anne a humiliating recantation, signed on 17 August. In the process, one of Anne's servants – her cloak-bearer Pierre de La Porte – was arrested and tortured but refused to implicate his mistress further. It was understandable therefore that La Porte in his memoirs would refer wryly to Louis as being 'as much the son of my silence, as of the prayers of the Queen and the pious vows of all France'.[13] It is certainly true that under these unpropitious circumstances some kind of miracle was generally felt to be necessary.

Of course there were, as there always would be, wags who suggested that the miracle had a more human origin. The aggrieved younger brother Gaston d'Orléans said that he was quite prepared to believe Louis Given by God had come out of the Queen's body, but he did not know who the devil had put him there. As to that, popular scandal was quite prepared to supply the name of the King's minister Cardinal Richelieu, simply because of his political power (a ludicrous misreading of the relationship between Anne and the Cardinal), with rhymes suggesting that the King had prayed 'to the saints, men and women' every day and Richelieu had prayed too but 'he succeeded much better'.[14]*

The religious of all sorts who prayed for the Queen's fertility were many of them, like rainmakers, ready to claim a successful result. A nun, a former favourite of Louis XIII named Louise Angélique de La Fayette, was said to have asked her priest to choose a great feast of the Church – presumably the Feast of the Immaculate Conception on 8 December – to remind her platonic admirer of his conjugal

---

* The name of Richelieu's Italian assistant, known in France as Jules Mazarin, later to be closely associated with the Queen, did not feature at this date in these scandalous satires, and he was in any case in Italy at the time of Louis's conception.[15]

duties: the result was the immediate conception of a more earthly sort.[16]

One story however does have the particular distinction of being believed by Queen Anne herself, and later by her son. This was the prediction in a Paris monastery of a monk named Brother Fiacre, to whom the Blessed Virgin Mary appeared in a vision on 3 November 1637. He was told by the Virgin to inform the Queen that she would shortly become pregnant; then he instructed the royal couple to make three novenas at the cathedral of Notre-Dame and the church of Notre-Dame-des-Victoires in Paris – and most importantly at the shrine of Notre-Dame-des-Grâces, an obscure chapel at Cotignac in Provence. (Cotignac may well have been one of the old pagan fertility sites, dedicated to forgotten goddesses, which had been transformed into a place of veneration for the Virgin.)[17]

In the end it was Brother Fiacre himself, accompanied by the sub-prior of his order, who made the pilgrimage to Cotignac. By the time Brother Fiacre was actually received by the royal couple on 10 February 1638 the Queen was already pregnant. This meant that it was not so much conception as the desired masculine gender of the baby which was now the object of concern. The importance of Brother Fiacre's mission was signified by the fact that the King gave orders for free board and lodging to be provided for the pilgrim pair on their way.

It is evident that Brother Fiacre's sincerity had made a great impression on Queen Anne when they met. Six years later she called the monk to her presence again with the words: 'I have not forgotten the signal grace you have obtained for me from the Blessed Virgin who gave me a son. I have had a great picture made where he [Louis] is represented in front of the mother of God to whom he offers his crown and sceptre.' And the monk duly travelled once more to Cotignac with the picture. Nor was this the end of the connection. Brother Fiacre, even as an old man, was allowed privileged access to Louis, for the role he was believed to have played 'in the happy birth of Your Majesty'. When the monk died, it was on the orders of the mature King (who paid for the journey) that his heart was taken to Notre-Dame-des-Grâces.[18]

That was the supernatural reasoning, one that the pious Anne clearly accepted, given the respect paid to Brother Fiacre. A more down-to-earth explanation was provided by a story involving Louis XIII, a hunting expedition near Paris cut short by an unexpected storm, and given that the King's separate apartments at the Louvre were not prepared, the need to take refuge in those of his wife on the night of 5 December 1637 ... The result of this unscheduled propinquity was Louis, born exactly nine months later. Unfortunately the *Gazette de France*, the official source of royal movements on any given day, does not confirm joint occupation of the Louvre on that particular night (although it is true that Anne was there).[19] The King and Queen were however together at their palace of Saint-Germain from 9 November for six weeks. The couple moved to the Louvre on 1 December, after which the King went hunting at Crône, and by 5 December was at his hunting lodge of Versailles. It was the prolonged period of opportunity in November which led the doctors to project a birth at the end of August.[20]

Leaving aside the supernatural, and given that the dates of the storm do not fit (unless the King made a speedy and unrecorded stop at the Louvre on his way to Versailles), the truth was surely more prosaic. The conjugal relations of a King and Queen were never subject to the ordinary laws of preference, attraction or even anger and disgust. The need for an heir had hardly diminished, and at some point in the autumn, following the summer crisis, relations were simply resumed with happy results. Yet even if Louis XIII himself

irritably if understandably observed: 'It is scarcely a miracle
if a husband who sleeps with his wife gives her a child,' the
circumstances of the conception, followed by the birth of
the long-desired son, were widely held to be extraordinary –
and above all by the baby's mother. 'Godgiven': it was a
view of himself as someone of special destiny that Anne
would impress upon the future Louis XIV.

On 14 January 1638 the royal doctor, Bouvard, informed
Cardinal Richelieu of the Queen's condition. Two weeks
later the news was broken in the *Gazette de France*. On 10
February – the occasion of Brother Fiacre's visit – Louis
XIII invited the whole kingdom to pray for a Dauphin
and placing it under the protection of the Blessed Virgin,
commanded the country to celebrate the Feast of her
Assumption on 15 August.* The Queen underlined the
connection by sending to Puy for a fragment of the Virgin's
holy girdle to aid her in childbirth. Other sacred relics, to
which Anne was in any case extremely partial, decorated her
private oratory.[21] The royal midwife, Dame Peronne, hitherto
sadly under-employed, was installed some months before
the expected date with her potions and her pots of pork fat
recommended for rubbing during labour. The royal birthing-
bed was readied: this was three feet wide, and consisted of
two planks between two mattresses, a double bolster for
use under the shoulders and two long wooden pegs on
either side for the Queen to clutch during her ordeal. Very
different from the elaborate great bed with its hangings and
embroideries in which the Queen slept, the birth-bed was
nevertheless an object of state, kept in a cupboard when
not in use and produced for successive royal ladies.[22]

The Queen's health was good. There was no threat this
time of a 'wretched miscarriage', in the King's phrase: only

* Still a major national holiday in France.

the high figure of infant mortality haunted Anne as it haunted all parents at the time – and in this case the whole court. It has been reckoned that roughly one in two children died, and those that survived the birthing process remained statistically at risk until their first birthday and beyond, so that burials of children under five were not recorded in the parish registers. The only irksome moment – one common to all fathers, not only kings – was when the baby failed to arrive according to Louis XIII's precise schedule: he was anxious to leave for Picardy. The King snarled at the Queen, but the dating of childbirth, although calculated then as now from the last *règles* (monthly period), has never been a precise art and it is easily comprehensible that the royal doctors erred on the side of caution.

It was on Saturday 4 September that the Queen finally went into labour at the royal château of Saint-Germain. This wondrous castle, adjacent to the small town of Saint-Germain-en-Laye, ten miles from Paris, was raised high over the curving banks of the Seine. The air was pure. There were gardens and terraces going down to the river, in which it was fashionable for both ladies and gentlemen of the court to swim. Close by lay the forests so vital to the main royal leisure pursuit of hunting. The old château was of twelfth-century origin but had been completely rebuilt in the sixteenth century by François I; then the adjacent Château-Neuf, a more intimate residence, was begun in 1557 by Philibert de L'Orme and transformed by Louis XIII's father Henri IV. The Queen's labour took place here, in a room overlooking the river.*

---

* Largely demolished during the French Revolution, the château was rebuilt in the nineteenth century and adapted for a Musée Gallo-Romain. The Pavilion Henri IV where Louis XIV was born remains however and is, appropriately enough, the site of a luxurious restaurant. A medallion on the terrace marks the birth of the future King with the inscription: '*C'est ici que naquit Louis XIV*'. It shows a cradle and a fleur-de-lys.

The labour took place in public, or at any rate in the presence of the court, as was the royal custom of the time, so as to prevent the possible substitution of a living baby for a dead one – or a son for a daughter. After all, in this case the King and Queen had evidently not made love under the waxing moon, let alone practised the physical constriction of the left testicle from which females were supposed to be generated – two contemporary suggestions for producing males. In view of this attendance, courtiers had to work out a private signal for indicating the vital sex of the child without vulgarly shouting it out. Whatever her use later in the dynastic matrimonial stakes, the birth of a girl was always a source of vivid disappointment at the time; one royal princess of this period, whose husband wanted an heir, volunteered crossly to throw her newborn daughter in the river.[23] Thus arms were to be kept folded for a girl, hats to be hurled in the air for a Dauphin.

It was at 11.20 a.m. on Sunday morning 5 September 1638 that the Queen's ordeal came to an end and hats were hurled violently, joyously, into the air. 'We have a Dauphin!' declared Louis XIII. It was 'the time when the Virgin was at her greatest strength', wrote an anonymous pamphleteer in *Le Bonheur de Jour* the next year. This was a reference not so much to the Virgin Mary, under whose protection the baby had been placed in the womb, but to the astrological sign of Virgo, which, stretching between late August and late September could indeed be argued to be at its zenith on 5 September. The sun itself was also said to be exceptionally near to the earth, as though to salute the future King, and it was of course the day of the Sun, a traditionally auspicious day. Racine wrote of the galaxy at that moment that it was 'a constellation composed of nine stars'.[24] The sun and stars did indeed look down upon, and the Virgin blessed, an exceptionally strong and healthy baby.*

* For the astrologically minded, an 11.20 a.m. birthtime at Saint-Germain-en-

The boy now shown to the gratified courtiers was the first legitimate male to be born into the Bourbon royal family proper (excluding the Princes of the Blood) for thirty years – that is, since the birth of Gaston d'Orléans. Gaston's daughter and Louis's first cousin, Anne-Marie-Louise de Montpensier, proud of her own Bourbon inheritance, referred to the 'natural goodness' which ran in the veins of all the Bourbons.[26] She contrasted it with the 'venom' which she believed ran in the blood of the Médicis – which Louis and of course Anne-Marie-Louise herself would have derived from their shared grandmother, Marie de Médicis, wife of Henri IV and daughter of the Medici Grand Duke of Tuscany.

It is true that physically there was an Italianate darkness in all the grandchildren of Marie de Médicis. It appeared most notably in another of Louis's first cousins, Charles II of England, who bore a remarkable resemblance to his ancestor Lorenzo the Magnificent. But there was an equally strong mixture of Spanish and Austrian Habsburg blood in the baby's veins. Anne of Austria was herself the child of a Spanish father and an Austrian mother who was actually her husband's niece. Other uncle–niece unions had occurred within the succession, to say nothing of the repeated marriage of first cousins to insure against outside dilution. A trace of Jewish blood, for example, had entered the royal family of Aragon in the fifteenth century via the mother of Ferdinand of Aragon: constant intermarriage meant that this trace was preserved rather than dissolved.

And so the child who had been mature enough to be born with two teeth – auspicious in a male, less so for his wet-nurses – embarked on his life with cries of joy ringing in his ears: first of the court, then in the

---

Laye gives Louis, apart from the Sun in Virgo, an ascendant sign of Scorpio, in conjunction with the planet Neptune.[25]

little town of Saint-Germain-en-Laye, gradually spreading through all France.

The infancy of Louis, the Godgiven child, was marked by two features, one common enough, the other anything but common. On the one hand he saw very little of his sickly father. That was not at all unusual by the standards of the time, any more than the increasing prospect of his father's death was outside the norm (Louis XIII had been only nine when his own father was assassinated, and in the previous century the accession of young kings had been the rule rather than the exception). Anecdotes survive of their relationship which designate irritability on the part of the father – but then Louis XIII, often in pain, was an irritable man. One story of the eighteen-month-old boy screaming at the sight of his father, and Anne of Austria's desperate efforts to retrieve the situation by demanding better behaviour from her son in the future, certainly has the ring of truth.

But then men, especially kings in their separate households, did not see much of their young children. Relations between the child's parents continued to flourish in one sense at least, for all Louis XIII's suspicion of his wife, since almost exactly two years after Louis, another boy, Philippe, was born on 22 September 1640; he was subsequently known as 'Monsieur', the traditional title of the sovereign's second son, and sometimes as 'Petit Monsieur' in the lifetime of his uncle Gaston.* (This birth has always constituted the best proof that Louis was not some changeling procured from an alien source; and that marital relations continued at least sporadically between the royal couple.)

What was both uncommon and significant was the amount

---

* Louis's brother Philippe was first Duc d'Anjou, then Duc d'Orléans; he will be designated as 'Monsieur' throughout to avoid the confusion of name changes.

the young Louis saw of his mother. Contemporaries drew the obvious conclusion: that Anne had found the love with her first-born son that she had never found with her husband. The result was, as the ever-present La Porte observed, that Louis not only saw much more of his mother than children of his class generally did, but also loved her much more. In his own memoirs, written mainly in his twenties, Louis confirmed the pleasure he always took in her company: 'Nature was responsible for the first knots which tied me to my mother. But attachments formed later by shared qualities of the spirit are far more difficult to break than those formed merely by blood.'[27]

It is true that Anne's own mother, Margaret of Austria, also noted for her piety, had seen more of her daughter (before her premature death) than most queens in the remote atmosphere of the hierarchical Spanish court. But Anne's involvement was quite exceptional. One of the Queen's attendants wrote that her mistress hardly ever left the child: 'She takes great joy in playing with him and taking him out in her carriage whenever the weather is fine; it is her great pleasure in life.'[28]

When the Queen woke up – at ten or eleven, except on days of devotion, very late by French standards – she went to her oratory and prayed at some length.[29] She then received ladies concerned with her various charities, philanthropy being one of the historic roles of a queen. After that, her sons came to her, enjoying their specially commissioned furniture: a little green velvet chair with fringes and gilded nails for Louis and a type of red velvet walker for Monsieur. At his mother's ceremonial rising, a court affair, Louis frequently handed her the chemise, traditionally the prerogative of a high-born lady, not a child, sealing the deed with a kiss.

Except when they were very small, the children took their meals with their mother. Anne loved her food: not only the proverbial Spanish chocolate but bouillon, sausages, cutlets and *olla* – a rich Spanish stew-pot of vegetables. One result of this happy indulgence was that with the onset of middle age and two late pregnancies, her voluptuous figure swelled. Loyal commentators pretended that it made no difference to her beauty – and besides, the greenish eyes still sparkled, the hair was still abundant, the long white hands were as graceful (and well displayed) as ever. The other result was a positive image of food and eating for the young Louis: in time his appetite would astonish Europe and burden his court.

There are many vignettes of Louis's joy in his mother's company: he would join her in her luxurious marble bath in her Appartement des Bains. This was decorated in azure and gold with the mythological theme of Juno, another great queen, as well as pictures of Anne's Spanish relations by Velázquez. The huge marble bowl had lawn curtains and pillows at the bottom of it, a little wood-burning stove providing hot water. Here the pair would lounge, dressed according to the general custom of the time, whether bathing or swimming, in long grey smocks of coarse linen. La Porte gives a picture of the little boy jumping with joy at the news that his mother was going to her bath and begging to join her.[30] No such delight greeted Anne's practice of visiting convents – a Queen of France had the right to visit even closed convents. The adult Louis would recreate the pleasures of the Appartement des Bains in a very different context but he never showed enormous enthusiasm for convents.[31]

A taste for the theatre was however something Anne handed on to her son (even in mourning, her passion was so great that she went privately). The family of the playwright Pierre Corneille was ennobled by the Queen and a pension granted; later a certain witty writer of 'burlesques' named Paul Scarron would also be granted a pension. In the case of Corneille, whose immortal *Le Cid* appeared the year before Louis's birth, the romantic yet stern values that he delineated were very much to the point with the Queen. These were recognisable characters to her: Chimène with her strong sense of her own *gloire* (another important word of the time, with many subtle meanings, in this case perhaps best translated as 'self-respect') and the message: 'Love is only a pleasure, honour is a duty.'[32] Louis grew up knowing all about Corneille, *Le Cid* and a prince's impulsion towards noble action. It remained of course to be seen whether like his mother he would accept the contrast between pleasure and honour in favour of the latter.

Queen Anne's love of the theatre accorded easily with the enormous value she placed on her own dynastic inheritance. It was something inculcated in her son. Queen Anne's 'Spanish pride' – as the French liked to call it – was the subject of much comment throughout her life, variously interpreted as arrogance or resolution, depending on the observer's point of view. Anne herself saw it as an integral part of her position as a great princess: unlike her predecessor Marie de Médicis, daughter of a mere Grand Duke of Tuscany, she was descended from a long line of monarchs including the Emperor Charles V. As Madame de Motteville wrote (obviously echoing the view of her mistress): 'by birth none equalled her.' Apart from the numerous rosaries made of pearls and diamonds which Anne collected, there was nothing she liked more as decoration for her apartments than rows of family portraits – her celebrated relations and ancestors.

At the same time Anne understood the obligations placed upon any person, however grandiose their position, by their faith. It was Queen Anne who patronised not only Corneille but also the great apostle of the poor Vincent de Paul, later canonised, known then as 'Monsieur Vincent'. By making him in 1643 her director of conscience, the Queen indicated her approval of his aim: this was to tap the charitable instincts of ladies who wanted to do good but did not want to become cloistered nuns. It was incarnated in an organisation known as the Daughters of Charity. Appearing at court in an old soutane and coarse shoes, Monsieur Vincent was a striking philanthropic figure, concerned to support the poor.

In general, with a parent who combined royal dignity and Christian goodness with a capacity for enjoying life, it is fair to say that Louis loved his early childhood. His father was no rival; he could be confident that he enjoyed what any son might want: the undiluted love of his mother. Of course this maternal love might have been shared with his brother. There are many theories as to why Anne not so much showed a clear preference for Louis (although she did) but also detached herself from any particularly close relationship with Monsieur.

Was it because Marie de Médicis had favoured her second son, Gaston, over Louis XIII and thus raised him up into inconvenient opposition? Was the delicate Monsieur, a pretty child with the bright black eyes of the Médicis, to be in effect neutered by being feminised, dressed in girls' clothes? Such a ploy is easier to detect with hindsight than for people present at the time. Monsieur did show homosexual leanings quite early in his life – but there is no reason to suppose that he would not have done so in any case. 'The Italian vice', as it was derogatorily known, existed at the French court at the time as at any other. The real answer seems to hark back to the cataclysmic effect of Louis's birth on the Queen: she simply could not go through those feelings again. After all, the birth of Monsieur was convenient (a second male heir provided security in the succession – and indeed a great many second sons had succeeded in French history including Henri II), but it could hardly be seen as a miracle.

*

Before Louis was five years old, his life was transformed. The death of his remote and querulous father, probably from tuberculosis, on 14 May 1643 can hardly have appeared as a tragedy to the child.* Louis XIII himself displayed his melancholic temperament to the end: when told he had an hour to live, he replied: 'Ah! Good news!' The sincere grief that the Queen experienced, at least according to Madame de Motteville, must also have been tempered with relief and even excitement at the new order. Change for Queen Anne had begun late the previous year when her old enemy Richelieu died in December. 'There is something in this man which rises above ordinary mankind,' a contemporary had written of the mighty Cardinal.[34] His designated successor Jules Mazarin was of a very different nature. He showed himself from the first far more accommodating to the Queen, as indeed prudence dictated in the developing situation of Louis XIII's illness.

It was a point made by Queen Anne in her first words to the new monarch, aged four years and eight months, as she knelt breathless before him: 'My King and *my* son' – emphasis added. (In her haste to pay him homage she had hurried on foot through the gardens of Saint-Germain.) In the practical fashion of the time, the corpse was then abandoned to its rituals at Saint-Germain while the living set off for Paris, the Queen and her two sons in an open carriage. The wild applause, the expressions of loyal sympathy, meant that the cortège was constantly delayed: it took seven hours to travel the short distance. As Madame de Motteville wrote: 'They saw in the arms of this princess whom they had watched suffer great persecutions with so much staunchness, their child-King, like a gift given by Heaven in answer to their prayers.'[35]

* There is a story that the dying Louis XIII asked little Louis his name; on being told 'Louis XIV' he replied: 'Not yet, my son'; but it is apocryphal, since kings never referred to themselves by their numeral.[33]

This popular notion that a golden age was dawning was dramatically reinforced five days after the death of the old King. It was said that the dying Louis XIII had had a vision of a French triumph over Spain. No one otherwise could have expected the dazzling victory which the twenty-one-year-old Duc d'Enghien secured over Spain on 19 May at Rocroi in the north-east, on the borders of the Spanish Netherlands.

Known to history as the Grand Condé (he inherited the princely title of Condé from his father three years later), this superb young soldier was seen by his detractors as having 'the air of a brigand' while others thought more admiringly that there was 'something of the eagle about him'.[36] Brigand or eagle as he might be, it was the future Condé's brilliant boldness which enabled him to defeat the Spanish cavalry on the left, leading the charge himself. On the field the Spanish troops, then thought to be the finest in Europe, slightly outnumbered Condé's. But at the end of the bloody day, their casualties far outstripped those of the French. Condé had brought to an end the legend of Spanish military invincibility and could report an extraordinary victory to his child-master.

CHAPTER 2

Vigour of the Princess

The vigour with which this princess sustained my crown
during the years when I could not yet act for myself, were
for me a sign of her affection and her virtue.

– Louis XIV, *Mémoires*

'I have come here to speak to you about my affairs; my
chancellor will tell you my wishes.' These carefully
prepared words were pronounced in a small high voice by
the four-year-old Louis XIV on 18 May 1643. The occasion
was the so-called *lit de justice* of the Parlement de Paris,
taking its name from the cushioned bed from which medieval
monarchs dispensed justice: this was the ceremony by which
the sovereign personally enforced the registration of edicts.
The King was so small that he had to be carried into the
chamber by his chamberlain, the Duc de Chevreuse, and he
was wearing a child's apron. But he had learned his lesson
well. At his side, the new Regent, Anne of Austria, was
draped in the deepest mourning, and it was for the sake of
her future – or, as she would have seen it, for his – that
she had brought her son to the Parlement.

In the end the dying Louis XIII had not denied his wife
her right as a Queen who had given birth to a Dauphin to
act as Regent, even if that Queen was as so often a foreign
princess and in this case a native of the country France was
currently fighting. But he had attempted to circumscribe her
power with a Regency Council, including his brother Gaston
Duc d'Orléans, no longer heir presumptive to the throne
but the senior adult royal male. This limitation Anne

proceeded to get removed with the agreement of the Parlement; furthermore she declared Cardinal Mazarin to be officially her chief adviser. With French victories accruing, and Mazarin at his mother's side to guide her – and perhaps as the years passed offering love as well as guidance? – in 1643 it looked as if Louis would have as happy a childhood as any healthy young prince could expect.

Mazarin, a year younger than the Queen, had in fact been recommended as chief minister to the late King by Cardinal Richelieu as he lay dying. He was an attractive man who had once been described teasingly by Louis XIII to his wife as bearing some resemblance to Buckingham: 'You will like him.' Born Giulio Mazarini and brought up in Rome, he came of a family that had served the princely house of Colonna; he himself had been used by Pope Urban VIII for diplomatic missions when quite young. Early on in his French service he had shown sympathy for Anne of Austria during her period of disgrace which had preceded Louis's birth. Be the resemblance to Buckingham as it may, Mazarin, who was made a cardinal in 1641, was civilised and courtly: he could speak Spanish with Anne, and indulge her femininity – always an important aspect of her character – by procuring her jasmine-scented gloves (for those famous white hands) from Rome.

It can never be known for certain what his true relationship was with the Queen, and there are many divergent theories.[1] If it became in time sexual (without marriage) then this apparently pious woman who continued to take communion frequently was an outrageous hypocrite: for she lived day by day in a state of mortal sin by the rules of the Catholic Church.* It is for this reason – the psychological

* Not only did sexual relations outside marriage constitute a mortal sin by the rules of the Catholic Church (putting the sinner in danger of hell if she/he died without repenting), but taking communion in such a state was a further grave offence. Anne however was noted for being a frequent communicant in an age when not many people were.

implausibility in terms of Anne's known character – that historians have preferred the explanation of a secret marriage.

Such marriages were very much of the period, as we shall see: valid in the eyes of the Church because they were held in an oratory or chapel in the presence of witnesses and blessed by clergy, they permitted all the intimacies of marriage, even if they were ignored in civil terms. It is true that the Cardinal had not actually taken priest's orders (which would obviously have prohibited any marriage) but was merely of clerical status: this was a position which was rare but not unparalleled at this date. However, a modern scholar has provided evidence that Mazarin had begun to think very seriously of being ordained before his death, something that a secret marriage would rule out.[2]

In any case, both these explanations ignore the third possibility that Anne, now in her early forties and with the experience of being unhappily married at fourteen, was not in such desperate need of sex as the cynics and balladeers determined that she must be. What she needed was advice, loyalty, protection and that precious gift *amitié* or even *amitié amoureuse*, a friendship which, as it grew, developed within it a great deal of love. Mazarin took a lot of trouble to aid the Queen in her duties as Regent – for which she was hardly trained – and to educate her into being the dignified figure who came to fill the role with such aplomb. The result was that Anne the Regent was a far more serious person than Anne the scorned and often controversial Queen. It was a change of personality noted by her intimate friends, such as the Duchesse de Chevreuse, who had been exiled at the time of the Queen's disgrace and was now allowed to return. It was motivated by Anne's passionate love for her elder son, but it was orchestrated by Cardinal Mazarin.

The crudeness of the balladeers was extreme and in

certain instances, as satire often is, contradictory. Mazarin, on grounds of his birth, was accused of 'the Italian (homosexual) vice', which meant that his couplings with the Queen – their 'dirty frolics' – had to be of an unnatural sort.* On the other hand, a rhyme entitled 'The Queen's Keeper Tells All' stated exactly the opposite. The admonition 'People, don't doubt that it's true that he f∗∗∗ her' was followed by explicit detail; Louis was supposed to remonstrate against the suggestion of castrating the Cardinal: 'Maman still has a use for them [his private parts].'[4]

In contrast to these, the distasteful snipings from which great persons can never be entirely free, the correspondence of Mazarin and Queen Anne, of which eleven of her handwritten letters have survived, bears witness to tenderness, devotion – love indeed, but with no discernible hint of sex. There are numbers as codes – Anne is fifteen or twenty-two and Mazarin sixteen, while Louis is known as 'the Confidant'. There are signs as symbols: Anne as a line with cross-bars, like an extended cross of Lorraine, and Mazarin as a star. There are endings of letters which betoken real love: Anne signs off: 'I will live' and adds the symbol for herself.[5]

How did the Queen react to the public slurs on her private conduct? Madame de Motteville for one believed that the Queen was too 'lofty' by nature to contemplate the interpretation which might be put upon her relationship with Mazarin (just as she had been naïve in her innocent addiction to 'gallantry' when she arrived in France). Anne knew the vulgar charges to be untrue – 'people who have

---

* In France there was a contemporary obsession with the idea of homosexuality being 'Italian'; Primi Visconti, born in Piedmont, was once told, to his great indignation, that 'in Spain the monks, in France the nobility, in Italy everyone' was homosexual. Primi Visconti's racy memoirs of the French court where he arrived in 1673 are a useful source, given that he was frequently in the company of Louis XIV.[3]

done nothing wrong, have nothing to fear' – and she simply maintained the intimacy which was so essential to her, both personally and in terms of government. The regular evening meeting between the two where Mazarin gave his advice was, finally, what mattered to the Queen.

Against this background of domestic companionship, Louis spent the first ten years of his life. Much later he would criticise his education – as people often do look back with a reproof for the previous generation which is not necessarily justified. He remembered his governesses as an idle lot who simply enjoyed themselves, leaving his care to the humbler waiting-women. But other people who were present remembered things differently. In any case, by the time of his adolescence he spoke and wrote elegant French, could manage Italian and Spanish, and even knew enough Latin to read the dispatches of the Pope.[6]

Detailed instructions for Louis's daily routine, the *Maxims and Directives for the Education of Boys*, were drawn up at Anne of Austria's request and dedicated to her (she was compared to the noble Roman mother of the Gracchi).[7] For example, he was not to sleep in an overheated atmosphere, since the brain needed cold air in order to develop. Classical allusions abounded. It was explained that Socrates had compared a child to a young horse, and at different points Aristotle, Plutarch and St Bernard were cited as well. Nevertheless the advice was all very practical. Plato had sent his disciples and his children to sleep with the aid of music: a gentle chant would help Louis to relax. He should be accustomed to sleep with the light burning, so as not to be frightened if he woke up. Hair should not be allowed to grow too long (Louis had 'the most beautiful hair imaginable', wrote his cousin Anne-Marie-Louise, thick, curling and a rich golden brown). As for washing, 'cleanliness is a quality to be much recommended in a young prince': nails were to be clean, and hands washed regularly with a wet cloth impregnated with *eau de Fontane*, a perfume. Swimming was highly recommended, just as the Greeks swam when fishing, and that role model of energy Henri IV owed his health to frequent swimming.*

Instructions for reading reflected the prevalent political climate. An interest in history was to be deliberately encouraged by Louis's reading matter. He must also study books about the provinces and towns of England and Spain – in case of future conquest – but written in French. Louis however never developed a particular taste for reading: what he loved even as a child were activities which he could practise himself. The royal passion for hunting was inculcated early (Anne had been 'an Amazon in the saddle' when young). So was the passion for sport generally: at the age of four Louis was chasing ducks with his dogs.

Then there were military matters. It was a militaristic age and it was not unusual for a royal or noble child to be obsessed with soldiers: Louis had a taste for silver and lead soldiers and toy forts. Combat was after all the obsession of most of the adult males who surrounded him: not only the nobles who generally went through a form of military service, but also the guards who surrounded him twenty-four hours a day. There was a cult of the warrior at the French court (where the great Henri IV was remembered as a warrior who had brought harmony). As the aphorist the Duc de La Rochefoucauld declared, no man could answer for his courage 'if he had never been in peril'.[8]

Another many-sided figure of the period, like the *galant*, was that of the *honnête homme*; this term essentially referred to the civilised man. One of his virtues was to be brave. Even before Louis had discovered for himself – or thought

---

* It was a type of breaststroke which was in question, with the face out of the water: proposed by the German professor Nicolas Wynman in his *Colymbetes* of 1538, as a protection against drowning.

he had – that 'war ... is the real profession of anyone who governs', in the words of Machiavelli, many of his amusements had something of the military about them. At five Louis drilled other children, and before he was seven he was reviewing real-life guards' regiments. Nor was there an implicit distinction between the masculine sphere of war and that of feminine domesticity: in the summer of 1647 Louis's beloved mother took him to the war front in Picardy to encourage the troops, an image of female presence on military campaigns which presaged his behaviour in adulthood.

All this concentration on the person, the health, the education, the welfare of the young King was further enhanced by Anne's continuing determination that her younger son Monsieur was to defer to Louis in games and treat him, in effect, as a *'Petit Papa'*. This was a phrase sometimes employed of elder brothers, and Louis himself used it to sign his letters to Monsieur. This constant reiteration of the pecking order did not prevent the brothers from having fights: one particular incident was related by the valet de chambre Du Bois in which a boyish romp turned into an equally boyish scatological contest, and Monsieur gave as good as he got. But in essence Monsieur was as firmly trained to occupy the second place as Louis was to rejoice in the first.

On the surface, the religious life of the child Louis was completely conventional. He was confirmed in November 1649 according to the custom of the time and made his first communion at Christmas. Only in the shadowed corners of his life, the dark places in his mother's oratories hung with crucifixes and saints' relics, did an absolutely contradictory sense of his worth prevail. On the one hand Louis was born to be a great King, with glorious possibilities: someone to whom all his subjects from his brother (his heir) downwards must bow according to the will of God. At the same time he himself must bow down to God, in whose eyes his soul was no more precious than that of the humblest peasant in the kingdom.

Mazarin sometimes criticised the Queen for the excessive nature of her piety – 'God can be worshipped everywhere, including in private, Madame,' he said, referring to her addiction to public rituals, to convents and chapel-visiting. But it was sincere. The several hours a day she spent in prayer meant a daily accounting of her spiritual state. Therefore when she educated Louis to believe that kings, however powerful, would one day have to account to God for what they did, it was a lesson he was not likely to forget. Evil, declared the *Maxims ... for the Education of Boys*, was to be pictured in a child's mind as 'a black stain' on a fine piece of cloth: and the cloth in this child's case was of the finest.[9]

In September 1645, political events, in particular the pressure of the war against Spain and others, expensive if successful, meant that it was thought necessary for Louis to appear again at the Parlement de Paris where the Regency had been decided in Anne's favour two years earlier. This time there was no need for the Duc de Chevreuse to carry him. At seven years old Louis walked boldly, although still dressed in the short jacket of a little boy. What he lacked in stature was however fully made up for by the appearance of the Queen Regent. She was the 'leading lady' of the show – and the show was carefully staged.[10] Anne was still draped in black, including a black veil (it was over two years since her husband's death but black suited her, quite apart from establishing her ceaseless mourning as a widow). Through the veil however gleamed a huge pair of earrings, gigantic diamonds mixed with equally vast pearls, all evidently of great worth. A large cross over her heart was equally impressive and equally ostentatious.

Mother and son had been escorted to the Sainte-Chapelle by a panoply of guards and courtiers, with soldiers lining the road from the palace of the Louvre. There they were received by four Presidents of the Parlement de Paris and heard Mass. The seating at the *lit de justice* was carefully arranged by the Queen. On her right she placed her brother-in-law Gaston, beside him the Prince de Condé, whose warrior son had been involved in another great victory at Nördlingen. Dukes and marshals of France were in their appointed places, as were Cardinal Mazarin and various princes of the Church. The Chancellor of France was there and other senior officials, while on the other side were royal ladies such as Condé's wife, the first Princess of the Blood, and the Queen's attendants. The only concession to the King's tender age was the presence of his governess Madame de Sénéce, one of Anne's supporters whom she had appointed on her husband's death; she stood at his side throughout the ceremony.

The grace with which the young King spoke at his mother's signal – everyone saw him glancing at her for approval before he began – caused a surge of prolonged applause. He made the same short introductory speech as he had made in 1643. What followed was a good deal less anodyne. The Chancellor, in 'an eloquent discourse', proceeded to set forth the needs of the state: the campaign against the Spanish must be pursued more strongly than ever, despite a series of splendid victories and despite the Queen Regent's understandable desire for peace.

The best way to secure this peace however was to impress the enemy by conquest. And for conquest, money was needed. At this the First President, Mathieu Molé, responded with lavish praise of the Queen, before holding forth on the needs of the suffering people of France. The Advocate-General Omer Talon also spoke of their tribulations in even more emphatic terms.

Later the Queen Regent, closeted as usual with Mazarin, asked Madame de Motteville whether the King had not done well – had she noted the tender way he turned towards her? – before furrowing her brow over the Advocate-General's speech. She herself cared very deeply for the common people, but all the same perhaps he had said a little too much ... The Queen then returned to discussing the question of peace with Mazarin, accepting his contention that peace, as so often, could only be secured by further fighting.

From the point of view of a boy of seven, such an appearance, such criticisms of his mother's (and Mazarin's) regime, such needs for money, meant that the apparently rock-like security of his home life was crumbling. Was there perhaps an unpleasant lesson to be learned from the presence at the French court of certain close relations who were in effect political refugees? The troubles of Charles I with his own Parliament – which had begun with resistance to taxation – had driven his wife, the former French princess Henrietta Maria, back to her native country. She arrived in the summer of 1644, destitute except for French charity, and was housed in the old quarters at Saint-Germain.

Two years later her youngest child, baptised Henrietta in July 1644 in Exeter Cathedral, was smuggled out of England by a faithful lady-in-waiting. It was symbolic of these unhappy royals' dependence on the French crown that the name of Anne was immediately added to that of Henrietta as a tribute to her aunt the Regent. The two-year-old princess became in the French fashion Henriette-Anne, appropriately enough since French would be her first language, and her first cousins Louis and Monsieur the stars of her childish firmament.* And she was also brought up a Catholic despite that Protestant baptism.

---

* The close family connection of the European royal families at this date is demonstrated by the fact that the young princes and princesses of France, England, Spain and Savoy were all first cousins, descended from the five

The arrival of Henriette-Anne's sixteen-year-old brother Charles Prince of Wales in June 1646 presented a more acute political problem than his helpless mother and baby sister. He was a tall, swarthy, gangling youth who met his difficulties with the only weapon at his disposal, a sense of humour – 'wit rather more than became a prince', wrote Halifax disapprovingly later.[1] Charles now attempted to solve his own financial problems by courting his first cousin Anne-Marie-Louise de Montpensier, the celebrated heiress. It was doubtful whether the wary Mazarin would have allowed such a vast fortune to leave France for the sake of solving the difficulties of the English King (Charles I was currently held by the Scots and would be handed over to Parliament in January 1647). In any case Anne-Marie-Louise herself was too conscious of her own position to waste herself on a penniless Protestant who might not even have a throne to offer in the future. Sentimentally she was more inclined to dwell on a future with her little husband, as she had laughingly designated Louis in childhood.

With Mazarin ambivalent about aiding the English King with French troops, it was not until mid-August 1646 that Charles was formally received by Louis XIV, half his age. He rode in a coach on his cousin's right hand: 'no point of honour being forgotten and nothing omitted that could testify the close ties of consanguinity'. After that it was back to Saint-Germain, and from Charles's point of view a hateful dependency on his mother's meagre financial allowance. Unfortunately Anne of Austria, deeply charitable as she might be towards her sister-in-law and little Henriette-Anne, was far more interested by the news of the death of her

---

children of Henri IV and Marie de Médicis: Louis and Monsieur (Louis XIII); Anne-Marie-Louise de Montpensier and her Orléans half-sisters (Gaston); Charles II, James, Henriette-Anne and Mary, wife of William II of Orange (Henrietta Maria); Infanta Maria Teresa of Spain (Elisabeth); Charles Emmanuel and Marguerite-Yolande of Savoy (Christine).

nephew Philip IV's only son than by events in England. This death meant that in November 1646 the eight-year-old Infanta Maria Teresa became heiress to the throne of Spain (with interesting possibilities for her future husband and children). Looking at the Spanish succession from another angle, Anne's ambitions were also aroused on behalf of Monsieur, half-Spanish by birth and now a possible candidate for the Spanish throne in his own right.

As it happened, the implementation of these hopes – or were they snares? – lay far ahead. What the Regent and the Cardinal had to deal with immediately was protest from the Parlement de Paris against the burden of taxation, something that the pretty speeches of the puppet-King could no longer curb.* In August 1648 the Grand Condé secured another brilliant victory at Lens, north-west of Arras, against the invading Austro-Spanish army. So the interminable shifting hostilities which had become the Thirty Years War ended for the most part with the Peace of Westphalia. That is to say, France settled its accounts with the Austrian Empire although remaining at war with Spain. In theory the French forces not occupied against Spain were now freed to deal with dissension at home. In practice the Queen's ineptitude (against the advice of Mazarin) in ordering the arrest of three popular members of the Parlement, led by the dis- tinguished elder Pierre Broussel, resulted in widespread rioting. The Queen and her children were forced to take refuge in the Palais-Royal, none too secure a place compared with the fortress of the Louvre, while barricades were put up all around them.

Worse was to follow. On 13 September 1648, a week after his tenth birthday, Louis had to be taken away from

---

* The Parlement de Paris was not a parliament in the English sense of the word but a High Court with jurisdiction over a third of the kingdom; there were other provincial Parlements.

Paris itself by his mother. The Queen's coolly resolute behaviour in the midst of many challenges to her authority impressed observers: she certainly justified her own pride in her descent from great rulers. The little family, with Monsieur recovering from smallpox, went first to Rueil and then to Saint-Germain. When members of the Parlement followed her in protest, Anne blandly explained that the Palais-Royal needed a thorough cleaning (not quite such a feeble excuse as it might sound, since royal palaces were generally vacated so that cleaning could take place). Besides the boy King wanted to enjoy the last of the summer in the fresh country air.

An accord with the Parlement, negotiated by Gaston d'Orléans in Paris, was signed by Anne at the end of October, and the Queen brought her children back to the capital. But this agreement, although signed by Anne on Mazarin's advice, outraged her sense of royal authority with its concessions, while in the event solving nothing. The next stage was from Louis's point of view still more alarming. The Queen and Mazarin were determined not to allow the young King to become the hostage of the Parlement. In an incident very far removed from the glorious circumstances of his birth, Louis and his brother with the Queen and a few trusted attendants were smuggled out of the Palais-Royal on the night of 5–6 January. They were taken to Saint-Germain once more, but this time the château was ill-prepared to receive them, since for secrecy's sake the news of their arrival could not be spread abroad, nor could any baggage accompany them. The first flight might have been presented to Louis, as to the Parlement, as a perfectly reasonable expedition; four months later it was impossible to put any such cosy gloss on what was clearly a desperate measure.

Yet it was still the Queen's high spirits in the face of danger which struck those present. At Christmas the satires against the Queen pinned up on the Pont Neuf had caused her much pain: she found the iniquity of the content deeply distressing and the credulity of the people in believing them horrifying. Now that there was need for action, Anne could not have been happier 'if she had won a battle, taken Paris, and hanged everyone who had crossed her'. Thus she celebrated the eve of the Feast of the Epiphany in traditional style with cakes and little games, laughing heartily when she was the one to be crowned 'queen of the bean'.[12] The King and his brother were duly put to bed. It was only when all was silence and darkness that they were awakened, taken to a wicket gate, placed in a closed coach and transported away out of Paris. Whatever the trauma of the occasion for Louis, there were lessons to be learned from his mother's behaviour: the need, not only for calm in the face of danger but also for utter secrecy when a bold plan was to be carried out.

This first stage of the many-stranded revolt later known as the Fronde (from the French word for catapult, weapon of choice for the Frondeur mob) was settled at the Peace of Rueil in March 1649, with compromise on the subject of taxation. Two months earlier Charles I had been executed in Whitehall, and the exiled Prince of Wales, greeted with the faltering words from his attendants, 'Your Majesty', had understood that he was now King. Thus the little French Queen of England, cowering in the old quarters of Saint-Germain, had become a widow, the four-year-old half-French Princess an orphan with little to commend her as a marriage prospect except her rank. As Madame de Motteville observed, 1648 had not been a good year for kings: it seemed that 'divine justice menaced' them all across Europe.[13]*

---

* In addition, the sudden death of Ladislas IV of Poland precipitating a crisis in the monarchy, the death of Christian IV of Denmark at a critical moment for his country and a revolt in Moscow against the Tsar Alexis meant that her comment of 1648 was fully justified.

Much of the popular venom now focused on the Cardinal, in a series of pamphlets or 'Mazarinades' which mixed scurrility with violent protest. The second stage of the Fronde consisted of serious armed uprisings in the provinces, notably Normandy, Guyenne and Provence, whose effect was to devastate the countryside. An appalling harvest led to soaring grain prices and only exacerbated the sufferings of the people. Then there was the popular hero, the Grand Condé, whose personal courage (courage attended by a series of victories) made him the ideal leader of noble dissent, coupled with the wealth and vast properties which gave him an enormous clientele. At first Mazarin had dealings with Condé which enabled the court party to defeat the Frondeurs. But Condé's personal arrogance infuriated the Queen. In January 1650, with his brother the Prince de Conti and brother-in-law the Duc de Longueville, Condé was committed to prison for a year.

As an expedient, once again it did not work. Condé had to be released, due to fierce agitation, and it was Mazarin who temporarily withdrew to Brühl, near Cologne. He left an agonised Queen, who poured out her suffering heart in that correspondence ending in coded symbols of affection to which allusion has already been made.

In the intricate pavane of changing alliances – and multiplying challenges to the royal authority – Gaston d'Orléans now moved across to the Frondeurs, and in a dramatic incident his defiant eldest daughter, the Grande Mademoiselle,* heroic as she stood at the head of her men, ordered them to fire from the Bastille. For brave, foolish Anne-Marie-Louise this was a defining moment in which she deployed all those great qualities she felt to be within

* The term 'the Grande Mademoiselle' will be used in future here to denote Anne-Marie-Louise, although it was in fact a title used later to distinguish her from her senior half-sister, meaning 'the Elder Mademoiselle', not a reference to her stature, moral or physical.

herself, daughter (actually granddaughter) of kings: she satisfied her sense of her own glory. Later the Grande Mademoiselle tried to justify her disobedience to her sovereign by citing the superior patriarchal claims of her own father.[14]

Unfortunately the incident was also a defining moment for her young cousin Louis. The Grande Mademoiselle had robbed herself of her little husband, said Mazarin coarsely. That was probably true: in the scales in which her wealth was neatly balanced against the eleven-year gap in their ages, the Grande Mademoiselle's Frondeur stand certainly weighed against her heavily. She would pay for it by five years of exile from the court, just as her father was dispatched to his château at Blois with his wife, his three younger daughters and their attendants.

And there was more to it than that. In his adulthood, Louis evinced a pronounced dislike of 'political' women. He went on record on the subject: 'the beauty who dominates our pleasures has never had the liberty to talk to us of our affairs.'[15] (Whether it was always true is another matter: Louis believed it was true.) The distasteful heroics of his older cousin, in virago-like opposition to Louis himself, set him on this course: women were undesirable elements in politics. There was one honourable exception: his own mother. In his praise for Queen Anne after her death, Louis made the point: 'The vigour with which this princess sustained my crown during the years when I could not yet act for myself, was for me a sign of her affection and her virtue.'[16] In short, total public and private support was acceptable, public defiance definitely not.

September 1651 marked a significant date: it was the young King's thirteenth birthday and, by the royal rules, his majority. The occasion was marked by a great procession through the heart of Paris. It was witnessed by the English diarist John Evelyn, who had fled the 'unhandsome' troubles of his native country, and he watched it from the balcony of another exile, the philosopher Thomas Hobbes. Evelyn noted 'the whole equipage and glorious cavalcade' including the Swiss Guards, led by two cavaliers in scarlet satin. Most glorious of all was the King himself, 'like a young Apollo' in a suit so richly covered in embroidery that nothing could be seen of the stuff beneath it: 'he went almost the whole way with his hat in his hand saluting the ladies and ambassadors, who had filled the windows with their beauty, and the air with *Vive le Roi*.'[7]

But Evelyn, in all the lushness of his description, also put his finger on an aspect of Louis's character, the Louis who lived through the complicated vicissitudes of the Fronde. His 'countenance' was sweet, but at the same time it was 'grave'. The impenetrable public composure which was to be such a marked characteristic of the mature Louis XIV was already in place.

The troubles of the Fronde were finally put to rest when the brilliant French soldier the Vicomte de Turenne, originally under the command of Condé, helped to defeat his former master on behalf of the court. In February 1653 Condé retreated to the service of Spain, and Cardinal Mazarin returned. A halcyon period lay ahead, in which the young Apollo was displayed by his mother in a series of godlike appearances, symbolic of peace not war. They also, of course, symbolised the power of the crown.

Dancing was the key element in all this. The importance of the dance at this time, as vital to young men as fencing, was considered to be so great that even the Jesuits saw it as necessary to instruct their pupils in the art. Among the various genres, that of the Court Ballet, developed in Italy and brought to France by Catherine de Médicis, needed a ceremonial dignity, at which Louis XIV had a natural talent: already by the age of eight he was described as dancing 'perfectly'. As a young man he excelled at the grave so-called Slow Courante and could perform the necessary turn-out of legs and feet with supreme elegance.*

In the *Ballet of the Night* at the carnival of 1653, Louis wore for the first time the costume of the rising sun, while one of the lines spoke of the 'coming marvels' to be expected of this glittering vision. Alongside him danced a young musician of twenty, born in Italy, now French, who had recently been in the service of the Grande Mademoiselle, Jean-Baptiste Lully. Professional dancers posed as beggars with bandaged wounds so that they could be 'cured' in the Court of Miracles. A few months later, in a ballet called *The Marriage of Peleus and Thetis*, Louis played Apollo himself, surrounded by the first ladies of the kingdom dancing the nine muses. Henriette-Anne, at the time of the Fronde reduced to shivering in her bed for lack of heat and food, was now thought suited to the role of Erato, muse of erotic poetry; she was not yet ten years old but her position as the first princess in France after her aunt and mother entitled her to the role. In case anyone missed the significance of these government exercises in propaganda, Louis, playing a sorcerer in the *Ballet of the Feasts of Bacchus*, was hailed with these lines: 'He is indeed the Master of the Future: / You only need to look upon his eyes and his countenance.'[19]

For once in royal annals, there was actually no need of exaggeration to hail the fourteen-year-old King in this manner. All contemporary accounts agree that he was astonishingly handsome at this stage. The beautiful, long, curling hair, sentimentally praised by the Grande Mademoiselle, was only one of his physical assets, but it was much prized at the time. (Queen Anne struck many a

---

* The turn-out of Louis XIV's time was 90 degrees, i.e. each leg turned out 45 degrees from the centre-line, rather than the 180 degrees which has become the norm.

graceful attitude combing thick locks which her son had inherited.) Louis's figure was described as 'tall, free, ample and robust' while his bearing was characteristic of 'those whom we speak of as having the blood of gods'.[20]* This particular eulogy went on: above all this nonpareil had to be seen dancing the ballet; then he appeared as 'Heaven's masterpiece, the gift of God to France'. It did not need the indulgent eyes of his mother and the court, relaxing at last after the divisive horrors of the Fronde, to see in the juvenile grace of Louis a triumphant presage – once again as at his birth – of a golden age.

On 7 June 1654 Louis XIV was consecrated King of France, according to the custom of his ancestors, in the cathedral at Rheims, north-east of Paris. Those princes present did not include his uncle Gaston, in exile at Blois, nor the Grand Condé, now serving his erstwhile enemy in Spain. But the array was magnificent, the ceremony prolonged, beginning at six in the morning, and the whole ritual ostentatiously holy and historic.† Seated in a specially constructed box, Queen Anne was radiant with her son's public triumph; only the presence of the widowed Henrietta Maria beside her provided a kind of *memento mori*.

But Louis XIV did not only look a romantic ideal at this point: he himself felt full of romance towards women. He

---

* Louis XIV is always mentioned as being tall by those who knew him, like the Grande Mademoiselle: in another account he was mentioned as half a head taller than Cardinal Mazarin, whom no one described as being short. The myth of the small King elevating himself on high heels is based on a misconception about fashion at the time. Charles II for example, who was well over six feet tall, also wore high heels. Historians now think that Louis XIV was probably about 5'9".[21]

† The attention paid to the mere fact of consecration in this period may be judged by the earnest dilemma of a young English Royalist, Mary Eure, in 1653. Needing to be touched for the King's Evil, as scrofula was termed, she could not decide between Louis XIV (as yet unconsecrated) and Charles II (a king without a throne).[22]

loved to play the guitar, the plucked stringed instrument introduced from Spain (where it had been brought by the Arabs).²³ He was originally influenced by his mother and the memories of the Spanish court of her faraway, idealised youth. But it was Cardinal Mazarin who saw to it that Louis had the best available teacher, a fellow Italian, Francisco Corbetta, who by the mid-century had published two guitar books for the rulers of the cities of Bologna and Milan, and probably another for the King of Spain.

Playing the guitar was a notably less ceremonious occupation than dancing in the formal Court Ballet: at the same time, what was the Spanish guitar if not a weapon of courtship in the hands of a gallant? It was significant in this context that the return of Mazarin meant the institution once again of a kind of home life, as had been enjoyed before the Fronde, but it was now a home life which included a host of Mazarin's female relations, a lively collection of Italian girls. For the Cardinal had a desire, laudable by most family standards (if not those of the jealous French), to surround himself with his own blood, and arrange ambitious marriages for them.²⁴

These Mazarinettes, as they were known, were seven strong, plus three brothers, and had started arriving in court in 1647. They included the Martinozzis, children of Mazarin's eldest sister; Laura, a few years older than Louis, would marry the heir to the Duke of Modena. Anna Maria married the Prince de Conti who was the younger brother of the Grand Condé.

The Martinozzis were blonde and pliant. The same could not be said of the Mancini girls, five of them altogether, whose ages in 1654 ranged from nineteen to five. These were the children of Mazarin's second sister Hieronyma, who had married up into a higher degree of the Italian nobility. With their zest for life, their combative high spirits, their intelligence and their dark 'Roman' looks, the Mancinis were very far from being the contemporary ideal, at least in theory. It was not so much that they were dark – although it was female fairness which was constantly praised as representing perfection. It was more the Mancinis' general disdain for conventions. Every preacher, every philosopher preached the need for feminine passivity and submission. As Hortense Mancini, the acknowledged beauty of the family, wrote in her memoirs: 'I know that the glory of a woman consists in never talking of herself.' Or as a certain governess would sum it up later, a woman born Françoise d'Aubigné: 'modesty should be the lot of women ... your sex obliges you to obedience. Suffer much before you complain about it.'[25] The Mancinis on the other hand were active and early on entered the courtly business of fascination.

The eldest was the sweet-natured Victoire – 'the only wise one' – who married the Duc de Mercoeur. Olympe, Louis's exact contemporary, was a famous charmer, quite as determined as her uncle to make the best of her chances. The beautiful Hortense, born in 1646 following two boys, looked 'like an angel'; she was easygoing but wayward; the novelist the Comtesse de La Fayette noted acidly that Hortense, unlike her sisters, had no wit but to some people at court 'that was yet another mark in her favour'.[26] Marianne, the youngest, who would marry the Duc de Bouillon, loved poetry and later saw herself as the protectress of poets, including La Fontaine.

There was however a Cinderella in the family, to quote the ancient folk fairy story which would be published in its French version towards the end of this century in Perrault's *Tales of Mother Goose*. This particular Cinderella was the middle child, a year younger than the sparkling Olympe. And the role of the vindictive Ugly Sister was played in her life not by Olympe or Hortense – the Mancini girls were always strongly supportive of each other – but by her own mother.

Marie Mancini was the darkest of all the girls and very slender. With her long thin arms and her wide mouth (at least she showed the contemporary rarity of perfect white teeth when she smiled), Marie appalled her mother with her lack of classical looks. The lethargic and anxious Hieronyma Mancini, inspired by a horoscope which predicted that Marie would cause trouble in the future, demanded on her deathbed that the Cardinal should shut Marie up in a convent and keep her there.

Surrounded by these young women in a pleasant domestic atmosphere, it was inevitable that Louis would fall in love with one of them. Or more than one. It was not a question of sexual initiation. There was a tradition among sophisticated European royals that this was the task – or privilege – of an accommodating older court lady. When Louis was hardly in his teens, the enchanting Duchesse de Châtillon, known as Bablon, was alleged to have set her cap at him. A dismissive rhyme was written on the subject by the sharp-penned Bussy-Rabutin: 'If you are ready / The King is not ... / Your beauty deserves more / Than a minority.' Now fifteen, Louis was ready. Just as Charles II, while still Prince of Wales, had been seduced by the opulent Mrs Christabella Wyndham, Louis is always supposed to have been initiated by one of his mother's most trusted ladies-in-waiting (she had taken part in the flight from the Palais-Royal on that fateful night). 'One-eyed Kate', as the Baronne de Beauvais was nicknamed, was about twenty-four years older than Louis, much closer to his mother's age than his own. The incident was said to have taken place as Louis was on the way back from the baths – 'she ravished him or at least surprised him' – and to have been enjoyable enough to be repeated on several more occasions.[27]

The evidence for this is, it is true, based on later gossip.

Primi Visconti and the Duc de Saint-Simon both mention the story with confidence, although the former first arrived in France in 1673 and the latter was only born in 1675. Nevertheless there seems enough support to give the story plausibility. Madame de Beauvais was rewarded with a house and pension – conceivably for services to the mother rather than the son, or possibly both. More cogently, the young Saint-Simon remembered her, wrinkled and by this time almost entirely blind, being treated with great respect at Versailles by Louis XIV and accorded that ultimate mark of favour, a talk with the King 'privately'.[28]

Where romantic flirtation as opposed to sex was concerned, Louis was originally captivated by Olympe Mancini, with her delicious *fossettes* or dimples and her 'eyes full of fire'. Olympe had a dubious reputation: she was described as having a nature 'little touched with Christian maxims', and there were rumours that Louis slept with her. It was certainly possible. It is true that this was an age when in the marriage-market all girls had to enter, virginity was highly prized and virgins closely watched: the Cardinal's men were after all everywhere. Yet Olympe's subsequent career would show her to be a bold and even amoral woman, not afraid to barter her physical charms for her own advantage – or for her own pleasure. There were always those who took the risk of breaking the rules, and Olympe was certainly among them. In the course of time she was rewarded with a semi-royal match to a Savoyard prince who became the Comte de Soissons. Olympe's condition was that she should remain at the French court. Here her Italian zest and voluptuous looks continued to be generally admired – not least by the King.

Olympe Mancini knew the rules – the rules of the court as laid down by Queen and Cardinal. Yet already Louis was beginning to challenge his mother's authority, especially where his own pleasures were concerned. In 1655, at a so-called Petit Bal held by Queen Anne in her apartments to honour her niece Henriette-Anne, the Queen instructed her son to open the proceedings by dancing with his cousin. Instead of agreeing, as protocol demanded, Louis made it quite clear that he preferred to dance with Victoire Mancini Duchesse de Mercoeur and took her hand, muttering something about not wishing to dance with little girls (Henriette-Anne was nearly eleven but small for her age). Her appearance, in Louis's graceless expression, reminded him of the bones of the Holy Innocents.[29]

It was a calculated affront not only to the English royal family but also to Queen Anne's own authority. Furious, she yanked Victoire de Mercoeur from her son's grasp. In vain poor Queen Henrietta Maria ran after Queen Anne with the polite fiction that her daughter had a bad foot and thus no wish to dance. Queen Anne insisted. Louis sulked but in the end the mother's will prevailed. The question must however have been in her mind as in that of other observers of the sullen seventeen-year-old boy: for how long?

CHAPTER 3

Peace and the Infanta

'Good news, Madame! ... I bring Your Majesty peace and the Infanta.'

– Cardinal Mazarin to Anne of Austria, 1659

By 1657, Louis XIV, approaching nineteen, was evidently of marriageable age. It could be argued that he was the most brilliant match in Europe: and if that was true, the one bride who was equal to him in her superb rank was his first cousin the Infanta Maria Teresa. This was the marriage for which Anne of Austria had prayed so fervently since the two, virtual twins, were in the cradle. Similarly Maria Teresa's French-born mother Elisabeth had impressed on her daughter the incomparable majesty of the role of the Queen of France: otherwise a great Spanish princess could well be happier in a convent. Unfortunately the two countries of France and Spain had been at war so long – and Spain now harboured the Frondeur rebel general the Prince de Condé – that there were considerable obstacles in the way of these wistful dreams.

Meanwhile there were many other royal parents to whom the young King of France appeared as the ideal son-in-law. For example, Louis XIII's sister, Christine Duchess of Savoy, made delicate enquiries about the prospects of her own daughter Marguerite-Yolande.[1] There was always much to be said for a Franco-Savoyard marriage (which is why so many of them took place down the centuries of the *Ancien Régime*). Savoy's geographical position between Austria north of its capital Turin and the Italian duchies of Modena and Tuscany made it of perpetual strategic significance to France. Another possible Italian bride was from the d'Este family: a daughter of the Duke of Modena whose heir had recently married the Cardinal's niece Laura Martinozzi. To almost any Catholic princess – and perhaps a few Protestant ones prepared as Henri IV had done to find the throne of France worth a Mass – Louis XIV represented a magnificent career opportunity.

One way-out suggestion was made by a French theologian presenting an address to the former Queen Christina of Sweden, who was on a European tour following her abdication.[2] Perhaps this maddening, eccentric, brilliant spinster, in her masculine wig looking 'more of a man than a woman', nevertheless with a highly feminine décolletage, might be the bride from heaven ... Christina maintained a steely silence at the suggestion, although the idea of such a marriage certainly represents a counterfactual delight.

What then of the French royal princesses? The Grande Mademoiselle, now thirty, had been recently welcomed back to court with elegant words from the King: 'let us talk no more about the past.' (Louis had learned early on the gentle and useful art of public forgiveness.) Her half-sisters, daughters of Gaston by a second marriage, were of more marriageable, or rather child-bearing, age by the standards of the time. Although the Grande Mademoiselle would have preferred the King's fancy to fall on any candidate other than these 'inferior' princesses, Marguerite-Louise at twelve was already 'beautiful as the day'.[3] Then there was the half-French half-English Henriette-Anne, who if scorned as 'a little girl' by her cousin Louis, still had to be found a bridegroom. Naturally Queen Henrietta Maria dreamed of what would be the greatest match of all, and Queen Anne, with her feeling for dynastic connection – remember all those family portraits – would have accepted the niece who had been her protégée since babyhood if the Infanta remained unavailable.

However, where Mazarin was concerned, neither the money of the Grande Mademoiselle, the beauty of Marguerite-Louise nor the impeccable royal breeding of Henriette-Anne counted in this situation. What was a career opportunity for a princess was a diplomatic opportunity for a King (and his advisers). The marriage of Louis XIV was destined, surely, to be an awesome matter of state. So his duty demanded.

Yet for a moment, a week, a month, perhaps a little longer, it seemed that the steady flame of duty in Louis's heart, so carefully tended by his mother since his birth, flickered dangerously as the far more exciting flame of romantic love flared up beside it. It was a question not so much of his feelings for the Mancini Cinderella, Marie, but his intentions towards her.

Louis was already showing himself susceptible to a pretty face, a languishing glance, and at court especially among his mother's junior ladies-in-waiting there were plenty of attractive girls glad to throw just such a glance in his direction. One of them was Anne-Lucie de La Motte d'Argencourt, who, while not a startling beauty, had a bewitching combination of blue eyes, blonde hair and naturally very dark eyebrows (black eyebrows, unlike black hair, were much admired at the time). Furthermore she shared Louis's 'violent passion' for dancing. Naturally the Queen frowned upon the flirtation, and although Louis gallantly offered to ignore his mother's criticisms, this proposal seemed to the girl to cast some aspersion on her virtue. In the end Queen Anne persuaded her son that it was all a matter of sin and he abandoned his romance for a while – before returning and sweeping Anne-Lucie away in a court dance. Anne-Lucie said afterwards that Louis trembled all the time he held her.[4]

The authority of Anne and Mazarin was however still in the ascendant. Brutally, Mazarin told Louis that Anne-Lucie had betrayed all his secrets, whereas the girl had merely tried to win Mazarin's esteem by discussing the King with him. Nevertheless, a combination of their anger and the jealousy of the wife of the lover Anne-Lucie actually preferred, meant that she was relegated to a convent at Chaillot. It is pleasing to report that unlike many girls thus dismissed in this period, Anne-Lucie found life there very much to her taste, received many visits (she was not an enclosed nun), and spent the next thirty-five years in total happiness.

Where Anne and Mazarin were concerned, Marie Mancini presented quite a different challenge. Contemporary observers agreed on three things about the Cardinal's niece (apart from the fact that in general they disliked her). These were their conclusions: first, that she was not remotely pretty; second, that she was intellectual, even bookish in a way most young girls were not; third, that for a season she was 'absolute mistress' of the young Louis XIV, in the words of the novelist the Comtesse de La Fayette, having 'compelled' him to love her.[5] Queen Anne also believed that Marie Mancini had woven a spell: furiously she compared it to that by which the enchantress Armide had captured Rinaldo in Tasso's *Jerusalem Delivered* and turned him to sensual pleasures.

And yet the pleasures Marie Mancini outlined do not seem to have been particularly sensual, unless taste for high romance in plays and novels be seen as such. What Hieronyma Mancini, the wicked Stepmother – actually mother – of Marie's story had missed was her daughter's originality by the standards of the time. Not only did she appreciate painting and music but she had an ardent love of literature. The heroic plays of Corneille, especially *Le Cid*, were a particular favourite: a taste, of course, that Marie Mancini had in common with Queen Anne. Here was a heady mixture of love, honour, duty and renunciation as Chimène passionately adores Rodrigue the killer of her father, yet feels compelled in terms of her personal *gloire* to demand his death. At the same time the proud Infanta Urraque is inspired with an equally unsuitable passion for Rodrigue, but in her case it is the need for royal to wed royal which inhibits her. 'Heaven owes you a king,' Urraque is admonished at one point, yet 'you love a subject'.[6] A female who was obsessed by Corneille and his lofty chivalric ideals was in a different class from most girls of her age for whom the prayer-book was enough, with the best-selling novels of Madeleine de Scudéry the far horizon of their reading.

The standard of women's education in France was not only low in the seventeenth century but unabashedly so. Even a clever woman like the Princesse des Ursins would boast of merely knowing her catechism and her rosary 'as good women do' (although she certainly knew a great deal more). Most women were held to have no need of such leisurely accomplishments as reading and writing. Physical weakness was equated with moral frailty to add to the presumed inferiority of the weaker sex: women were by nature disorderly beings not even responsible for their own actions (with of course no status at law).[7] What need of education for them?

Estimates of the number of women who could actually sign their own name in this period vary between 34 and 14 per cent. 'Oh, that I were but a Man, I should study Night and Day,' wrote the English pamphletist Elinor James. But since they were not men, as a whole the female sex accepted its virtually illiterate destiny. For women of the upper classes, a convent education, provided by inspiring individual nuns, offered growing possibilities as the century progressed. But even here a clever woman like Madame de Sévigné looked down on the quality of the teaching supplied: she rejected the idea of a convent for her daughter's child, telling the daughter, Juliette de Grignan, to whom she wrote so constantly and so richly: 'you will talk to her [the child]. I think that is worth more than a convent.' Conversation, declared the great letter-writer, was better than reading.[8]

The fact was that, as Madame de Sévigné's remark indicates, there were clever women in France – in Paris – and it was the art of conversation which was their principle organ of expression. In the salons of the brilliant, witty, cultured, refined women later nicknamed by Molière the *Précieuses*, ideas flowed during conversation. And from ideas came a special kind of excitement, making other more stolid company unendurable. Madeleine de Scudéry, for example, suggested that a woman in conversation should demonstrate a marvellous rapport between her words and her eyes, while she should of course be careful not to sound 'like a book talking'; she should rather speak 'worthily of everyday things and simply of grand things'.[9] But these women and their male admirers deliberately constituted their own kind of society with their private nicknames and their codes, which had little to do with the court, particularly during the troubled years of the Fronde.* In short, the young Louis XIV did not know many sparkling young women. Thus Marie Mancini constituted his introduction both to the arts, which made a lifelong impression, and to a kind of chivalric love.

It helped that Marie was not entirely preoccupied with things of the mind. She was a wonderful rider, and her

---

* The name *Précieuses* was first used for these preternaturally clever women in 1654, not in denigration but descriptively. It should not therefore at this date be identified with the English word 'precious' or affected. Molière's play of that name which poked fun at young women with highfaluting ideas about their own accomplishments (not women's education as such) dates from 1659. Its success had the effect of changing the meaning of the word to something humorously critical.

slender figure – scrawny, some said rudely – meant that she had a marvellous air dressed up in boy's clothes on her horse, where the plumper beauties fashionable at the time might not have made such a pretty picture. In black velvet edged with fur, including a matching hat above the huge dark eyes which were her best feature, she was irresistible. It was certainly not a coincidence that the King's early loves were all superb equestriennes, able to outdistance the court if necessary, since riding in the forests and glades round the various royal châteaux represented some of the few opportunities for privacy that Louis had.

As for the Cinderella element in the story, the King's eye first fell upon the neglected Marie when her disagreeable mother was dying in late 1657 and he paid a series of courtesy visits to his chief minister's sister. According to Marie, the King appreciated the frankness she showed in their talks: 'the familiar way in which I lived with the King and his brother [due to the intimacy of Cardinal and Queen] was something so easy and pleasant that it gave me the opportunity to speak my thoughts without reserve.'[10]

Louis was able to taste the delights of knightly rescue: the beguiling thought that he had transformed Marie's life with his attention. As she wrote much later in her memoirs,[11] it was a pleasure for Louis to be so generous to her: the King saw them as Pygmalion and Galatea, the sculptor and the marble statue that he brought to life. In other words, from her own point of view (that of an ordinary young woman of little or no fortune) 'it was the love of a God'. The Court Ballet *Alcidiane and Polexandre* of 14 February 1658, founded on a novel by Marin de Gomberville, contained these lines: 'Your Empire, Love, is a cruel empire / All the world complains, all the world sighs.'[12] But in these early months of their relationship, neither Louis nor Marie found Love's Empire anything but delightful.

What Marie Mancini really offered Louis in the heady

days before that inevitable royal marriage – or was it really inevitable? – was something totally new to him in an upbringing which had at times been traumatic but in private terms always carefully cloistered. Of course there was her unconditional love for *him* as opposed to his crown, a tribute which like any young man born to a great position, Louis found immensely seductive. But there was more to her hold over him, the 'spell' she had cast, than that. Marie, in her 'witty, bold and wanton' way offered independence from the clearly stated wishes of his mother and the Cardinal.[13] Even their disapproval must have been exciting because it was new.

The situation to outsiders was especially baffling since it seems quite unlikely that Marie and Louis ever slept together. Once again contemporary commentators, no friends to Marie, combined to doubt the fact. The abdicated Queen Christina of Sweden spent a week at the court at Compiègne and longer than that – rather longer than expected – in France. She had a low opinion of Marie Mancini's looks: she told the Grande Mademoiselle that it was a shame the King could not be in love with someone more attractive. Nevertheless Christina doubted that 'he [Louis XIV] has even touched the tip of Marie's finger'. Perhaps it was not *quite* that platonic: the discreet Madame de Motteville probably expressed the truth when she wrote that the relationship was 'not altogether without its limits'.[14] Subsequent events would show that Marie's nature was romantic and impetuous, in contrast to her frankly carnal and charmingly calculating sisters Olympe and Hortense. A physical affair – however far it went – with Olympe Mancini or the rash Anne-Lucie de La Motte d'Argencourt was something that could be tolerated as harmless (if sinful, as the Queen never failed to point out) and then quietly ended with all the weapons of society at the disposal of Cardinal and Queen. But the winning card of God's thunderous disapproval could hardly be played against a platonic friendship, however intense.

It was when Louis began to reflect dreamily on the possibility of marrying Mazarin's niece that the dangers of the situation came home to the Queen and the Cardinal. In spite of the malicious suggestions of his enemies, there is no evidence that Mazarin ever entertained the idea of the family union seriously and a great deal of evidence that he did not. He loved Louis, who was his godson, his creation, the summit of his gift to his adopted country, and he did not particularly like Marie. While Louis dallied with Marie Mancini, the Cardinal was involved in a series of resourceful manoeuvres aimed at peace between France and Spain – peace and the Infanta.

The serious illness of Louis in the summer of 1658 served to concentrate the Cardinal's mind on the need for a royal marriage. On the surface it was a time of joyous French victories. The shifting alliances of Europe in the middle of the seventeenth century were illustrated well by the fact that in their shared contest against Spain, France had recently joined up with Cromwellian England (despite the close relationship of the French to the exiled English royal family). At the Battle of the Dunes on 14 June 1658, which led to the seizure of Spanish-held Dunkirk, the celebrated commander the Vicomte de Turenne headed the French, aided by six thousand English infantry under Sir William Lockhart. The Spanish forces under Don Juan José of Austria included not only Turenne's former commander the Grand Condé, but also the younger brother of Charles II, James Duke of York.

The French King, who believed in sharing so far as was possible the rigours of a campaign with his troops, insisted on lodging at nearby Mardyck despite the discouragement of Mazarin. The Cardinal pointed out that the courtiers were eating the food from the countryside needed by the army. But Louis would not listen. As Mazarin commented wryly to a colleague: 'He is the master, but nothing will prevent me from telling him always what I believe would be in his interest.' It was extremely hot and Mardyck was notoriously unhealthy, with the lingering odour of corpses all about, some new (there had been four thousand Spanish casualties alone), but also the half-buried dead of battles long ago. Wrote Madame de Motteville of these unwelcome presences: 'the dryness of the land' preserved the bodies.[15]

Louis fell ill, probably with typhoid fever. Even now he argued with Mazarin about the need to retreat to Calais. But once there his fever flared up hideously and many of those around him – in an age when sudden death from a disease like typhoid was a common phenomenon – feared the worst. For about ten days he was in extreme danger. There was something like panic. (The point has been well made that the contemporary concentration on the eldest son 'took no account of sudden death'.)[16] The sight of this nineteen-year-old royal sun in eclipse led to court attention focusing on the new light on the horizon: seventeen-year-old Monsieur. It was at this moment that the remarkable subjugation of Monsieur's spirit – subjugated since birth – was evinced. For Monsieur himself never wavered publicly and privately in his despair at his brother's illness and his total loyalty to him personally. In turn this critical moment in Louis's life cemented his own feelings of protection and loyalty to his brother. Monsieur's evident homosexuality – for which Louis had no time in others – did not come between the brothers.

Louis XIV recovered. His cure was attributed to doses of wine laced with emetics such as cassia (an inferior kind of cinnamon) and senna. The ecstatic gratitude of the whole country, spared 'the most grievous loss France could have' in the words of a gazette, left Cardinal Mazarin with two problems.[17] One was the need for a suitable royal bride (and royal mother of future kings) sooner rather than later. The other was, of course, the problem of his spritely niece Marie Mancini, who was found weeping at Louis's bedside during his illness. An expedition to Lyon in the autumn of 1658 was intended to solve both problems, although at the time it appeared to solve neither. It was intended to bring together two young people in a very public manner to see if a marriage could be arranged. The people concerned were Louis King of France and – to the unconcealed disgust of Queen Anne – his first cousin, Marguerite-Yolande of Savoy. As the court trailed south to Lyon, Queen Anne was alternately morose and furious (her lovely Spanish or Spanish-accented voice became extremely shrill when she was angry). And Marie Mancini went along too in the great caravan of the court.

Once Lyon was reached, the King continued his ostentatious attentions to Marie. They laughed together. They gossiped: Marie's mocking style made her a good gossip. They whispered conspiratorially. Marie Mancini sang to the music of Louis on his beloved guitar while the Italian-turned-French musician Lully composed airs for her. They danced and rode together. And Queen Anne remained torn between her disapproval of her son's defiant conduct and her dismay at the Cardinal's Savoyard project (so much less appealing to her than that shimmering vision of the Infanta ...).

When the French and Savoyard royal families encountered each other, formal kisses were exchanged, denoting Duchess Christine's previous status as a princess of France. Marguerite-Yolande proved to be pleasant enough, if extremely shy: 'the most demure and reserved person in the world'. Her appearance was derided by the Grande Mademoiselle, who generally found something unpleasant to say about younger women, on the grounds that her head was too big for her body. But she had beautiful eyes, even if her nose was rather large. Marguerite-Yolande's main defect was her 'sun-burnt' complexion. This was an age when a white skin was so highly prized that women of society wore masks outdoors to protect themselves, especially when out hunting: Marguerite-Yolande had evidently not worn a mask. Naturally Marie Mancini, like the Grande Mademoiselle, disparaged her in private to the King.

Nevertheless the solemn ritual dance of seventeenth-century royal encounters was carried out. Other marriages were mentioned. The Grande Mademoiselle for the young Duke Charles Emmanuel of Savoy? In her teens Anne-Marie-Louise had been attractive enough, given her material endowments, if rather masculine-looking: her appearance had fitted her for her warrior-queen stance at the Bastille during the Fronde. It was true that she was big-boned with a prominent reddish nose and bad teeth in a long face: but she had the fair hair and blue eyes admired at the time. Now she was thirty-one and the fair hair was already greying. It was a trait the Grande Mademoiselle told Queen Anne with characteristic pride of race that she inherited from both noble families from which she was descended: although in principle she saw herself as far more Bourbon than Montpensier, referring to her mother's mother dismissively as 'my distant grandmother: she was not a queen'.[18] Madame de Motteville loyally remarked that the Grande Mademoiselle's pink and white complexion had not faded, but it was hardly surprising that Charles Emmanuel did not leap at the opportunity. Later he married her pretty little half-sister Françoise-Madeleine d'Orléans.

Poor Marguerite-Yolande! Far from being the future Queen of France, she was the present victim of the Cardinal's machinations. He bestowed a present of diamond and black enamel earrings upon her. This was intended as a consolation for the fact that all the time tectonic plates were moving beneath the surface of dynastic Europe, which would not be to her advantage. As the Savoyard match looked ready for conclusion, King Philip IV of Spain acted in dramatic fashion.

'That cannot and will not be,' he said angrily to his courtiers. The Cardinal had won his game of bluff: the Spanish King refused to contemplate the prospect of a Franco-Savoyard block of territory so hostile to his own interests. Within a remarkably short time, given the bitterness and length of the military dispute between the two countries, an envoy, the Marquis de Pimentel, was sent offering the hand of the Infanta. As for Marguerite-Yolande, some care was taken to gloss over the fact that she had been rejected, since a seventeenth-century princess had a certain market value which was not enhanced by this kind of incident. The fiction was maintained that Savoy not France had ended the marriage negotiations.

There was universal relief in France at the prospect of peace, even though the negotiations for the marriage between King and Infanta which would bring closure to the past were protracted. As one Frenchman wrote of the possible union with Maria Teresa to a friend on 1 January 1659: 'Everyone who is a good Frenchman wants this very much. That will put an end to the war and she will be the Queen of Peace.'[19] These popular feelings were matched by a spirit of hectic gaiety at the court which was on a less statesmanlike level. Anne of Austria's own relief at the ending of the Savoyard negotiations and her hopes for future ones with Spain were marred by her disgust at her son's behaviour. Much later Marie Mancini gave a nostalgic account of the revels which ensued: every lovely lady had her cavalier and every gallant cavalier his lady: 'we were all easily persuaded that love was the only thing that mattered, which was the spirit of these festivities.'[20] So in various allegorical ballets Marie played the character of Venus, a Summer Star, a Fairy, a Goddess and even on one occasion 'my Queen', as Louis murmured in her ear.

One incident left a special impression on all the courtiers who witnessed it. 'His Majesty wishing to give me his hand,' wrote Marie later, 'and mine having struck against the pummel of his sword, hurting it slightly, he drew the sword briskly from the sheath and threw it away.' She added: 'I will not try to tell with what an air he did this; there are no words to explain it.'[21]

Was Louis XIV still dallying with the unthinkable: marrying for love a girl from a modestly noble Italian family, who owed her social prominence entirely to the fact of being the niece of the King's unpopular adviser? At one point Mazarin told Anne that Marie was boasting that her hold was so great she could actually force the King to marry her. At this, Anne of Austria positively screeched at the Cardinal: if the King was capable of such a 'despicable' action, all France would rise up against the Cardinal 'and I would head the rebels'.[22] But was he capable of it? The answer seems to be the proverbially indecisive yes and no.

On the one hand the Queen's agitation is only explicable in terms of Marie Mancini's demonstrable power over Louis, that Armide-like enchantment she was said to have exercised. On the other hand Louis always knew in his heart of hearts that his mother and the Cardinal were there to rescue him. Voltaire put the situation eloquently in his history written in the following century: Louis XIV 'loved [Marie] enough to marry her and was sufficiently master of himself to separate himself from her'.[23] This however was with the benefit of hindsight, full knowledge of the famously self-controlled man Louis would become. But perhaps it was not so much Louis's mastery over himself at this point, as Anne and Mazarin's mastery over him, the training in duty which he could not and finally did not want to cast aside.

The spring and summer were spent by Mazarin in peace

negotiations, accompanied by parallel discussions for the hand of the Infanta. Certainly the Cardinal, in failing health, tortured by gout, saw the 'Peace of the Infanta' as his ultimate gift to his adoptive country. Anything less advantageous either to his own reputation or France's future than marriage with his niece was hard to imagine. It was a crude, cruel truth: great kings simply did not marry girls like Marie Mancini, however bold, however amusing. They made them their mistresses.

Still Louis rejected this alternative – which was probably not on offer anyway – and spent the summer racked by tears, by hopes and by his mother's reminder of his obligations. The two vital scenes which put an end to the crisis both had their symbolic element. Anne of Austria, taking a flambeau, conducted Louis into her Appartement des Bains, her intimate chamber of relaxation to which the King as a little boy had run so eagerly and where he had romped so happily. (The Appartement had a secondary purpose, as a private retreat; for example, it was there that Anne received Don Juan José, the illegitimate son of her brother Philip IV, on an unofficial visit to France.) Mother and son spent an hour alone together. Later Queen Anne, confiding in Madame de Motteville, gave vent to that classic parental prophecy: 'One day Louis will thank me for the harm I have done him.'[24]

As for Marie Mancini, her final desolate words when she realised the romantic game of love was over – that the empire of love was indeed a cruel one, in the words of *Alcidiane* – were simple: 'You love me, you are the King and I go.' They were later to be adapted by Racine in his play *Bérénice*. The Emperor Titus referred sadly to the 'inexorable' need for glory which pursued him and was 'incompatible' with his marriage to the foreign Queen. As Bérénice understood that her tearful royal lover was dismissing her, she exclaimed sadly: '*Vous êtes empereur, Seigneur, et vous pleurez.*' ('You are the Emperor, Sire, and yet you weep.')

Louis's own view was perhaps best expressed by the celebrated aphorist of the period, the Duc de La Rochefoucauld, who declared 'the greatest admiration for noble passions, for they denote greatness of soul ... they cannot rightly be condemned'. Louis had exhibited what he saw as his greatness of soul in his noble passion and did not think he should be condemned. Now he moved on. The Comtesse de La Fayette wrote that having broken with the spellbinding Marie, for ever after Louis remained master both of himself and his love.[25]

Marie's last interview with the King at which these sad words were spoken took place on 13 August 1659. She was dismissed with the wonderful pearls of Queen Henrietta Maria which Louis got Mazarin to purchase from the poverty-stricken widow – surely an unlucky gift. More endearingly Louis gave Marie a spaniel puppy bred from Queen Anne's favourite Friponne with 'I belong to Marie Mancini' engraved on its silver collar. Marie went to the country and awaited what marriage her uncle would now provide for her. The eventual choice, an extremely grand Italian, Prince Colonna (proud Marie did not wish to linger as damaged goods at the French court), was surprised to find his wife a virgin. As the Prince said, he did not expect to find 'innocence among the loves of kings'.

The Treaty of the Pyrenees between France and Spain was signed on 7 November 1659. By it, France gained territories such as Gravelines, most of Artois, part of Hainault and some places south of Luxembourg as well as Roussillon including Perpignan. Just as important was the state of peace between the two countries, and the opportunity for recovery from the inevitable depredations of war on both sides of the Pyrenees. The Grand Condé returned to the French court in January 1660, doing homage at Aix while Queen Anne and King Louis were making a southern tour. Once again, as with the Grande Mademoiselle, Louis showed himself master of the graceful words of reconciliation which promised forgiveness and even forgetfulness. Another relic of past troubles, Louis's uncle Gaston, died in February. This allowed Monsieur to assume the Orléans dukedom, traditional title of the second Bourbon son as well as its wealthy *apanages* or territories. As 'Monsieur' he was already the first man in France after the King; just as any future wife would be known simply as 'Madame', in its very simplicity the most honorific female appellation of all, barring that of the Queen.

In the course of this tour Anne and Louis visited the shrine at Cotignac to which his mother attributed the 'gift from heaven' of his conception – and his male gender. Together mother and son knelt for a long time in silent prayer in the chapel of Notre-Dame-des-Grâces before placing a blue ribbon of the Saint Esprit at the foot of the statue of the Virgin. Queen Anne also paid for six masses to be said in perpetuity. Then they passed through Carcés on their way back to Brignoles.*

Meanwhile many positive reports were being disseminated by the Cardinal about the character of the Infanta Maria Teresa. She was after all a major part of the deal, as the Cardinal's dialogue with Queen Anne demonstrated:

'Good news, Madame!'

'What! Is there to be peace?'

'There is more than that, Madame. I bring Your Majesty peace and the Infanta.'[26]

The girl's childish attachment to the idea of her cousin

---

* A visit still commemorated in a vivid fresco of the royal party opposite the Mairie. Apart from King, Queen and Cardinal, it shows a musketeer – perhaps d'Artagnan – and two Mazarinettes, presumably not including Marie.

was stressed, and how that youthful hero-worship had ripened into something more tender with the years. Here was a young woman who blushed at her cousin's portrait, and the allusions of her ladies-in-waiting, half joking, half prurient, to her possible future with him. The fact that Louis had shown an early predilection for an intelligent, spirited woman, not a great beauty but one who understood the new art of agreeable conversation, was quite forgotten. But it provided a valuable clue for his behaviour in the future: this was a man who needed, no, *expected* to be amused. Infantas, after all, did not amuse people: that was not their role, and certainly not this sweet-natured, secluded girl who had been brought up according to the ruthless etiquette of the prison-like Spanish court. The restrictions placed upon her can be deduced from an anecdote told about the Infanta some years later. When a nun asked her if she hadn't wished to please the young men at her father's court, the former Infanta replied: 'Oh no, Mother! For there was no king among them.'[27]

In family terms it had been more of a desert than a prison. Her mother Elisabeth de France died when Maria Teresa was six, her only brother Don Balthasar Carlos when she was eight. After that Maria Teresa was heiress presumptive to the Spanish throne (it will be remembered that females could inherit it) until the birth of a half-brother Philip Prosper from her father's second marriage in 1657; there was also a half-sister Margarita Teresa born in 1651, famously painted as a little girl by Velázquez. Unfortunately this second marriage to Philip IV's own niece, Marianna of Austria, did not offer Maria Teresa the harmony for which her affectionate nature craved. Many stepmothers at this time of high maternal mortality stepped easily into the real mother's place and provided loving support for the existing family. The new Queen, only a few years older than Maria Teresa herself, was lazy and rather greedy: she was also resentful of her stepdaughter's position and her father's tender feelings for her.[28]

Under the circumstances, it was touching how the young Infanta, in her formal interviews with the French plenipotentiary, emphasised her respect for her future mother-in-law Queen Anne. 'How is the Queen my aunt?' was the first thing Maria Teresa asked the Duc de Gramont in Madrid. This was the message she wished to send: 'Tell my aunt that I will always be obedient to her will.'

Maria Teresa's references to Louis XIV were a great deal more formal. The young couple had already been allowed to exchange portraits, and Louis was now permitted to write to Maria Teresa. Addressed 'To the Queen', Louis's letter began: 'It was not without constraint that I yielded up till now to the arguments which prevented me from expressing to Your Majesty the sentiments of my heart.' Now that matters had fortunately changed, 'I am delighted to begin to reassure her by these lines that happiness could not arrive at anyone who more passionately wishes for it ... nor anyone feel themselves happier in possessing it.'[29]

The sheer rigidity of the Spanish court may be judged by the fact that Philip IV pronounced it 'too soon' for this respectful if stilted letter to be delivered. A coy interview between the Infanta and Louis's emissary, the Bishop of Fréjus, resulted in the latter whispering in her ear that he had a secret to tell her. And he displayed the banned letter which had been hidden in his hand. Maria Teresa made no attempt to establish its contents (as many young women, including princesses, might have done) but merely repeated that her father had forbidden her to receive it. The most she allowed herself to say was that the King her father had assured her that everything would soon be arranged.

Yet with Marie Mancini gone from his side, no longer whispering sweet and malicious nothings in his ear, unable to denigrate the Infanta, Louis seems to have adopted the idea of his marriage with some enthusiasm. With that sense of his own grandeur inculcated since birth, he was glad to be marrying a great princess. The fact that Maria Teresa was said to have long been in love with him (and France) was also very much in her favour. In getting married, a state of which he officially declared himself in urgent need, Louis was also abandoning sin. On the contrary, he was happily adhering to the rules of the Church which wanted young people of suitable degree to get married and procreate children: exactly what Mazarin and Anne wanted him to do. In terms of Church teaching, he was getting peace for his conscience, peace and the Infanta.

According to the custom for European royals, there were to be two marriages. A proxy marriage, at which a Spanish dignitary Don Luis de Haro played the part of the bridegroom, took place at Fuenterrabia inside the borders of Spain on 3 June 1660: the venue was a simple church, although distinction was lent to it by the fact that the décor, including specially imported tapestries, was arranged by the ageing Spanish court painter Velázquez. The King of Spain, giving away his daughter, was pale and dignified in the sombre colours – grey and silver – favoured by the Spanish court. The most remarkable thing about the bride's appearance, as she was transformed from the Infanta Maria Teresa into Queen Marie-Thérèse,* was her bizarre (by French standards) bouffant hairstyle. Many jewels and a mass of false hair, topped by a further disfiguring 'sort of white hat', completely extinguished one of her great advantages, which was her marvellously thick blonde hair. The description was that of the Grande Mademoiselle, who chose to attend the proxy wedding incognito and left a satisfyingly malicious account of it.[30]

Apart from her hair, Marie-Thérèse had another much-

* By which name she will be designated in future.

praised beauty of the period, translucent white skin, the protected white skin of a supreme aristocrat on which no ray of common sun would fall. Her forehead was rather too high and her mouth rather too big. However, her protruding 'Habsburg' lower lip, a trait believed to be inherited from the great heiress Margaret of Burgundy which would plague the Habsburg family for generations, was not considered a disadvantage at the time; more of a badge of royal descent. Her eyes, if not large, were of a particularly brilliant sapphire blue. But although charitable observers did discern in Marie-Thérèse a resemblance to Queen Anne, still beautiful on the verge of her sixtieth birthday, the fact was that this new Spanish bride lacked that preeminent quality of her predecessor which struck everyone, friend or foe: her queenly dignity.

Marie-Thérèse, like Anne, tended to plumpness, but being much shorter than her aunt, she appeared dumpy. The enormous wide skirts she wore, extended by padded and boned petticoats called farthingales but described by a Frenchwoman as 'monstrous machines', did not help matters. Just as she had not been taught French – a shockingly insensitive omission for an innately shy and bewildered girl – she had not been brought up to understand the importance of dance, an increasingly vital element of the French court, given the King's passion for it. (And incidentally one of the few public occasions when men and women could act in conjunction.) Marie-Thérèse was not badly educated, but it was teaching which had never encouraged any true interest in the arts that her future husband was beginning to love. With her jewels, her false hair and her huge touch-me-not skirts, Marie-Thérèse was a hieratic figure; but she was neither a graceful nor an alluring one.

By the time of her proxy marriage, Marie-Thérèse as future Queen of France had already renounced her rights to the

Spanish throne in a document which took one and a half hours to read. Among those present, some certainly took note of one particular clause in the marriage treaty demanded by the French: if the Infanta's dowry of 500,000 écus d'or was not paid by Spain, these rights of succession would revert to her ... But few would have predicted the ominous long-term consequences of this apparently not-unreasonable provision.

In early May the royal party of France had set out southwards for the second, 'real' marriage scheduled to take place at St Jean-de-Luz, near Bordeaux, on 9 June.* A visit paid along the way pointed respectively to the future and the past. A courtesy call was paid to the château of Blois, where the King was much admired by his three young cousins, the beautiful Marguerite-Louise and her younger sisters Élisabeth and Françoise-Madeleine. One of their attendants, a fourteen-year-old girl called Louise de La Vallière, also gazed in awe at the man she had been brought up since childhood to regard as close to a god, and whose portrait dominated the salon of her family's home. But while the Orléans girls were encouraged to accompany their cousin onwards, the awe-struck Louise remained at Blois.

By now Queen Anne was in a state of great happiness: she was on the verge of a triumph for which she had hoped and prayed for so long. She had written a letter to Maria Teresa in March (the Infanta was allowed to receive this one) which began with the salutation: 'Madame, my daughter and my niece' and went on 'Your Majesty can easily believe the satisfaction and the joy with which I write to her, giving her the name [i.e. daughter] which I have desired to give her all my life.'[31] Like Simeon in the temple, Queen Anne

---

* At roughly this date, Charles II was due to be restored to the throne of England on his thirtieth birthday (29 May by English reckoning, which lagged ten days behind that of the Continent in the seventeenth century). Unlike 1648, 1660 was a good year for kings.

saw herself as departing in peace from the duties of the Queen of France she had carried out for so long, in favour of her hand-picked successor.

The first sighting that the young couple had of each other demonstrated that Louis XIV had not forgotten every lesson of romantic courtship inculcated in him by Marie Mancini (herself still languishing in France at this point, waiting for her Italian marriage to be finalised). The sighting came about as the result of the formal – extremely formal – meeting at Fuenterrabia on 4 June between brother and sister, King Philip and Queen Anne. They had not seen each other for forty-four years, during which time their respective countries had for a long period been at war.

It was another testimony to Spanish rigidity that King Philip merely inclined his head, instead of giving the embrace that Queen Anne, with her stiff Spanish years long behind her, might have expected, although both of them had tears in their eyes. When it came to the question of the war, however, King Philip provided a satisfactory, even theological explanation: 'It was the devil that did that,' he pronounced in Spanish.[32] From this position, however, the brother and sister (who had themselves married a sister and a brother) moved happily on to a discussion, also in their native Spanish, of the future which was a great deal more relaxed.

'At this rate,' said Philip, 'we shall soon have grandchildren.'

'Yes indeed,' replied the Queen. 'But I want a son for my son more than I want a bride for my nephew.' She referred to Philip IV's son and heir by his second marriage, Philip Prosper, now three. It was all quite jocular, and there was even badinage on the subject of patriotism.

'I am sure Your Majesty will pardon me for being such a good Frenchwoman,' remarked Anne, referring to the recent war. 'I owed it to the King my son and to France.'

To which Philip replied that the Queen, his late French wife, had been just the same in reverse: 'only wanting to please me'.

In the meantime Louis had been given permission to ride past the windows of the great chamber where all this was taking place, so that bride and groom could inspect each other: at a distance and in silence. Instead Louis sent a message to Mazarin that he was coming to the door of the conference chamber in the guise of 'an unknown man'. Queen Anne readily agreed to this apparition, but once again King Philip intervened heavily: Marie-Thérèse was not even to acknowledge the unknown's salute. 'Not until she has passed through that door.' The mischievous Monsieur did however secure the admission from a nervously smiling Marie-Thérèse that 'the door looks to me very fine and very good'.

Nevertheless the pseudo-encounter was a success. Louis declared that Marie-Thérèse would be 'easy to love' and Philip pronounced him a fine-looking son-in-law. As for Marie-Thérèse, in public she contemplated life in another country with 'the door' in silence; but in private she admitted: 'He is certainly very handsome ...'

For all that, Marie-Thérèse departed from Spain on 7 June in floods of tears, moaning to her chief lady the Duchess of Molina: 'My father, my father ...' Like Philip, the newly designated Marie-Thérèse knew that they were unlikely to meet again in their lifetime. It was not customary for foreign princesses to revisit the land of their birth: emotional ties were supposed to be severed. Marie-Thérèse's return to Spain would only be in exceptional circumstances, such as the failure and annulment of her marriage.

Two days later, the 'real' or French marriage took place in the little thirteenth-century church of St Jean-de-Luz which had recently been rebuilt. So august was the event felt to be, that the main portal through which the bridal pair passed was blocked up afterwards.* Marie-Thérèse, already technically Queen of France, wore a gown covered in the royal fleur-de-lys; her uncovered hair proved so thick that it was difficult to attach a crown to it. Her train was carried by two of the younger Orléans princesses. Louis looked both dashing and dignified in black velvet, richly jewelled. Having played his part with the aplomb demanded by custom and his own growing feeling for royally appropriate behaviour, Louis was now keen to cut, as one might say, to the chase: consummation of a royal marriage was quite as important a part of the ceremony, if not the most important, as the religious rites and the courtiers' agreements.

Immediately after dinner, he suggested retirement. Marie-Thérèse gave vent to a few maidenly demurs – it was too soon – but on being told that the King was waiting for her, changed her tune and begged her ladies – 'Hurry, hurry!' – to speed up the elaborate rituals, dressings and undressings thought necessary for a Queen to meet a King for the first time in bed. Appropriately enough, it would be Louis's mother who closed the bed-curtains on bride and groom before departing.[33]

The wedding night was a success, unlike most royal wedding nights throughout history. The marriage so ardently desired by Anne of Austria for over twenty-one years looked set fair to fulfil all her hopes.

* And remains blocked up to this day, with a plaque stating the reason.

CHAPTER 4

Our Court's Laughing Face

Our court rediscovers its laughing face.

– La Fontaine, 'Ode to Madame' (Henriette-Anne)

On 26 August 1660 the King and the new Queen paraded through the streets of Paris in the traditional ceremony of the Royal Entry. It was a magnificent display of panoply and power, both spiritual and temporal. That is to say, it was the Church which led the procession: priests and monks brandished crosses and chanted the litanies of the saints, before the soldiers and courtiers followed. Marie-Thérèse was borne along in a chariot drawn by six grey horses, her person draped in gold, so richly embroidered, every inch of the cloth covered in precious jewels, that she dazzled the eye. Since the Queen would have no separate coronation – it was considered unlucky because Henri IV had been assassinated immediately after the coronation of Marie de Médicis – this was her introduction to her husband's subjects. Marie-Thérèse smiled graciously, acknowledging the cheers. The handsome figure of Louis, riding on a spirited bay horse whose harness also sparkled with jewels, left a deep impression on the multitudes who witnessed the parade.

Amongst these, watching from a balcony, was the twenty-five-year-old Françoise d'Aubigné, wife of the playwright Paul Scarron. 'I don't think there could be a finer sight in the world,' she wrote the next day. 'And the Queen must go to bed tonight well content with the husband she has chosen." Her last remark may have been an unconscious reflection on her own very different marriage to the invalid playwright (who would die six weeks later). But it was also an allusion to Louis as the symbolic bridegroom of France, marrying a bride from Spain who brought 'peace as her dowry': an allegorical arch at the beginning of the Pont Notre-Dame, one of many such, had as its theme the conquest of Mars, the God of War, by Conjugal Love. Another young woman, Louise de La Vallière, still in attendance on the Orléans princesses, gazed in silent rapture at her hero.

If Conjugal Love had not exactly conquered the God of War for ever – as Louis's subsequent history would amply demonstrate – it was certainly holding sway in the first months of his marriage. The wedding had been followed by a leisurely two and a half months' progress from the south. During this time and in the seasons to come, Louis paid assiduous court to his young wife, as indeed he continued to do in his own fashion for the rest of her life. In the previous century, the celebrated ancestor of Louis and Marie-Thérèse, the Emperor Charles V, had seriously advised his son Philip II to 'keep a watch' on himself and not indulge too much in 'the pleasures of marriage' lest he damage his health. This was not the advice which was tendered to Louis XIV, nor would it have been welcome to his bride. There is a story that Marie-Thérèse used the opportunity of the wedding night to make the King swear never to abandon her but to sleep every night at her side.[2] While it would be surprising if the former Infanta had at this point sufficient worldly knowledge to extract such a brilliantly aimed promise, it is true that the King did end up almost every night – including some very late ones as time went on – in his wife's bed. In the morning he would depart for his own official *lever* or dressing ceremony, leaving Marie-Thérèse to that longer, lazier Spanish sleep so beloved of

Queen Anne. When love-making took place, Marie-Thérèse made it clear that she was 'well content with the husband she had chosen', in Françoise Scarron's phrase: blushing, rubbing her little white hands together, and accepting teasing the next morning. She would also ritually take communion to indicate a royal conjunction the night before, with prayers that the result might be a child in nine months' time.

The marriage therefore did not go wrong in the bedroom. And at first Louis basked in the general approval for his course of virtue, headed by that of his mother and the Church. As Madame de Motteville, observer of all this, noted: he enjoyed 'the legitimate passion' that his wife felt for him.[3] (The passion that Marie Mancini had felt for him was not 'legitimate', nor was the adolescent rebellion connected to it.) A few years after his marriage, Louis, drawing up instructions for his baby son for the future, told him to ask of God 'a princess who was agreeable to him'.[4]* In this sense at least, God or Louis's advisers had certainly succeeded. The trouble was that Marie-Thérèse was dull. Uninterested in the arts, she formed a little Spanish-speaking Castilian world of her own, with her pet dogs and her equally pet dwarves, the traditional companions of a Spanish infanta as seen in Velázquez's portraits. Her one enthusiasm, for gambling, although a frequent pastime at all courts – both Anne and Mazarin gambled – could hardly be called inspiring.

In time she would display a possessive and jealous streak, so perhaps that wedding-night demand was actually true, but Louis XIV was perfectly capable of interpreting such jealousy as flattering to his ego. It was Marie-Thérèse's innate reluctance to accept the public role of Queen of

---

* *The Memoirs for the Instruction of the Dauphin* by Louis XIV, begun in 1661, went through several versions; although the King received considerable assistance, he always had an essential role in the publication, thus the sentiments are his.[5]

France in its fullest implications which weakened her in her husband's eyes. (It is ironic that she would actually have made a very good Queen of Spain.) Louis XIV did not as yet know quite what he did want in his first lady – some kind of star to reflect the light of his radiant sun – but the instinct to explore the situation was there.

As it was, the person whose highest hopes were actually fulfilled was Anne of Austria. Just as Marie-Thérèse found the mother to whom she was determined to submit, so Anne found her royal 'daughter', that name she had desired to give Marie-Thérèse all her life, as she wrote in March. Both immensely devout, the two Queens had an excellent time visiting convents, praying together and taking part in other religious practices. There was, it turned out, no question of Anne's Simeon-like retirement. They formed a kind of pious unit, speaking to each other entirely in Spanish (as a result of which, Marie-Thérèse's French never really improved, so that it was fortunate that the King could speak some Spanish). All of this could of course have been far worse. The Queen duly fell pregnant in early 1661, thus fulfilling what many, if not Louis XIV, might have thought was her only function. The pregnancy however left her young and active husband with a lot of energy to spare.

Providentially, as it seemed at the time, royal protocol was about to furnish him with a playmate. Furthermore, she was one ideally equipped to act as the First Lady of the Court: although she was in fact only the third lady at the court in the lifetime of Queen Anne. This was Henriette-Anne, married off to her first cousin Monsieur in March 1661; one of those alliances, like the ending of a Shakespeare play, intended to solve the destinies of the remaining unattached characters in the drama. (One of the other major players, Marie Mancini, finally got married to Prince Colonna a few weeks later and departed for Rome: even here she was an instrument of her uncle's policy, for Marie by this time would have preferred Prince Charles of Lorraine, but it was not to be.)[6] As the wife of the King's brother, Henriette-Anne was now styled by the proudly simple title of 'Madame'.

At sixteen Henriette-Anne, Duchesse d'Orléans, rated the best dancer at the court, was a very different creature from the little waif of a princess once scorned by her cousin Louis. No one would scorn Madame now, not so much because they would not dare, but because no one would wish to. Everyone now was falling chivalrously in love with Henriette-Anne: she herself would say wryly of this period that even Monsieur had been in love with her for six weeks. The Comtesse de La Fayette commented that the court was amazed by the sparkle of the young woman who had once been a silent child in the corner of her aunt's room.[7]

Where her looks were concerned, youth certainly played some part in her allure: versifier Jean Loret, author of *The Historic Muse*, described her as 'this springtime beauty'. Madame de Motteville waxed lyrical about the natural bloom of her 'roses and jasmine' complexion, her perfect teeth, the sparkle of her eyes, dark like her mother's (her fair hair had darkened too).[8] Henriette-Anne had grown tall, and her slender figure had filled out, her natural grace helping to conceal the fact that her back was slightly crooked. She was a wonderful rider as well as dancer, with a passion for swimming which was perhaps one of the few things she owed to her English heritage. Charles II, the elder brother she reverenced and had recently visited in England to mark her future marriage, was a fanatical swimmer. Somehow she never seemed to need sleep, going to bed late and waking her people at dawn, in contrast to the somnolent Marie-Thérèse.

Where her tastes were concerned, Henriette-Anne had a passionate love of gardening, something she shared with the King: appropriately graceful swans floated in the ornamental water of her gardens at the Palais-Royal. She had a fine picture collection, including a Van Dyck of her English family and a Correggio of the penitent Magdalen. Henriette-Anne also loved to act as a muse to writers. The young Racine (born the year after Louis XIV) dedicated his play *Andromaque* to her, complimenting her not only on her intelligence but on her benign influence where the arts were concerned. 'The court regards you', he wrote, 'as the arbiter of all that is delightful.'[9]

But Madame de Motteville pinpointed the real secret of the attraction which everyone (including, briefly, her homosexual husband) felt for Henriette-Anne: it was her charm, that 'something about her which made one love her', a 'certain languishing air' she adopted in conversation, in the words of Bussy-Rabutin, which convinced people she was asking for their love 'whatever trivial thing she said'. In short, she had not been able to become a queen – as she and her mother had devoutly wished – but 'to remedy this defect it was her wish to reign in the hearts of honest men; and to find her glory in the world by the charm and beauty of her spirit'.[10] Protocol dictated that this self-styled Queen of Hearts should, in the absence of the real Queen, head every entertainment, indoors and outdoors, with her brother-in-law, the real King.

'Our court / Rediscovers its laughing face / For while Mars flourished / Love languished ...', wrote La Fontaine in his 'Ode to Madame'.[11] But before that rediscovery could be complete, the new mode of the governing of France had to be established in the spring of 1661. The health of Cardinal Mazarin had grown progressively worse and it was clear that he must be dying long before his actual death took place on 9 March 1661. (He was fifty-eight.) This meant that the King was granted an extended season in which to decide who would replace the great minister, he who had in effect controlled France ever since Louis could remember. Queen Anne, after weeping inconsolably, commissioned an enormous marble tomb for her loyal friend.* To the astonishment of Louis's advisers, he announced that there was to be no replacement for Cardinal Mazarin. In future he himself would preside over his own government.

It was a decision based, one imagines, on a long-held desire to be his own master, which only the prospect of Mazarin's decease fully revealed to him. Some people secretly believed this decision to be the King's latest caprice, to be rescinded shortly: a reading of his character which would prove to be totally wrong. Of course, Louis was assisted by his Council. Some of its members were according to convention senior aristocrats, or warriors, or a combination of the two. But Louis was also aided by highly intelligent ministers such as Jean-Baptiste Colbert. Here was a man in his early forties at the death of Mazarin, whose father had been a failed merchant but who had, by diligence and efficiency, worked his way up the French bureaucratic system. As the Cardinal's confidential man of affairs Colbert had already shown himself capable of trust in intimate matters such as the business of Marie Mancini (and he had a trustworthy wife too). Colbert's orderly mind meshed perfectly with that of the King. His dual ambition was to advance himself and sort out the finances of France, bedevilled like those of any country involved in prolonged warfare. Then there was the Intendant of Finance, a man who had perhaps expected to replace Mazarin: the intelligent, powerful – and powerfully corrupt – Nicolas Fouquet. It remained to be seen what surprise the King, who had already surprised everyone with one decision, had in store for him.

---

* It can still be seen today at the palace of the Institut de France, a magnificent monument, spared the depredations of the French Revolution because it was used as a grain store.

The power of the King of France at this date was in theory absolute but in practice it was not absolutely unlimited. The Estates-General, composed of the three classes of society, noble, religious and commoners, had not met since 1614 (and would not meet, incidentally, until the summer of 1789). But the various *parlements* in the provinces led by the Parlement de Paris in the capital were certainly not without the power of protest over matters such as taxation, as the latter's behaviour at the time of the Fronde had demonstrated. The lessons of the Fronde and its suppression, the dangers of a turbulent aristocracy, could not fail to be fresh in everyone's minds including that of the King, whose boyhood had been branded by it. Sensibly or insensibly, the Sun King set out to make it clear that outside the hedonistic warmth of the rays he spread at court lay coldness, impoverishment – and personal failure.

Yet the kind of kingship he now proceeded to display was as much marked by his industry as by his hedonism. Where the industry was concerned, 'all admired the extraordinary change' according to the Chevalier de Gramont and there was general surprise at 'the brilliant emergence of talents' which the King had kept hidden. Certainly, it would be very far from the truth to see in Louis XIV the type of amused indolence which characterised his first cousin Charles II, now safely established across the Channel. Charles yawned and wrote notes in council meetings and wondered when it would be time for him to go hunting. Louis did not yawn and write notes, and as to hunting, in a fanatically well-organised day, that too had its place, but never to the detriment of his long hours of work. Not only was Louis hard-working as such, but he showed an obsessive interest and command of detail. This extended not only to military orders and decisions but to matters of architecture and decoration, down to the smallest points. For example, he criticised the figures on the royal fans and had them altered – this baton should be held higher, too many dwarves on one (a dig at Marie-Thérèse?), too many dogs on another (Louis adored dogs, so this was purely a design flaw).[12] In his relentless industry, a lifelong pursuit, Louis XIV resembled his work-obsessed ancestor Philip II of Spain.

On the other hand the austere Spanish King surely never enjoyed a season like that first brilliant summer of the King's personal rule. They had all known hard times, even Marie-Thérèse with her sad childhood. Now they were free. And everyone was so young. Louis and the pregnant Marie-Thérèse were both twenty-two; Monsieur was twenty; Henriette-Anne's seventeenth birthday was in June. The ladies-in-waiting to Madame such as Louise de La Vallière, who had managed to join her service, were very young too, a fact reflected in the nickname given to these female attendants: 'the flower garden'. There were picnics. There were moonlight expeditions. Ballet as ever was the centre of graceful amusement. On one particular occasion at Fontainebleau, there was a Court Ballet in which the chief dancers were the King, Henriette-Anne and 'the handsomest man at court', the Comte de Guiche (although much fancied by Monsieur, the Comte had declared himself in theatrical fashion in love with Madame: not welcome news to one of Monsieur's jealous temperament). A mechanical way was found to move the stage slowly from one sylvan alley to another so that 'an infinity of persons' approached imperceptibly in an endless dance, as it were, to the music of time.[13]

There is one unforgettable image which emerges from that celestial season that comprised – time would show – the happiest hours Henriette-Anne would ever know. Madame had gone swimming with her ladies, as she did every day in midsummer, travelling by coach on account of the heat. But she returned on horseback, followed by her ladies 'in gallant attire, a thousand feathers nodding on their heads', accompanied by the King 'and all the youth of the court'. Then there was a supper and to the sound of violins, they drove in carriages round the canals for the greater part of the night.[14] The only prominent person in all this who was not young was the now-dowager Queen Anne. Increasingly she was alienated from the joyous revelry, and it was at this point that the advanced age at which she had borne her sons began to tell: for she would be sixty in October.

If Henriette-Anne really was the Queen of Hearts, her ambition, it seemed to royal-watchers at court – and who was not permanently gazing at the King? – that one heart she had captured was that of her brother-in-law. There can be no question that at some point in that summer Louis and Henriette-Anne fell gently, happily in love, perhaps not even understanding what had happened to them for a while. Each incarnated the other's ideal. As Marie-Thérèse would have made a good Queen of Spain, Henriette-Anne, gracious and cultivated, would certainly have made a wonderful Queen of France. The private life of Louis XIV might indeed have read very differently if, by some diplomatic twist and chance, the Infanta had not actually been available. Anne of Austria would have promoted her other niece instead, and given the restoration of Charles II to the English throne in 1660, might well have succeeded. This is not to postulate improbable lifelong fidelity on the part of Louis XIV. Nevertheless the respect he subsequently felt for his intelligent sister-in-law, and the true, deep affection he always bore her – a letter from him years later attests to it* – reveals the best of his attitudes to the female sex. And she was a princess. Somewhere an opportunity was missed.

At the time the romance flourished by day and by night –

---

* The King wrote from Dijon in 1668: 'If I didn't love you so much I wouldn't write because I have nothing to say to you after the news which I've already given to my brother.'[15]

or at any rate much of the night. Much of it took place at Fontainebleau: this had been the favourite residence of François I, who had transformed it into a Renaissance palace in the sixteenth century. Now, with its extensive park and magic forest close by – 'a Desert, noble and beautiful', Loret called it – Fontainebleau seemed made for private pleasure. The court stayed there from April to December 1661 (it would prove the longest sojourn of the entire reign).[16]

Louis, for all his marital complacency, had by no means lost that romantic streak which had been so fatally aroused by Marie Mancini. Henriette-Anne's marriage to Monsieur, following those halcyon few weeks when she had enjoyed his passion, had settled into a series of little jealous games on the subject of their mutual admirers. Monsieur, anxious to provide himself with a son and heir for the new house of Orléans, was at least assiduous in his marital duties. So that was not the issue. The problem was: who – even his wife – could concentrate on Monsieur when there was an opportunity of enjoying the chivalrous admiration of his elder brother . . .?

The romance was however short-lived. And it remains open to question whether that short period encompassed a full-blown love affair. One recent writer on the subject has asked: what on earth would have stopped them?[17] That might be true of two modern celebrities, but the answer for a seventeenth-century monarch and his brother's wife was: a great deal. Significantly, the phrase 'sister-in-law' did not exist: such relationships were considered straightforwardly incestuous. In the eyes of the Church, and thus in the eyes of both Louis and Henriette-Anne by innate training, they were now brother and sister. One may suppose therefore that there were kisses and perhaps a little more, but not the full consummation which would have put both of them in an alarming state of mortal sin. Since a favoured method of birth control at this time was coitus interruptus, drawing back from the ultimate act was something which was understood.

The Comtesse de La Fayette who wrote down her memories of Henriette-Anne, and whose great novel *The Princess of Cleves* concerned a romantic, illegitimate (but unconsummated) love, analysed the relationship as follows. It had all been too easy for them, she wrote, two people born with gallant, that is to say flirtatious, temperaments, thrown together every day in the midst of pleasures and entertainments. Louis and his sister-in-law were 'on the point of falling in love if not further'. Yet there was an innocence about it all, certainly on her behalf. Henriette-Anne believed that she only wanted to please Louis as a sister-in-law, but 'I think she was also attracted to him in another way. Similarly she thought he only appealed to her as a brother-in-law although he actually attracted her as something rather more.'[18]

The end of the affair came with a twist which would have recommended itself to Jean-Baptiste Poquelin, that 'excellent comic poet' and playwright known as Molière. He enjoyed his first great success with *Les Précieuses ridicules* in November 1659 when he was in his late thirties (in 1663 he would receive a pension of a thousand louis from the King). It was of course the appalled reaction of Anne of Austria which precipitated the drama: how could she not be shocked by conduct which struck at the very heart of her religion – and her family?

Using Madame de Motteville as her intermediary, Queen Anne began by warning her niece-cum-daughter-in-law of the dangers of her misplaced conduct, those night-time expeditions 'against propriety and health' and so forth. Henriette-Anne promised to improve, but in true comedic fashion actually wove a plot with Louis by which they could continue their flirtation in secret. 'Her natural sentiments were against prudence,' commented the lady-in-waiting sadly.

The stratagem was for the King to feign admiration for one of the young ladies in Henriette-Anne's 'flower garden' and under this pretence come calling as often as he pleased. It can hardly be a surprise that in the true manner of such cheerful conspiracies, Louis actually fell for the girl who was supposed to be the cover.[19]

This was Louise de La Vallière. She was not the first candidate: that was Mademoiselle de Pons, who was recalled to Paris to look after her uncle Maréchal d'Albret, after which Louis turned his attentions to Mademoiselle de Chémérault before finally fixing on Louise. In the event she was considered particularly suitable because she had such an evident, touching crush on the King. What Saint-Simon was to denounce angrily a generation later as 'the eager homage, the near-worship' felt 'against all reason' for royalty was already experienced in the heart of this young girl.[20] Perhaps it was the portrait of the King in her home in the Touraine which had ignited it, perhaps it was that visit the handsome young man paid to the château of Blois on his way to his marriage.

Observers were apt to scrutinise the texts of the Court Ballets as well as the Ballets themselves for pointers to the future. At the *Ballet of the Seasons* of 23 July 1661 Henriette-Anne danced the goddess Diana surrounded by nymphs. One of these was Louise. Her appropriate role was that of Spring; in the lines of the poet Benserade: 'This beauty only just born ... It is Spring with her flowers / Who promises a good year.'[21] The Ballet was such a success that it was repeated five times in one month. Unknown for the next few weeks was the fact that Henriette-Anne had conceived her first child by Monsieur on or around the same date (Marie-Louise d'Orléans was born on 27 March 1662). Monsieur's jealousy and indignation at the behaviour of his wife and brother took the form – as his jealousy continued to do where Henriette-Anne was concerned – of relentless marital attention. Besides, he needed a son, or failing that a daughter, who in true Bourbon fashion would make an excellent royal marriage.

Louise-Françoise de La Baume Le Blanc de La Vallière was born on 6 August 1644: she was thus a few weeks younger than her mistress Madame and nearly six years younger than Louis. She came from a stoutly royalist family, minor nobility from the Touraine. Her father was a soldier who had been notably brave at the Battle of Rocroi, fought a few days after Louis XIV's accession. Louise, with one brother two years older, enjoyed a happy if austere childhood at the little manor of La Vallière at Reugny, north-east of Vouvray, until her father's death when she was seven. Her mother then married again, the Marquis de Saint-Rémy. Perhaps the chant of the Carmelites next door to her childhood home made a permanent impression upon the sensibilities of Louise. She certainly showed all her life an ardently religious temperament and a seriousness on the subject which put to shame many of her contemporaries at the French court.

It may therefore seem surprising that she did not opt for a convent in youth (a decision which would have spared her on the one hand great personal torment and on the other hand the delights of the most glamorous lover in her known world). But this is to misunderstand the financial circumstances in which a girl entered a particular convent. She needed a dowry. It is true that the dowry for a nun – the bride of Christ – was by custom much less than that needed for a bride of a more humdrum human being; which is why in large families with many daughters, the eldest might be lucky enough to get a husband, the youngest lucky enough to enter an agreeable not-too-harshly-restricted convent. Looks were important: convents could be regarded as useful dustbins, remembering how Marie Mancini's mother had thought her plainness designated her for the convent, not marriage, although she was the middle sister. Personal preference did not as a whole come into it: the Duc and Duchesse de Noailles, who had nine daughters, were praised for being 'so Christian and so tender' for allowing them the choice of the veil or not. The continual denunciations of the preachers against parents who shut unwilling children up in convents shows how common the practice was.[22]

But nunneries were not the only option. A seventeenth-century young woman of no fortune above the working class (whose females simply found work wherever they could) could also look for a richer household where she would serve in a genteel way. There she would be maintained; there, having formed the vital social connections, she might eventually find a husband.

In the case of Louise, her first entry, as has been noted, was into the household of the three younger Orléans princesses (Gaston's daughters) at Blois, who were roughly her own age. Sharing their lives, she was educated, and even more to the point, she was instructed in royal ways, learning for example that vital court art of dancing.[23] And of course all the little princesses planned in a dreamy way, led by the eldest Marguerite-Louise, to marry their august cousin Louis XIV when they grew up.

Louise had a sweet, submissive character. She was eager to please, eager to obey, all this coupled with a natural modesty which was very much to the contemporary taste in a young woman entering society: the description 'a violet hidden in the grass' was applied to her by Madame de Sévigné with approval.[24] However, this hidden violet had from her country upbringing a tomboy side: she was a notably good rider, able to control a Barbary horse bareback with only a silken cord to guide it. A riding accident in youth had resulted in the fracture of her ankle and she walked with a slight limp, but this did not, it seems, affect her dancing or her riding. As we have seen with Marie Mancini, the ability to ride with skill and daring was an important aspect of the early loves of Louis XIV because it ensured a certain privacy (Henriette-Anne was another excellent equestrienne).

As for looks, nobody ever called Louise beautiful but everybody called her appealing: 'the grace more beautiful than beauty', as the Abbé de Choisy wrote in his memoirs, quoting La Fontaine.[25] Her evident vulnerability – here if ever was the innocent virginity which the preachers constantly emphasised as the ideal state of every young girl – was also part of the package. A local admirer, Jacques de Bragelongue, had been dismissed by Louise's mother as being too poor but there was no question of anything damaging in the relationship.* This innocence was something that attracted the Church and the seducer in equal measure, if for precisely the opposite reasons.

If Louise had a fault physically by contemporary standards, it was her lack of the properly lavish bosom. To conceal her flat-chestedness she was wont to wear neckties with floppy bows acting as a kind of padding.† A childishly thin throat gave an air of defencelessness. On the other side of the coin she had very pale, almost silvery fair hair, huge blue eyes with what was generally held to be a melting regard, and a soft voice.

The King's assault on Louise's virtue was estimated to have lasted six weeks before she granted him what *The Loves of Mademoiselle de La Vallière*, an anonymous pamphlet, described euphemistically as 'that ravishing grace for which the greatest men make vows and prayers'.[26] At this point the King was not free from that perennial problem of illicit

---

* Alexandre Dumas, in the third novel of *The Three Musketeers* series published in the mid-nineteenth century, *The Vicomte de Bragelonne* (*sic*), builds on this story, before passing on to her subsequent fate in *Louise de La Vallière*.
† A *lavallière* is still noted in Larousse as a necktie with a large bow.

love-making: where to do it. Louise, as a mere maid-of-honour, lived with her colleagues under the watchful eye of a duenna, and the King's apartments were a kind of public concourse where people flocked, anxious to establish their rank by their presence close to the sovereign. The answer was the apartment of Louis's good friend the Comte de Saint-Aignan: like all the courtiers in favour, Saint-Aignan was granted an in-house room, in this case conveniently on the first floor (many of the courtiers slummed it in tiny attic rooms in order to preserve that precious proximity to the royal scene). Here Louise pleaded, according to the same pamphlet: 'Have pity on my weakness!' And here the King, after an appropriate duration of siege, showed no pity.

Louise's initial resistance was not a charade. Her piety was genuine and in order to sacrifice her virginity she had somehow to convince herself – or be convinced – that sleeping with the King was a kind of holy duty. But of course this maidenly reluctance by no means discouraged her suitor, especially as he was well aware that his prey was madly in love with him 'for himself'. A story comes down from the eighteenth century of a pastoral incident, where the appropriate author might be Marivaux rather than Molière. Louise sat in the shade of an arbour with some other ladies and confided to them on the subject of the King: 'The crown adds nothing to the charm of his person; it even diminishes the danger [of falling for him]. He would be altogether too much for an impressionable heart to resist if he was not King.' Surprise! Louis himself was actually concealed behind the arbour with an equerry and heard everything.

But if the provenance of the story is uncertain, since Versailles figures in it (not yet reconstructed), it strikes exactly the right note for Louis's initial pursuit of the girl, her sense of danger coupled with her bashful admission that this particular king needed no crown to make him attractive to women. It was not a question of the aphrodisiac of power, but the aphrodisiac of his person: that was the message Louis had found so beguiling in Marie Mancini and once again in Louise. Bussy-Rabutin, impressed by Louise's passionate devotion, wrote that she would have loved the King just as much if their positions had been reversed, with her the Queen and he but an ordinary gentleman.[27] True or not, Louis believed it to be true. And of course throughout the days, weeks of this pursuit (temporarily complicated as an amazed and indignant Henriette-Anne finally understood what was going on) Louise wept. Her tears of anxiety, tears of agonised indecision and finally tears of submission were also a satisfying part of this classic seduction.

One of the original aspects of Louise's character was her lack of materialism, or what many would have thought at the time was actually a lack of proper care for her own interests and those of her family and circle. But she had no circle and did not try to make one. In this she stood apart from virtually every other woman in Louis's life. This singularity, which sprang perhaps from her need to feel her motives for loving the King were pure and even in some way holy, was not at first appreciated by those around her. Fouquet, the Intendant of Finance, was already under threat as Colbert determinedly presented the King with copious evidence of his money-making at the state's expense. Fouquet, unaware of the trouble brewing, thought he had identified a subtle method of keeping in with the King by bribing Louise.

Louise was outraged and the King likewise, the latter believing wrongly that Fouquet had actually tried to make love to the girl whereas his aim had merely been to establish a useful line of communication to his master. None of this helped the future of the minister who chose to give a splendiferous feast on 17 August at his vast palace of Vaux-le-Vicomte, built for him by the architect Le Vau in the late 1650s.*

King and royal family attended. It was all aimed at honouring Fouquet's young master, with a sideshow of demonstrating the wealth and magnificence of a great man. But was it so wise to demonstrate wealth and magnificence in excess of that of the sovereign? In the era before the construction and official habitation of the palace of Versailles, Vaux-le-Vicomte was evidently more splendid than any of Louis's own residences. The week before the feast, Fouquet was told that Queen Anne had made the following comment on his lifestyle to which the Intendant of Finance should perhaps have paid more attention: 'The King would like to be rich and does not appreciate those who are richer than he is, because they can set about undertakings which he cannot afford; in any case he is quite certain that the great wealth of such men has been stolen from him.'[28]

With ruthlessness – a new quality in the King's behaviour – and the secrecy taught to him by his boyhood, Louis attended the great feast with every sign of pleasure. Then in September Fouquet was arrested, charged with corruption and imprisoned (under harsh conditions) for life. It was true that this was only the public face of Fouquet's fall. There were private reasons to do with Mazarin's vast fortune and the dubious methods by which it had been acquired that Louis (who had inherited it) and Colbert (previously in Fouquet's employ) were anxious to mask. Yet it was symbolic that the King also confiscated, as it were, Fouquet's artistic imagination. The architect Le Vau, the painter Charles Le Brun and the incomparable garden-designer Le Nôtre, the team that had brought Vaux-le-Vicomte to Fouquet, were shortly to create Versailles for Louis XIV.

*

* Vaux-le-Vicomte remains to this day a magnificent monument to the high style of the so-called grand siècle – and to the perils of Icarus trying to fly higher than the Sun King.

On 1 November, the propitious Catholic feast of All Saints, Queen Marie-Thérèse 'by a happy deliverance' gave birth to a son, Louis de France, a Dauphin to whom his father gave the new title of 'Monseigneur'. During the twelve-hour labour, Spanish actors and musicians danced a ballet beneath the royal windows, with harps but also guitars and castanets to remind Marie-Thérèse of her native land. It is to be hoped that these Spanish sounds diverted the poor Queen, who kept crying out in her native language: 'I don't want to give birth, I want to die.'[29] However, within a few months she had fallen pregnant again.

Five days after the birth of the Dauphin, Marie-Thérèse's stepmother also gave birth; the twinship of these two babies might have echoed the twin births of Louis and Marie-Thérèse if they had been of opposite sexes, and marriage would have been immediately envisaged as Queen Anne had foretold at Fuenterrabia. Instead Carlos became the new heir to the Spanish throne (his elder brother Philip Prosper had died), demoting both his half-sister Marie-Thérèse and his full sister Margarita Teresa in the line of succession. But for how long? From babyhood, it seemed evident to the doctors that the Infante Carlos was not destined for a long life. Although this turned out to be a singularly inaccurate prediction, the doctors' analysis of his frail condition, both mentally and physically, was on surer ground;* in particular his lack of proper development would raise questions about Carlos's ability to beget children. So the question of the future Spanish succession was already lurking. The Dauphin,

* Modern scientific and genetic knowledge enables us to see that the desperate intermarrying of the Habsburgs, for reasons of state, was not calculated to produce healthy offspring (Carlos was the son of an uncle and niece). Marie-Thérèse and Louis, first cousins on both sides, got lucky with the healthy Dauphin, although their luck did not last. At the time frequent infant deaths in the children of great persons were attributed more sternly to the wrath of God with the parents concerned.

a large and remarkably healthy baby, described by the enthusiastic versifier Loret as 'a living masterpiece',[30] was the nearest male heir, after the sickly Carlos – except of course that his mother had renounced her rights of succession.

Meanwhile Louis's undercover love affair with Louise de La Vallière flourished. In theory it had to be conducted in secret because of the sensibilities of the two Queens, the mother and the wife, although very little was ever secret at the French court. But a far more experienced and wily opponent to Louis's illicit amours was now about to engage him in battle, a contest that would last for the next twenty-odd years with neither side conceding defeat or receiving total victory, although both had their triumphs. This was the Catholic Church.

The power of the Church in seventeenth-century France over the conscience of its followers, who were the vast majority of the population, was enormous and should not be underestimated even where an 'absolute' King was concerned. The betrayed Marie-Thérèse, with the sensitivity of a woman in love, probably became aware of what was happening sooner than most people thought, despite difficulties of language and her grand isolation. In the autumn of 1662, on the eve of the birth of her second child, she made some public remarks in Spanish about 'that girl, the woman the King loves' which indicated that for some time she had not been fooled. Ignorant of the art of intrigue, however, there was nothing much Marie-Thérèse could do about the situation, beyond bemoaning it to Queen Anne, particularly as the King's promised conjugal ardour did not diminish.

Queen Anne, an altogether more doughty operator, as witness her dismissal of Marie Mancini, had a different perspective. In a sense she had brought the La Vallière affair about by her horrified reaction to the over-close friendship with the King's 'sister' Henriette-Anne. No one knew better than this majestic survivor that great men tended to have mistresses, even if her own husband's loves had been platonic. The Spanish kings, including her brother Philip IV, had had numerous entanglements, and as for the French! It was significant that the most popular king in French history was Louis's grandfather Henri IV, the role model of manliness and swagger, who had been a philanderer on a serious scale. But Queen Anne was not a cynic and she was sincerely pious. What worried her was the thought of Louis's immortal soul, the state of sin into which he had plunged himself. There was no resignation here, only a helpless sadness.

The Catholic Church however was not helpless. And Louis's religion, in which he had been so carefully trained by his mother, might be simple, as commentators sometimes pointed out, but it was sincere: and because it was simple it was not for that reason shallow. He understood, since it had been constantly reiterated to him, that kings had been put in charge of their peoples by God, but that kings were for this reason answerable to God. These feelings, incidentally, were in quite a different category from his attitude to the Church in France as an organisation, and its connection to the overall government of the Pope in Rome. His relationship with Louise was adulterous (that is to say, as a married man he was committing adultery while she of course was not).

It was the matter of an adulterer receiving Holy Communion that became the symbolic battlefield of this epic struggle, since the King publicly attended the Mass daily – in his entire life, he only missed attending daily Mass two or three times – and any falling away in receiving Communion drew public attention.[31] The reason was not really very difficult for outsiders to perceive. Already Fouquet, in his unwise approaches to Louise, had noticed the royal 'backslidings' where taking Communion was concerned and drawn the correct conclusion. This was a mini-scandal for those who cared to note it. But ahead of King Louis, as the year 1662 dawned, loomed an annual occasion which became central to the drama of his illicit affairs: the occasion when he made his Easter duties (*faire ses Pâques*). By the rules of the Catholic Church, a professing Catholic had to make his or her confession at Easter or thereabouts, followed by Communion.* This was an extremely public event for a monarch, a testing time. What was more, notable prelates were invited to preach the Lenten sermons, not always as compliant to weakness as the private confessor.

Every king had his personal confessor, and the Jesuits, traditionally confessors to the kings of France, had a more relaxed approach to the subject of human frailty than some of the mighty monastic orders who did not. A quick confession and a firm promise of amendment, totally sincere at the time, could be followed by Absolution and Communion; the confessor would hope that a soft approach would bring the (moderately) penitent monarch to virtue by slow degrees.

The Jesuit Father François Annat, over seventy at the time of this first crisis of the King's marital life, had been Louis's confessor since he was sixteen, and as was his duty had nursed him through his various adolescent troubles. He practised discretion and detachment: the confessional was after all secret, and as Louis approvingly remarked later, he did not get mixed up in any intrigues. Father Annat was a great enemy of extremism in the Catholic Church, so-called

* Easter Communion had been obligatory in the Catholic Church since the fourth century and is still today a precept that must be fulfilled at least once a year 'during paschal time' unless there is good reason to the contrary. Even the seventeenth-century state prisoner known as 'the Man in the Iron Mask' was allowed to doff his mask to receive communion at Easter.[32]

'Jansenism'.³³* He had written a work attacking the type of austere Catholic who thought that 'those not chosen were predestined to damnation' – a doctrine of grace close to Calvinism – some twenty years earlier, *Quibbles of the Jansenists*. Saint-Simon later denounced Father Annat as a 'supple Jesuit' responsible for tolerating much wrongdoing. It is difficult however to see how a less 'supple' confessor would have survived so long at the King's side, with the aim all along of one day drawing in the long rein and bringing him back to the path of virtue.

The views of the great prelates were, on the other hand, a great deal less supple. What went on in private in the confessional, promises made and broken, did not concern them. What went on in public, to the edification or scandal of the entire nation, did. The celebrated series of Lenten sermons which led up each year to the great public feast of Easter with the absolute necessity of a public Communion from the monarch (if in a state of grace, that is) were very different from the private counsels of Father Annat. It was a crucial factor in the first phase of the affair of Louis and Louise that the Lenten sermons of 1662 were to be given by the rising orator and theologian Jacques-Bénigne Bossuet.

Aged thirty-five in 1662, Bossuet was a follower of St Vincent de Paul, whose attitude to the poor he much admired and promulgated in a series of sermons: 'No, no, oh rich men of our time!' he once declaimed in the face of a large body of them. 'It is not for you alone that God causes his sun to rise.' Queen Anne (herself an admirer of St Vincent de Paul) heard Bossuet preach with approval in 1657 and he was then made preacher-extraordinary to the King. In 1659 he delivered a sermon in Paris on 'The

* The name was applied by the hostile Jesuits to the beliefs of the followers of the Dutch theologian Cornelius Jansen. Jansenism was not therefore a body of doctrine.

outstanding dignity of the poor in the Church'. At his first court sermon he announced to the great ones before him that 'honours' would not follow them into the next life. It will be obvious that in an age when flattery was the daily bread of court life, this man was not a flatterer. At the same time his lessons were delivered in such magnificent style that everyone flocked to hear them. Sainte-Beuve, in a happy image, would describe his style of oratory as 'like the stops of a huge organ in a vast cathedral nave'. His solemn, handsome countenance only enhanced the impression Bossuet made.[34]

All this time, while the King made love and both Queens lamented, there was one person whose attitude to her religion was quite as literal as that of the two pious royal women. This was Louise de La Vallière herself. After a few months, she could hardly bear her sense of her own sinfulness, so painfully coupled with her abject devotion to the King. On top of it all, Louise, who was no court politician, had become unwittingly involved in an intrigue between Henriette-Anne and the dashing Comte de Guiche when details of it were confided to her by a fellow maid-of-honour, Françoise de Montalais.[35] Louise incurred the temporary displeasure of Louis, who could not believe that his sweet little mistress had kept anything from him. All this acted further on a palpitatingly guilty conscience.

On 2 February Bossuet began preaching his series of Lenten sermons at the Louvre. On the one hand he commended Queen Anne, comparing her to Saint Anne, the mother of the Virgin Mary. On the other hand he was soon ripping into the King's immoral behaviour, under the scarcely disguised figure of the biblical David who had in his early life been swayed by unlawful passion for another man's wife. (There was no perceived connection here with the 'other' David, a soulful figure praising the Lord with his harp, of whom a portrait bought from the Mazarin estate hung in the King's own room.) Biblical imagery was and remained a convenient ruse for denouncing the all-powerful sovereign of the country: not only David but Solomon and Ahasuerus were royal wrongdoers who could be usefully cited.[36]

It was all too much for Louise. On 24 February she bolted from the court to the Convent of the Visitation at Chaillot.

CHAPTER 5

Sweet Violence

Beauty embraces me wherever I find it, and I can easily
yield to the sweet violence with which it sweeps me along.

– Molière, *Don Juan*, 1665

On 24 February 1662 Louis XIV was in the midst of receiving the Spanish envoy, come to congratulate him on the birth of his son the previous November, when the news was whispered to him: 'La Vallière has taken the veil!' The stately diplomatic visit was hurried along in a way that was hardly consonant with the dignity of Spain. And then Louis, swirling a dark grey cloak about him to cover his face, mounted his fastest horse. He galloped the three miles to the convent at Chaillot where his mistress had taken refuge.

The tearful reconciliation was sweet to both sides. Louise confessed all she knew about the tentative intrigue of Henriette-Anne and Guiche. A carriage was commanded and Louise returned to the court. She was in time for the rest of Bossuet's Lenten sermons: the general theme was the horrifying fate of those, especially kings, who died impenitent. According to Christ, Dives, the sinful rich man, was in Hell, Lazarus, the good beggar, in Heaven. One who did not die impenitent was of course the saint Mary Magdalen. And the organ-voiced orator preached about her too. His terms were resounding: 'the heart of Magdalen is broken, her face is all covered in shame ...' In spite of, or more probably because of, her own sense of shame, Louise was among the many people – men as well as women – in seventeenth-century France who adopted Magdalen as their favourite saint.[1] Some of the most beautiful motets by Marc-Antoine Charpentier, suitable for women's voices, were titled *Magdalen Weeping* and *The Dialogue between Magdalen and Jesus*: 'Weep, lament, Magdalen,' commanded the plangent texts. 'That is what the love of the sweet Saviour asks of you.'[2]

It has been noted that Henriette-Anne, not a noticeably Magdalen-like figure to the outward eye, had a painting by Correggio of the subject; the widowed Françoise Scarron had another version. With the exception of the Virgin Mary, no saint of either sex was painted so often at this period. There was even a tradition that Magdalen, fleeing persecution, had come to rest at Saint-Maximin-la-Sainte-Baume near Aix and had been buried there: the road to La Sainte Baume was one of the most popular routes in France for pilgrims.* Somehow the figure of the Magdalen expressed the obsession of the times with sin – sin and salvation following penitence.

In fact the saint represented a collage of various women from the Gospels. In the sixth century Pope Gregory the Great had announced that Mary Magdalen, Mary of Bethany and the penitent woman in St Luke's Gospel who used precious ointment on the feet of Christ were all the same *beata peccatrix*, blessed sinner, redeemed whore. Since women loved to be painted in the role of the Magdalen, it was an important part of the representation that Magdalen's long hair, with which she had dried the feet of Christ, could be painted as flowing down across her bosom, sumptuously and of course penitently (long hair was the sign of a virgin, and married women were not generally painted with their

---

* In 1683 a huge altar was erected there by Lieutaud, a pupil of Bernini; iron grilles featured the emblems of France and suitably enough the arms of Louis XIV; in the crypt a nineteenth-century casket is said to preserve the relics of Mary Magdalen.

tresses so erotically visible). It was significant that all the chief lovers of Louis XIV were painted as the Magdalen at one time or another; and so were the four chief mistresses of Charles II, whose first and longest-serving lover Barbara Villiers prided herself on her beautiful hair.[3]

The affair of Louis XIV and Louise de La Vallière flourished on her return and for the next year without further interruptions; the tears of Marie-Thérèse, shed in front of her mother-in-law, and the embarrassing discussions she was insisting on having about fidelity by the summer of 1663 did not really count. Queen Anne also wept and prayed, but no official cognisance of the situation had to be taken: Louise was a secret love, not a *maîtresse en titre* like Barbara Villiers. As for the girl herself, she continued to assure the King of her devotion, which left her asking for nothing more than his love. How happy they could have been in another world where he was not the monarch, she was supposed to have exclaimed. And as for Louis, if not exactly in love with her at this point, since his maximum point of love was probably in the weeks and days before he conquered her resistance, he was happy enough with his young and charming mistress.

An English observer, Edward Browne, who was touring France with Christopher Wren, was charmed by the sight of her: 'returning to Paris, the King overtook us in a *chaise roulante* with his mistress La Vallière with him, habited very prettily in a hat and feathers [probably the hat trimmed with white feathers which was part of the new uniform designed for the King's friends] and an especially fashionable jacket called a *Just-au-corps*.' To the Englishman the pair looked settled and content. In another incident whose 'condescension' on Louis's part deeply impressed the courtiers that witnessed it, the King covered Louise's mass of tumbling fair hair with his own hat when she lost hers out riding. Such chivalrous gestures recalled the moment in his youth when he had thrown away his own sword because it had accidentally caused hurt to Marie Mancini.[4]

But there were incipient problems. First, the King liked to give: it was part of his nature, his concept of his role, that the Sun King was bountiful. Louise however was neither greedy nor extravagant and thus gave him few opportunities for that warm feeling of generosity beloved of wealthy men. Her brother, the Marquis de La Vallière, benefited and received a position at court, but someone else, less of a hidden violet, could provide the Sun King with the opportunity to spread his rays further. Second, while the King might not consciously be seeking another serious entanglement at this point, he understood the feelings expressed by Molière's Don Juan: 'Constancy is only good for fools. Every beautiful woman has the right to charm us ... As for me, beauty embraces me wherever I find it, and I can easily yield to the sweet violence with which it sweeps me along.'*

The third problem was of a different nature. In late March 1663 Louise de La Vallière fell pregnant; this could not have been totally unexpected, since there is no reason to believe that the King used contraception at this or any other moment.

Contraceptive knowledge did exist, and given that the need was as old as society, always had. The condom, made of animal membranes, although generally seen as an eighteenth-century prophylactic invention, was already in use in the middle of the seventeenth century, as recent archaeological discoveries have demonstrated.[6] Of more ancient and more universal provenance were tampons made of different materials, sponges soaked in vinegar or other astringents, or similarly constituted douches. These had

---

* Molière's *Dom Juan ou le Festin de Pierre* (*Don Juan or the Stone Banquet*) was first performed on 15 February 1665; the play became the basis for Mozart's opera *Don Giovanni* in the next century, although the original source of the story was Spanish.

LOVE AND LOUIS XIV

always been used by prostitutes, and where the necessity existed, a too-rapidly-increasing family or an extramarital affair, doubtless by many others. Madame de Sévigné believed that her beloved daughter fell into the former category. 'What, haven't they heard of astringents in Provence?' she enquired bitterly after the birth of Juliette's third child. Saint-Simon mentioned with approval that French duchesses rarely had more than two children, compared with the over-fertile Spaniards: in France, dukes knew how to limit their families. Then, as has been mentioned, there was the practical preventive of coitus interruptus, what the French Church called disapprovingly *étreinte réservée* (embrace withheld). Denunciations by the preachers of this so-called 'sin of Onan', a biblical character who was suppose to have wasted his seed on the ground, makes it clear that withdrawal was widely used and, given a cooperative male, certainly the easiest method of avoiding conception.[7]

Royal procreation, even outside marriage, like royal virility, was somehow different. There was a primitive instinct to regard a fertile king as symbolic of a fertile and successful country. The archetypal monarch Henri IV had left enough bastards for the survivors to be among the honoured members of society, even if Louis XIII had not added to their number. In 1663 you found César Duc de Vendôme, son of the fabulous mistress Gabrielle d'Estrées, and his sister the Duchesse d'Elboeuf; the Duc de Verneuil, Governor of Languedoc, was Henri's child by another woman and Jeanne-Baptiste, the powerful Abbess of Fontévrault (appointed as a mere child), by yet another. Rank was not an issue. Under the entry 'Royal bastards' Antoine Furetière's magisterial *Dictionnaire Universel* stated baldly: 'the bastards of kings are princes.'

Louise, a girl without a husband, may possibly have tried to avoid conception by some of the whispered artificial expedients, although coitus interruptus was surely not part of the Sun King's vision of himself. It is more likely that she accepted the inevitable consequences of the King's sinful (but rapturous) love-making as part of the price. This would have been combined with just a *soupçon* of pride: after all, her children would be royal, and they would be *his* children. In a muddling way fertility was also considered one of the female virtues, even if the consequences might be awkward: as a saying on the subject had it, 'A good land is a land that gives a good harvest.' Similarly, abortifacients, like contraceptives, were known since ancient times and passed from generation to generation of women: wormwood, hyssop, rue and ergot were all believed to be effective.[8] But there is no evidence that anyone ever tried to abort one of the King's children, regardless of the mother's marital status. What did happen in Louise's case was an attempt at concealment.

At the *Ballet of the Arts*, performed in the early part of 1663, Louise was still being described, in the lines of the poet Benserade, as the most beautiful shepherdess in the show, with that special 'sweet languor' in her melting blue eyes.[9] But as her pregnancy advanced before an expected birth-date in December, Louise was bought a house in Paris where she passed her time entertaining the court and playing cards. Did Queen Anne know? Most likely some rumour reached her. And Marie-Thérèse? Probably not. In any case the Queen herself was similarly occupied. After the births of her first two children, a boy and a girl of whom only the Dauphin survived, Marie-Thérèse would give birth to another daughter Marie-Anne in 1664 who died after six weeks, yet another in January 1667, a little Marie-Thérèse known as 'the Petite Madame', and the desired second son Philippe Duc d'Anjou in August 1668. With La Vallière entering the maternal lists, the King would be found by August 1668 to have been responsible for no fewer than nine royal or quasi-royal births in six and three-quarter years.

Leaving aside the paternity of their offspring, however, the experience in childbirth of the two women, the wife and the mistress, was very different. The accouchement of the Queen of France was witnessed by as many people as could cram into the chamber: that was the custom. When the Dauphin was born, Louis himself flung open the window to the waiting crowds in the courtyard and shouted: 'The Queen has given birth to a boy!'

On 19 December, Louise also gave birth to a boy, but in the greatest secrecy in a house in Paris. There was a story that the fashionable doctor Boucher who attended was escorted in an anonymous carriage and entered though a garden gate with his eyes bandaged. There he helped a masked lady give birth ... [10] It was a story told of more than one mysterious beyond-the-law-of-the-Church birth. In the case of Louise, it may even have been true.

What is certain is that the boy was smuggled away by the loyal minister Colbert and his wife. It was Colbert who sent a note to the King: 'We [sic] have a boy' – contradicting reports that Louis was actually present, lurking, also masked, in a corner of the room. The baby was baptised Charles, registered under a false surname, given suitably obscure parentage and brought up far from his mother. Louise returned to the court and, only a few days after a long and painful labour, was back in attendance at the midnight Mass on the eve of Christmas. Not for Louise the long lying-in period of recovery granted to the Queen of France, who would recline, surrounded by congratulatory crowds, for several weeks. Even Madame de Sévigné's daughter did not move till the tenth day, a period of rest generally thought essential to the preservation of youth and beauty, especially a graceful figure.

This child Charles died some two years later, not of neglect, but the victim of one of the many childhood maladies which plagued rich and poor alike. Nevertheless, there is evidence from her later life that Louise always regarded the children of her sin with more pious regret than maternal solicitude. She was soon back in her way of life as the King's pliant, submissive and allegedly secret mistress.

The year which followed was cruelly frustrating for the virtuous at court. None of the issues, foremost among them the King's adultery but including Louise's status, was either resolved or put aside. Louise for her part angrily spurned the idea of an arranged marriage to some complaisant nobleman of a certain age. This suggestion was not quite as gross or insensitive as it might seem, especially when Louise became pregnant with her second child in April. Kings and others were expected to provide cover – or security – for their unmarried mistresses. For example, the Duke of Savoy was congratulated by one of his ambassadors for having married off Gabrielle de Marolles so well: not only was his behaviour generous in itself but it might act as a 'fish-hook', pulling in future mistresses.[11] But the whole idea upset Louise's romantic susceptibilities. As a married woman she too would have been committing adultery (like the King) and the whole fantasy of her quasi-holy devotion to the King would be shown up for what it was.

At Easter for the first time the King did not make his public Communion. Father Annat, worldly-wise but not a cynic, threatened to give up his post as confessor if such a blatantly false penitence was proposed on the part of his royal master in order to receive the Sacred Host at Communion. Luckily the royal pew at St-Germain-l'Auxerrois, the parish church of the palace of the Louvre, had heavy curtains so that the royal embarrassment, if revealed on his face, was concealed from the congregation.

As if in defiance of the holy laws, the prolonged and

glorious Fête entitled *The Pleasures of the Enchanted Isle* took place in early May. It was planned and carried out by Louis XIV 'in the manner in which he did everything, that is to say the most gallant and the most magnificent way you could imagine', in the words of Bussy-Rabutin. The planning also showed Louis XIV's attention to detail: he was personally shown a mock-up of the stage machinery which was intended to be a startling feature of the celebration, and all the outdoor stages proposed. Only then did he hand matters over to the First Gentleman of the Bedchamber, the Comte de Saint-Aignan.[12] This early facilitator of life with Louise was a noted impresario of the ballet. The theme chosen was from Ariosto's *Orlando Furioso* and the Fête was supposed to be dedicated to the two Queens, Marie-Thérèse and Anne. But everyone knew the true dedicatee was Louise, in attendance as one of the maids-of-honour of Henriette-Anne.

Apart from the gorgeousness of it all, and the titillation of Louise's presence, there was a special excitement to be had because this was the first official court entertainment held at Versailles. Ironically enough – in view of what was to become of it – the charm of Versailles at this point was its modesty. Since there was limited accommodation, only those who were nominated by the King were present: as the Grande Mademoiselle reflected, this made Versailles particularly agreeable. Certainly it was convenient for Louis to use it to entertain his intimates, including Louise; it was no wonder that by 1663 he was reported as having 'a special affection' for the place. Queen Anne was beginning to love it too, for her apartments were decorated with two things for which she had a passion: gold filigree and jasmine plants.[13]*

* Jasmine – the name was Arabic in origin – had been brought to Spain by the Moors, and so to France in the last century by Spanish sailors.

Modest as Versailles might be at this stage, by the standards of the future, the gardens, designed by Le Nôtre, were already ravishing and there was already a delightful menagerie full of rare birds, pelicans and ostriches, to be viewed from a balcony; wild animals would be added later. And already the King had been seized by the mania for building which would hardly leave him in the course of his reign, so that as in some Sisyphean labour he would turn a modest château into a vast palace, only to resent the lack of privacy, and start all over again with a modest château ...

In the three years up to the end of 1663, Louis had spent 1,500,000 livres on Versailles (about 5 million pounds in today's money). The winter of 1663 was a hard one and the deep frost delayed the plasterers. Undeterred by religious observance, Louis sent a message to the parish priest of Versailles to ask him to let the men work on the Feast days of the Church which were normally holidays. In 1664 alone he would spend nearly 800,000 livres. And the pillaging of Fouquet's creative legacy continued while the erstwhile minister languished in captivity.

Louis XIV, a fanatical gardener, had a special interest in orange trees, whose subtle but distinct perfume he adored. Perhaps the golden globes were connected to his self-mythification as the Sun King. Now twelve thousand seedling orange trees were transferred for the new orangery at Versailles, designed by Le Vau. As time went by, the King's gardeners would keep a number of them in bloom all the year round, replacing them at fifteen-day intervals; specimens would be brought from Flanders and even Santa Domingo. And they were not cheap: the Duchesse de La Ferté was paid 2,200 livres (over seven thousand pounds in modern money) for twenty orange trees. One, known as Le Grand-Bourbon, traditionally planted in 1421 by the Princess of Navarre, was moved by François I to

Fontainebleau and by Louis XIV to Versailles.[14]*

The pleasures of the ballet's enchanted isle – allegedly it lay somewhere off the coast of France – were supposed to be enjoyed by a company of knights held there in a rather agreeable form of captivity by the enchantress Alcina. Louis, flashing with the jewels which studded his silver breastplate, flame-coloured plumes nodding from his head, took the role of their leader Roger, and rode the finest horse among his troop. Saint-Aignan played Gaudon the Savage and the Duc de Noailles Olger the Dane. 'A small army' of actors, dancers, musicians and stage-hands also took part. The vast number of tapers and candles needed to light the whole proceedings over days had to be protected from the wind by a specially made dome.[16]

There was a tournament at which Louise's brother, the Marquis de La Vallière, won the prize of a bejewelled sword, presented by Queen Anne. There was a play written specially for the occasion by Molière, *The Princess of Elide*, in which the playwright acted. And there was a new ballet composed by Jean-Baptiste Lully, who since 1662 had been in charge of all the music and musical activities at court.

Louis's heartfelt patronage of these two artists may be seen in the fact that he volunteered to act as godfather to the sons of both men (a coveted honour). In the case of Lully, this patronage survived the composer's extramarital dalliance in the Paris underworld: a *bon mot* by Saint-Évremond on the difference between Orpheus and Lully suggested that Lully would have picked up some criminal young man and left Eurydice behind.[17] As for the theme of Molière's play, that was very much to Louis's current taste, for it celebrated young love – in royalty. A courtier went so

* It is possible to imagine that the trees one sees at Versailles today in the Orangery, some very gnarled but still fruiting, include specimens which belonged to the Sun King; in 1966 Nancy Mitford recorded that there were eight such still at Versailles.[15]

far as to commend the hero, Euryale, King of Ithaca, for his passionate nature, 'a quality I like in a monarch' and especially 'a prince of your age'. A shepherd's song proposed that 'There is nothing that does not surrender / Before the sweet charms of love.'[18]

At the end of the festival, there was a huge display of fireworks. Alcina's palace, dome and all, was reduced to cinders and vanished into the waters of the ornamental lake where it stood.* Everyone talked of the marvels of these feasts, wrote the poet La Fontaine, the palace which had become gardens, the gardens which had become palaces and the suddenness with which it had all happened. Certainly that notorious Fête of La Fontaine's former patron Fouquet at Vaux-le-Vicomte in August 1661 was thoroughly eclipsed – that was surely part of the point.

And still the jollity was not over. The King decided to hold an extravagant Court Lottery at the end of dinner, on a scale to match the splendour of what had gone before. These lotteries were in effect a gallant way for the Pasha Louis XIV to present some favourite ladies of his Seraglio with cash, jewels, or even on occasion silver and furniture. Thus in 1659 Marie Mancini, at the height of her influence, had won some awesome rubies in a Court Lottery.[19] On this occasion the number of *billets heureux* (lucky tickets) equalled that of the ladies present, although Queen Marie-Thérèse got the biggest prize – five hundred pistoles (over fifteen hundred pounds today).

On 12 May 1664, as the Fête ended, Molière presented another play, entitled *Tartuffe*. King Louis found it 'most amusing', this study of the impostor and hypocrite who managed to dupe the foolish Orgon (played by Molière himself). But it was symbolic of his growing differences with

* The site of the Basin of Apollo in present-day Versailles.

his mother that Queen Anne on the contrary found the piece deeply shocking. A prodigious row ensued in which the highly vocal ultra-devout party represented by the Confraternity of the Holy Sacrament (to which Bossuet ministered) shared the Queen Mother's point of view and denounced 'this wicked play'. In the end Louis compromised. *Tartuffe* was banned from public performances: however, private performances were permitted on the élitist grounds that the aristocracy could cope with satire where the 'little people' could not.[20] The Prince de Condé became a patron, and five years later the Grande Mademoiselle offered a performance to celebrate the wedding of a lady-in-waiting.

In the event, Molière did not suffer from the gesture of demi-banning by which the King tried to conciliate the *dévots* and his mother. In August 1665, his troop of actors was made into the King's Company. No doubt Louis appreciated the lines of *Tartuffe*'s supposedly happy ending when the hypocrite is unmasked: 'We live under a King who hates deceit / A King whose eyes see into every heart / And cannot be fooled by an impostor's art.'[21]

Queen Anne was not so easily mollified. In June mother and son had a painful, angry showdown in which both sides wept copiously: but unlike that previous encounter, five years earlier, when Louis had given way over Marie Mancini, he did not now give way over Louise de La Vallière. Instead he talked honestly enough about the 'passions' which possessed him and were too strong for him to control: yet he loved his mother as much as ever and had not been able to sleep all night on hearing that she wanted, out of sheer misery, to withdraw from court to the convent of Val-de-Grâce. Anne for her part harped on the gloomy theme of Louis's eventual 'salvation', which was in grave peril; how would God judge him if he died in a state of mortal sin? And she threw in some harsh maternal words on the subject of Louis's overweening sense of his own grandeur (although

Anne of all people should not have complained of what she had inculcated in her son since his earliest days).

In the end Anne was the one who weakened. 'Oh these sons, these sons,' she moaned to the Duchess of Molina. But she told the Duchess that she could not bear to be estranged from either of them (Monsieur's dalliance with his elegant male favourites such as the Chevalier de Lorraine was hardly more to her taste). In spite of their sins, they brought her more consolation than suffering.[22]

The Queen Mother's best hope lay in time: advancing years would perhaps diminish the unlawful ardour of the gallant King. It was a point he made himself to his wife, who, heavily pregnant, flew into a jealous passion at the thought of an expedition to Villers-Cotterets from which her condition barred her. (It did not bar Louise, a mere six months on her way.) Louis promised Marie-Thérèse that when he reached thirty, he would quit acting the gallant and act instead the good husband: this was the age in men when 'the flower of life' was considered to be over and in principle at least, promiscuity was supposed to wither away too.[23] In the event things did not quite work out like that. Nevertheless, it is worth noting that even at this point, when he was in his mid-twenties, Louis, the sincerely religious man, only too conscious of his wrongdoing but unable to give it up, had in mind some vague notion of eventual reform.

The trouble was that such a reformation would very likely come too late for Queen Anne to witness and rejoice. The Queen's health had been frail for some time: the previous year she had felt a great 'lassitude', with aches and pains in her limbs and a fever which made it difficult to fast severely in Lent according to her usual custom. Louis, ever the devoted son, had watched over her on that occasion, spending several nights on a mattress at the foot of her bed, a revival of his childhood intimacy. Now, in May, shortly before the battle with her son which she had lost, Queen

Anne showed the first symptoms of the breast cancer which
would almost inevitably – at that time – kill her. Fearfully
apprehensive on her behalf, with an attack of nerves his
doctors called 'vapours', Louis took refuge in swimming to
try and calm himself.

The treatment for tumours of this sort was rudimentary:
bleeding and purges (the usual prescriptions for every illness),
which were supposed in theory to restore the natural balance
of the body, but in practice merely weakened the patient.
Some medical textbooks mentioned the possibility of a
mastectomy, but what Queen Anne actually endured was
less radical: the application of hardening agents such as
burnt lime paste so that the diseased tissue could be gradually
cut away.[24]

At Christmas, the doctors pronounced the cancer incur-
able. In a moving scene the Queen Mother broke the news
to her two sons: she was determined to be steadfast in her
coming suffering. Although the pain made sleep almost
impossible, she decided at first that it was 'by the orders of
God' that the remedies of man were useless in trying to
cure her body; later she believed that she was being punished
for the pride she had always felt in her own beauty. The
following year was marked by a series of hideous ordeals in
which even such a pious woman's resolution was tested to
the utmost; by the summer erysipelas – inflammation of the
skin – covered half her body and her arm was so swollen
that the sleeve of her chemise had to be cut off. An attempt
at lancing the visible tumour ended in disaster and caused
yet more suffering. In all this time her courage never deserted
her, nor, touchingly, did her feminine love of fine things:
she could bear only the finest batiste against her skin. This
recalled an erstwhile joke by Cardinal Mazarin, that if she
went to hell, there would be no greater torture for her than
being made to sleep in coarse linen sheets.[25]

Everyone at court could see that the Queen Mother's

death, whenever it came, would bring great changes. The King for one would no longer have that emotional tug towards his mother's approval which had, at least in part, guided his behaviour. Anne's death might see the return to the French court of the *maîtresse en titre* last seen in the reign of Henri IV. It was significant that in October the King had dared to introduce Louise into the usual crowd in the Queen Mother's salon for a game of cards. Although Anne was horrified and withdrew into an inner sanctum, she made no official objection. Louise gave birth on 7 January 1665 to a second son, Philippe, who was smuggled away in the same fashion as the first and like him died in infancy. Louis's gallantry, or *galanterie* in that useful French term, was however leading him in new directions. While the court reacted predictably: if the King was sexually available, perhaps he was available to more women than one?

The reason *galanterie* was a useful term at this period was that it had no single meaning and could therefore be discreetly employed to cover a number of modes of behaviour. The range was considerable. To the Comtesse de La Fayette, gallantry was merely 'a polite or agreeable manner of saying a thing'. For Madeleine de Scudéry, analysing the subject, it all began with a wish to please and thus style was all-important. A gallant man with a certain 'worldly *je ne sais quoi*' could say out loud things that other people would not dare mention. At the same time the word definitely had other darker and more exciting meanings, from amorous conduct, the 'sweet badinage of love', to passionate flirtation and outright sex. In her famous Map of Love, included in her best-selling novel *Clélie*, Madeleine de Scudéry was quick to admit that the River of Inclination flowed all too fast into the Sea of Danger and beyond this Sea lay 'the Unknown Lands'.[26]

Just as gallantry itself was an ambivalent term, it was not always clear how far the King's own gallantry with particular ladies actually went. What exactly transpired when the King was *chez les dames* late of an afternoon, as the contemporary euphemism had it? (His own apartments were never used for such rendezvous.) A seventeenth-century dictionary actually defined a *chambre* or bedroom as 'a place where you sleep and receive guests'.[27] Thus beds were everywhere and ladies happily entertained from them according to the manners of the time. The *ruelle* was the name for the space between a bed and the wall where a gallant might conventionally sit enjoying his lady's conversation. But it was a remarkably short hop from *ruelle* to bed.

For Louis, there was a brief affair, as it probably was, with the saucy and malicious Princesse de Monaco, sister of the Comte de Guiche.* Another candidate for a fling was the rather more agreeable Anne de Rohan-Chabot, Princesse de Soubise, with her reddish hair, white skin and her slanting brown eyes. '*La belle Florice*', as she was known to her friends, maintained her beauty by a strict diet, surprising for her time, of chicken and salad, fruit, some milky foods and water only occasionally tinctured with wine. A devoted wife, still very young, at this stage she probably did reject the advances of the gallant King in favour of a flirtatious friendship.

Olympe Mancini, now Comtesse de Soissons and Superintendent of the Queen's Household (her husband's family, the Carignans, were Savoyard royalty), was another candidate. Whether their youthful affair had been consummated or not, there was nothing to stop Olympe and Louis now, and she should surely be included among his periodic mistresses. Amusing and lively company, which was very much to Louis's taste, time would show that Olympe had an Italian taste for intrigue, which was not. Then there were the

---

* The Princesse spitefully marked her failure to establish something more permanent by describing the King's 'sceptre' as 'very small' – or so she said.[28]

younger girls propelled forward by those who believed it would be advantageous all round to supplant Louise: Charlotte-Eléanore de La Motte Houdancourt, another maid-of-honour, was one of these, although the incipient romance was nipped in the bud by the sternly virtuous Duchesse de Navailles, Marie-Thérese's Dame d'Honneur, who had special grilles put over the windows of the maids-of-honour to eliminate late-night junketings.

It was to the King's discredit that, furious with the distinguished Duchesse, who was after all only doing her duty of protection, he banished her and her husband from court, despite pleas on their behalf by Queen Anne. His treatment of the Duc de Mazarin, granted the title because he was married to Hortense Mancini, was more in keeping with the high standards of a great monarch. When Mazarin impertinently remonstrated with Louis over his conduct, the King merely tapped his forehead: 'I always thought you were mad,' he said, 'and now I know it.'[29]

More important than these variegated philanderings was the first death in the royal family: not, as expected, that of Queen Anne but of her brother Philip IV. The Spanish King died at the age of sixty on 17 September. He left a troubled legacy. The four-year-old child who now became King Carlos II was, as has been mentioned, a dismal prospect for a long life. Since Marie-Thérèse had renounced her rights to succession, Philip in his will designated as heiress presumptive his other daughter, Margarita Teresa. Long promised in marriage to her Habsburg cousin the Emperor Leopold, she would wed him at the end of the following year.

Louis broke the news of Philip's death personally to Marie-Thérèse, and he did so gently; wherever possible he treated his betrayed wife with the greatest courtesy and tenderness, as he sympathised with her sorrow over the death of her third child Marie-Anne, born in November and dead by Christmas. He knew that Marie-Thérèse had loved her father; he also knew that she disliked her stepmother, the new Regent Marianna, and had no feeling about the brother Carlos born after she left Spain. Marie-Thérèse might be sequestered but she had a fine Castilian sense of what was due to her.

Louis's own preoccupation was also with his wife's rights. There were two points here: the non-payment of her dowry which might render the whole renunciation void, and the so-called Law of Brabant by which children of the first marriage, such as Marie-Thérèse, preceded those of the second, Carlos and Margarita Teresa. Here was an opportunity to increase French security in its northern borders by grabbing certain territories of the Spanish Netherlands under the guise of law.

As his mother's health suddenly deteriorated at the beginning of January 1666 Louis was still undecided on the direction of his future foreign policy. He had in fact been bound since 1662 in a defensive alliance with the Dutch, already at war with England over naval supremacy and maritime trade. As he recounted his cogitations in his memoirs, the King initially held back from the prospect of engaging two great powers, Spain and England, at the same time. In the end he decided to use fighting the English as a smokescreen for his real intentions: the Dutch, who wanted his assistance against England, would in the future be fervent in their support against the Spaniards. 'But while I prepared my arms against England, I did not forget to work against the House of Austria [Louis equated Spain and Austria] by all the means that negotiation favoured.'[30]

Queen Anne survived until late in the month of January. Madame de Motteveille wrote loyally that she had never been so beautiful as when on her deathbed. Even when the unfortunate woman had been subjected earlier to that public cutting of the tumour, the faithful lady-in-waiting still found something to admire in her breast, lacerated as it was. In spite of her sufferings, the Queen Mother attempted even now to retain some of the lightness of touch in desperate situations which had endeared her for so long and over so many crises to her household.

'I am not crying, this is just water coming out of my eyes,' she said to the Duchess of Molina. 'In truth Your Majesty is very red,' the Duchess replied, also in Spanish. 'Well, Molina, I've got a good big fever,' said the Queen, still trying to speak lightly.[31]

It could not last for ever, this frightful ordeal in a room where even a profusion of perfumed sachets could not altogether conceal the smell of illness. The Queen's beautiful hands of which she had once been so proud were swollen beyond endurance. (After her death, she was found to possess over four hundred pairs of gloves: none of them now wearable or bearable.) Looking at them, the long white fingers now unrecognisable, she said at last: 'So it is time to go.' At this point even Madame de Motteville had to admit that her adored mistress, by now more alabaster than flesh, looked old rather than beautiful. The relics of Sainte-Geneviève, the patron saint of Paris, once used to solace her in childbed, were brought to her aid yet again, but in vain. The Grande Mademoiselle, seeing the crystal cross and candlesticks, brought from the chapel as a kind of comfort, contrasted the brilliance of the crystal with the approaching darkness of death.[32]

Quite apart from the grief of the onlookers, a deathbed was, in the religious sense, the most serious moment of a seventeenth-century Catholic life. It was considered crucial for a person to face the fact of their impending death in order to repent fully and ensure that salvation on which the Queen herself placed such emphasis. The ideal frame of mind was to be 'neither fearing nor desiring' the end, in a line of the poet François Maynard quoted with approval by Madame de Sévigné.[33] The Last Sacrament was to be administered and Extreme Unction applied. (Hence the contemporary horror of sudden death, which gave no such opportunity.) In theory the living lay people no longer had any role to play, only the clergy, intermediaries with the next world. But when were the doctors to announce that the end was coming? It was a fine call to make for those – everyone – in awe of the King. Louis, who once again had a bed installed in his mother's room, was enraged when he felt that she was being denied her due out of servility.

'What!' he exclaimed. 'They would flatter her and let her die without the sacraments, after months of sickness. I will not have this on my conscience.' He made the point again, strongly: 'We have no more time for flattery.'

Queen Anne finally expired just after six o'clock in the morning on 20 January 1666. Monsieur was with her; the King was in the next room with the Grande Mademoiselle, where he had been taken, 'half fainting', in the course of the night. As his mother's hand had slipped from his own for the last time he gave a great cry. In the Queen's last audible words, she asked for a crucifix to hold.

Anne of Austria was in her sixty-fifth year. Her example, the prudence, dignity and virtue of her conduct, would leave an indelible mark on Louis XIV, whether he followed it or not. In his affliction, he paid his mother an unparalleled tribute from a son to one who had also ruled the country: Queen Anne was to be numbered, he said, among the great *kings* of France. The years had slipped away and as happens with the death of a parent, his memories went back to his youth, when 'the vigour of the princess' had preserved him on his throne. It was fitting that an inventory of the Queen's belongings after her death included, among the list of brilliant many-coloured gems, a bracelet containing the hair of the infant Louis.[34]

'I never disobeyed her in anything of consequence,' he said. Whether of consequence or not, at some date very close to the deathbed of the Queen Mother, Louise de La Vallière conceived her third child. With the dark cloud of Anne's disapproval dissipated for ever, there was no reason for Louis not to yield to 'the sweet violence' of love when and where he wished. Its only rival was that other violence, the violence of war, or as Louis would have it: the glory of the martial contest. On 26 January, less than a week after his mother's death, Louis XIV declared war on England allegedly in support of the Dutch. In the words of Racine, he went in search of 'the glory and the joy / That a first victory brings to a young man's heart'.[35]

PART TWO

Summer

CHAPTER 6

The Rise of Another

In the human heart new passions are forever being born;
the overthrow of one almost always means the rise of
another.

— La Rochefoucauld, *Maxims*

'There is a rumour going round the court that the King
is dreaming a little of Madame de Montespan': this
was the Duc d'Enghien writing to the French-born Queen
of Poland on 2 November 1666 with the gossip about her
native country. Nine months later, the Comte de Saint-
Maurice, the Ambassador of Savoy, reported that Louis
could think of little else except the scintillating Marquise.
By September 1667, Saint-Maurice was convinced that wherever the King happened to be, he made three (long) visits
to the Marquise every day.[1] Thus far had Athénaïs, born
into the Mortemart family, travelled in the affections of the
King, regardless of the fact that she was now very much a
married woman, and the mother of two young children by
her husband, the Marquis de Montespan.

Louise de La Vallière's third child, Marie-Anne, had been
born on 2 October at the royal château of Vincennes (was
it tenderness, tactlessness or sheer indifference that gave the
baby the same name as the Queen's daughter who had died
at Christmas the previous year?). The circumstances of the
birth still had to be discreet, so far as was possible in
the ritual intimacy of court arrangements. Henriette-Anne
happened to be passing through her maid-of-honour's

chamber on her way to the chapel just as Louise was experiencing the first pangs of childbirth.

'Colic, Madame, an attack of colic,' Louise managed to gasp out. Keeping up the required fiction, Louise urged Dr Boucher, the *accoucheur*, to make sure the birth was successfully accomplished before Madame's return. Her room was filled with tuberoses so that their delicious, dominating perfume would cover up anything else in what had now become a delivery room. The doctor, who was by now after all a veteran of these natural–unnatural crises, succeeded. Louise, pale and exhausted, even managed to make that midnight court supper known under the Italian name of *medianoche*.[2]

Nevertheless, Marie-Anne's life was to be very different from that of the brothers who had been spirited away. Cared for at first by Madame Colbert, she grew up to be petted and adored; gifted with exceptionally pretty looks from childhood, graceful like her mother, she bade fair to be her father's favourite child. The little girl's status as the child of the King by his acknowledged mistress was made possible by the death of Queen Anne. Her mother's fortunes on the other hand were improving only in theory, not in practice. No semi-official rank could atone for the pain Louise felt and continued to feel at the King's 'infidelities', which mocked the holy love she had believed they enjoyed (and paradoxically kept her in a state of sin). At least fatherhood was a claim that the King honoured: thus Louise rapidly conceived her fourth child after the birth of Marie-Anne. Unfortunately this also meant that Louise spent the vital year during which Athénaïs developed her ascendancy, yet again in a physically burdened state.

Françoise-Athénaïs de Rochechouart de Mortemart was born on 5 October 1640.* She was thus about twenty-six

---

* She was baptised Françoise but became known as Athénaïs, from Athena

when the King's eye first lit upon her in any context except that of an attendant on his wife. This was not the first flush of youth in a society where looks were supposed to decline after twenty. Athénaïs however was made to be different. She was astonishingly beautiful. She had long, thick, corn-coloured hair which curled artlessly about her shoulders when she was in a state of *déshabille*. Her eyes were huge, blue and very slightly exophthalmic; she had a pouting mouth. There was something at once sexy and imperious about her appearance that ravished the eye while her lus-ciously curved figure appealed to contemporary taste in contrast to that of slender Louise. This voluptuousness makes plausible at least one story by which Louis plotted to spy on her at her bath disguised as a servant; awestruck, he gave away his presence, at which Athénaïs laughingly dropped her towel.[4]

But Athénaïs was far, far more than a mere beauty, of whom there were, after all, large numbers at Versailles. She was high-spirited and amusing, with a special kind of drollery known as 'the wit of the Mortemarts' which her family made famous. There were catchwords which baffled the uninitiated: *Bourguignon* for example stood for everything dull and dreary, due to one sister's dislike of her husband's Burgundian estates. A judgement would be delivered by a Mortemart with seeming innocence, even naïvety, what Saint-Simon called a 'witty languishing manner', and yet in its own way it would be quite devastating.[5] And certainly where Athénaïs was concerned, this lovely rose had thorns: later courtiers would dread passing under her windows at Versailles for fear of the comments she might make. Mad-eleine de Scudéry had commended elegant mockery as the consummate social weapon in an essay 'Of Raillery'. 'To

the Goddess of Wisdom, while moving in the sophisticated Parisian circle of the *Précieuses*, and never looked back.[5]

mock well,' she wrote in 1653, 'you must have a fiery intelligence, delicate judgement and a memory full of a thousand different things to use on different occasions.' All this was possessed by Athénaïs.[6]

The Rochechouart-Mortemarts of Lussac in Poitou were of ancient lineage and proud of it, the two grand families having been joined together by marriage in the thirteenth century.[7] Gabrielle Marquise de Thianges, Athénaïs's clever elder sister, was known to tease the King on the subject: the Bourbons, with their Médicis merchant blood, were really a great deal less distinguished ... In the meantime her love of opera and the theatre made Gabrielle intelligent company for the King, someone with whom he could enjoy readings by Racine and Boileau. Perhaps the cleverest sister of all was the third, Marie-Madeleine, who was obliged to discover she had a religious vocation by their father (he was having a problem paying dowries for so many daughters). She subsequently ran the convent of Fontévrault, where with her strong character and her remarkable learning – Latin, Greek and Hebrew were among her accomplishments – Marie-Madeleine was considered 'the pearl of abbesses'. Louis liked her company too. A fourth daughter Marie-Christine really did discover her vocation; she spent her life as a nun at Chaillot, in a state of greater contentment no doubt, if less excitement, than her elder sisters.[8]

Then there was the single brother Louis-Victor Marquis de Vivonne before he inherited his father's title of Duc de Mortemart. Vivonne, two years older than the King, had been one of his Children of Honour, just as the Duc had been a boyhood companion of Louis XIII. Vivonne was so fat so young that he became the butt of the royal sense of humour. 'Vivonne' – to use his surname alone was an extremely familiar form of address – 'you get fatter every time I look at you,' said the King. 'Ah, Sire,' replied Vivonne, 'what a slander. There's no day when I don't walk four times round my cousin Aumale' (notoriously the fattest man at court). But Vivonne, bulky as he might be, was an intelligent man and a good soldier: one of his annoyances about his sister's rise to favour was that his career advancement might be attributed to it instead of to the talents on which he prided himself.[9]

The close royal connections of the Rochechouart-Mortemarts concealed the fact that their parents' marriage was not only unhappy – like so many arranged marriages of the time – but also upsettingly scandalous. One can see in the character of the father of Athénaïs all the unashamed sensuality which she would later make her own. The Duc de Mortemart was a hedonist to whom all pleasures were welcome: music and literature, food and drink, hunting – and of course sex. Diane de Grandseigne, the Duchesse de Mortemart, had been a lady-in-waiting to Queen Anne; a wise woman who loved music and the arts, she was also renowned for her piety and virtue. Instead of staying yoked in a marriage of convenience (which had bred five children), the Duc lived quite openly with his mistress, Marie Tambonneau, the wife of the head of the Paris Chamber of Commerce, in a way that flouted the conventions, loose as they were. Eventually the Duchesse retired to Poitou.

It is easy to look on Athénaïs as echoing the career of her father as a sensualist. But the profound embedded influence of her mother should not be forgotten, a woman who made an exceptionally holy death in 1664, surrounded by monks and priests. A pious mother was something she had in common with Louis XIV, and in fact the two women, the late Queen and the Duchesse de Mortemart, had been close friends. As a girl Athénaïs showed remarkable religious devotion, and as a young adult was noted for taking Communion once a week – that badge of virtue.

Yet for all her beauty, her intelligence and her vitality, which surely entitled her to a high position, there was something disappointed about Athénaïs at the moment she caught the King's eye – or perhaps, as we shall see, deliberately rolled her own magnetically large blue eyes in his direction. She was already twenty-two when a betrothal was arranged with Louis-Alexandre de La Trémoïlle. For Athénaïs and her sisters were not heiresses whose fortune made them objects of desire, despite their vaunted noble blood, and, as has been noted, the cheaper solution of religion had to be chosen for two of them.

Then the betrothal went wrong in a startling fashion. Her fiancé got involved as the second in a duel in which the Marquis d'Antin was killed, and he had to flee France.* The man left to pick up the pieces of this broken romance was Louis-Henri de Gondrin de Pardaillan, Marquis de Montespan, brother of the dead d'Antin, who paid Athénaïs a visit of condolence. As a result of his visit, this rearranged bridal couple were married at the church of Saint-Sulpice in Paris on the eve of Lent 1663. Athénaïs said later in her amusing way that she had forgotten to bring the proper cushions for them to kneel on, and on sending in a hurry to the family home received some dog cushions from the porter ...

Certainly the dog cushions brought no luck to a marriage which was clearly difficult from the first for two reasons. The first of these was debt: the young couple did not really have the wherewithal to meet the considerable expenses in terms of dress and entertainment of an aspiring court lady. The second, probably not unconnected to this comparative poverty, was the prickly character of the new husband. Good-looking in a saturnine way, Montespan was a Gascon, a traditionally proud and touchy race, the poorer the

---

* Duelling, the curse of a noble society, was strictly illegal in France at this point, successive kings making their disapproval felt in terms of strong punishment. Nevertheless it took place.

prouder.* Where religion was concerned, he had Jansenist connections: his uncle Henri de Pardaillan, Archbishop of Sens, was a man of rigid piety with suspected Jansenist sympathies. This explained the fact that there were no royal signatures to the marriage contract, a favour which would normally have been bestowed on the daughter of the Duc and Duchesse de Mortemart.

Under these circumstances, there was not much for Montespan at court: his own character if not Jansenist was certainly unbending. For Athénaïs, from the first, the court had a great deal to offer. And as time would show, she was far from being the kind of woman derided by Madeleine de Scudéry in *Sapho*: someone who believed she was put on earth only to sleep, get pregnant, look beautiful and talk 'foolishness'. Nor for that matter was she the type described by a Father Garasse in *La Doctrine Curieuse* for whom the choice was the distaff, the mirror or the needle (for men, it was book, sword or plough). Athénaïs had an irrepressible life force.[10]

Her first child Christine was born on 17 November 1663 and a son, Louis-Antoine, Marquis d'Antin (his dead uncle's title), the following September when the marriage was scarcely eighteen months old. Already Athénaïs was showing herself a goddess of fertility, yet child-bearing did not deter her. Two weeks after the birth of Christine, Athénaïs was dancing in a Court Ballet, just as she had danced immediately after her wedding. Then she enjoyed the sophisticated circles of the Hôtel d'Albret, where clever women such as Madeleine de Scudéry, Madame de Sévigné and Madame de La Fayette discoursed with clever men at their feet – here was *galanterie* in its purest sense.[11] Athénaïs formed friendships there: one of her friends was a young widow in

---

* D'Artagnan, a real-life character immortalised in Dumas's *Three Musketeers*, exemplified this kind of Gascon arrogance and awkwardness.

struggling circumstances, Françoise Scarron, whose propriety, intelligence and moderation made her an agreeable
member of any circle, if never the centre of it.

It was debt which caused the Marquis de Montespan to
break away from the unsatisfactory court life and, along
with his brother-in-law Vivonne, set off for a military career
in the south.[12] The measure of the Montespan poverty can
be seen in the fact that the couple found it very difficult to
raise the money for the equipment needed (officers paid for
their own uniforms, horses and so forth) and in 1667
Montespan sold his wife's diamond earrings. In the end
Montespan was able to depart, leaving Athénaïs, the reigning
beauty of the court, alone with two small children. It was
at this point that she may have looked round at her limited
opportunities as the aristocratic wife of a poor man, and
seen that there was one magnificent opening: to become
the mistress of the King.

Louise de La Vallière was clearly falling from favour, and
in any case was once more pregnant. In disappointment at
what piety and virtue had brought her, it seems that Athénaïs
decided to take her destiny in her own hands. Why not?
She was old enough to know her own mind. She was not a
royal parcel like Marie-Thérèse or a timid virgin like Louise.
It was a brilliant solution to a life that Athénaïs did not feel
was quite brilliant enough (she may not have anticipated
exactly how brilliant – or how notorious – her new life was
going to be).

The evidence is a story of the King being overheard
saying to Monsieur: 'She does what she can but I myself
am not interested.' Possibly he instinctively ducked away
from a woman who however beautiful was clearly not
submissive. By November 1666 the report from the Duc
d'Enghien quoted earlier showed that he had changed his
mind. Somewhere between November 1666 and July 1667
Louis XIV seduced the Marquise de Montespan. Or was it

THE RISE OF ANOTHER

the other way round? Either way, the great sexual adventure
of his life was about to begin.

One of the maxims of the Duc de La Rochefoucauld which
was peculiarly appropriate to Louis XIV in 1667 was his
reflection on the human heart where 'new passions are
forever being born; the overthrow of one almost always
means the rise of another'.[13] But it was not only the passion
for Athénaïs which was beginning to consume Louis. There
was also the question of his personal glory: something to
be established in the suitably glorious sphere of war.

Gloire was an important word of the time, not only for
the King, although he might seem to incarnate the general
glory of France. Sometimes it could be equated with ambition, as Madame de Castries, daughter-in-law of Vivonne,
was described as *glorieuse* for her husband. Generally it meant
personal honour. Young girls at Saint-Cyr would be told to
treasure their *'bonne gloire'*, which meant never doing base
things. In a king however, and above all for Louis XIV,
glory meant military glory. Years later he would declare that
'the passion for glory was definitely the leading passion of
my soul'; he was talking the language of Corneille's military
leader Le Cid, which had been impressed on him in youth.[14]
At the same time there was the glamour of possessing the
most blatantly beautiful mistress: this was another kind of
glory in the eyes of the world, including foreign ambassadors.
The new Gallery of Apollo in the Louvre, started in 1662
(following a fire), was centred by the artist Charles Le Brun
on the device of the sun, symbolising the reputation of the
young King;[15] in the same way the gorgeous Athénaïs
symbolised the richness of his private life. Both contributed
to the *gloire* of Louis XIV.

When Louis XIV set out in the direction of Flanders on
a military campaign in May 1667, he could fairly be said to
be combining two new passions: he was commanding (if

not leading) his troops and he was also accompanied by Madame de Montespan. The declaration of war on England the previous year in support of the Dutch had not, to the great relief of Charles II's government, been followed by the use of French troops in this cause. Henriette-Anne, sister of one King, sister-in-law of the other, was coming into her own as a discreet intermediary. Both men saw that under the guise of affectionate familial correspondence, messages could be given and received. Both men trusted her and indeed, in the years which followed as Henriette-Anne developed her role, her loyalties were probably about evenly divided. She adored her brother Charles and at the same time she loved and honoured Louis, her King.

Louis now came clean about his real intentions. With the aid of useful legal advice about the Law of Brabant which favoured Marie-Thérèse's succession to certain properties in the Spanish Netherlands (as the child of the first marriage), he established a war-centre at Compiègne. From here Turenne was to push with the French army against Spanish-ruled Flemish fortresses that were ill-prepared to defend themselves in the so-called War of Devolution. This was realpolitik in the seventeenth-century world: Louis and his ministers equated both branches of the Habsburg family, Spain and Austria, as one, and convinced themselves of the danger of encirclement. Only a really satisfactory defensive border would do. The scenes on the way to Compiègne, and at the court established there, had however something of the pageant about them.

There were tents of silk and damask – Louis had one tent of Chinese silk – hung with rich embroideries. A tent would contain three rooms and a sleeping-room: 'the most handsome and pretentious suites that anyone could ever see'. And there were the ladies. Of course women always went to war: cooks and prostitutes and on this occasion courtiers. This was not just the whim of Louis XIV. Turenne was generally followed by a great train of ladies, including their vast wardrobes and mules to carry them all. It has been seen that Anne of Austria had taken her son on campaigns when he was quite small. But where the Sun King ruled things tended to be carried out on a larger-than-life scale – including the presence of women. Marie-Thérèse was there, playing an important symbolic role when she was introduced to her future subjects as the Spanish heiress. Athénaïs was there, her pretext the fact that she was lady-in-waiting to Marie-Thérèse. Henriette-Anne was also there. One observer compared the style of it all to 'the magnificence of Solomon and the grandeur of the King of Persia'.[16]

When the King advanced to the front, he returned after a short while to Compiègne, ostensibly to see his wife, actually, as everyone perfectly well knew, to see the woman with whom he was now besotted. It is sometimes suggested that the pair first slept together in Flanders. The logistics of this seem dubious compared with the endless possibilities of the royal palaces beforehand. Life at Compiègne was in essence camping, although magnificent camping.

Two actions now focused universal attention on the rivalry of the ladies in Louis XIV's life. The first of these was the King's step, unprecedented in this reign, of creating Louise a duchess and bestowing upon her land in the Touraine and Anjou. Furthermore he legitimised six-month-old Marie-Anne – 'our natural daughter' – and designated her Mademoiselle de Blois, a semi-royal title. The letters patent which were duly registered by the Parlement were lavish in their praise for 'our dear and well beloved and most trusty' Louise, Duchesse de La Vallière; her 'infinity of rare perfections' were stressed, which had long aroused 'a most singular affection' in the King's heart and were now to be publicly expressed by a title and an income derived from properties. There was mention of Louise's descent from 'a noble and ancient house', conspicuous for its zeal in the service of the state, while emphasis was placed on the modesty which had made her oppose such material endowments. Marie-Anne de Bourbon, Mademoiselle de Blois as she had become, was declared to be the future heiress of Louise's lands, together with any other descendants 'whom we have declared legitimate' (Louise was of course expecting her fourth child at this point).[17]

Legitimisation was a fully acknowledged process at this point: the term used – *légitimer* – indicated that such persons, despite their irregular status at birth, had subsequently been *made* legitimate. Furetière in his *Dictionnaire* devoted five long entries to the subject, of which the main thrust was that legitimisation was to be used for children, born out of wedlock, whose parents subsequently married. This was hardly the case here. The King was a married man, even if Louise was not a married woman, and he had undoubtedly been married to another woman at the time of Marie-Anne's birth. However, Furetière, writing towards the end of Louis's reign, had to recognise the reality of what had taken place over the last thirty years: therefore he pronounced that the King was even able to legitimise adulterine children, and thus 'efface the turpitude of adultery', since he was master of the civil state.[18] Yet no action taken by Louis would arouse more criticism from the devout on one hand, the snobs of the French court on the other. This was because the *légitimés* also became princes and princesses – who might outrank honest courtiers born in holy wedlock.

Louis, in his memoirs written for the Dauphin, justified this advancement of his mistress and her child as being a decision taken on the eve of war: since he had no intention of avoiding danger, 'I thought it was only just to assure this child of the honour of her birth,' while giving the mother an establishment which matched 'the affection I had had for her for six years'. The court, on the other hand, saw the whole thing as a golden farewell: Louise was now expected to accept gracefully that her reign, such as it was, was over. Advantage was taken of her pregnancy to dispatch her to Versailles while the court went to war. In the course of a long reflective letter to a confidante Louise wrote sadly that of all the King's great qualities it was 'his crown' which had attracted her the least.[19] It was the old song, her passion for the man not the monarch. But it no longer resonated as it had once done, in view of 'the rise of another', in La Rochefoucauld's phrase.

But Louise was not finished yet. The second even more dramatic action which focused the attention of the court on the current rivalry was taken by herself. Louise's nickname in the witty Sévigné circle might be 'The Dew' – Athénaïs was 'The Torrent' – but The Dew was certainly capable of impetuous gestures, as her precipitate flight to Chaillot had demonstrated three years earlier. Now Queen Marie-Thérèse was spending the night at La Fère, on her way from Compiègne to join the King at Avesnes according to his orders, when a piece of startling news was brought to her. The equipage of the new Duchesse de La Vallière was on its way. There was general consternation. There was also disgust, some of which had a hypocritical ring as the Queen's ladies, including Athénaïs, denounced Louise for reducing Marie-Thérèse to violent bouts of weeping.

The next morning the Duchesse swept a low curtsy to the Queen, according to protocol. Marie-Thérèse did not even acknowledge her presence. Nor was any food provided for her, until the maître d'hôtel took pity on the starving Louise and served her privately. When all the ladies gathered round the Queen resumed their places in the carriage and travelled on to their rendezvous with the King, the conversation never left the subject. What effrontery to present herself to Her Majesty without being sent for! Thus Athénaïs. She was echoed by the others. Athénaïs even went further, with her own brand of effrontery: 'God save me from being the mistress of the King! But if I was, I should feel thoroughly ashamed in front of the Queen.'

It was the encounter with the King himself which was however the high point of the drama, at once pitiful and embarrassing. Louise flung herself trembling on the ground before him. Only then did his glacial reception – she had defied his explicit orders to stay at Versailles – convince her of her terrible mistake. 'How much inquietude you might have spared me, had you been as tepid in the first days of our acquaintance as you have seemed for some time past! You gave me evidence of a great passion: I was enchanted and I abandoned myself to loving you to distraction.' The poignant words were those of a young woman in a convent, seduced and abandoned by a French officer, in the celebrated best-seller of the time, *Letters of a Portuguese Nun*.[20]* They might have been spoken word for word by Louise.

Louis XIV was a philanderer, but he was not a monster. He disliked disobedience but he did not like cruelty and humiliation either.† The next day it was he, not the recriminatory and in many cases hypocritical ladies, who invited Louise to join the Queen and her ladies in her carriage. His gesture was so imperious that Marie-Thérèse dared not say a word. That night Louise was invited to take supper at the royal table. None of this stopped Louis's assiduous attentions to Athénaïs, so that the Queen observed out loud that he sometimes only came to bed at four o'clock in the morning. 'Working on dispatches,' replied the King smoothly, but the

---

* Allegedly written in Portuguese in 1667–8 by Mariana Alcoforado, and translated into French, *Letters of a Portuguese Nun* was actually composed in French by Gabriel-Joseph de Guilleragues.[21]

† It is for this reason that one should reject the apocryphal story of Louis rushing through Louise's room to reach Athénaïs, hurling the latter's spaniel, called Malice, for Louise to tend as he went. The manners of the Sun King were something on which he prided himself; the story is only important for calling attention to the physical intimacy in which they all lived.

Grande Mademoiselle noted that he had to turn away to hide a smile.[22]

The King returned to his armies, which took the major Flemish fortress of Lille after a nine-day siege; the Spanish troops fell back on Brussels and Mons. The Queen and her strange entourage returned via Notre-Dame-de-Liesse, where Marie-Thérèse wished to pray. Nothing demonstrated the extraordinary interweaving of Queen, paramours – two of them – religion and intrigue more than the fact that Athénaïs and Louise now both went to confession at the same place to the same priest. Presumably they confessed the same sin, of sleeping with the King, though of course it was still true that Athénaïs had committed adultery and Louise had not.

Louise gave birth to her fourth child, a boy, at Saint-Germain on 17 November 1667. He was legitimised in February 1669 and the title of Comte de Vermandois was to be his. Later that year he was created Admiral of France under the conveniently bland name of 'Louis, Comte de Vermandois', the King having rejected anything more explicit such as 'Bastard of France', 'Louis, natural son of the King' or even 'Louis, Légitimé of France'.[23] Honours could not conceal the fact that emotionally the King had moved on. Even poor Marie-Thérèse was found in floods of tears after receiving an anonymous letter informing her of the shift in her husband's affections; perhaps she had entertained a wistful hope that the demotion of Louise would have meant the return of Louis permanently to her side.

By the Peace of Aix-la-Chapelle between France and Spain in May 1668, Louis acquired various towns in Flanders which he had recently conquered, including Oudenarde and Lille. But Franche-Comté, lying further south on the borders of Switzerland, which had been overrun by French troops under Condé, was for the time being handed back. The Peace also brought King and court back to Saint-Germain.

Louis renewed his frenzied enthusiasm for the elaborate rebuilding of a new Versailles. There in July he staged another vast celebration known as the Grand Royal Entertainment, ostensibly to celebrate the Peace, but in court opinion actually to honour the new favourite. Over three thousand people were present, including the Papal Nuncio and numerous ambassadors. One of these, the Savoyard Comte de Saint-Maurice, described the chaos: even the Queen was forced to wait for half an hour for her entry, while some ambassadors never got in at all. The lucky entrants marvelled happily at the enormous artificial 'rooms' made of foliage and hung with tapestries; thirty-two crystal chandeliers illuminated them.[24] Many trees were hung with fruits including oranges from Portugal; a huge palace of marzipan and sugar looked so tasty that the crowd subsequently tore it to bits and ate it.

Molière's offering on this occasion was a merry tale of a cuckolding: *George Dandin or the Astonished Husband*. Generally pronounced 'the height of comedy', it told the story of a peasant who married above himself and found it a strange experience, including the fact that his 'lady' wife betrayed him. At first the peasant wanted to drown himself in one of the numerous handy fountains at Versailles; in the end however he was persuaded to drown his sorrows instead of himself − in drink. The line 'You asked for it, George Dandin' became a catchphrase.[25]

Peacetime also brought an unwelcome visitor to court in the person of another, if nobler, 'astonished husband', the Marquis de Montespan, who came from the lesser war on the borders of Spain itself. It was now that Louise, Duchesse de La Vallière, tasted the full measure of her invidious position, something that her religious nature began to construe as a fit punishment for her sinfulness. Where once Louis had courted her to conceal his feelings for his sister-in-law, he now used her continued visible presence to distract public attention from his relationship with Athénaïs. Thus Louise was once again cast in the role of decoy, a penance to be weighed in the balance against six years of sinning.

The trouble was the matter of Double Adultery, and the arrival of the disagreeable Montespan only emphasised the fact. Double Adultery was odious to the Church. Adultery was after all specifically forbidden in the Ten Commandments, unlike fornication, which was not mentioned; quite apart from the fact that adultery itself was a criminal offence for which a woman could be locked into a convent for life. Montespan's uncle, the Archbishop of Sens, for example, had preached an angry sermon on the subject and made a woman in the same circumstances as Athénaïs do penance. What could just be pardoned in a King with a pretty young girlfriend – with suitable recourse to a Jesuit confessor tolerant of man's failings along the road to salvation – could not be pardoned in a married woman involved with a married man, even if he was a King. (This was one of the reasons Louise had rejected the offer of a smokescreen marriage.) The practical if not doctrinal solution was a complaisant husband.

Unfortunately nothing about Montespan was in the slightest bit complaisant. Not for him the sophisticated attitude suggested by some highly topical lines of Molière in an entertainment of January 1668. This featured the story of Jupiter and Amphitryon, husband of the beautiful Alcimène. While Amphitryon was away at the war, Jupiter had assumed the husband's shape in order to sleep with Alcimène. He then proceeded to console Amphitryon as follows: 'Sharing with Jupiter / Has nothing dishonourable about it. / Certainly it can be nothing but glorious / To find oneself the rival of the king of the gods.' To Montespan, sharing with Jupiter was anything but glorious.[26]

Charles II, who had his own troubles with Barbara

Villiers' husband, wrote teasingly on the subject to Henriette-Anne: 'I am so sorry to find that cuckolds in France grow so troublesome. They have been very inconvenient in all countries this last year.'[27] And troublesome was a light word for Montespan's behaviour once he realised what had been going on, and was still going on with his Alcimène. Where members of both the Montespan and Rochechouart families shrugged their shoulders, ready to enjoy the good fortune which Jupiter's attentions would surely bring them, Montespan raged loudly and publicly.

The comparison of Louis XIV to King David in the Bible was one which had already been covertly made by Bossuet, on the grounds of David's pursuing another man's wife, Bathsheba. It was now openly proclaimed from Montespan's lips. Well-wishers such as the Grande Mademoiselle tried to calm and divert him. But Montespan was not to be calmed or diverted. Denouncing Jupiter in Jupiter's own kingdom was so evidently self-destructive that there would even have been something quite magnificent about his behaviour; except for the fact that Montespan in his own private life showed an unpleasant contempt for the female sex, mixed with bouts of physical violence.

Montespan now announced in a two-part plan that he was regularly using whores in the filthiest brothels in order to become infected and thus pass on the disease to the King via his wife. Part one of this plan was easy enough; part two involved forcing himself upon Athénaïs (although a husband was entitled by law to compel his wife to have sex, the violation of Athénaïs would by any decent standards have been nothing less than rape). Athénaïs managed to elude this fate but could not avoid various scenes when the grossest insults were hurled at her. In the meantime Montespan's wrath also fell upon the Duc de Montausier, recently appointed governor to the young Dauphin because of his wife's friendship with Athénaïs. The Duchesse de

Montausier – long ago *'la belle Julie'*, protected daughter of the celebrated *Précieuse* the Marquise de Rambouillet – also found herself involved in Montespan's outrageous denunciations. Nor had the Marquis lost his propensity for physical threat: at one point this sensitive, sixty-year-old woman thought she was going to be thrown out of her own window. Her nerves never really recovered from the ordeal.

But at this point the angry Amphitryon had gone too far. Embarrassing as the whole situation certainly was for Jupiter, no subject could criticise the sovereign's decrees and get away with it. The abuse loaded on Montausier's appointment to the Dauphin gave Louis his opportunity. He sent Montespan to prison to cool his heels (or stop his mouth) by a *lettre de cachet* – that is to say, the simple order of the King, no duration of stay indicated and no judicial process involved. After a week Montespan was let out (a longer stay would have become increasingly awkward) on condition that he went into effective exile on his estates in the south. So Montespan departed, taking his son Louis-Alexandre to join his daughter Marie-Christine at Bonnefont, where his own mother cared for them.

There were rumours, not proved, that he was helped on his way by a sum of money to pay his prodigious debts. If so, Montespan still did not quieten down even in his own home. He had the gates to the château taken down on the grounds that his cuckold's horns were too high to let him pass through. And Marie-Christine, Louis-Antoine, the old Marquise and all the servants were treated to the spectacle of a full funeral with black-draped carriages where Montespan declared that his wife was henceforward dead to him.

Back at court, Athénaïs was very far from being dead or even – unlike poor Julie de Montausier – permanently shattered. But she was extremely anxious. The real reason for her anxiety, visible in a momentary dimming of her generally triumphant beauty, was the fact that she was pregnant. Athénaïs must have conceived the child at the end of June, and been aware of her pregnancy during the ghastly period of Montespan's imprecations. Obviously her state had to be kept a complete secret, since Montespan was and remained her lawful husband. This meant that there was an ugly possibility that, to spite the lovers, he would claim the baby as legally his. Fashion and her own enterprise came to her aid. Athénaïs developed a method of concealment as her figure bloomed: wearing looser and looser dresses known, not altogether appropriately, as 'the Innocent *Déshabillé*'. The baby was born at the end of March: probably but not certainly a girl.[28] Arrangements were made for the birth to take place in the same obscure fashion as had been used for Louise. Athénaïs was installed in a little house in the rue de l'Échelle, near the Tuileries. Three months later the mistress was pregnant again. As Saint-Maurice drily observed: 'The lady is extremely fertile and her powder lights very quickly.'[29]

This routine – as it became – of pregnancy did not prevent the development of a magnificent lifestyle for the Marquise. She also took her chances of providing for her own Rochechouart family. Athénaïs, unlike Louise, was greedy for everything that life or rather the King could grant her. She owed it to herself and the King owed it to her. Like Versailles, she was expensive – and glorious. It was characteristic of Athénaïs's exuberance that her apartments were full of animals, not only birds but more surprising pets for indoors such as goats, lambs, pigs and even mice, which she allowed to run about all round her and displayed on her navel. Flowers she adored, and found a perfect outlet for her natural extravagance. She employed twelve hundred gardeners at Clagny and in one season had eight thousand daffodils planted, not a cheap enterprise. Part of her greed also, or at least her extravagance, was an enjoyment of food and drink, perhaps unwisely so for a member of a family which included such an overweight phenomenon as the Marquis de Vivonne.

Another area of pleasure for Athénaïs was sex or *commerce* (literally 'having dealings'), which was the contemporary phrase for intercourse. This was not how women were supposed to feel. For once it was not the Catholic Church which was responsible. It was true that in theory laid down by St Paul, conjugal sex was intended purely for the procreation of children, and the fathers of the Church had further denounced over-amorous conjugal exertions. Between them St Jerome and St Thomas Aquinas managed to designate roughly a hundred days in any given year, including the whole of Lent, when sex between married people was not allowed. But by the fifteenth century, sex for pleasure between husband and wife was tolerated so long as there was no question of birth control. And there was a theory at least that the female orgasm helped on conception, being expressed in the language of male desire: *'Je coule, je coule'* ('I flow, I flow').

It was the women of the tribe, those who endured it or who were enduring it, who spoke of having *commerce* as a burden. It was generally thought of as the 'conjugal debt', or in the words of Madame de Sévigné (constantly advocating separate rooms to her daughter) a duty that her daughter owed her husband, not something from which she could expect pleasure. Of course not all women disliked having *commerce*. An anonymous seventeenth-century verse in English, 'Sylvia's Complaint', drew attention to the fact that females did feel sexual desire but 'Custom and modesty / Strictly forbid our passion to declare.' A future Duchesse d'Orléans would write in some surprise of her daughter's recent marriage: 'She is already quite used to the thing and does not dislike it as much as I did ...'[31] Athénaïs went further and was an enthusiast.

There was a danger in all this, the height of sexual

enterprise which Louis and Athénaïs indulged in together, sometimes three times a day for long sessions. Louis was now verging on his thirtieth birthday (5 September 1668). He certainly showed no sign of that reform promised four years earlier, rather the contrary. There might come a time when such excess, by normal standards, was not so easy. The temptation might arise to provide or indulge in artificial stimulants.

That lay ahead. The public face of Athénaïs was now as the dazzling creature, the brightest star in the galaxy which surrounded the Sun King, the one for whom, without knowing it, he had always craved to complete his image in the world at large (if not the world of the Catholic Church). Her second child by the King, a boy named Louis-Auguste, was born at the end of March 1670. He turned out to be clever, sharp, and amusing like his mother; unlike Athénaïs he was not physically perfect, being born with one deformed leg which made it very difficult for him to learn to walk.

Obviously proper attention had to be paid to these secretly housed children even if they could not for the time being figure at court – Montespan's behaviour was still raw in everyone's mind and the legal situation unchanged. The solution was surely a governess, someone of good but not grand birth, someone known for her virtue rather than her glamour, intelligent and attractive nevertheless, someone who would be able to inspire children; and someone discreet. In this casual way Athénaïs's choice fell upon her friend Françoise d'Aubigné, the Widow Scarron. She could have no idea – nobody could, least of all Françoise herself – where the new path of this modest thirty-five-year-old widow would lead her.

The little crippled boy, Louis-Auguste, was handed to Madame Scarron shortly after birth. She stood in a waiting coach and received in her arms a sacred trust.

CHAPTER 7

Marriages Like Death

Marriages are like death. The time and season are marked,
you can't escape.

– Liselotte, Duchesse d'Orléans

Neptune, God of the Sea, and Apollo, God of the Sun,
were the last two roles Louis XIV danced in a Court
Ballet. The occasion, once again a joint effort of Molière
and Lully, was entitled *The Magnificent Lovers*; it was held at
the château of Saint-Germain-en-Laye on 7 February 1670.
Appropriately enough, in view of the ballet's title, it was
Athénaïs who had made the choice of Molière; she could
not however dance herself, given that she was nearly eight
months pregnant. Two men were needed to take over
Louis's parts: a week later Neptune was danced by the
Comte d'Armagnac and Apollo by the Marquis de Villeroi.[1]
  The King had been dancing with much-praised skill for
twenty-odd years. What prompted his decision? There was
a rumour that some lines in Racine's *Britannicus*, first staged
a few months earlier, had irked him. In the play the Emperor
Nero, in a hostile portrait, was accused of 'wasting his life
on the theatre'. But Racine was a jovial courtier in his
approach to the King, rather than a critical artist; it was a
distinction made with approval by Saint-Simon: 'There was
nothing of the poet in his conversation and all of the
civilised man.'[2] He remained popular with Louis, who made
him one of his two Historiographers Royal.
  More to the point was the King's own sense of *gravitas*.
He was now in his thirty-second year, and one remembers

the emphasis that had been put on his thirtieth birthday as marking the end to gallantry. Even if that had not been the case, the art of the Court Ballet was an increasingly complex one: it demanded more of him in public than love-making did in private. And there were his responsibilities of government, the pursuit of martial glory in the cause of national security: that perennial formula which has enabled nations to invade their neighbours throughout history. For the Peace of Aix-la-Chapelle, it became evident, was merely a truce in France's struggle (as she saw it) to improve her boundaries with the Spanish Netherlands.

One should realise that this patriotic militarism was a development which aroused much admiration at the time in Europe: pacifism was not after all a common emotion among kings – or peoples. Samuel Pepys for example spoke at a dinner in late 1668 of 'the greatness of the King of France and of his being fallen into the right way of making the Kingdom great, which none of his Ancestors ever did before'. A few years later there began to be a nostalgia for Cromwell in England, at the expense of Charles II; it was expressed in lines written by Andrew Marvell: 'Though his [Cromwell's] government did a tyrant resemble / He made England great and his enemies tremble.'[3]

At the end of April, the entire court – or so it seemed – set out at the King's behest to Flanders. As before, the cortège was more majestic than 'warlike'; the public reaction of bafflement to the royal relationships may be judged by the fact that even Athénaïs got some cheers. The ostensible reason was that the Queen needed to display herself to those new subjects gained by the Peace of Aix-la-Chapelle; the presence of her eight-year-old son the Dauphin, heir to her own rights, gave plausibility to the idea. The real plan was to provide cover for an important diplomatic mission on the part of Henriette-Anne to her native England.

The past years had not dealt gently with the charming,

pleasure-loving girl who had enchanted Louis XIV that summer of 1661. An idyllic scene inscribed on a fan showed Henriette-Anne with the brown-and-white spaniel Mimi she adored which had been given to her by Charles II (she even danced a Court Ballet with Mimi in her arms). There was a boy musician in attendance, as Madame had her hair dressed.[4] The reality was not so happy. Not yet twenty-six, Henriette-Anne already showed upsetting signs of ill health. Repeated pregnancies, eight in nine years, had not helped. There were several miscarriages; her only son died as a child and she was left with two daughters, Marie-Louise born in 1662 and Anne-Marie born on 27 August 1669. The death of Madame's mother, Queen Henrietta Maria, three days later brought another little princess to her household: this was her niece Anne Stuart, daughter of James Duke of York and his wife Anne Hyde.* Anne had spent the previous year in France with Henrietta Maria to consult French doctors about her chronically weak eyesight; at the age of four and a half she moved over to her Orléans first cousins. Little Anne loved France, retaining a French Huguenot servant for the rest of her life; she also preserved feelings of closeness for these particular Catholic cousins.

Unlike the robust Athénaïs, Henriette-Anne never felt well during pregnancy, and needed various pain-killing remedies including opium. But the real cause of her melancholy and distress was the unkindness of her husband. This cruelty was the repeated theme of her letters, either to her brother Charles, or to her old governess, Madame de Chaumont. It was not imaginary. The English Ambassador, Ralph Montagu, wrote to a colleague at the end of 1669 that if Madame had married an English country gentleman with

---

* The future Queen Anne was already third in line to the British throne at this point after James and her elder sister Mary, since Charles II had no legitimate children.

five thousand a year, she would have led a better life than she did in France, for Monsieur 'takes pleasure in crossing his wife in everything'.⁵ Compared with this malevolence, often taking the form of public rudeness, her husband's sexual preference hardly upset her. There had to be a certain kind of philosophic acceptance of such matters in an arranged royal marriage (especially as he performed his marital duties regularly with the aim of begetting an heir).

Under the circumstances, Charles, although not seen for nearly ten years, became the lodestar of her existence and the idea of Franco-British friendship, of which she would be the private conduit, immensely important to her. All this suited Louis XIV perfectly. The carousel of European alliances was on the move again. Louis was anxious to detach England from its defensive alliance with Holland – the so-called Triple Alliance including Sweden – on the grounds that sooner or later he would have to attack the Dutch. Charles II was equally anxious to move closer to France having made peace with Spain and Portugal in 1668. Who better than Madame, the beloved younger sister, to promote a secret treaty, and by her presence with a large entourage provide cover for the signing? In theory against women's interference in politics, in practice Louis was happy to be the beneficiary.

There was only one flaw in all this: Monsieur's spitefulness towards his wife was expressed in his determination that she should not visit England, since that was what she so passionately wished to do. Her last pregnancy, ending with the birth of Anne-Marie, had effectively grounded Henriette-Anne and Monsieur was quite prepared to use the same biological ploy again. It all came down to Monsieur's slavish love for the courtier his wife described as 'the man who is the cause of all my sorrows, past and present'. This was Philippe de Lorraine-Armagnac, a minor member of the Guise family, generally known as the Chevalier de Lorraine.

The Chevalier was about three years older than Monsieur and in the contemporary *cliché* 'beautiful as an angel'. He was also intelligent, very amusing and utterly unscrupulous. Everything had to be done according to his wishes, Monsieur even going so far as to suggest to Madame that he could not love her 'unless his favourite is allowed to form a third in our union'.[6]

Fortunately the Chevalier de Lorraine, rather like the Marquis de Montespan, overreached himself in a way that enabled Louis XIV to take action. The King absolutely refused to allow the Chevalier to take over the income from some bishoprics theoretically in Monsieur's gift, on the grounds that his dissolute private life made him unsuitable. The furious Chevalier made a feature of denouncing the King, and as a result was speedily imprisoned on Louis's orders on 30 January 1670. Public criticism of the monarch could not be tolerated; it provided the King with an excellent excuse to defend Henriette-Anne without appearing to do so. The incident was the equivalent of the King condemning Montespan for his words about the Dauphin's governor when he could not protect Athénaïs outright from her husband's violence.

In a passion of anger and loss, Monsieur withdrew to his distant property of Villers-Cotterets, dragging his wife with him. 'We go today,' she wrote miserably on 31 January, 'to return I know not when,' and Henriette-Anne spoke further of 'the fear I feel that the King may forget me'. This departure again Louis could not stop outright – the rights of the husband were paramount – but he certainly showed no sign of forgetting his sister-in-law. He bombarded the exile with presents from some mythical Court Lottery: caskets full of cash, jewelled garters, perfumes and gloves, even some country walking shoes with lavishly expensive silver buckles.[7]

In the end there was a compromise. The Chevalier was

allowed out of his prison on parole and vanished for a while to Italy. Monsieur's restlessness with the delights of provincial Villers-Cotterets provoked him into returning to court and granting, albeit sulkily, permission for Henriette-Anne to make a brief visit to England. As for her, when the King asked her whether she had been very bored, she replied, with a flash of her old spirit, that she had spent her exile learning Italian but was glad she had not had to stay at Villers-Cotterets long enough to learn Latin.

To outsiders, the great caravan of Louis XIV which set out for Flanders in 1670 might appear awesome. Jean Nocret, a painter who specialised in allegorical compositions, painted the entire royal family this year at the request of Monsieur.[8] There they all were as gods and goddesses, ineffably dignified and handsome in their robes: from Louis and Marie-Thérèse, blonde locks flowing, patting the head of an equally golden-haired Dauphin, Monsieur and Henriette-Anne, the Grande Mademoiselle as Diana with a crescent moon in her hair, down to the half-naked children with their lyres and wreaths. The reality was rather different and had its absurd side. On rolled the vagabond court including the Queen, the Duchesse de La Vallière, the Marquise de Montespan, the Grande Mademoiselle, and of course the Duc and Duchesse d'Orléans. Molière and Lully went too so that civilisation should not be altogether abandoned, and Racine was present in his role of Historiographer Royal. There were thirty thousand others when all the soldiers were included. But none of this travelling majesty was proof against the weather.

Waterlogged roads impeded progress. On one occasion the river Sambre, a tributary of the Meuse, had so far overflowed its banks that the royal party could not pass. Marie-Thérèse screamed out in terror at the rising water and Henriette-Anne, who felt so ill that she could swallow nothing but milk, fainted. Refuge had to be taken in a

primitive farmhouse at Landrecies. The Grande Mademoiselle got stuck in the mud carrying the Queen's train.
The food was uneatable. There was only one room and
everyone had to share it. 'Sleeping all together is dreadful!'
cried the indignant Queen. Only Athénaïs's sister Gabrielle
retained her equilibrium and, with that sweet Mortemart wit,
said that hearing the noise of cattle lowing outside the
window, with straw inside, made her think of the birth of
Christ.

All in all Henriette-Anne cannot have been sad to part
from the court at Lille before travelling to Dunkirk, where
a British squadron awaited her for the journey to England.
She had a long interview with Louis before departure and
he clasped her hand tightly and tenderly in farewell. The
disagreeable mood of Monsieur had not lifted: referring to
his wife's marked pallor, he ' chose to meditate on the
message of an astrologer who had predicted that he would
marry several times ... He duly made a last-ditch attempt
to block the expedition, and made no affectionate sign of
farewell.

Henriette-Anne arrived at the cliffs of Dover at dawn on
26 May.* She got an ecstatic reception not only from her
brothers King Charles and James Duke of York with his
wife Anne (whose little Anne was currently in her household
in France) but also from James Duke of Monmouth, Charles's handsome, twenty-one-year-old illegitimate son. To the
annoyance of Monsieur, Henriette-Anne had had one of
her light-hearted flirtations, an exercise in gallantry, with
Monmouth at the French court.

Jollifications, many of them by sea, where the 'fearless
and bold' Henriette-Anne walked on 'the edge of ships',

---

* The following dates are given in French New Style as opposed to English
Old Style which, as has been noted, lagged behind that of the Continent at
this period.

covered the diplomatic negotiations considered vital by both kings.[9] The way had been well prepared in advance and accord was reached by 1 June. And joy of joys, Louis XIV (not Monsieur) had agreed to an extension of her visit, so that Henriette-Anne actually remained in England until 12 June.

The Secret Treaty of Dover, as it became known much later, was literally a secret from all but Charles's closest advisers. For all the lip-service paid to the Peace of Aix-la-Chapelle concluded by France with Spain, Charles agreed to support Louis's further claims to his wife's alleged possessions in Flanders. England's theoretical fidelity to the recently signed Triple Alliance was equally ignored: the two Kings agreed to attack the Dutch together. Linked to this notional aggression was however a crucial clause in which Charles, being convinced of the truth of Catholicism, was resolved to reconcile himself publicly with the Church of Rome *as soon as the welfare of the kingdom will permit* (italics added). In return he was to receive generous financial subsidies from his French cousin.[10]

It will be obvious that the italicised clause, although sometimes held to prove Charles's determination to turn Britain Papist, in fact did no such thing; the timing was left to him to decide in the future, the money came at once from Louis.* Was this secret religious clause put in to please Henriette-Anne? Raised a Catholic in France (after her Protestant baptism in England), she was however not a noticeably ardent one. Although it remains in the realm of conjecture, it seems more likely that Louis XIV, an ardent Catholic if an ardent sinner as well, supported the clause as putting him on the side of the (Catholic) angels.

---

* To look ahead, one should note that the 'welfare of the kingdom' never did permit Charles to declare himself a Catholic until he was lying on what was manifestly his deathbed.

The château of Saint-Germain-en-Laye where Louis was born in 1638.

Louis XIV aged about
twelve; the beauty of the boy
King – the 'Godgiven' child –
was the subject of general
comment, and his flowing,
golden brown hair (which
darkened with age) particularly admired.

Louis XIV dancing the role
of Apollo, God of the Sun,
at the age of fourteen; the
image of Louis as the
'Sun King' was carefully
cultivated.

Anne of Austria as a young woman was vivacious and attractive, also a noted
equestrian, a taste Louis inherited; she had many admirers including the Duke
of Buckingham although her intimates believed these flirtations remained
chaste.

Louis XIV in his early twenties, about the time he began his personal rule. By Nicolas Mignard.

The figure of Reputation holds a medallion of Louis XIV.

The Grande Mademoiselle as Minerva, patroness of the Arts; she holds a portrait of her father, Gaston Duc d'Orléans.

Marie Mancini (*right*), the first love of Louis XIV, with her sister Hortense; although Cardinal Mazarin was her uncle, he was horrified at the possibility of the King making such a comparatively lowly marriage.

Philip IV greets Louis XIV on the occasion of his wedding to the Infanta
Maria Teresa, 1660; her stiff ceremonial attire symbolizes her formal and
restricted upbringing at the Spanish court.

Two Queens of France: Anne of Austria with Marie-Thérèse who
was her niece as well as her daughter-in-law, with the Dauphin,
from birth a remarkably robust child.

Queen Marie-Thérèse and her only surviving child, the Dauphin Louis de France, by Pierre Mignard.

Anne of Austria, mother of Louis XIV, as a widow (her husband died when she was in her early forties); she retained her love of magnificent jewellery, her bracelets in particular drawing attention to her famously beautiful hands.

HET WEDER KEEREN VAN LODEWYK DE XIIV MET SYN HOF G

The triumphant figure of Louis XIV depicted on a warhorse outside Maastricht which he besieged successfully in June 1673; a new militaristic image as his plans for conquest increased.

As European opinion turned against Louis XIV and his military ventures became less successful, there were numerous satirical attacks on him. An anonymous engraving of 1693, 'Louis Retreats with his Seraglio', shows him with a column of ladies behind him.

LA RETRAITE DE LOVIS XIV AVEC SON SERRA

Louise de La Vallière, the virginal young girl whom Louis made his mistress and who bore him several children; no one described her as beautiful but everyone found her appealing.

Louise de La Vallière as a huntress: despite her seemingly frail physique, Louise was an accomplished rider, something which made her an ideal companion for the King.

Athénaïs de Rochechouart de
Mortemart, Marquise de
Montespan, who was the King's
maîtresse en titre for seventeen
years; her beauty, including the
curling hair admired by Madame
de Sévigné and her large blue eyes,
dazzled contemporaries. By Louis
Elle Ferdinand II.

Athénaïs reclining in front of the
gallery of her château at Clagny;
her frequent pregnancies meant
that she adopted elegant and
languorous loose clothing to
conceal her figure.

Athénaïs by Pierre Mignard.

The Appartement des Bains where Madame de Montespan and the King relaxed, with a marble bath and couches; depicted on a fan.

Satirists were happy to mock Athénaïs's voluptuous figure as it thickened with age; seen here feasting with Louis XIV and attendant goblins and devils. By Joseph Werner.

Angélique de Fontanges became the King's mistress at the age of eighteen when he was forty; she died two years later after a traumatic experience in childbirth; some people thought she was the most beautiful girl ever to come to Versailles – 'like a statue' – but she lacked intelligence.

Françoise de Maintenon, showing the attractive young woman whose dark hair and dark eyes were much admired; she also loved fine clothes, contrary to later sneers that she was a prude who always dressed in black.

MARIE ANGELIQVE D'ESCORAILLES
DE ROVSSILLE DVCHESSE DE
FONTANGE.

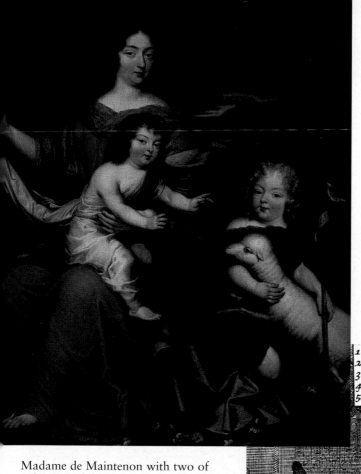

1. *La Maintenon*
2. *Scarron*.
3. *Ragotin*.
4. *La Rancune*.
5. *La Rapiniere*

Madame de Maintenon with two of Athénaïs's children to whom she acted as governess in a secret house in the rue de Vaugirard: the Duc du Maine, her favourite, and the Comte de Vexin who died young.

Engraved frontispiece to the satire *Scarron appearing to Madame de Maintenon*, 1664; the middle-aged playwright whom she married at the age of sixteen and who died nine years later here regards his widow in all her court finery with dismay.

Madame de Maintenon with her niece Françoise-
Charlotte, daughter of her reprobate brother Charles
d'Aubigné; she made Françoise-Charlotte her heir,
married her to the Duc de Noailles and gave her the
Château de Maintenon.

'May your fidelity be inviolable to the
end…' The 'Secret Notebooks' of
Madame de Maintenon which she
kept from about 1684 onwards;
noting religious texts, bibilical
quotations and sayings of
the Saints.

Madame de Maintenon painted as Saint Frances of Rome; contemporaries wondered whether the 'queenly' ermine indicated that she was secretly married to Louis XIV; when asked about the fur, the King commented that Saint Frances certainly deserved ermine.

King David playing on his harp by
Domenico Zampieri which Louis
acquired from the possessions of
Cardinal Mazarin; it shows a more soulful David than the lecherous biblical
King regularly denounced by preachers as
a covert way of attacking Louis XIV's
adulteries.

A miniature based on the Saint Frances
portrait which Louis XIV carried in his
pocket until his death.

All too soon Henriette-Anne had used up her extended leave and had to return to the French court – and Monsieur. As she departed, her brother Charles was in visible anguish, rushing back three times to embrace her, seemingly unable to let her go. The French Ambassador commented that he had not realised until he witnessed this scene that the cynical English King was capable of feeling so much for anyone.

Eight days after returning to France, Henriette-Anne went with Monsieur to their château at Saint-Cloud, a short distance from Paris. The next day she complained of pains in her side as well as the stomach ache 'to which she was subject' in the words of the Comtesse de La Fayette.[11] But she was oppressed by the summer heat (it had rained in England) and determined to bathe in spite of her doctors' advice. On Friday 27 June Henriette-Anne did bathe; on the Saturday however she felt so much worse that she had to stop. The Comtesse arrived in Saint-Cloud later that Saturday night to find Madame looking ghastly and admitting that she felt even worse than she looked. (This was from someone famous for her patience in the face of suffering.) Nevertheless, her nervous energy had not altogether departed: Henriette-Anne walked in the moonlit gardens until midnight.

On Sunday morning she went to Monsieur's apartments and had a long talk: he was planning to return to Paris. She visited her daughter Marie-Louise, whose portrait was being painted. Dinner took place. Afterwards Henriette-Anne, feeling terrible, lay down as she often did, and put her head in the lap of the Comtesse de La Fayette. The Comtesse was wont to think her mistress beautiful in all her attitudes, but now Madame's face seemed to have changed and she looked quite plain.

About five o'clock that afternoon her true ordeal began, a horrifying process of torment which would not terminate for over nine hours. First Henriette-Anne asked for some chicory water, which was prepared for her by one of her most trusty waiting-women and administered by a similarly devoted lady-in-waiting. Immediately she started to cry out: 'Ah, what a pain in my side! What agony! I can't bear it!' As the hours passed, her pains only grew worse until the doctors who had begun by assuring everyone that there was no danger were forced to change their tune totally, and admit that Madame was actually near to death. Her limbs were icy, her expression glazed, although she never lost consciousness. The bleedings from the foot which were the recommended panacea of the time added to her sufferings.

It was distressing both then and afterwards that in her agonies Henriette-Anne cried out that she had been poisoned by the chicory water and must be given antidotes. Monsieur showed no signs of guilty dismay (the Comtesse de La Fayette admitted with shame that she watched his expression). There was a suggestion that a dog might be given the chicory water until a lady-in-waiting came forward and said she had drunk some without ill effect. The antidotes such as powder of vipers were however administered – without doing more than, once again, increasing the pain.

In spite of her torments, Henriette-Anne managed to retain that graceful quality which had marked her all her life. Now the court rushed to their adored Madame's side, Louise and Athénaïs among others. To Monsieur she said sadly: 'Alas, you have long ago stopped loving me, but I have never failed you.' The scene with the King was more affecting. He embraced her and embraced her again as the tears fell. She told him: 'You are losing the truest servant you ever had.'

Given the seriousness of a deathbed at the time, already mentioned with regard to Anne of Austria, the Grande Mademoiselle worried that the sacraments were not being brought.[12] The stern Father Feuillet, a local priest of Jansenist sympathies, was introduced. He provided little solace: when

Madame was convulsed with suffering, he suggested that this was a suitable punishment for her sins. Then the greater-souled Bossuet, now a bishop, arrived. It was Bossuet who gave her the Sacrament and Extreme Unction and promised her forgiveness. Later the English Ambassador, Ralph Montagu, arrived. It was typical of Madame's good manners that she tried to tell him in English about an emerald she wanted to bequeath to Bossuet lest the Bishop be embarrassed. Finally she kissed the crucifix Bossuet held out. Henriette-Anne, Princess of England and France, died at two o'clock in the morning on 30 June. She was just past her twenty-sixth birthday.

It was inevitable, in view of the state of the Orléans marriage, and Madame's unfortunate involuntary cry after drinking the chicory water, that accusations of poison should be flung at the widower. Although the Machiavellian Cheva-lier de Lorraine was absent, there were many who thought that he was indirectly if not directly responsible. But it has always been regarded as proof of the Chevalier's innocence that Louis allowed him back to court despite his behaving in 'so insolent a manner towards the Princess, whilst she was living', in the words of the English Ambassador. In fact these accusations were endemic at this time, as we shall see.

The truth was simpler and sadder. Henriette-Anne's health had been wrecked by childbearing and exacerbated by her own misery. The prospect of taking permanent refuge in England was not one a princess of her time would have contemplated, given that it involved abandonment not only of her children but also of her honoured place at the French King's side – he for whom she had just acted the ambassadress so triumphantly. Modern opinion inclines to the view that she died of acute peritonitis following the perforation of a peptic ulcer. It was a tortured end but it was not the result of a criminal deed.[12]

Monsieur's mourning took the form of extreme attention

to etiquette (he was rapidly becoming the private arbiter on such matters, if the King remained the supreme public source). Marie-Louise, aged nine, was draped in purple velvet, the mourning of a princess, and received the condolences of the court in a long procession. That was suitable enough. She was joined by the five-year-old English Princess Anne, similarly attired; with the death of her aunt, she would shortly sail back to England to join her parents, armed with two splendid pearl and diamond bracelets given her by the French King. Even the baby Anne-Marie, less than a year old, was similarly bundled up in purple velvet and had to receive compliments, which she can hardly have registered.[13]

In order to assuage the horrified grief of Charles II, Louis ordered a state funeral as for a Queen of France, while one of Henriette-Anne's rings was delivered back to her brother. In an even greater departure from tradition, Louis sent Queen Marie-Thérèse to the ceremony incognito. (The King himself by custom never attended such rituals.) It was Bossuet's oration at these obsequies in Saint-Denis on 21 August which crowned the life of Henriette-Anne with the nobility it deserved.[14]* He stressed the shortness of her life: 'Madame passed at once from morning to evening like the flowers of the field.' He harked back to her early years in France: how 'the misfortunes of her House could not crush her in her youth and already at that time we saw in her a greatness which owed nothing to fortune', she who had a head and heart even above her royal birth. But now: 'O disastrous night! O frightful night! When there arrived all at once this astonishing news: "Madame is dying! Madame is dead!"' And the Bishop told Louis XIV that Madame had been 'gentle towards death as she was to all the world'.[15]

* Compared by Lytton Strachey in the twentieth century to 'molten lava'. There was always a considerable gap between a death and a state funeral, the corpse having been embalmed and the vital organs removed to be interred elsewhere.

Just as La Fontaine had saluted Henriette-Anne for the recovery of 'our court's laughing face', so Madame de Sévigné wrote to her cousin Bussy-Rabutin that 'all happiness, charm and pleasure' had departed from the court with her death. The Comtesse de La Fayette put it quite simply: it was 'one of those losses for which one is never consoled'.[16]

A few days after Henriette-Anne's death a scene took place which might seem bizarre by any standards except those of the French court created by Louis XIV. The King was devastated by the death of his brother's wife: his thoughts dwelled on her perennial youthfulness as he remembered it (never mind what had happened to her in recent years), her devotion to him seen in her embassy to England. Above all Henriette-Anne was the first beloved contemporary to die, an epochal moment in the life of any human being, including a king.

Finding himself with the Grande Mademoiselle, Louis indicated to her that there was now what in modern terms would be called a job opportunity: the position of Madame was vacant and she might wish to fill it.[17] Anne-Marie-Louise was forty-three years old and her childbearing capacity, which had been doubted in her thirties, had certainly now vanished. The King was therefore thinking along two lines. On the one hand he was, as ever with the unfortunate heiress, eyeing those rich properties coveted by so many over the years, and wondering about their fate after the Grande Mademoiselle's death. On the other hand he sincerely believed in the necessity of a new Madame to replace the old one. As a future incumbent would say later, 'being Madame' was a *métier*, a profession. Effectively the second lady at court – Louis's surviving legitimate daughter, known as 'the Petite Madame', was only three – Madame had a role to play in the royal order of things.

As it happened, both the spinster-bride and the widower-bridegroom had other priorities. Monsieur definitely wanted a son and heir whereas the Grande Mademoiselle had for some time harboured the extraordinary, even exotic design of marrying a courtier named Lauzun, who was by no conceivable means a proper match for her. Anne-Marie-Louise therefore told the King that she *had* thought of marrying without specifying whom she had in mind.

Antonin Nompar de Caumont, Comte de Lauzun, was now in his late thirties, a man of good family connections and much favoured by Louis himself. Unalluring to the eye of posterity, he clearly possessed considerable sex appeal, despite being described as 'very diminutive' by the Duke of Berwick, who was baffled by his attraction. Perhaps it was the charm of outrageous, even *louche* behaviour which benefited him in such regimented society. Not all his reported remarks to his would-be fiancée were chivalrous: for example he criticised Anne-Marie-Louise for going to the ballet and parties at her age when she should be praying and doing good works. He also disapproved of an over-youthful red ribbon in her hair. The Grande Mademoiselle took a different line. 'People of my rank are always young,' she once said.[18] At any rate he caught her eye and somehow (the potential rewards to him were enormous) suggested in her emotionally virginal mind the dazzling prospect of marriage. That is to say, it was dazzling to this long-term spinster in romantic terms, otherwise horrifyingly daring and even foolhardy.

Astonishing most of his court, Louis did give permission for the marriage, essential for public acknowledgement of the union (a secret marriage with the Church's blessing was another matter). Queen Marie-Thérèse and Monsieur, both sticklers for the formalities, were vociferously opposed to the match. Yet it was significant that the shock, horror at the news of this fearful *mésalliance* was felt most keenly by the Grande Mademoiselle's own servants. Three days later, on 18 December, with a heavy heart but conscious of the duty of the sovereign, Louis rescinded his permission, to the devastation of Anne-Marie-Louise. His excuse – given in a memorandum on the subject – was that Anne-Marie-Louise had pretended falsely that he, the King, had promoted the marriage: 'my reputation was involved.'[19] But court disapproval was the major reason. Whether Louis had been weak in the first place in giving in to her desire so strongly expressed, or was acting weakly now in cancelling his decision, was a matter of opinion. Most people at the time thought the former.

Louis, having broken the poor woman's heart in the cause of the royal order in which he believed so passionately, now showed himself at his most supportive. When Anne-Marie-Louise broke down at a ball, it was the King himself who went to her aid, thus preempting the unpleasant ridicule of the courtiers. 'Cousin, you are not well,' he said and personally escorted her away. So the Grande Mademoiselle remained with her fortune – who would now inherit it? The subject did not go away as she grew older – and her high position at the court. Louis also retained Lauzun in his favour, even using him on a confidential mission, until the rakish count, in a highly melodramatic manner, brought about his own disgrace.

It was a question of the reputation of Athénaïs. Lauzun asked the favourite to intervene on his behalf with the King on the subject of the marriage and then hid himself under her bed when Louis was *in situ* to make sure she had carried out her mission. Athénaïs, believing herself in private, did no such thing. She then lied about it to Lauzun. He was a man of whose violence people at court tended to be frightened, and for good reason. Furious at what he saw as a gross betrayal (never mind his own gross invasion of the lovers' privacy), Lauzun now shouted at the King that he himself had slept with Athénaïs. Louis, with the greatest difficulty mastering his seething outrage, broke his own cane in half and threw it out of the window 'lest he strike a gentleman'. (His self-control would later incur the ultimate approval of that courtly purist Saint-Simon.)[20] Lauzun ended up in prison in the south, in the company of the disgraced minister Fouquet, where he languished for ten years.

All this left the problem of Monsieur's second marriage unresolved. It was the eventual solution, in November 1671, which brought to the court of Louis XIV not only its most original female member but also its most entertaining observer, rivalled only by Saint-Simon (but the new Duchesse d'Orléans had over twenty years' start on the great memorialist).* The person in question, known to history by her family name of Liselotte, was Elisabeth-Charlotte, daughter of Charles Louis, Elector Palatine.

At first sight Liselotte was an obscure German princess, very far from being the greatest match in Europe as Marie-Thérèse had once been. Nor was she a King's sister, and that King an important European player, like the first Madame. But the Palatinate, a principality on the Rhine with its capital at Heidelberg, had considerable geographical importance where the plans of Louis XIV to the east were concerned. The Wittelsbach dynasty had acquired the Palatinate in the thirteenth century, and by the beginning of the seventeenth the Palatinate was the leading Protestant German state. However, it suffered much devastation during the Thirty Years War. Liselotte's marriage contract, if not fulfilled, offered rights over and opportunities in the Palatinate, in a grim parallel (from the point of view of that country) with the rights of Marie-Thérèse in the Spanish Netherlands.

---

* The copious correspondence of the second Madame to her relatives and friends at home starts in 1672 and constitutes a first-hand record which did not benefit from hindsight. Saint-Simon's own personal memories begin in the 1690s, and were written down from 1739 onwards.

Liselotte was born on 27 May 1652 and was thus nearly twelve years younger than her future husband. Her interesting ancestry included her paternal grandmother Elizabeth Stuart, the daughter of James I, known as the Winter Queen, who was herself the granddaughter of Mary Queen of Scots, the most romantic femme fatale in history.* Liselotte however was neither beautiful nor romantic. She was stolid, not to say earthy, and even on occasion downright vulgar. In her letters home Liselotte would cover these vulgarities with the airy words: 'By your leave, by your leave', when she gave vent to such comments as this: 'With my cold, I shall probably look like a shat-on carrot.' More entertaining was her frequent use of folksy proverbs: 'The snow falls as easily on a cow-pat [Kuhfladen] as on a roseleaf' was one of them. 'When the goat gets too frisky, she goes dancing on ice and breaks a leg' was another.

It will be seen that in a world where style and dignity, everything possessed by the first Madame, were so highly esteemed, Liselotte was the exception. The Grande Mademoiselle deplored her 'lack of a French air' due to her German origins. Certainly she must have spoken French with a strong German accent, as her phonetic spelling of some French words indicates. And Liselotte positively hated dancing, the art which distinguished the French court, starting with the exceptional skill of the King himself. This 'confounded ball' she exclaimed in exasperation on one occasion, probably the only person at court to feel that way (Monsieur like his brother was an excellent dancer). Nor was she a romantic. Bérénice's lament over losing Titus in Racine's eponymous play did not move her: 'All the howlings she sets up about this make me impatient.'[21]

In the matter of her appearance, the second Madame was

* Liselotte's great-granddaughter was Marie Antoinette: she thus provides the direct blood link between the two tragic queens without resembling either.

also at the opposite end of the spectrum from her predecessor. Where Henriette-Anne was graceful and slender,
getting thinner with the years, without ever sacrificing her
charm, Liselotte was big and got bigger. A vivid interest in
food and drink helped on the process: she never lost her
taste for German food and drink such as sausage, sauerkraut
and beer, which had to be sent to her by her favourite aunt
Sophia. Liselotte was the first to describe her face in comic
terms — it was a 'badger-cat-monkey' face and her nose a
'badger's snout'. As for her complexion, the apple-cheeked
freshness of her youth quickly gave way to a coarse weather-
beaten appearance, her skin prematurely wrinkled and 'red
as a crayfish' due to her mania for hunting all day and every
day without the conventional mask to protect her. All this
was very far from Henriette-Anne's legendary complexion
of 'jasmine and roses'. As her weight increased Liselotte
once again pronounced the best verdict on her appearance:
'I would be good enough to eat if I were roasted like
sucking-pig.'[22] Nor did her clothes help: Liselotte boasted
of taking no interest in them; no alluring *déshabille* for her,
either cumbersome court clothes or serviceable hunting
costumes, nothing in between.

The peculiar circumstances of her family background
surely explain the excessive attention the adult Liselotte
would come to pay to what Saint-Simon called 'honour,
virtue, rank, nobility', with the emphasis on the last two. In
time this attention would have something quite hysterical
about it, especially about the status of the royal bastards:
'mouse-droppings in the pepper' was her blunt way of
describing them.[23] Yet Liselotte had been raised against the
background of a highly unusual marriage, or rather two of
them. The constant disputes of her parents led in the end
to the disappearance of her mother from court. Already
Charles Louis had installed his mistress in a room above his
own, and she had given birth to several of his children;

Charles Louis now bigamously married this mistress in the lifetime of his wife to 'legitimise' them.

The happiest times of Liselotte's childhood were the seven years spent with her beloved aunt Sophia, her father's sister, married to the Elector of Hanover.* Sophia, to whom many of Liselotte's letters were later addressed, took the girl on a prolonged visit to The Hague, where her grandmother Elizabeth the Winter Queen had taken up residence. It was here that Liselotte got to know her cousin William of Orange, two years older and like herself a Protestant. It had been Liselotte's wistful hope to marry him eventually. Now, for reasons of realpolitik, she was not only marrying elsewhere, but marrying a Catholic, in consequence of which she had to change her own religion. Nobody in her family circle seemed to see anything odd about this, including the stoutly Protestant Sophia: the French King's brother was a splendid match for someone like her niece. One simply had to make sacrifices ...

Liselotte said later that she had only agreed to conversion in order to honour her father. It certainly cannot be said that Catholicism was ever really imprinted on Liselotte. Once again this was something which set her apart from those at the French court, forever worrying about their own salvation. The torments of a Louise de La Vallière were unknown to her. Louise wrestled with a Catholic conscience; Liselotte did not. It was something she faced in herself: she was not devout and did not have the kind of faith that moved mountains. The most Liselotte could do, she declared, was try to keep the Ten Commandments. As for God Almighty, she conceded that she did admire Him 'although without understanding Him'.[24]

* This feisty twelfth child of Elizabeth the Winter Queen was born in 1630, the same year as her first cousin Charles II, with whom she had flirted in 1648 when he was in exile. As a granddaughter of James I, she was of course within the English succession, which admitted females, although at this point there were many candidates between her and the throne.

Over the years Liselotte became by inference quite anti-Catholic: 'the boredom of all that Latin whining', she wrote privately of one particular long-drawn-out Easter. Any sermon longer than fifteen minutes sent Liselotte unashamedly to sleep. Perhaps her cynicism had begun with the day of her proxy marriage in the Gothic cathedral of Metz where a plethora of sacraments was rained down on her in a very short space: conversion, communion, confirmation and marriage. (At the time her conversion was said to be due to 'the Holy Spirit'.)[25]

On arrival at the French court Liselotte did have one great asset which for the first few years outweighed her disadvantages of style: she amused the King who had, as it were, commissioned her arrival. Her frank speaking was an agreeable novelty, as people in power always do enjoy frank speaking until it wounds them. Her enthusiasm for the outdoor life, whatever it did to her complexion, was very much to his taste too. Liselotte, who had once wanted to be a boy, was a marvellous rider – not a graceful Diana of the chase as Marie Mancini had been, but an Amazon. The gazette *Mercure Galant* wrote that 'few men were as vigorous in pursuit of this exercise' and certainly Madame was capable of hunting from five in the morning until nine at night. Liselotte also liked to walk, unlike most people at the French court, who she complained were left 'puffing and panting' twenty paces behind her, with the exception of the King. Like Louis himself, Liselotte was also passionate about the theatre.[26]

Louis therefore showed his new recruit to court great kindness from the beginning, when he introduced her to Marie-Thérèse: 'Courage, Madame,' he said gently. 'She is far more frightened of you than you are of her.' He also liked the fact that Liselotte was virtuous. No gallantries were to be expected from this Madame, and when the sophisticated Princesse de Monaco, a swinger *avant la lettre*, suggested a lesbian affair, Liselotte was outraged. If she was, as some suspected, a little platonically in love with the King, that was only to be expected from one of 'these other stars' which surrounded the sun 'like a court' in the words of Louis's memoirs, and hardly displeasing to him.[27]

Contradictory as it might seem, Louis XIV had a great taste for virtuous women whom he could admire whole-heartedly as he remembered admiring his mother. One of these was Colbert's daughter, Jeanne-Marie, married to the Duc de Chevreuse, Liselotte's contemporary with 'her admirable virtue which never failed her in any predicament'; she was incidentally one of the few fellow walkers Liselotte discovered, so perhaps virtue and exercise went together. Later Louis would admire Saint-Simon's young wife, daughter of the Duc de Beauvillier, for her mixture of modesty and noble bearing. The supreme example was the beautiful dark-eyed Italian princess, Mary Beatrice d'Este, who passed through France at the age of fourteen in 1673 to marry James Duke of York. On this occasion Louis described himself paternally as her 'godfather', but he did not forget Mary Beatrice, that vision of Catholic youth and beauty, even if he could scarcely have predicted the circumstances in which they would next meet. Then there was his children's governess, Françoise Scarron, whom Louis was getting to know, in clandestine visits to the Parisian house of her little charges: she was nothing if not virtuous.

Liselotte's take on the whole subject of marriage was expressed like this: 'Marriages are like death. The time and season are marked, you can't escape. That's how Our Lord wished it and how we must do it.'[28] It was a view which her predecessor would have shared, just as Liselotte quickly came to share Henriette-Anne's dislike of the Chevalier de Lorraine, who now proceeded to humiliate the second wife wherever possible just as he had humiliated the first. As for

Monsieur himself, the best Liselotte could do, describing him to her aunt Sophia, was to call him 'not ignoble', with his hair, his eyebrows and lashes all very black, his large nose and his small mouth.

But in one crucial respect, the marriage of Monsieur and the second Madame was a success. Liselotte conceived her first child, a son, less than a year after marriage. 'Very soon there is going to be a big bang,' she wrote in her merry way in May 1673. Although this boy did not live long, a second and healthy son Philippe, given the title Duc de Chartres, was born in August 1674. His horoscope predicted that he would be pope, 'but I am very much afraid that he is more likely to be the Antichrist', added Liselotte.* A daughter, Élisabeth-Charlotte, followed two years later, who evidently took after her mother: she was 'as fat as a Christmas goose and large for her age'. After that, by mutual agreement, Monsieur and Madame ceased marital relations. Monsieur had found them, it seems, even more testing with Liselotte than with Henriette-Anne, when he had after all been a decade younger. From Liselotte's confidences we know that Monsieur needed the inspiration of rosaries and holy medals draped in appropriate places to perform the necessary act.†

Liselotte's satisfactory fertility was in contrast to that of the unfortunate Queen. There was a sad catalogue of royal infant deaths around this time: three in just over a year. The little Duc d'Anjou died at the age of three in July 1671; his brother, born the following year, was dead by the beginning of November; then the Petite Madame, an especially beloved child, died at the age of five in March 1672. The line of royal succession now led from the Dauphin to Monsieur,

* Philippe, forty years later Regent of France, did not fulfil either prophecy, although from the single point of view of personal profligacy he was nearer the latter than the former.
† Since Monsieur begot at least eleven children in the course of his life, the rosary was evidently effective.

and so to the new baby Philippe. There were evil tongues which ascribed the deaths of the Queen's children to the scandal of her husband's philanderings, although as has been noted, repeated intermarriage was the more likely explanation.

There was a further, even more marked contrast, to set the tongues wagging again, between the Queen's experiences and those of the Ceres-like goddess of fertility Athénaïs. A second boy, Louis-César, was born to her in 1672 (very shortly after Marie-Thérèse's son who died) and a second daughter Louise-Françoise in June 1673. With Louis-Auguste, born in 1670, and her two children by her husband, Athénaïs had given birth to six children in under ten years, only one of whom, that mysterious baby of 1669, had died in infancy. It was a prodigious record, especially when combined with the sensual duties of a mistress, and as it turned out Athénaïs's ready powder would be lit again in the future.

There was however a question mark over these little pledges of love – or symbols of royal, even national virility as many of less censorious disposition would have seen them. How long would they remain in the comfortable obscurity of the rue Vaugirard, tended by the virtuous Françoise Scarron? This was especially true after Athénaïs gave birth to Louise-Françoise on 1 June 1673 at Tournai, while the whole royal cortège of war was once more in Flanders.

Louis had declared war on the Dutch in 1672 in pursuit of solidifying his north-western dominions. This so-called Dutch War was expected to end in another triumph for Europe's most dazzling military monarch. But for once the victorious French armies had met their match. The heroic resistance of the Dutch took the form of opening the dykes and flooding their own country, making further French advances virtually impossible. All this was done under their newly appointed leader, the young Prince William of Orange (that Protestant nephew of Charles II Liselotte had once hoped to marry).* The French were obliged to withdraw in early 1673.

In the new season's campaign Louis was engaged in the siege of Maastricht, the court remaining at nearby Tournai. The Queen and Louise de La Vallière occupied the Bishop's house while Athénaïs gave birth in the town's citadel. This distinction of dwelling hardly made for concealment.

---

* William, born in 1650, was the posthumous son of another William of Orange and Princess Mary Stuart, daughter of Charles I and Henrietta Maria; he was thus Louis's first cousin once removed.

CHAPTER 8

A Singular Position

I have already got a singular position, envied by the whole world.

– Françoise Scarron

On 18 December 1673 a baby girl of six months was baptised at the church of Saint-Sulpice on the Left Bank in Paris. This was the important parish church for those living in this 'countrified' area, as Madame de Sévigné called it.[1]* These included Madame Scarron and her mysterious charges. The child was given the names Louise-Françoise by her godmother – who was none other than Louise-Françoise Duchesse de La Vallière. No one mentioned the fact that these two names also linked those of the King and Françoise-Athénaïs de Montespan. The parish priest stood proxy for the three-year-old godfather, the baby's elder brother.

Two days later something more unusual than a mere parish baptism took place. The King issued an edict, duly registered by the Parlement, legitimising Louise-Françoise and her brothers Louis-Auguste and Louis-César. They received titles: Mademoiselle de Nantes, Duc du Maine and Comte de Vexin respectively. The edict referred to 'the tenderness which Nature leads us to have for our children',

---

* Saint-Sulpice, much simpler then than it is today, was built in 1646 on the site of a previous structure and enlarged from 1670 onwards. The present imposing classical front dates from the eighteenth century; many further embellishments and additions were made in the eighteenth and nineteenth centuries.

an echo of the edict which had legitimised Marie-Anne and the Comte de Vermandois four years earlier, as well as 'the many other reasons' which increased such feelings.² There was however no repeat here of the profound tribute which the King had paid on the previous occasion to the 'virtues and modesty' of the children's mother. In fact there was no mention of the mother at all: unless she was to be counted among those 'many other reasons'. These, it seemed, were miraculous children born to a father only, and that father the King.

The reason was not far to seek. Athénaïs was still officially married to the Marquis de Montespan although a judicial separation was being sought to tidy up the situation as far as was possible, given that divorce in the modern sense did not exist. Annulment was recognised by the Catholic Church, meaning that no valid marriage had ever taken place; but this was embarrassing to put forward when Athénaïs had borne two children to her husband. Judicial separation, which had to be ratified by Parlement, was the best possible solution. That separation would not, as it turned out, be granted until the following July.

In the meantime Athénaïs reigned triumphant. 'She must have whatever she wants,' was the King's constant assertion to his minister Colbert. No wonder that the nickname 'Quanto' ('How much?') was added to that of 'The Torrent' by Madame de Sévigné. Jewels were showered upon her, pearls, diamonds, earrings 'which must be fine', settings of different-coloured gems which could be interchanged: 'It will be necessary to go to some expense over this but I am quite prepared for it.'³ In an instruction about the terraces of Saint-Germain, a birdcage for her birds and a fountain from which the birds could drink were commanded on one terrace, while another would have earth, and would be made into a little garden. From 1671 onwards, Athénaïs had one of the finest suites of apartments in the palace, of positively regal splendour. At Versailles they were situated at the top of the Grand Staircase with five windows onto the Royal Court (those windows under which courtiers feared to tread for fear of her tongue) and had, naturally, direct access to the King's own apartments. She had a special gallery with her own collection of pictures.

As Versailles took shape in a perpetual flurry of building works, so did Athénaïs's own arrangements, which included a little pleasure-house decorated with blue-and-white Delft tiles on the walls by Le Vau and a new residence of her own at Clagny, close by Versailles, reconstructed by Mansart. (The first changes at Clagny had been rejected by the superb Athénaïs as only fit for a chorus girl ...)[4] Once again the watchword in its construction was the will of the mistress. 'I have no answer at present as I wish to ascertain what Madame de Montespan thinks about it,' replied Louis when his minister Colbert tried to consult him about Mansart's plans. Athénaïs filled Clagny with her favourite rococo furniture. The result was certainly a paradise and a fertile paradise at that, compared by Madame de Sévigné to the palace of the enchantress Armide and by Primi Visconti to the House of Venus. Here tuberoses,* jasmine, roses and carnations bestowed their perfume, to say nothing of the King's trademark orange trees, expensive gifts which he showered upon the favourite in large quantities. The home farm, suitably enough, contained 'the most amorous turtle doves' and 'cows that yielded an abundance of milk ...'[5]

Athénaïs's irrepressible mocking wit continued to be a feature of her relationship with Louis. One typical exchange occurred when the Queen's carriage fell into a stream on one of the campaigning journeys. 'Ah, the Queen drinks!'

---

* At Versailles the smell of tuberoses of a summer's night was sometimes so strong that the court was driven indoors; as has been noted, it was sometimes a convenient cover-up perfume indoors.

cried Athénaïs. 'Madame, she is your Queen,' said the King reprovingly. Athénaïs was quick to retort: 'No, Sire, she is *your* Queen.' Similarly, her taste for literary and theatrical patronage – something Marie-Thérèse had never displayed – made not only her company but the company around her a source of stimulation. Athénaïs was the patron of La Fontaine, to whom the second edition of his *Fables* was dedicated with the favourite apostrophised as Venus: 'Words and looks, everything is charm with you.'[6] Molière's rehearsals for *Le Misanthrope* were held in her apartments in November 1673 and it was hardly surprising that the wickedly amusing *Tartuffe*, which had shocked Anne of Austria, was much to her taste. Personally she loved to play the harpsichord, but she also acted as the generous centre of the elaborate musical entertainments that the King appreciated.

Despite this artistic atmosphere, which pleased the King and impressed ambassadors, Athénaïs's real power consisted in the sexual thrall or '*empire*' – the word generally used – which she exerted over the King. There were tales that his passion was so great that he could not even wait for his mistress to be properly undressed by her ladies, before starting to make love to her. To her mocking wit, Athénaïs added a further tempestuous element whenever she did not have exactly what she wanted: perhaps this added yet further spice to the relationship.

In any case, the characteristic image of Athénaïs the mistress was surely an intimate one: lounging, voluptuously dressed, wearing her favourite high-heeled mules in her fabulous Appartement des Bains. There was nothing Spartan about this scene. Paintings by Le Brun, sculptures by Le Hongre, bronzes, were set off by brocades showing shepherds and shepherdesses having pastoral fun. Here the couple could have their own fun: they could disport themselves on couches, surrounded by orange trees in silver pots, and enjoy the huge octagonal bath cut from a single block of marble, in the Cabinet des Bains, lined with linen and lace.[7]*

In this supremacy of the senses and the intellect on the part of Athénaïs, it remained notable that the Duchesse de La Vallière was still at court. Her needs were considered with elaborate courtesy: where public display was concerned, there were even demonstrations of equality between the two ladies in order to preserve the fiction of the unmarried Louise as *maîtresse en titre*. In 1669 specific orders were given to the architect Jean Marot for the two ladies to have identical grottoes, two each, decorated in the rococo style.

None of this made any difference to Louise's private feelings of humiliation and despair, prompting another comparison to the confession of the rejected Portuguese nun: 'I was not fully acquainted with the excess of my love until I resolved to use all my strength to be cured of it.' On Ash Wednesday she made another bolt for the convent dedicated to her favourite saint Mary Magdalen at Chaillot and asked for shelter. This time the King did not seize a grey cloak, mantle his face, ask for his fastest horse and gallop after her. He simply ordered her to return, sending Lauzun (still in favour) to the convent. A feeble defence for this cynical gesture can be put up: Louise had not sought permission to leave the court. In reality Louis was reacting as impatiently as Orgon in *Tartuffe* when his daughter Marianne pleaded on her knees to retire to a convent: 'Everyone / When once her love is crossed must be a nun. / Get up!'[8] The truth was that the need for her as a cover was still paramount. It was not the King's finest hour; the measure of the cynicism of the situation is that Louise eventually pleaded with Athénaïs to persuade the King to release her ...

---

* Still to be seen at Versailles today, although moved to the Orangery: a remarkable souvenir of bygone amours.

It was about this time that Louise began her practice of wearing a hair shirt beneath her court robes as a penance. She had lost a lot of weight and looked quite haggard to unsympathetic observers. The hair shirt was less onerous than the daily strain of living in the greatest intimacy with her former lover and his current mistress. It is not clear exactly when sexual relations between Louis and Louise ceased: he certainly wept with emotion when Louise returned to court on his orders in 1671, but then Louis wept easily, and no one had ever doubted his affection for Louise, if it was not on the same scale as hers for him. Athénaïs wept too. The whole scene was highly sentimental if diverting to worldly observers.

While Louise attempted to leave the galaxy, a former star attempted to rejoin it, equally in vain. Marie Mancini had not been happy in her marriage of convenience to Prince Colonna; he turned out to be a brute for all his noble ancestry. In 1672, deprived of her children, she tried to return to the French court, perhaps with some nostalgic notion of fascinating the sovereign yet again with a glance of those mesmerising black eyes. She lurked at Grenoble, awaiting a positive message.

It was not to be. For once both Queen and mistress, Marie-Thérèse and Athénaïs, were in accord. There was a disastrous expedition to Fontainebleau – there where Louis and Marie had loved and hunted fifteen years before – in which Marie gambled on the drawing-power of memory. Instead, a cool message came from the King: Marie should return to Grenoble. Louis did send her a large gift of money: 10,000 pistoles (over three hundred thousand pounds in today's money). But he declined to receive her.[9]

Marie Mancini had not lost all her spirit. She had heard of ladies being given money to gain access to them, she remarked, but never to keep them away. Eventually she was allowed to withdraw to the abbey of Lys, near Lyon. Alas, poor Marie, who had always detested convents, was once more condemned to reside in one. No wonder she observed in her memoirs that 'fortune always seemed to be interested in persecuting me'.[10]

It was the summer of 1674 which saw the formalisation of the new order at court, as it was intended to be for the foreseeable future (although few would have predicted the consequences of this new order). There were two steps. First, at the age of nearly thirty, Louise was at last allowed to have the wish she had harboured on and off for over ten years and take the veil. Bossuet played his part in persuading her but as he wrote, if the words were his, the deeds were hers. She made her departure in a style which was generally admired: she insisted on a last interview with Marie-Thérèse in which she begged the Queen's pardon for all the wrongs she had done her. Although the Queen's lofty attendants tried to prevent this scene taking place as being unsuitable, Louise retorted: 'Since my crimes were public, so should my penance be.' With her gentle manners, Marie-Thérèse raised Louise from the floor where she had abased herself, kissed her on the forehead and told her that she had been forgiven long ago.

The interview with the King was tearful: his eyes were still red with weeping at Mass the next day. He wept, no doubt, for his youth as well as from the fidelity Louise had shown him over thirteen years in which she placed her King above her God, an order which was now to be reversed for ever. In future she was to be counted among those ladies for whom, in the words of Saint-Évremond, God was 'a new lover, that comforts them' for what they had lost.[11] Louis then set off immediately with the court towards Franche-Comté, which had been handed back to Spain in 1668. Once more, with its capital Besançon, Franche-Comté was easily overrun. It all represented the push towards further European conquest, since that unexpected check by the Dutch.

Louise for her part left behind a picture specially commissioned from Pierre Mignard which showed her with her two children, Marie-Anne and the Comte de Vermandois. It featured the discarded vanities of the world, including a casket of jewels and a large gambler's purse, at her feet. The words SIC TRANSIT GLORIA MUNDI – thus passes the glory of the world – were inscribed in large letters on a pillar behind her: the rose in her hand, like Louise herself, looked rather battered. That night at the Carmelite convent in the rue d'Enfer in Paris, Louise cut her famous blonde locks to indicate the end of her old life.

Louise was officially 'clothed' in her postulant's garments at the beginning of June. Present were the Queen, Monsieur and Madame, Marie-Louise d'Orléans, Monsieur's daughter by his first marriage, the Grande Mademoiselle and many other dignitaries. In a brilliant move, Louise had transformed herself from humiliated duchess to respected nun. The new Sister Louise de La Miséricorde was a penitent, and there was nothing the seventeenth century liked more than a penitent, be it the remote but venerated Mary Magdalen or the King's former mistress.

It was of course relevant to Louise's adoption of her new life that her children, the product of her shame as she saw them, were well established. Marie-Anne in particular had created a sensation by her dancing at the carnival celebrations earlier in the year, a delightful vision in black velvet and diamonds. Madame de Sévigné described how the King was enchanted with her and everyone else eagerly followed his lead.[12]

At seven and a half Marie-Anne was already wise to the priorities of the court. In the middle of the ball, she went up to the Duchesse de Richelieu and enquired anxiously: 'Madame, can you let me know if the King is pleased with me?' She also understood the need to be amusing. 'All sorts of things come out of her pretty mouth,' Madame de Sévigné went on; 'she fascinates people with her wit of which no one could have more.' The little girl's partner in the dance was a young Prince of the Blood, the thirteen-year-old Louis-Armand, son of the Prince de Conti. 'Ah, the little fiancés!' murmured the courtiers, for such an elevated match was not out of the question for Louise's daughter. Symptomatic of the hierarchy of the King's natural children and their mothers now emerging was the fact that Louise called Marie-Anne (who had legitimised royal blood) 'Mademoiselle' but was herself addressed as '*belle Maman*'.

A few weeks after Louise's departure, and shortly after the formal registration of Athénaïs's separation, the next batch of natural children was presented at court. It must have been obvious to that observant world that Athénaïs would fairly soon be adding to their number: her fifth child by the King, Louise-Marie, created Mademoiselle de Tours and nicknamed 'Tou-Tou', was born in November. (Tou-Tou was fortunate to be born after the official separation and was therefore, unlike her brothers and sister, not the fruit of that tricky Double Adultery.) Louise-Françoise, the Duc du Maine and the Comte de Vexin were in the charge of their governess Françoise Scarron. The baby girl had to be carried and so did Maine, who with his lame leg could not yet walk at the age of four and a half. It was an anxious moment for Françoise, this thirty-eight-year-old woman of modest birth, with a marriage to a mere playwright behind her. But apart from the friendship with Athénaïs which had secured her position, Françoise already had another ally at the court. That was the King.

Françoise d'Aubigné was born on 27 November 1635: she was thus three years older than the King, five years older than Athénaïs and nearly ten years older than Louise de La

Vallière. From the first the circumstances of her life were unusual; indeed, one might go further and say that, by the standards of the time, they were adverse. Although she was not exactly born in a prison, as her enemies would later suggest, her father Constant was in prison at the time at Niort near Poitiers. Françoise was probably born close by his place of confinement.* Constant's crime was conspiracy against Richelieu, but this was not in fact his first spell in prison; earlier he had been accused of abduction and rape.

Françoise's ancestry was not undistinguished: her grandfather Agrippa d'Aubigné, who died before she was born, had been a celebrated poet – but a Huguenot (Protestant) poet. Although Huguenots were still legally tolerated in the France of the 1630s following the Edict of Nantes forty years earlier, Richelieu had already annulled some of the political clauses to their advantage; Huguenot descent once again, like her father's disgrace, made Françoise an outsider. There was certainly a contrast with the conventionally Catholic upbringing of Louise, daughter of soldiers who served the King bravely, or the grandeur of Athénaïs's birth, a duke's daughter with her much-vaunted Mortemart blood.

Françoise's mother, Jeanne de Cardhillac, a girl of sixteen when she got married, was the daughter of Constant's jailer. She was a Catholic, and Françoise had a Catholic baptism a few days after her birth at which her godmother was Suzanne de Baudéan, daughter of the governor of the town, the Baron de Neuillant.[14] The event itself and the connection were to stand Françoise in good stead. Although raised in the first instance as a Protestant, the essential Catholic baptism meant that she could always recover the official religion of the state without a ceremony of abjuration; while Suzanne, only nine at the time, would grow up to

* A plaque marks her suggested birthplace, at the Hôtel du Chaumont, 5 rue du Pont, Niort.[15]

honour her commitment as godmother in proper style.

Jeanne had already given birth to two sons, Constant and Charles, when the little girl who would be known in childhood as Bignette arrived; Constant died under mysterious circumstances at the age of eighteen but Charles d'Aubigné, only a year older than his sister, would grow up to constitute the kind of affliction no family needs and many families have. In any case, Bignette's true family life was not lived in the insalubrious atmosphere in and around the prison (although she visited her father on Sundays, watching him in silence as he played cards with his jailers). The magic place she loved, not only then but in recollection all her life, was the château of Mursay, where rivers met in a forested valley at Parthenay, not far from Niort.

Beloved Mursay was the home of Constant's sister, the Marquise de Villette, who, in view of Constant's distressing circumstances and Jeanne's poverty, took Bignette in. Apart from her aunt and kindly uncle – 'you acted as my Father in my childhood', as she wrote to the Marquis de Villette later – there were the three pretty fair-haired daughters, all older than herself, and the only son Philippe de Villette, born in 1632, who became an important brother figure.

To the Marquise de Villette, little Bignette was in effect a fifth child. But she was a fifth child who was also a poor relation.* It was a state of affairs hardly likely to lessen Bignette's natural feelings of insecurity. Brought up in touch with luxury, she knew that it would not necessarily last into adulthood given that she was unlikely to have the dowry which even life in a convent necessitated. To accustom her to this, Bignette had no fire in her room, cast-off bonnets which had belonged to her glamorous cousins, and wooden

---

* A classic combination of intimacy and inequality best captured by Jane Austen describing the position of Fanny Price at Mansfield Park in the eponymous novel.

shoes which began by being too big, so that she could grow into them – till then she must stuff them with straw. Nevertheless Bignette loved the Villettes, felt grateful to them and in general remembered these days at Mursay as the happiest times of her childhood.

In time Constant was released. Relaxation and domesticity did not follow: rather, adventure and hazardous travel. When Bignette was eight and a half, in the spring of 1644, she rejoined her family in order to travel to the French West Indies.[15] The two months of sea crossing were ghastly for all parties. Much later the former Bignette would tell the Bishop of Metz of how a fever on board apparently left her for dead; her corpse was about to be thrown overboard when her mother, giving her a last kiss, saw signs of life. 'Ah, Madame,' commented the Bishop portentously, 'one does not come back from such a distance for nothing.'

They landed first at Guadeloupe. There however life did not radically improve. Jeanne was a strict mother. Bignette was given little liberty to taste the delights of a wild island and a different culture. Her education was conventional, pious (still Protestant) and took place indoors. Meanwhile the post of governor of the Isle of Marie-Galante turned out to be vacant. But after a brief sojourn there, the family settled in Martinique.* The unsatisfactory Constant returned to France, leaving Jeanne to be 'both father and mother' to her children, as she put it herself. Forever combating poverty, Jeanne was a strong role model of female endurance under difficult circumstances for her daughter. Nor would it be surprising if Bignette, both from observation of her father and in conversation with her mother, derived a less than perfect image of the male sex.

---

* Next to the Maine of Prêcheur, one of the most ancient villages in Martinique, a little plaque on the side of the church commemorates the presence there of Françoise d'Aubigné during her childhood.[16]

Another frightful journey followed when Jeanne took the family back to Europe in 1647 to join their father. But Constant was dead by the end of August. For Bignette at least it was back to the delights of Mursay and the mingled intimacy and hard work: for it was at this period that she was set to work in the farmyard and elsewhere, herding turkeys, going barefoot on occasion, although taking care to preserve her precious lady's complexion with a nose-mask.[17]

It was what happened next which created, even if briefly, a real trauma in her life. It will be remembered that Bignette had been baptised a Catholic, although educated according to the Protestant mode with instruction on the Psalms and the Bible. Nevertheless Madame de Feuillant, mother of her godmother Suzanne, seized the opportunity to petition Anne of Austria about the fate of this little lost soul, and succeeded in taking her into a Catholic convent with a view to restoring her to the true faith. Bignette did not like the convent and there was a considerable struggle for her soul until, significantly, her true affection for one of the nuns there, Sister Céleste, persuaded her to (re)join the Catholic Church.

Bignette made her Catholic First Communion for the sake of Sister Céleste, she said, not out of any religious principle. 'I loved her more than I could possibly say. I wanted to sacrifice myself for her service,' she wrote later.[18] Once again it was a different trajectory from the innate piety of Louise and the devout family background of Athénaïs, at any rate where her mother was concerned.

It was Madame de Feuillant who now brought Françoise, as Bignette had become, on a visit to Paris at the age of sixteen. There she was introduced to the intelligent, sophisticated ladies and gentlemen of the Marais whose patronage and friendship were to have a significant effect on her fortunes. It was not difficult to be friendly towards Françoise because she was by any standards an attractive young woman. The society of the Hôtel Rambouillet, and elsewhere at the homes of the *Précieuses*, liked what it saw: a serious, modest young person whose best feature was a pair of large, wide-set dark eyes. Madeleine de Scudéry waxed eloquent about them in a character sketch of Françoise under the name of Lyriane: 'the most beautiful eyes in the world', she called them, 'brilliant, soft, passionate and full of intelligence'. Furthermore 'a soft melancholy' pervaded the charms of Lyriane: her gaze was gentle and it was slightly sad.[19]

Françoise's complexion – 'pleasing if a little dark', Madeleine de Scudéry called it – must somehow have become in a measure tanned, despite all her precautions, for she was awarded the sobriquet of '*la belle Indienne*'. Her mass of lustrous dark hair was however unqualifiedly admired. Françoise's face was a delightful heart-shape and if her nose was a little long, her mouth a little small and her chin a little plump, yet the general effect, as contemporaries agreed, was most appealing.

It helped that Françoise when young was discreetly feminine in her tastes. Perfume, for example, played an important part in her life, and so did clothes, when she could afford them: a skirt of pink satin, black velvet corselets worn over white blouses, handkerchiefs of Genoese lace. Her confessor once pointed to her taste for fine petticoats (invisible but not inaudible): 'You say you only wear very ordinary stuffs but when you fall to your knees at my feet [in the confessional] I hear the rustle of something rather out of the ordinary.'[20]

Her docile and apparently pliant character also made Françoise agreeable to the society in which she found herself. The years of dependency had filled her with a profound desire to please. Late in her life Françoise told Madame de Glapion: 'I was what you call a good little girl,' always obedient and in particular loved by the servants because she tried to please them as well as their masters and mistresses. While her difficult upbringing might have made a subversive of some women, Françoise had on the contrary a strong sense of the hierarchy of society according to the divine will. A characteristic instruction to girls in her care was to avoid murmuring against the rich: 'God has wanted to make them rich as He has wanted to make you poor.'[21] (It was of course a philosophy which could also cover an upward trajectory in society: that too could be seen as according to the divine will.)

Furthermore, she was desperate to secure the good opinion of respectable people: 'That was my weakness,' as she put it. But it was of course a weakness which made her excellent company for these same respectable people she was so anxious to please. Equally her fervent concern for her own reputation – 'it was my good name that I cared about' – meant she constituted no danger or challenge to other women.[22] Or so it seemed then.

It was during her expedition to Paris that Françoise first met the playwright Paul Scarron, who already by 1648 had described himself as 'a condensation of human misery' thanks to the acute rheumatoid arthritis which twisted him unbearably. Later Scarron was amused and impressed by her letters, written from the country to a Mademoiselle de Saint-Herment, one of those useful female friends Françoise had acquired.* These letters were not what one expected from a girl 'brought up in Niort' or, worse still, 'the isles of America', as the West Indies were generally termed. So, in a sense, Scarron's relationship with Françoise began as the epistolary romance beloved of novelists in which letters to one party actually cause another party to fall in love.[23]

Perhaps the playwright, twenty-five years older than

---

* The writer the Chevalier de Méré, who lived in Poitou and knew Françoise when she was young, may have helped with advice over these letters, although he subsequently much exaggerated his importance in Françoise's life.

Françoise and physically tormented, did not exactly fall in love. It was too late for that. What he did do in 1652, with the cheerful, worldly kindness which was one of his characteristics, was offer the poverty-stricken Françoise, whose mother had died two years earlier, a solution to her life. He would either provide the dowry necessary for a convent or he would marry her. And Françoise, for all her piety, was no fan of convents. Her first surviving letter of 1648 or 1649, imploring her aunt Madame de Villette to rescue her, had run: 'You can't imagine what hell it is for me, this so-called House of God.'[24] So she chose marriage.*

It is unlikely that Scarron was able to consummate the marriage fully if at all by this time. It was a question raised by the priest at their wedding, to Scarron's annoyance. 'That is between Madame and me,' he retorted. That was true enough, and finally the details of what happened between Monsieur and Madame Scarron must remain a mystery. The fact that Françoise emerged from the experience of marriage at Scarron's death eight years later with a lifelong indifference if not aversion to sex, as being something rather unpleasant that men expected of women, might indicate that activity of some limited sort took place. Much later Françoise would write of herself to her scapegrace brother Charles, when giving marital advice, as 'a woman who has never been married'.[25] If she was being honest, that makes full consummation unlikely. Nevertheless it is only fair to point out that Françoise's attitude to sex within marriage, though weary at best, was a great deal more common among women of her generation than the free-wheeling enthusiasm of Athénaïs.

Françoise certainly had no good words to say about marriage itself; when in August 1674 she was offered a

---

* They lived in a house in the rue de Turenne, near the Place des Vosges in the Marais; it is now a sports shop.

convenient marriage to an unsavoury old duke she replied: 'I have already got a singular position, envied by the whole world, without seeking out one which makes three-quarters of the human race unhappy.' Twenty years later she was still preaching the same gloomy if realistic doctrine: 'Don't hope for perfect happiness from marriage.' The female sex would always be exposed to suffering because it was dependent: marriage was 'the state where one experiences the most tribulations, even in the best'. And she had after all had early contacts with the high-born Parisian ladies who from their privileged positions sighed and complained of marriage as 'slavery'.[26]

The death of Scarron, on 6 October 1660 (shortly after that triumphal entry to Paris of Louis and his Queen which Françoise witnessed), left his widow once again plunged into poverty, and with debts in addition. But Françoise had preserved her precious reputation. It would have been easy for the pretty young wife of a cripple to enjoy romances; on the contrary, Françoise made a point of avoiding such encounters, going to her room after dinner when the company got too raucous. The story that she took part in 'gallantries' with the rakish Marquis de Villarceaux has no contemporary backing and a great deal of evidence to the contrary, starting with Françoise's obsession with her virtue.*

The woman who told it thirty years later, claiming to have lent her own accommodation for the affair, was the famous courtesan Ninon de Lenclos. Once so beautiful that she could seduce any man of any age, fathers and sons a

---

* The drunken ramblings of Françoise's jealous brother Charles – 'a madman who should have been shut up', in the opinion of Saint-Simon – on the subject of her debaucheries in the Scarron days should certainly be ignored: this was Charles's payback for his lifelong dependence on her.[27]

speciality, and perhaps grandfathers too, such was the longevity of her reign, Ninon in old age became jealous of the august position of her erstwhile modest friend. And in her report, Ninon managed to have it both ways. Françoise had indeed had an affair, but she had been 'clumsy' in her love-making (unlike Ninon was the implication).* La Rochefoucauld had a maxim on the subject of ladies and their gallantries which seems relevant to the case of Françoise. Plenty of women, he wrote, had no affairs at all, but there was seldom a woman who had only one.[29] Since Villarceaux was the sole named candidate (and that so many years later), Françoise was surely in the former category.

Laminated by her virtue, Françoise was able to enjoy the patronage and friendship of other women, one of these being Athénaïs. Queen Anne was persuaded to grant her a pension. Aristocrats such as the Duchesse de Richelieu and the Marquise de Montchevreuil had her to stay for periods in their country houses unofficially acting as something between a secretary and a housekeeper. One of the Montchevreuil children was lame in the leg: a foretaste of the problems of the Duc du Maine.

Françoise was pliant but she was by no means weak and she had a strong practical streak. Above all, she loved being with children, teaching them to read and seeing to their welfare, including their spiritual welfare, by teaching the catechism. This addiction might sound an obvious feminine trait, but in fact there was no sentimentalisation of children at this date; such a profound liking for and interest in children was yet another characteristic which made Françoise unusual for her time.

* A painting of a naked woman, optimistically described as Françoise, which belonged to Villarceaux, is sometimes put forward as proof of the affair; it actually looks rather more like Ninon (who definitely had an affair with Villarceaux); even if it does depict Françoise there is no proof that she posed for it.[28]

In the course of her work with and for children, Françoise also encountered several of the illegitimate ones of whom there were many examples in society, not only in royal circles. Scarron's sister, also called Françoise Scarron, was the mistress of the Duc de Tresmes-Gescres, having been seduced by him at fifteen; she had five illegitimate children. At one point Françoise d'Aubigné spent a year in the same house as her sister-in-law and family.* In 1667 she included her brother Charles's bastards Toscan and Chariot in a little nursery.

In so many ways therefore Françoise seemed the ideal person to take on the prestigious – but tricky – post of governess to the royal bastards. Where her religious nature was concerned, the fact that in 1666 she took on a confessor in the shape of the Abbé Gobelin made her even more suitable. Gobelin, whose correspondence with Françoise would become a vital source for her true feelings, was not only profoundly spiritual himself, but also intellectually brilliant. He demanded – and got – Françoise's obedience over many years, for that was part of the bargain. As Françoise confided to the Marquise de Montchevreuil, she knew that once she had chosen Gobelin, she must obey him in everything.

It was thus to Gobelin that Françoise put the proposition of her new post. The Abbé's reply was to tell her to make sure that they really were the King's children, not the byblows of a great court lady's love affair with an unknown noble: there was a rumour that the Duc de Lauzun was involved, due to the secrecy in which the household was cloaked. If they were the King's offspring, then tending to them could be seen as some kind of duty ... even a holy

---

* It has been suggested that the coincidence of the two Françoise Scarrons, one of whom certainly had a colourful private life, may have been responsible for later slurs.[10]

destiny (Gobelin was very interested in the individual's search for his or her holy destiny). Thus the connection in Françoise's mind between religious duty and her role as semi-royal governess was there from the first. Above all, said Gobelin, Françoise must distinguish between Madame de Montespan and her lover: 'She is neither here nor there but he is the King.'[31]

So Françoise did accept: another rather unusual decision in an unusual life. By the time she was welcomed with her ennobled and legitimised charges to the court in the summer of 1674, she had spent four years running an unorthodox but comfortable and welcoming household, mainly at 25 rue de Vaugirard, near the Palais du Luxembourg in the parish of Saint-Sulpice.* Madame de Sévigné, who visited the house, described it as having large rooms and a necessarily large garden in which the children (still officially hidden from the world) could play in safety. Unfortunately this need for secrecy meant a lack of domestic help and even builders: Françoise would later describe how she had rushed about, painting, scrubbing, decorating ... all unaided for fear of inviting dangerous speculation. Nevertheless she created, as she was able to do, a happy domesticated atmosphere.

It was here, at this out-of-the-way house, 'in the shadows', as Saint-Simon put it, that Louis XIV, who had seduced so many women, was himself in quite a different way seduced: although the process was not intentional. He would pay unannounced visits on his way from hunting. He found a charming, tender mother figure, with one child on her lap, another at her shoulder, a third in a cradle, reading a book aloud. 'How good it would be to be loved by a woman like

---

* The Allée Maintenon, reached from no. 108 rue de Vaugirard, commemorates that lost time: a quiet leafy cul-de-sac off the busy traffic-ridden street, it is guarded by a door; the courtyard inside contains various houses including a Quaker mission.[32]

that,' he mused. In the modern sense of the word, Françoise was cool – something expressed in the nickname given to her in the Sévigné circle: 'The Thaw', where Louise had been 'The Dew' and Athénaïs 'The Torrent' among other names.

To her genuine maternal instinct, Françoise added another very different quality, that of conversation, and its concomitant, the art of being a good listener. It was Madame de Sévigné, no mean judge of the subject, who attested to Françoise's abilities in this respect. Louis, who in principle disliked blue-stocking women and had thus been prejudiced against Françoise at the start, was quite won over by the gentle social arts she had learned among her *Précieuses* friends. Françoise understood perfectly well the force of that observation by Madeleine de Scudéry that a woman should never sound like a book talking.

Of course Françoise in her thirties was still an attractive woman. Did the King, according to his wont, make a pass at her at this early stage? A letter of March 1673 in which she complained of 'the master' and his advances, how he went away 'disappointed but not discouraged', is certainly forged, with the benefit of hindsight.* The importance of the bond between them by the time she reached court and stayed there in 1674 was its basis in his admiration for her virtue, her respectability, her femininity, exactly those qualities which Françoise prided herself on possessing. It was a happy match of temperaments.

Unfortunately there was a loser in this, and that loser was Athénaïs, the mother of the children. It was not a question of sexual jealousy: the issue was the perennial jealousy of the (mainly absent) parent for the (ever-present) nurse or

---

* Unfortunately an eighteenth-century editor of her letters, Angliviel de La Beaumelle, behaved 'without regard to honesty', rearranging and even forging documents; later nineteenth-century editors built on this material.[33]

governess. Athénaïs surely loved her children as much as grand ladies did and could, especially one whose role in life – richly rewarded – was to amuse the King. Equally Françoise gave vent to correct sentiments: 'Nothing is more foolish than to love to excess a child who is not mine' (although her love for her darling, Maine, was certainly to excess). This common sense did not prevent her experiencing her own jealousy for the beautiful, dominating mother whose behaviour towards her children was, in Françoise's opinion at least, disruptive. Françoise considered that Athénaïs spoilt the children with sweets and other treats; Athénaïs believed that Françoise was trying to divide her children from her. It was the classic struggle.

And no one had ever suggested that Athénaïs, fascinating as she might be, was easy to get on with. By September 1674, Françoise was complaining regularly to the Abbé Gobelin of the royal mistress's rages and caprices: surely it was not the will of God that she should continue to suffer in this way? Françoise began to talk wistfully of retirement. She even threatened to become a nun, although she quickly retracted the threat: 'I am too old to change my condition.'[34]

When the King rewarded Françoise for all her faithful care with a large sum of money towards the end of 1674, she was able to begin the purchase of a property at Maintenon. This lovely water-girt château, twenty-five miles from Versailles, thirty-five miles from Paris, reminded her vividly of the lost paradise of her childhood, Mursay.* Medieval in origin, it had been embellished and added to over the years, principally in the sixteenth century. Françoise described it to her brother Charles in January 1675 as 'rather a beautiful house, a little too big for the household I intend

---

* Today the Foundation of the Château de Maintenon, created in 1983, thanks to the generosity of collateral descendants of Madame de Maintenon, means that the château is accessible to the public. It is beautiful and tranquil in its watery setting.

to have, in an agreeable situation'. Here she dreamed of retirement, Françoise told Gobelin, leaving 'the sinful court' behind. She loved everything about this country retreat, *her* butter, *her* apples, *her* linen (which had to be stored with lavender as fragrance, not rose petals). And she could swim in the river Eure, whose waters lapped the ancient stone tower.[35]

But she would retire under the name of Madame de Maintenon. The King had given her permission to use the designation taken from 'my land' as she proudly called it (the title of Marquise came later). That name of Scarron, with its faintly disreputable tinge, was left behind. Even if the dream of retirement was to remain just that, something to which the new Madame de Maintenon would refer sorrowfully when things at court were not going according to her plan, she had already, as she said herself, achieved 'a singular position', she who had been first a poor relation, then a poverty-stricken widow.

What neither Françoise, Athénaïs nor Louis XIV could foresee was that the Easter of 1675 would bring an extraordinary threat to the *maîtresse en titre*, affecting all their destinies. Athénaïs's true adversary turned out to be not the upwardly mobile governess she had chosen but the Catholic Church itself.

CHAPTER 9

Throwing Off a Passion

You speak of throwing off a passion as if it was as easy as
changing a chemise.

— Angélique de Fontanges to Françoise de Maintenon,
1680

On 10 April 1675, the Wednesday of Holy Week, an obscure priest in the local parish church of Versailles named Father Lécuyer refused absolution to Madame de Montespan. The sacrament of penance was an essential preliminary in order that Athénaïs should 'make her Easter': that is, take the requisite Holy Communion as ordained by the Church for practising Catholics.

Father Lécuyer issued this brave prohibition in a dramatic fashion. Through his grille he demanded: 'Is this Madame de Montespan who scandalises all France? Go, Madame, abandon your shocking life and then come and throw yourself at the feet of the ministers of Jesus Christ.' This was not the sort of advice that the startled and indignant favourite was used to. An appeal was made to Father Lécuyer's superior, Father Thibout, but – horrors! – he backed Father Lécuyer. It turned out that even the King could not simply order the 'ministers of Jesus Christ' to break their own laws, and in order to solve the impasse, Bishop Bossuet was brought in.

Altogether, the Catholic Church showed no signs of giving up on its campaign for the salvation of the sovereign since those early days when Bossuet's sermons had dwelt with uncomfortable emphasis on the sins of that biblical philanderer King David. Bossuet himself had even been endorsed, as it were, by being appointed preceptor to the nine-year-old Dauphin in 1670. But the most celebrated prelate now preaching to the court was Father Louis Bour-daloue, a man in his early forties, who had originally run away from home to become a Jesuit. No stranger to the art of moral denunciation, Bourdaloue would give ten cycles of Lent and Advent sermons at court in the 1670s and 80s, more than any other preacher. His success in Paris, where he arrived in October 1669, had been immediate and he was first invited to the court in 1670. In the view of Madame de Sévigné, 'he surpassed everything we had heard' and on Good Friday 1671 she could not even get into the church where he was due to preach because it was full of the lackeys who had been there since Wednesday keeping seats for their masters.[2]

It might be supposed that such a popular preacher would give the sinful courtiers (and their sinful King) the kind of dulcet message that was easy to accept. On the contrary, Bourdaloue was famously strict in his judgements, pointing out how the morality preached by Jesus Christ was in direct contrast to that of the world; on occasion he juxtaposed the virtues of pagans with the laziness of Christians. He stressed the need for frequent Communion and the serious prep-arations a Christian should make for it: 'Tomorrow I must approach the [Communion] table.' But Bourdaloue, a man of exemplary piety himself, who placed emphasis on char-itable visits to the sick and prisoners, understood how denunciations of sin could be allied with gentleness – but not indulgence – towards the sinners. His manner was friendly rather than stern, and as a result the general effect was compelling. He was widely regarded as an *honnête homme* or civilised man, that supreme contemporary word of praise, with his 'probity, prudence and penetration', in the words of the introduction to a book of his sermons in 1707. Later the King would say of the charismatic priest: 'Father, you have made me dissatisfied with myself.'[3]

The rise of Bourdaloue was not good news for Athénaïs. Above all, Bourdaloue hammered home what the essential goal should be: 'Live as a Christian king,' he told Louis XIV, 'and you will merit salvation.' It was that same salvation which Queen Anne had declared in peril in 1664, making her son weep. It was still in peril (and for the same reason). Now, in the interests of a double salvation, where there had once been a Double Adultery, the King and Athénaïs abandoned their relationship. It was a decision which amazed sophisticated Parisian women such as Madeleine de Scudéry. The pair had broken up, she wrote to Bussy-Rabutin on 20 April, 'purely for a principle of religion'. Such a reaction was very far from Father Bourdaloue's advocacy of Magdalen as a role model: 'Love as Magdalen loved' and, from this, 'inner peace would be born' out of the severity of penitence.[4]

By this time there was another woman also interested in the 'project' of Louis's salvation. Maternal, already middle-aged by the standards of the time (she was forty in 1675), virtuous and intelligent, Françoise de Maintenon had developed a benevolent but controlling character, suitable for dealing with children. As her correspondence with her confessor Gobelin shows, she found it easy to adapt these qualities to the new situation in which she found herself: being the discreet governess to the King's children was not so many steps away from discreetly advising if not governing the King himself.

Yet as her relationship with Louis developed, Françoise was in no sense acting as a substitute for Athénaïs. Françoise was pleasant company, everyone said so, natural sweetness combined with years in a subservient position had seen to that, but she was not especially witty or even amusing. And whatever the King's roving eye, in 1675 he was still in sexual thrall to Athénaïs.

The following vignette is significant, since the source is Madame de Maintenon herself, who confided it many years later to her protégée Marguerite de Caylus, daughter of her cousin Philippe de Villette. The quarrels of Athénaïs and Françoise had continued and there were some 'terrible exchanges' between them, as the governess told Gobelin. The uncomfortable intimacy thrust upon them with all the outward show of friendship – it was Athénaïs that Françoise took on a 'camping' expedition to Maintenon in April – did not help matters. Finally Françoise, provoked out of her usual serenity, succeeded in speaking to the King alone, something Athénaïs had tried to circumvent. Then Françoise poured out her troubles with the children's mother to their father, to the man Gobelin had encouraged her to regard as her true employer.[5]

She outlined Athénaïs's frequent and tempestuous fits of jealousy (of which Louis himself had had ample experience in the last eight years). The King responded: 'Haven't you yourself often noticed, Madame, how her beautiful eyes fill with tears when you tell her about any generous or touching action?' They were the words of a man still in love and can scarcely have soothed the indignant governess, more accustomed these days to seeing Athénaïs's beautiful eyes flashing with anger than with adorable compassion. And perhaps Françoise herself had just a little pang of jealousy for the triumphant beauty of her erstwhile friend, something, with all her attraction, she could never rival.

For all these upsets, the women were of course destined to remain in a kind of spurious intimacy, of the sort which had once united Athénaïs and Louise. That was the way of the court, the will of the King. Now that Athénaïs was duly separated from the King as a result of that ecclesiastical ambush, Françoise took care to preserve her neutrality –

and her reputation – by taking the five-year-old Duc du Maine on a long trip to the thermal baths at Bourbon in the hopes of doing something for his unfortunate physique. It was an action she performed from the heart, since the helpless Maine was probably the human being Françoise loved most in the world, but it also placed public emphasis on her motherly tenderness.

In the meantime Bossuet devoted himself to the struggle for Athénaïs's soul, as well as the soul of the King, and for the continued separation of two people who had certainly not lost their deep attachment to each other. Louis was still determined that his mistress – or rather his former mistress – should have every whim indulged. In 1675 alone Colbert was obliged to spend nearly 23,000 livres on orange trees, those palpable signs of Louis's favour, for her house at Clagny. It was an explicit royal command: 'Continue to take the most beautiful [to her] ... in order to please me.'[6]

Bossuet acted as the go-between, a task made easier by the fact that the King departed for Flanders campaigning. The Dutch War begun in 1672 had not yet brought him the victories of the earlier War of Devolution. The optimistic Bishop suggested that Providence would now reward him for his sacrifice with victory: the implication being that previous military troubles (like the deaths of so many of his legitimate children) had been the divine vengeance on his philandering.[7]

By a joyous coincidence – from the *dévot* point of view – the final vows of Louise de La Vallière as Sister Louise de La Miséricorde took place on 3 June 1675. A great crowd attended, including the Queen herself, only too happy with this spectacle of the penitent mistress, and undoubtedly wishing that Athénaïs would follow suit. All commented on the new spiritual beauty of Louise in her dark vestments. A few years later she wrote, with some help from Bossuet, who edited the manuscript, a religious tract: *Reflections on the*

Mercy of God. Her rank was not quite forgotten, for the author was described as a 'Carmelite Nun, known in the world as the Duchesse de La Vallière'. A rhyme used as a prefix described how Sister Louise had once given 'her heart to the Earth' until a flash of holy light had obliged her 'to declare war / On the World and the Devil in order to merit Heaven'. Throughout Sister Louise declared her devotion to the penitent saint who was her role model: 'above all regard me without cease as Magdalen. Like her I will wash your feet with my tears ...'[8]

Meanwhile Bossuet was not finding it altogether easy dealing with that other Magdalen whose penitence, it seemed, was incomplete. Was the Bishop the right man for the task? 'He has plenty of intelligence,' wrote Françoise, 'but it is not the worldly wisdom of the court.' Nor did he quite appreciate that Athénaïs might be a hard habit to break. There is an indication in his correspondence in the summer of 1675 that even the forty-eight-year-old prelate, a man of exemplary piety, felt her physical attraction. In an ambiguous letter on the subject of his heavy burden, he asked the Marquis de Bellefonds to 'pray for me' and 'may God make all the man in me die'.[9] To Louis, Bossuet reported that Athénaïs was calm enough, occupying herself with good works (as time would show, another aspect of her undoubted energy was an appetite for philanthropy). But he had come to understand that ending the liaison – stamping out 'a flame so violent' – was not the work of a day. The King returned from campaigning in August, but surely there was no danger: Madame de Montespan, no longer at court, resided at Clagny. It was Bossuet who observed with some foreboding: 'Yes, Sire, but God would be more satisfied if Clagny was seventy leagues from Versailles.'

Bossuet was right. The thought of poor Athénaïs languishing was too much for the King; she was allowed back to court, but with some touching if slightly ludicrous caveats.

The couple would never be alone together, or if they were, it would be in a room with glass windows so that the court could supervise their conduct and make sure it was sufficiently proper.

But perhaps the caveat was not so ludicrous after all. In May 1676 Athénaïs went on a restorative trip to the thermal baths at Bourbon, for the sake of her health (and figure). Bourbon, near Moulins in the Bourbonnais province southeast of Paris, was a spa which had been known since Roman times when its waters – *aquae Borvonis* – were praised by Vitruvius. There were other spas such as Vichy and Barèges, but this was the most fashionable one.* And Athénaïs was duly given an extremely lavish welcome, with loyal addresses in every town through which she passed. The status of the King's *maîtresse en titre* surely demanded it. Ironically enough the local governor was Louise's brother, the Marquis de La Vallière. Athénaïs herself however was more interested in her new outlet, good works: she endowed twelve beds at the local poor-house and gave a considerable amount of money to local charities.[10]

In July however a scene took place at Clagny worthy of the most successful playwright at court, Racine. Great care was taken that 'respectable ladies' should be present as chaperones, and at first Louis spoke to his former mistress in grave tones as though he was some kind of cleric – a Bossuet. Athénaïs interrupted him: 'It's useless to read me a sermon: I understand that my time is over.' Then gradually the pair – who had not been alone together for fifteen months – withdrew to a windowed alcove, while the courtiers, including the respectable ladies, remained at a respectful distance. The conversation grew more intense, and later still

---

* Madame de Sévigné, attending for rheumatism, described a regime of thermal baths interspersed with painful jets of boiling hot or icy water, which was much like that of modern hydros. The little underground 'theatre' where this took place made her think of Purgatory.

more tender. 'You're mad,' said Athénaïs. 'Yes, I am mad,' replied Louis ardently, 'since I still love you.' After this avowal, both King and Athénaïs 'made together a profound reverence to these venerable matrons'.[11] Then they withdrew to her bedroom ... This was the moment feared by Bossuet and Madame de Maintenon alike.

Athénaïs proceeded to make short work of some of the objects of the King's gallantry during his absence from her bed. The Princesse de Soubise proved not to be quite so virtuous a mature married woman as she had been as a teenager: there was a rumour that one of her children was the King's. Her husband however was remarkably complaisant about the association. After all, in the words of Saint-Simon: the family's rise was all due to the beauty of the Princesse de Soubise 'and the use to which she put it'.

Isabelle de Ludres with her statuesque body and striking red-gold hair was a more serious contender. This royal affair began in the course of a minuet. The King gazed rapturously into Isabelle's beautiful blue eyes: 'I am sure, Madame, that these *fripons* [rascals] have caused plenty of damage in their time.' Isabelle was ready with the appropriate gallant response: 'Not as much as I would wish, Sire, for I know someone who still defends himself too strongly against their force.'[12] Sure enough the King proceeded to lower his defences. What the Princesse de Soubise and Isabelle de Ludres lacked, it seemed, was the intelligence or wit to hold the King even if they had the spirit to capture him. Nevertheless, before Isabelle de Ludres could be thoroughly defeated, the court drama of her rivalry with Athénaïs had to take expression on the stage, in true Versailles fashion. *Isis*, an opera by Quinault and Lully, made a clear allusion to Isabelle as Io, who aroused the rage of Juno for daring to seduce Jupiter; Athénaïs was obviously caricatured as the jealous Juno to whom in the end Jupiter promised to be faithful. The whole court sang Io's lovely song from Act

III: 'It is a cruel offence / To appear beautiful / To jealous eyes,' and Madame de Sévigné knew it by heart.[13]*

There were two visible mementos of the King's rapprochement with Athénaïs. As one observer summed it up in fairly crude terms: 'And along came the second Mademoiselle de Blois and the Comte de Toulouse.'[15] It was true. Athénaïs was very soon pregnant again, and her daughter Françoise-Marie, conceived in August, was born on 10 March 1677. She was created Mademoiselle de Blois like Marie-Anne. It was an example of the intimacy of Athénaïs and Françoise, as well as the delicacy of the renewed relationship with the King, that the little girl was actually born at Maintenon (although Françoise was by now too grand to look after these latter children). Athénaïs's sixth child by the King, Louis-Alexandre, created Comte de Toulouse, was born on 6 June 1678. 'You have had Augustus [Maine] and you have had Caesar [Vexin],' said Athénaïs to her lover. 'Now of course you have to have Alexander.'

No more martial heroes were however to be commemorated in the names of Louis's children. There is good reason to believe that the King ceased to have sexual relations with Athénaïs after the birth of Toulouse. Ungallantly, but realistically, the cessation may have had something to do with Athénaïs's increasing weight in her thirty-eighth year, on which the courtiers were beginning to comment. The kindly Madame de Sévigné noted that her 'angelic' face was as beautiful as ever, with the delicious blonde ringlets, 'a thousand of them', which were made to frame it in a style called *hurluberlu*, so flattering that even the Queen copied it (maybe the blondness now owed something to art but the effect was still stunning). Malicious Primi Visconti

---

* The librettist Quinault was briefly sacked for the satire, giving the Mortemarts an opportunity to push forward their favourite La Fontaine, but Lully did not suffer, Louis acting as godfather to his son shortly afterwards.[14]

on the other hand described one of her legs as being as big as his own thigh, although he added, as though to soften the insult: 'I have lost weight lately.'[16] Athénaïs's physical family inheritance, remembering the notorious girth of her brother Vivonne, had proved a fatal combination when her large appetite and repeated pregnancies were added to it. She was endlessly massaged and perfumed: it made no difference against these more potent factors.

Louis still visited Athénaïs in his orderly way for the regulation two hours daily and she continued to enjoy her sumptuous apartments at Versailles. But his passion had passed on.

The Dutch War was concluded at last in 1678. By the Peace of Nijmegen of 1678–9, Franche-Comté, originally conquered ten years earlier, was formally annexed to France from Spain. Louis XIV now had leisure for two new enthusiasms. In the first place he concentrated once more on Versailles. His new official architect Mansart was given sums to spend which rose sharply over the next few years, reaching $5\frac{1}{2}$ million livres in 1680 from a mere three-quarters of a million in 1676 (eighteen million and $2\frac{1}{2}$ million pounds respectively in modern money). The aim in all cases of modifications and additions was grandeur, grandeur in the eyes of all Europe, the continent where the Peace of Nijmegen had made him the visibly preeminent monarch. Liselotte as a resident of the palace had another take on the subject: 'There is nowhere that hasn't been altered ten times,' she wrote of Versailles. The unpleasant smell of wet plaster was something with which all the grand ladies of Versailles had to contend, to say nothing of the inevitable dirt and noise of perpetual building works.[17]

The second enthusiasm was of the familiar sort. The King fell in love. Her name was Angélique. But since this was the love of a forty-year-old man for a girl of eighteen there was a new aspect to it: sheer infatuation with her youth, her blonde, ethereal, unsullied looks; wit or intelligence was no longer demanded. There was even an embarrassing aspect to it all, as the courtiers watched the Sun King, who passed his fortieth birthday on 5 September 1678, become a fool for love, devoting himself to a girl who was the same age as his son the Dauphin and twenty years younger than his *maîtresse en titre* Athénaïs.

Perhaps the warrior in him deserved this delightful reward: this was certainly the line taken, albeit satirically, by Bussy-Rabutin. As Louis seduced the virginal Angélique against a background of Le Brun's tapestries depicting his military victories, he could regard her as his latest conquest. Naturally Angélique fell madly in love with the King: in this, wrote Liselotte, she was more like the heroine of a novel. And if she was also stupid – Louis 'seemed ashamed every time she opened her mouth in the presence of a third party' – her sweetness was a pleasant contrast with the tartness of Athénaïs, by no means decreasing with age.[18]

Angélique de Scorailles de Roussille, Demoiselle de Fontanges, came of an ancient family in the Auvergne region where her father, the Comte de Roussille, was the King's Lieutenant. She was indeed very pretty, something of the same type as the young Louise de La Vallière although her features were more classically perfect: she looked 'like a statue', said the scornful Athénaïs. Others said more flatteringly that she was the most beautiful woman ever to appear at Versailles. Angélique arrived at court in October 1678 as a maid-of-honour to Liselotte. According to Liselotte later, the girl had had a prescient dream about her own fate which she duly recounted to her mistress: how she had found herself ascending a lofty mountain, but on reaching the peak, she was suddenly enveloped in an enormous cloud and plunged into total obscurity ... Angélique awoke from this vision in terror and consulted a local monk. His interpretation was scarcely reassuring: the mountain was the court, where she was destined to achieve great fame, but this fame would be of short duration. In short, said the monk, 'if you abandon God, He will abandon you, and you will fall into eternal darkness'.[19]

Although Liselotte's recounting of the dream surely owed something to hindsight, it was true enough that Angélique ascended the 'mountain' remarkably quickly: by February Bussy-Rabutin, a gossip but an accurate one, predicted 'changes of love at court'. Madame de Maintenon was of course horrified. She contributed her own analogy, also taken from dramatic scenery. 'The King,' she told Gobelin on 17 March 1679, 'is on the edge of a great precipice.'

What was happening now to his famous salvation, on which she, Bossuet and Bourdaloue were working so hard in their different ways? Happily indifferent to this important subject, intoxicated with the air at the peak of the mountain, Angélique flaunted her success. Her carriage was drawn by eight horses, two more than Athénaïs had ever commanded. Her servants wore grey livery to match the celebrated grey of her sea-nymph eyes. La Fontaine had paid tribute to her in verse with the permission of Athénaïs (who saw in Angélique less of a threat to her personally than Françoise). She was installed first of all in a pavilion of the Château Neuf at Saint-Germain and then in an apartment close to Louis's own. Undoubtedly the exquisite Demoiselle de Fontanges briefly aroused the King's flagging sexual powers in a way that Athénaïs, with all her arts, had failed to do in recent years. The men of letters knew all about that kind of excitement. It was a case of 'the charm of novelty ... the bloom on the fruit', in the words of La Rochefoucauld. Saint-Évremond discoursed on the difference: 'In a new Amour you will find delights in every hour of the day,' whereas in a passion of long standing 'our time lingers very uneasily'.[20]

In striking contrast to the King's pampering of his youthful mistress was his cruel imposition of dynastic duty upon another girl of roughly the same age. This was Marie-Louise, Mademoiselle d'Orléans, the seventeen-year-old daughter of the late Henriette-Anne and Monsieur. In the absence of war, Louis XIV turned to that other convenient method of boosting a nation's power, the strategic marriage alliance. In 1679 an impartial observer would not have considered King Carlos of Spain promising bridegroom material. At the age of eighteen Carlos was notorious for his gross, even brutal behaviour to his courtiers. He had a high eunuch's voice and disgusting eating habits, with an over-long tongue which lolled from his mouth and loose lips above a receding chin; his thick fair hair, his best point, was generally left matted and dirty. To marry such a man was a ghastly prospect for any girl – unless one took the line that he was the greatest *parti* in Europe and that could never be a ghastly prospect for any girl who was a princess.

The obvious bride in dynastic terms would have been Louis's daughter, the Petite Madame, but after her death in 1672, Louis turned his attention to the senior Princess at the French Bourbon court, his niece Marie-Louise. He was especially anxious, as ever, to win the race against any Habsburg candidate. Frankly, all the doubts about Carlos's physical ability to beget an heir remained unresolved; however, in the autumn of 1678 the Spanish court announced that he was in fact eager to be married.

In his capricious way, Carlos took a violent fancy to his pretty cousin's portrait. (Both were descended from Philip III.) And Marie-Louise *was* pretty. With her large sloe-black eyes and black hair, she had inherited the Médicis looks of her grandmother Henrietta Maria; in other ways she resembled her famously charming mother, if a darker version. Her bearing was superb: 'She deserves a throne,' whispered the French courtiers. A formal proposal came in January, followed by a proxy marriage and the planned departure of Marie-Louise for her new kingdom.

Marie-Louise was devastated. She too had envisaged a royal destiny to which as a Granddaughter of France she considered herself entitled. But her preferred bridegroom, the one she had believed since infancy would be hers, was her first cousin, the Dauphin Louis. A robust fellow, whose fair looks favoured his mother, the Dauphin was more interested in hunting than anything else except possibly his food. He was capable of much ingenuity in pursuit of his passion, only failing when he tried to hunt a weasel in a granary with basset hounds. He had however no intellectual tastes, and a brutal governor in childhood had left him terrified of authority in the shape of his father. But the Dauphin was essentially good-natured and popular with the people as well as the court.

In the royal lottery any princess could do a lot worse than drawing him for her mate, quite apart from the prospect of being Queen of France in the future. Like any French princess, Marie-Louise considered this the highest possible destiny. Her mother Henriette-Anne, although fobbed off with Monsieur, had certainly believed it; it was the same view that the French-born Queen of Spain had inculcated in Marie-Thérèse. Unfortunately, in his ruthless way where such matters were concerned, Louis XIV intended his son for a German princess to secure his position in the east still further.* To the weeping Princess, Louis remarked that he could not have done more for his own daughter. 'Yes, Sire,' replied Marie-Louise, in sad reference to her dashed hopes of marrying the Dauphin. 'But you could have done more for your niece.'[21]

---

* Louis XIV had once considered Mary, elder daughter of James Duke of York, for his son, although (like Liselotte) she was a Protestant; it is an interesting speculation what the consequences of this union would have been. Mary's actual marriage to William of Orange led to the Protestant takeover and the rule of King William and Queen Mary.

Marie-Louise paid a series of farewell state visits, including to the convent of Val-de-Grâce where the heart of her mother was interred; she was perpetually in tears. She even flung herself at the feet of the King, who was on his way to Mass, crying: 'Don't make me go!'

'Madame,' joked Louis, 'it would be a fine thing if the Most Catholic Queen [of Spain] prevented the Most Christian King from going to Mass.' His true indifference to her suffering in the interests of 'glory' was made clear when Marie-Louise said her last goodbyes. It was the case of the Grande Mademoiselle and Lauzun all over again: the dynasty must come first, whatever its demands. 'Farewell,' said the King, firmly. 'For ever. It would be your greatest misfortune to see France again.' He referred to the tradition by which a princess married to a foreign sovereign never returned to her native country except in circumstances of disgrace or failure. Yet Louis was extremely fond of this unhappy young woman, originally for her mother's sake and now for her own. He simply put duty as he saw it – her duty to uphold the interests of France in Spain – above human feelings. And expected others to do so.

So Marie-Louise departed to a life quite as miserable as she had anticipated. By the rules of the repressive Spanish court she was so confined that she could not even look out of the window. She was obliged to spend at least four hours a day in private prayer, quite apart from the prolonged rituals of the services. As for the local entertainment of watching heretics being burned by the Inquisition, that, as the French Ambassador in Madrid drily observed, 'gives horror to those not accustomed to it'. At first Carlos himself was obsessed with his young wife and highly jealous of her; then he started to dislike her for her (unsurprising) inability to conceive. He took to kicking the pets with which she tried to console herself: 'Get out, get out, French dogs.' By coincidence, another victim of Louis XIV's sense of duty had fetched up in Spain in a convent in Madrid: Marie Mancini, still warring with her husband. Queen Marie-Louise took her for rides in her carriage: two women, one of forty, one of seventeen, who pined for France.[22]

The fate of that other young woman, Angélique, whose duty was no more than to divert the King of France, was in the end not much better, if less protracted than that of Marie-Louise. In this case Louis XIV cannot be blamed entirely, since Angélique was essentially a willing victim who had used her charms to aim at a high position. She duly became pregnant, like all the other mistresses, but not for her the triumphant fertility of Athénaïs. On the contrary, her baby boy died at birth, and in the process of the confinement Angélique herself received injuries which made her, as the cruel courtiers said, 'wounded in the King's service'. As sex faded, so did the King's love, and the imprudence of the whole episode became apparent. Religion was playing an increasingly prominent part in the scenario of the court. The celebration of the Mass would find both women with a claim on the King, Athénaïs and Angélique, praying hard on their knees and jangling their rosaries. Athénaïs and her children would be on the right, Angélique on the left. 'Truly,' wrote Primi Visconti, 'court life provides the funniest scenes imaginable.'[23]

In the end Angélique was made a duchess: the traditional farewell gift of the sovereign. She also received a visit from Madame de Maintenon, who argued with her for two hours about the need to give up the guilty relationship. At one point the wretched Angélique exclaimed: 'You speak of throwing off a passion as if it was as easy as changing a chemise!'[24] A romantic if foolish character herself, who loved to dress in colours which matched the King's clothes, she could not understand the pious practicality of someone like Françoise. Angélique's ill health increased, and she began to show signs of lung disease. She retired to the convent of Port-Royal and endured a protracted death, probably caused in the end by a pulmonary abscess.

Louis's general policy was to ignore those mistresses who left the court: he never, for example, visited Sister Louise de La Miséricorde in her convent. (That was left to Athénaïs, who on one famous occasion made the sauce for the convent meal, food, as has been noted, being one of her interests in life.) But Louis, either out of tenderness or a bad conscience, did pay a visit to Angélique *in extremis* on his way from hunting. She saw the tears in his eyes – how could anyone, let alone Louis, fail to cry at the sight of a girl of twenty about to die? – and according to one story, reconciled herself to death as a result: 'I die happy since I have seen my King weep.' It was guilt, perhaps, that made Louis give money for an annual service in Angélique's memory, something once again he would do for no other mistress. *Sic transit gloria mundi*, commented Madame de Sévigné: it was the same allusion to the transitory nature of worldly glory which Louise had had inscribed on the pillar of her farewell picture by Mignard.[25]

The withdrawal of Angélique, and the effective ousting of Athénaïs from the King's intimate affections, paved the way for the more public ascendancy of Françoise. Athénaïs received the rank and rights of a duchess (she could not receive the actual title because her separated husband refused to be elevated from his Marquisate). She was also given the post of Superintendent of the Queen's Household, the most prestigious female office at court, something Louis had always declined to accord her. But the public role which pointed to the future was that given to Madame de Maintenon.

· January 1680 saw the arrival in France of the Dauphin's bride, the Bavarian princess who had taken the place so much coveted by Marie-Louise. A new royal meant a new household: it was Madame de Maintenon who was made the Dauphine's Second Dame d'Atour (Mistress of the Robes). She now had in public estimation that respectability and status which by her own admission meant so much to her. This appointment was a tribute to those conversations, perhaps two hours a day, which the King was beginning to have with her. This man who had experienced most forms of heterosexual relationship was, wrote Madame de Sévigné, tasting for the first time the delights of friendship. In consequence of her appointment Françoise had to adopt the grave costume which went with the post: 'Now I belong to a princess I shall always wear black,' she told Gobelin.[26]*

Marianne-Victoire, Princess of Bavaria and now Dauphine of France, was a year older than her bridegroom. She had little to commend her by the standards of the French court except French blood: her grandmother had been Christine de France, Duchess of Savoy. She was on her way to being an intellectual, speaking German, French and Italian with some knowledge of Latin. Marianne-Victoire was uninterested in the hunting which was her new husband's passion (she disliked exercise of any sort), nor in the gambling which the court loved; she preferred poetry and music. The trouble was that she was distinctly plain: Liselotte called her 'horribly ugly', an exaggeration perhaps, but then Liselotte was now displaced from being the Second Lady at Versailles to being the Third. Madame de Sévigné wrote more detachedly that it was odd how Marianne-Victoire's various features did not combine to make an attractive whole, her forehead being too high, her nose a little bulbous, even if she did have lively and penetrating dark eyes. But the fact that Marianne-Victoire was interested in the new art of conversation

---

* From this regulation court dress, which she had to wear for ten years, sprang the many slurs on Madame de Maintenon as a crone forever clothed in black. Françoise in fact preferred brightness to black, and when young loved blue above all other colours.[27]

endeared her to the King, who not only respected her rank (the Second Lady would always have been sacred to him), but positively enjoyed her staid but intelligent company.[28] And she was devout too, something that was becoming more and more important to him, as in his conversations with Françoise.

There is a comparison to be made at this date with another gallant King who was at last settling down – with his mistress. Charles II was eight years older than his first cousin, and thus celebrated his fiftieth birthday in May 1680. He too had led a life of extreme profligacy, in which one *maîtresse en titre* was surrounded by a changing cast of lesser mistresses. For many years the resplendent foremost position had been occupied by Barbara Villiers, Duchess of Cleveland, whose sensual beauty in youth, 'the sleepy eye that spoke the melting soul', made her one of Lely's favourite subjects. She had much in common with Athénaïs, including high fertility, an awkward husband and a tempestuous nature which alternated torrents of jealousy and high-spirited laughter.

But Charles, with the growing indolence of age, had settled for a quieter life. His current *maîtresse en titre*, Louise de Kéroualle, Duchess of Portsmouth, was a highly domesticated little Frenchwoman, nicknamed 'Fubbs' (Chubby) by the King for her plump figure and childish face; he even named one of his ships the *Fubbs* in her honour. Charles's unhappily barren Portuguese Queen, Catherine of Braganza, found Fubbs a great deal more congenial than the insolent Barbara: she even protected her when Fubbs was attacked publicly for her Catholicism. There was therefore something like a contented domestic triangle in what proved to be the last years of Charles II's life. In France a contented domestic triangle was also in the making.

Louise Portsmouth's relationship with King Charles had been sexual in origin, however cosy it had become. To

return to Louis XIV in 1680 and his demure con-
versationalist Françoise (who was incidentally fifteen years
older than the French mistress across the Channel): was he
by this time sleeping with her? In short, was the role of
Mistress of the Robes to the Dauphine, accorded to her at
this date, a reward or a recognition of a new role? Or was
it perhaps neither of these things, but an inducement to
adopt a new role in the future? There is considerable
difference of opinion among biographers over the date on
which the pair first became lovers, and a ten-year range of
suggested timings, starting as early as 1673.[29]* In the absence
of any absolute certainty, two things become crucial: Françoise's known character, developed over the forty-five years
of an often troubled life, and her correspondence with her
confessor.

Taking her character first, Françoise was certainly capable
of feminine jealousy as we have seen, including rivalry for
the attentions of the King with her erstwhile employer
Athénaïs. But she was no female Tartuffe, a scheming
hypocrite who outwardly preached one thing and lived
another. Her piety was sincere and her concern for the
King's salvation was genuine. So was the friendship she
offered him. At the same time life had made of her a realist.
If occasionally priggish, she was not a prude, as her down-
to-earth advice to girls in her care would show. She mocked
one who was horrified when her father used the word
'culotte': as if a mere 'arrangement of letters' made something
immodest. And she laughed at those who could only bring
themselves to discuss pregnancy in whispers – despite it
being mentioned in the Bible.[30] In any case, six years at
court, if nothing else, had surely convinced her that the King
would be with difficulty weaned away from the pleasures of
illicit sex altogether.

* The main theories and their supporters are listed in the Notes.

In a significant step the new Mistress of the Robes actually persuaded the King to 'return' to his wife in the summer of 1680 and sleep with her again from time to time: something which made Marie-Thérèse intensely happy.* This good deed was all part of Françoise's picture to herself (and her confessor) of the work-for-salvation policy she was committed to at court. Gradually it became evident that there might be some kind of price to pay for all this good work. Angélique might fade and lose her charms but it was by no means out of the question that the King's eye would fall upon another pretty moppet at court. There might be further bastards (how providential that Angélique's son had died!): after all, as the cheerful Gascon proverb had it, 'A man can beget as long as he can lift a sheaf of straw.'[31] Perhaps friendship – that hitherto unknown territory to the King, was not quite enough to keep the King safe.

The evidence of Françoise's correspondence with Gobelin points delicately to the possibility of compromise some time in the future. In a letter of 27 September 1679 for example she wrote that she was determined to profit from the instructions he had sent to her 'and make up by charities for the bad things I am doing'.[32] This is of course the conventional language of a penitent to her confessor, but it also points to the bargain Françoise was beginning to make with herself (and hopefully God, via her confessor). Good deeds could atone for other deeds which were not quite so good; in short the motto of the Jesuits might be discreetly applied, that the end justified the means.

All this was not immediate. It is surely inconceivable that Françoise was sleeping with the King at the time when she was lecturing Angélique on the need to throw away her

_____

* Marie-Thérèse, at nearly forty-two, had last given birth eight years previously; one supposes that the King had ceased his marital attentions when the fact that she was past childbearing became evident.

passion in March 1680. The appointment to be the Second Mistresss of the Robes was therefore a reward for her services and a recognition of her value to the King – that value not yet, if it ever would be in the true sense of the word, sexual. Significantly, Louis made a public Communion at Pentecost 1680, which coupled with the decline of Angélique's charms and his staged return to the Queen's bed, seems to indicate at least a partial repentance for past misdeeds.

At the same time Madame de Sévigné reported in early June that Madame de Maintenon's long interviews with the King were 'making everyone wonder'; her favour was growing all the time, and that of Madame de Montespan was diminishing.[33] It was true. At the start of 1680, that inviolable position Athénaïs had attained for herself, with her apartments, her children, her regulation hours of talk with the King every evening, was apparently under threat. But the danger in this case did not come from the Catholic Church. It came from the heart of seventeenth-century evil: allegations of poison.

CHAPTER 10

Madame Now

Madame de Maintenon is now Madame de *Maintenant*.

– Madame de Sévigné, September 1681

The Marquise de Brinvilliers, a notorious poisoner, was tortured and executed in July 1676; her tiny body was then burnt in a colossal fire, and her ashes scattered to the winds. It says something for the customs of the time that Madame de Sévigné, the most civilised woman of her age, took great pains to watch the process and was disappointed that the packed crowds meant that 'I only saw a mob-cap'. Madame de Sévigné went on to fantasise about the effect of the dispersal of the murderess's ashes: 'so we shall inhale her, and by absorbing the little vital spirits we shall become subject to some poisoning humour, which will surprise us all.'[1]

Whatever the mythical potency of the guilty Marquise's remains, it was certainly true that during 1679 a first-class crisis brewed on the subject of poisonings and poisoners, in which some celebrated names were mentioned by notorious criminals already under threat of death. And for one moment the ashes blew close to the King with the invocation of the name of the Marquise de Montespan. So began the temporary implication of Athénaïs, banished from royal favour but not the royal presence, in that brutal labyrinth of an episode known as the Affair of the Poisons.*

* The most recent book in English, Anne Somerset, *The Affair of the Poisons* (2003), gives a lucid account of it all.[2]

214

The arrest of Catherine Monvoisin, known as La Voisin, on suspicion of witchcraft (a capital offence) in March 1679 was the effective start of it all. La Voisin was a supplier of potions of many different sorts to the great ladies of the court, and has as a result been felicitously described as 'a duchess among witches'.[3] La Fontaine airily summed up her various talents: whether you wanted to keep your lover or lose your husband, straightaway you went off to La Voisin for assistance. The solution to both these annoying problems might be powders, aphrodisiac or the reverse, and certainly La Voisin supplied a great many powders in her time. There was also the question of horoscopes, spells, black magic and even that blasphemous use of inverted ceremonial known as a Black Mass. The contemporary view of black magic in any aspect was expressed by Furetière in his *Dictionnaire Universel* as follows: 'A detestable art which employs the invocation of devils and uses them to accomplish things beyond the force of nature.'[4]

Here a distinction must be drawn between the various functions La Voisin was supposed to perform. Supplying aphrodisiacs, which might or might not work, was a very different matter from providing poisons. Similarly, a visit to La Voisin to enquire about the future – of a love affair, for example – was a harmless activity; consultation about a horoscope might have something naïve about it but it was hardly evil (otherwise a great many people down the ages to the present day would have to be condemned). To take part in a Black Mass on the other hand, with its use of the human body as an altar, with a murdered child's body and blood as sacraments, was something so blasphemous by the standards of the seventeenth century (to say nothing of its horror by any standards) that no Catholic could have done it without the deliberate intention of rejecting conventional religion.

La Voisin described herself as 'a practitioner of

chiromancy, a student of physiognomy', arts she said she had learned at the knee of her mother, also a sorceress. She named an enormous number of suspects on her arrest and was finally executed a year later. As a result of her revelations a tribunal unofficially but graphically known as the Chambre Ardente (Burning Chamber) was set up under La Reynie, the Chief of Police. It sat until July 1682. Over four hundred cases were heard, over three hundred arrests were ordered, thirty-four people were executed, nearly thirty more sent to the galleys or banished. Crimes varied, like the penalties, from poisonings to the use of horoscopes: it was, quite literally, a witch-hunt.

The court began to feel the heat when the name of Marie Mancini's elder sister Olympe, Comtesse de Soissons, was mentioned as having poisoned her husband, who died in 1673. Although the latest research on the subject suggests that Olympe was not guilty, she fled to Flanders in January 1680 and later on to Spain, leaving her large family of children behind. She had long lost the favour of the King – memories of the amorous past they had shared had faded, while her mischief-making caused Louis intense irritation. Olympe had lost her position as Superintendent of the Household and Louis was surely relieved to see her go. Another Mancini sister, Marianne, the 'spontaneous and bold' Duchesse de Bouillon, was 'unperturbed' by similar charges of planning to harm her husband: she appeared in front of the tribunal accompanied by the aforesaid husband as well as the lover who was supposed to benefit. It was a gesture of high style which succeeded. The Duchesse did not flee.[5]

The name of Athénaïs was not introduced until comparatively late in the proceedings, by which time La Voisin was dead. Crucially, La Voisin had never mentioned the favourite under torture, although she implicated twenty other people. Another conspirator named Falastre, who did name Athénaïs (under torture), withdrew the allegation on the eve of his death. La Voisin's evidence on the subject of the favourite came second-hand via her daughter Marie-Marguerite. This was not a very convincing route, since Marie-Marguerite was desperate to do something, anything, which would spare her torture and execution.

The suggestion that Athénaïs had taken part in a Black Mass, her voluptuous naked body stretched out as an altar, with a rogue priest performing the 'ceremony', was frankly preposterous. Athénaïs's piety was genuine, as much part of her character as the radiant sexuality which had charmed the King for so long. She once gave a memorable dismissal to the Duchesse d'Uzès, who queried her sedulous church-going in view of her immoral life: 'Because I commit one sin [i.e. adultery] it does not mean that I commit them all.'[6] This declaration should always be borne in mind where Athénaïs is concerned. In the years to come she would show herself almost as devout as Louise de La Vallière, although her expression of her piety was less extreme. If employing black magic – 'the invocation of devils' – put a seventeenth-century Catholic in danger of hell, participation in the murderous blasphemy of the Black Mass would have condemned anyone beyond a doubt – not only in the eyes of the Church but in the fearful imagination of Athénaïs, the Catholic in question.*

Equally preposterous were the allegations that the *maîtresse en titre* had also procured poisons 'to accomplish things beyond the force of nature', in Furetière's phrase – that is, with the intention of killing the King. How on earth would the death of Louis have benefited his long-term mistress? Her entire position in material terms depended on his

* The index of books prohibited to Catholics after the Council of Trent in 1564 included (*Regula IX*) works on necromancy, chiromancy (palmistry), the preparation of magical drafts or poisons, auguries and magical incantations. 'All these things are utterly forbidden.'

favour, her lavish lifestyle, including her splendid apartments, her gems, her money, her house at Clagny; furthermore, status was equally important to her self-esteem, and the King was showing every sign of respecting that, even if the sexual bond had been broken. There was no question that the accession of the Dauphin to the throne (with her abiding adversary Marie-Thérèse as Queen Mother) would have led to disgrace and probably banishment from court.

As to allegations of other poisonings – did Angélique receive a bowl of poisoned milk? – these were so endemic to the French court, and indeed the society of that time, that any hostility expressed, followed by some kind of illness or death, was all too easily transformed into an accusation of poisoning.[7] (Remember how the Chevalier de Lorraine had been falsely accused of poisoning Henriette-Anne simply because they were on bad terms at the time of her death.) Liselotte for example, who had a vindictive streak in her apparently jolly, extrovert nature, accused Madame de Maintenon of poisoning both the minister Colbert and the architect Mansart. Athénaïs was of a far higher rank than the wretched old women who got into quarrels with their neighbours and were duly burnt as witches when the same neighbours collapsed from some common malady of the time. But her situation was essentially the same. Her unsurprising jealousy of Angélique, her role as furious Juno to Angélique's innocently lovely Io in the opera *Isis*, was all too easily transformed into an accusation of poisoning when the lethal ashes of the Marquise de Brinvilliers were blowing in the wind.

Where Athénaïs, like many of her friends, was probably guilty, if that is the right word, was in seeking aphrodisiacs from La Voisin: 'powders for love'.[8] The mention of her waiting-women in this connection, the saucy Demoiselle des Oeillets, who had probably had a child by the King in 1676, and another known as Catau, is perfectly plausible. No doubt they visited La Voisin on behalf of their mistress (and perhaps Oeillets on her own account too), especially since one date cited was 1678, when Athénaïs was losing her sexual hold over the King. Catau was said to have had her palm read: another fairly innocent pursuit despite the Church's prohibition. The name of Athénaïs's sister-in-law the Marquise de Vivonne was also cited. This behaviour might be louche but it was hardly heinous.

Aphrodisiacs were a subject of prodigious interest in the seventeenth century, as indeed they have been in every century down to the present one: like contraception, the need brought the solution, or hopefully the solution. (The same is true about recourse to horoscopes in time of personal anguish.) Cantharides – taken from the wing covers of the 'Spanish fly' beetle – and other ground-up substances were advocated, including extract of toad and snake. When Margaret Lucas, one of Queen Henrietta Maria's maids-of-honour, was married off to the future Duke of Newcastle, thirty years her senior, she found him in the unfortunate position of being both impotent and in need of an heir. Since the popular remedy of 'heating [i.e. spicy] foods' failed to do the trick, the Newcastles turned to Europe. From Rome Sir Kenelm Digby reported a cure by an apothecary who regularly killed three thousand adders to make his medicine: 'By long use of such flesh of vipers,' he wrote, men who had turned eunuchs through age 'become Priapus again'. (It did not work with the Duke; there was no male heir; the Duchess of Newcastle turned to writing.)[9]

There was an underworld market for such things in Paris. Nor was it only the great ladies or their maids who ventured there. All his life the King had plenty of discreet access to it. One of the most important men in the intimate life of Louis XIV was his chief valet, Alexandre Bontemps, whose reticence was so famous that keeping silent on a subject was proverbially known as 'doing a Bontemps'. A huge fat man, nearly twenty years the King's senior, Bontemps was adored by Louis for his total loyalty, also his adept way of carrying out private missions for which he used a special royal coach without armorial bearings. Bontemps was without malice. After his death, it was said of him that he had never spoken an ill word of anyone and, even more remarkably at Versailles, had never let a day pass without speaking well 'of someone to his master'.[10] But for all his good nature, Bontemps was not without his contacts in the underworld.

Another of the King's devoted valets, François Quintin de La Vienne, had been a celebrated swimmer and became a *baigneur*, something between a bath attendant and a barber. He conducted an *étuve* or bath-house where the King had been in the past to be bathed and perfumed. (Being rubbed down with eau de toilette was the most fashionable form of hygiene in an age when water was widely distrusted, with good reason.)

These *étuves* had many of the same assets as a modern health club with their facilities for bathing and massage. But under the alibi of being bath-houses, they also performed – discreetly – some of the same functions as a brothel. Everyone knew what was meant by the discreet phrase *coucher chez le baigneur* (sleeping at the bath-house). The women in attendance might be available for further services. Young men used them as places of rendezvous, especially with married women whose husbands had to be kept in ignorance. There was also a medicinal aspect to such establishments: people went to be cured of the problems brought about by 'great pleasures', that is, venereal diseases. They were certainly places where aphrodisiacs might be obtained. It was La Vienne who was credited with supplying the King with 'fortifiers' when Louis found he could no longer achieve 'all he wished' in his love affair with Angélique. The genial La Vienne, always elegantly turned out, was a popular member of Louis's inner household.[11]

All this is to say that the King, a man of terrific sexual energy in youth, encouraged to further heights in his thirties by the inspirational Athénaïs, was beginning to fall back just a little from the high standards he had come to expect as he approached forty. He therefore had recourse to stimulants. Athénaïs may have provided some of these 'powders of love' from La Voisin via her maids or in her own right. (The point has been made that former *maîtresse en titre* Athénaïs had bodyguards installed by the King who would certainly have monitored such discreditable visits and reported them.) But Louis also had his own network of discreet servants when such things were required.

There is certainly no evidence to link the King's periodic fits of '*vapeurs*' with the potions supplied, let alone with poisons. The English word 'vapours', with its hysterical female connotation, does not cover these royal attacks: they were more like mini-collapses. For example, Louis had an attack when his mother first fell really ill in the summer of 1664 (he cured it by going swimming). And he would have an attack in April 1684, long after Athénaïs had either opportunity or motive to administer a drug. These fits were perhaps nervous in origin, a periodic short-lived weakness due principally to his extraordinary daily schedule, which certainly included love-making (latterly with stimulants), but also hours in Council planning policy at home and military strategy abroad. As we shall see in the next chapter, other illnesses were on their way, including the dreaded gout to which both his father and grandfather had been subject. In the meantime the doctors' frequent purges and *lavements* (enemas), recounted in fearful detail in their industrious journals, were enough to weaken the strongest man and cause him collapses.

*

The reaction of Louis XIV to the 'revelations' of La Voisin's daughter, and her unsavoury accomplices, also under arrest, was immediate. A freeze was put on all the papers relevant to the Marquise de Montespan. At the orders of the Council, all documents relevant to Athénaïs, her sister-in-law Madame de Vivonne and her maid Oeillets were to be taken out of the dossier. The criminals themselves were separated and put into dungeons where their voices could not and would not be heard. The King kept the papers himself for twenty-five years and then burned them. His conduct towards Athénaïs did not alter – the daily visits – and that alone is the most convincing proof that he believed in her innocence.

Louis XIV was a fanatic for order and a good public show, but he was also human. Had these charges of poisoning and the Black Mass been believed, the former *maîtresse en titre* would certainly have been told to retire from court, either to the country or abroad like Olympe Comtesse de Soissons. There is another proof, quite apart from the psychological implausibility of it all already stated. Colbert, the King's chief minister for his whole personal reign so far, the wise and prudent Colbert who had in the past handled the question of the bastards, did not believe in the charges either. He quoted the Latin tag that a single (unsupported) accusation meant no accusation: *Testis unus, testis nullus.* And he had examined all the evidence.[12]*

There was also a political dimension to the Affair of the Poisons which Colbert thoroughly understood. He had a long-standing rivalry with Louvois, Louis XIV's Minister of War. Athénaïs had always belonged to the Colbert camp, being connected to him by marriage; she disliked Louvois, who in turn resented her influence with the King. Colbert,

* There is a comparison to be made between the Affair of the Poisons and the Affair of the Diamond Necklace, in which Marie-Antoinette was pilloried, one hundred years later. People at the time (and historians later) believed in the guilt of Athénaïs and Marie-Antoinette if they wished to do so.

absolving Athénaïs for good reason, was also protecting his own interests.

So, where Athénaïs was concerned, 'all the external signs of friendship and consideration were maintained', wrote Voltaire in his history of the King's reign. He added: 'although it offered her no consolation'.[13] It was true. Athénaïs's long reign was at last well and truly over, not because of the Affair of the Poisons, which was a deeply unpleasant but temporary embarrassment, but because Françoise was now established in her place. The Affair of the Poisons did not help Athénaïs's position but it was a position lost in any case. It could even be argued that the King's resolute defence of his former mistress indicated the continuing depth of his feelings for her – affection if no longer passion.

Athénaïs de Montespan was of course the mother of Louis's children, and the court of France was increasingly dominated by the presence of the younger generation. Or, to put it another way, since this was a King-centred court, the King's role as patriarch was beginning to be glorified. In January 1681 a ballet was danced at Saint-Germain-en-Laye in honour of the Dauphine. If officially dedicated to Marianne-Victoire, it has been described as 'a sort of celebration of the royal paternity'. Devised by the familiar team of Quinault and Lully, it is seen as the first true Opera-Ballet, and was later, slightly altered, performed in Paris at the Academy Royal. Love was the ostensible theme but the triumph of youth was also proclaimed. Louise-Françoise, the nine-year-old daughter of Louis and Athénaïs, played Youth itself. At the end of the performance she sang sweetly: 'Reserve your criticisms for old age / All our days are charming / Everyone laughs at our desires.'[14]

Louise-Françoise was already a mischievous little creature: 'a pretty cat, while you play with it, it lets you feel its claws.' In a few years' time – two months before her twelfth birthday* – she would be married off to a Prince of the Blood, the Duc de Bourbon, heir to the Prince de Condé and at court known as Monsieur le Duc. Her official title therefore, by which she was always addressed, was Madame la Duchesse.† The Duc de Bourbon was extremely small and his head was very large; he was singularly charmless, and arrogant on the subject of the rank which was his sole claim to distinction. At the time the Marquis de Sourches exclaimed that 'it was a ridiculous thing to see these two young puppets' getting married.'' The bride did not however long remain a puppet. The wilful Madame la Duchesse, irreverent and rather lazy, would come to exhibit the new values of Versailles, where everyone laughed at the behaviour of the young, or so the young thought.

It was however her half-sister Marie-Anne, daughter of La Vallière, who was the star of this particular ballet. She was newly married to another Prince of the Blood, the Prince de Conti,‡ a match that excited courtiers had predicted for 'the little fiancés' when they first danced together. Marie-Anne's ravishing looks fully justified the promise of her childhood: her perfect heart-shaped face and huge wide-set eyes were celebrated at every ball, including the masked balls when Marie-Anne often declined to cover the famous eyes, lest their 'fire' should be doused. (Like many beauties,

* These marriages of state, made at such a young age (the Duc de Bourbon was seventeen to his bride's eleven), were not however consummated until a more appropriate time; in this case a year later, when Louise-Françoise was not quite thirteen.

† Louise-Françoise will henceforth be mainly designated as 'Madame la Duchesse', in view of the quantity of similar forenames.

‡ The royal houses of Bourbon-Condé and Bourbon-Conti in this period descended from two brothers, respectively Prince de Condé and Prince de Conti, born to Henri II Prince de Condé and Charlotte de Montmorency in the 1620s. The Prince de Condé (known as Monsieur le Prince as his heir was Monsieur le Duc) was the elder of the two; thus he was the senior Prince of the Blood. Intermarriage of the cousins would make them further inextricably entwined.

Marie-Anne was extremely short-sighted: the kind of beguiling person who 'lost' her magnifying glasses because she had pushed them on top of her head.) 'The goddess Conti' was how she was often described, and was she not after all 'descended from Olympus', 'the Daughter of Jupiter', as La Fontaine apostrophised her? Her scented chamber was known as 'the shrine of Venus'. Perhaps her bastard birth was even responsible for her allure. When Marie-Anne unwisely commented on the reclining Dauphine: 'Look at her, just as ugly asleep as awake,' Marianne-Victoire opened her eyes and said: 'Were I a love-child I would be as beautiful as you.'[16]

This paragon of grace, with no reason to be tormented by the spiritual anguish of her mother, was rated the best dancer at court; according to one contemporary she eclipsed the dancers of the Paris opera. In this ballet Marie-Anne danced the nymph Ariane in the plumes and luxurious embroidered costume which were considered suitable nymph-wear at the time. The poet Benserade described her as 'effacing all the other flowers / Even to the lily of her origin'.[17]

The lily in question was her mother Louise, now in her convent, who had duly received a visit from Marie-Anne on the occasion of her marriage, as well as congratulations from the court. (Madame de Sévigné found Sister Louise as lovely as ever, if even thinner; her grace was unimpaired, as well as 'the way she looked at you'.) Although her daughter was making a prestigious match, Louise's attitude to her 'children of shame' remained ambivalent. A few years later Bishop Bossuet had to break to Louise the news of the death of her son, Vermandois, at the age of sixteen, under unsavoury circumstances: there had been some kind of homosexual scandal. Louise responded chillingly: 'I ought to weep for his birth far more than I weep for his death.' Both children were to the nun, in her own words in her book, reminders of her 'deplorable [former] life, all the more deplorable because it caused me no horror'.[18]

Like Madame la Duchesse, Marie-Anne belonged to a very different generation; after all she could not remember the distressing circumstances of her birth, her mother having to make an appearance in chapel only a few hours later. Marie-Anne set the tone for a new kind of emancipated princess when she complained on her wedding night that her husband 'lacked force' and she preferred his brother. Courtiers wondered how, exactly, at the age of thirteen, she was able to compare the two; but Marie-Anne had begun as she meant to go on. During a short-lived marriage (the Prince de Conti died in 1685) Marie-Anne troubled him constantly with her wayward behaviour, according to Primi Visconti, who seldom heard a rumour he wouldn't pass on. The Prince de Conti complained to her father. But Marie-Anne would fling her arms around the King's neck and be forgiven for her prettiness, her charm and above all for amusing him with her adorable if naughty ways.[19] As the King marched steadily, if at times laggardly, in the direction of virtue, there was a lesson here. The hard-working potentate still had to be amused.

After the death of her young husband, the eighteen-year-old Marie-Anne showed no signs of marrying again. Secure in her position, she was prepared to live a life of pleasure at court, enjoying the special friendship and favour of her half-brother the Dauphin. And there was one asset Marie-Anne enjoyed that was denied to Madame la Duchesse (Louise-Françoise). Although both were married to Princes of the Blood, Marie-Anne's mother had not been the wife of another man at the time of her birth; Madame la Duchesse on the other hand, for all her *hauteur*, was for ever stigmatised as the fruit of Double Adultery.

There were other princesses born in the seventies waiting in the wings: none of them showed signs of being docile. The

King's younger surviving daughter by Athénaïs, Françoise-Marie, the fruit of their reconciliation, was a little tearaway. Liselotte's daughter Elisabeth-Charlotte, a Granddaughter of France, was described by her mother as 'so terribly wild' and 'rough as a boy'. There was something like pride in the way in which Liselotte added: 'I think it must be the nature of all Liselottes to be so wayward in childhood.'²⁰ (Her half-sister Anne-Marie, child of Henriette-Anne, a gentler and sweeter character, was married off to the Duke of Savoy in 1684 and left France.) Then there were the Princesses of the Blood, the tiny daughters of the Prince de Condé and a Bavarian princess – nicknamed 'the Dolls of the Blood' – such as Anne-Louise-Bénédicte de Bourbon-Condé, sister of Monsieur le Duc. Bénédicte made up for her lack of size with a sharp wit and a ranging intelligence which was quite prepared to challenge the orthodoxies of the court of Louis XIV.

All this was for the future, when the girls one might term the dragons' teeth of Louis XIV, with all their rivalries of birth and position, grew up.* In 1682 however the important family event was seen with reason to be the accouchement of the Dauphine. To Marianne-Victoire was entrusted the responsibility of producing a male heir in the direct line (if the Dauphin had no son, the succession went to the Orléans branch: his uncle Monsieur and so to the latter's only son Philippe Duc de Chartres), and she had already suffered two miscarriages.

On 6 August 1682, therefore, the tension was considerable as she went into labour, using the famous royal plank between two mattresses on which both Louis XIV and the Dauphin had been born. Louis was in attendance, taking

---

* In the classical myth, Cadmus slew the dragon guarding the spring sacred to Ares; when he sowed some of its teeth in the ground on the orders of Athena, they sprang up into warriors.

his turn in promenading the Dauphine round the room as the hours passed. Also present among the host of courtiers exerting their rights to be in on important occasions of state were both Athénaïs and Françoise: the former as Superintendent of the Queen's Household, the latter as Second Mistress of the Wardrobe of the Dauphine herself. It was ordered however that no one wearing perfume should be admitted to the birthing-chamber: overwhelming scents were thought dangerous in this situation. Sniffer-dogs were posted at the door to make sure there were no back-slidings.

In attendance was the royal *accoucheur* (man-midwife), the calm and competent Julian Clément: he had already performed the same function for Athénaïs. When the baby was finally born shortly after ten o'clock in the evening, he answered the King's question about its sex according to a prearranged code: 'I do not know *yet*, Sire.' This meant a boy. ('I do not know, Sire' was code for a girl.) It was therefore the suddenly radiant King who cried out: 'We have a Duc de Bourgogne!'[21] The baby was put on a silver platter and examined – successfully – for perfection.* 'The little Prince', as Bourgogne was known, was promised a splendid destiny according to his horoscope, with the Sun in the sign of the Lion, Saturn in the eleventh house at the hour of Jupiter. From Louis XIV's point of view, the dynasty was now secure, especially since Marianne-Victoire became pregnant again without mishap a few months later. As a forty-four-year-old grandfather (little older than his parents had been at his birth) he could now relax. He personally had no more need to produce further legitimate heirs.

The King's patriarchal contentment contrasted with the

* Julian Clément, whose career as a royal *accoucheur* flourished, was finally ennobled in 1711. Given the strain of royal births, with their dynastic implications and the frenzied hope for boys, no one deserved it more.

mood of Liselotte. In July 1682 she described herself as
'miserable as an old dog'. Everyone went on about her being
so sad, she wrote, 'when they themselves are the daily and
hourly cause'. Once again, as with Henriette-Anne, it was
not Monsieur's homosexuality which was at issue, since for
the last four years, following the birth of a healthy son and
daughter, 'I have been permitted to live in perfect chastity.'
(A few years later she decided that abstinence had actually
made her 'a virgin' again.) It was Monsieur's slavish adoration
of the Chevalier de Lorraine which upset the balance of
what could have been a perfectly acceptable condition.
There were also rumours, probably spread by Monsieur's
supporters, of Liselotte's own gallantry with the Chevalier
de Saint-Saëns: quite untrue, since Liselotte much preferred
her dogs ('the best people I have come across in France, I
never have less than four about me ... no eiderdown could
ever be as cosy').[22]

In her unhappiness and her indignation Liselotte asked
to retire to a convent where one of her Palatine aunts was
a Catholic Abbess. But Louis refused. He gave her three
reasons. 'First of all, you are Madame,' he said, 'and obliged
to uphold that position. Secondly you are my sister-in-law
and my affection for you will not allow me to let you leave.
Thirdly, you are my brother's wife and I cannot let him be
touched by scandal.' To this Liselotte had no alternative but
to submit with the words: 'You are my King and thus my
master.' King, Monsieur and Madame all three embraced.

With the genuine affection he felt for her, Louis now
assured Liselotte that although he had taken his brother's
part and would always do so, on all other issues he would
take hers. It had to be enough. The number of Liselotte's
dogs increased: her Mione, 'the most beautiful little dog in
the world', her Rachille behind her chair, her Titti near the
writing-table, her Mille Millette on her feet, her Charmion
beneath her skirts crying to be close to her mistress, her

Charmante also under her skirts on the other side, her
Strabdille, her Charmille ...[23]

There was a subtext to Liselotte's dissatisfaction, and that
was her growing jealousy of Madame de Maintenon, a
woman not only inferior in birth and with a questionable
marriage behind her, but seventeen years her senior. Liselotte, in her frank and often extremely vulgar allusions to
Françoise, never stopped harping upon her age: she was '*die
alte Zott*' (the old trollop), and in future years old prune,
frump, chambermaid, hag, whore, garbage and ordure (an
extremely coarse German word was used for this). A handy
German proverb was quoted: 'Where the devil cannot go,
he sends an old woman.'[24] It was the beginning of a duel
which would only end with the death of the King.

Others, accustomed to the royal mistress being in her
prime of beauty, were simply baffled by the spectacle of the
King's attentions to a woman now nearer fifty than forty.
Primi Visconti, for example, wondered if Françoise might
be 'a skilled person whom the King would use to help him
rewrite his memoirs'.[25]

Madame de Maintenon was not helping Louis with his
memoirs, but the question remained open (and will always
be subject to speculation) as to exactly what their relationship
was at this point. It was in September 1681 that Madame
de Sévigné made her famous pun on the French word for
'now': Madame de Maintenon was 'Madame de *Maintenant*'
(Madame Now).

The following summer marked the date when Louis XIV
officially designated Versailles the seat of his court and
government. According to the Marquis de Sources, on 6
May 1682 the King left Monsieur's château of Saint-Cloud
to establish himself in Versailles, where 'he wishes to be for
a long time although it is still full of masons'.[26] Despite the
presence of the masons and the plasterers which upset the

great ladies, the disposition of apartments at the new official residence declared a great deal about the current state of his relationships. Françoise's rooms, for example, were of an ambivalent status, parallel to her own ambivalent position.

Queen Marie-Thérèse had immense and splendid rooms on the south face of the central block of the Parterre du Midi. The Dauphin and Dauphine were also on the royal floor, the latter annoying the King by her grumbling about the builders. Athénaïs, still theoretically *maîtresse en titre*, had four principal rooms on the same floor, looking out over the Cour Royale. Then there was the plethora of courtiers up above in cramped conditions occupying what would now be seen as attic rooms, obliged to share a common kitchen some way away, even if they had their own privies: nearness to the sovereign was preferred to spacious living.

But Françoise's accommodation fell into neither category. She had some little square rooms facing north and not very well heated (she suffered from cold, with the beginnings of arthritis, and loved cosy Maintenon for its warmth). The cabinet containing the *chaise percée* or commode was small enough to be extremely inconvenient: filling and emptying the copper bath tub would also not have been an easy task. A tiny wooden staircase led up to the landing where Françoise's faithful servant Nanon Balbien, her companion since the old Scarron days, kept Françoise's wardrobe in a single cupboard. The windows actually faced those of Athénaïs, but there was no comparison between the two suites of rooms: one demonstrated splendour, the other intimacy.[27]*

As late as August 1682 Françoise was still taking care to separate herself from the position formerly occupied by Athénaïs. 'People are saying that I want to put myself in

* Today these apartments, occupied by Madame de Maintenon for thirty years with certain modifications and adaptations, still have a poky feel.

her place,' she wrote, with her usual sensitivity to gossip about her reputation. 'They don't understand my distance from these sorts of *commerce* [sex] nor the distance which I want to inspire in the King.'[28] The battle for the King's salvation was not certainly won: there had been some earlier talk of his flirtations with pretty younger women. Françoise was evidently bearing in mind the warning in Madeleine de Scudéry's Map of Love on the subject of the fast-flowing River of Inclination which led into the Sea of Danger. Her aim, she said, was to be Louis's 'best friend'. The evidence is, however, that shortly after Françoise wrote these words, she decided that a best friend's duty to Louis XIV did unfortunately include sleeping with him, in order to prevent other more frivolous, less religiously focused people doing it without her own pure motives.

She did not of course put it like that to herself: six years earlier Françoise had criticised the King's confessor Father La Chaise for being content with 'a demi-conversion' and commented to the Comtesse de Saint-Géran how 'the atmosphere of the court spoils the most pure virtue and softens the most severe'. Now she herself had been softened. Much later, Françoise could look back with more detachment and tell her confidential secretary Marie-Jeanne d'Aumale that the King 'would have looked for his pleasures elsewhere if he had not found them with me'.[29] Her take on Marie-Thérèse was along the same lines: the Queen was a saint but 'not very intelligent', since she was always at prayer when the King needed her. But at the time her avoidance of public Communion in September caused her perturbation; still more did she agonise over the need to 'make her Easter' in 1683.* She told Madame de Brinon that it was true that

---

* This did not mean that Françoise never took Communion at all during this period; it was as ever the public nature of Easter which was the issue: to 'make one's Easter' when the whole world knew that adultery was being committed (by the King) or the lesser sin of fornication (by the widowed Françoise).

she had taken her Easter Communion 'after a very troubled night shedding many tears' although she knew only too well that they might be considered affected. Françoise then mentioned her charities as distinguishing her from other people in her position: an unfair allusion to Athénaïs, who was nothing if not charitable. But then Françoise could not bring herself to be generous about her effective predecessor. Something about past slights still rankled: Athénaïs was, Françoise wrote in May 1681, 'fatter by a foot' than when last seen.[30]

There was therefore from the first something bleak about the sexual relationship of Louis XIV and Madame de Maintenon: a necessity for two middle-aged people, but from completely the opposite point of view. For Louis it was the passion he could not master, for Françoise the passion she had to endure for the higher good. For Louis XIV there was no urge for conquest as with Louise, no rampant lust as with Athénaïs, no resurgence of youth as with Angélique. Whatever Françoise's sexual experiences with Scarron twenty-five years earlier, they had not given her a high opinion of men in that particular respect. How dominated they were by their physical urges! As she would reflect years later: 'Men, if passion does not guide them, are not tender in their friendships.'[31] Madame Now on the contrary specialised in tender friendship in which physical passion played no part.

With a serene – if still theoretically sinful – private life, Louis XIV was free to concentrate on the further glorification of Versailles, for which the expenses peaked at over 6 million livres (20 million pounds sterling in today's money) in 1685. A place where strict hierarchical values reigned, Versailles was conversely the scene of extraordinary disorder. It was not just the perpetual building-works, scaffolding everywhere, the smell, the dust, the noise. Security was also non-existent by modern standards. The gold fringes of the

King's own bed were cut off, the crime discovered only when an anonymous packet containing them was dumped on the royal dinner-table with a message for the valet Bontemps from the thief: 'Take back your fringes, Bontemps, the pleasure is not worth the bother. My compliments to the King.' As the royal doctor examined the returned fringes for possible traces of poison, the King himself remained cool, merely observing: 'What insolence!'[32] Which was true enough.

Yet Versailles was, as Louis had intended it to be, glorious.[33] Perhaps the King's favourite silver furniture symbolised the apogee of this glory: the glittering silver chairs and tables, the shining silver pots, for example, which held the beloved orange trees in the Orangery, more and more added yearly, many of them brought from Fontainebleau. The relation of dark to light at Versailles was also symbolic. The outer corridors were dark, and servants had to guide visitors and residents with torches. Yet Versailles itself, the state apartments, lit up by night by a myriad of candles and flambeaux, was a majestic, unforgettable sight.[34]*

The King's militant and militaristic foreign policy was also part of his concept of personal glory. In 1682 two young Scots lords, sons of the Marquess of Queensberry, admired the huge gilded ship named the *Grand Louis* at Toulon: the legend on its hull ran: 'I am unique on the waves / As my master is in the world.' This was how the French King was beginning to see himself. Unfortunately both aspects of the King's will – the creation of Versailles as the centre of Europe and his quest for military glory –

---

* It would be wrong in this context to see today's Versailles, a tourist mecca, a maelstrom of different races, as representing something totally alien to the Versailles of the seventeenth century. Enormous crowds of carriages and other horse-drawn vehicles once thronged the areas which are now car-parks and bus-parks; as to race, Asiatic princes paid ceremonial visits and Africans were popular as pages and guards, as can be seen from the portraits of the period.

demanded enormous sums of money: and money was finite, even if it did not seem so at the time to the Sun King.[35]

The fragile Peace of Nijmegen of 1678 which ended the Dutch War was fractured as Louis indulged by stages in the annexation of certain cities and territories he considered to be justly French. This subversive policy of *reunions* was enough to lead to another Grand Alliance against France in 1682. The Habsburg Emperor, Spain, Holland and Sweden were involved and war was surely on the horizon. It was the arrival of the Turks at the gates of Vienna in 1683 which distracted the Emperor and the Christian Kings, and it was John Sobieski, King of Poland, who saved Europe from the Muslim invasion, not Louis XIV: he for his part, much less helpfully, saw his opportunity to foment revolt in Hungary. It was in this atmosphere of impending European chaos that a totally unexpected event took place in both the public and the private life of Louis XIV which was to have an irrevocable impact on its future course.

In the last week of July 1683 Queen Marie-Thérèse was seen happily wandering in the gardens of Versailles, admiring the play of the new fountains. Her health appeared to be perfect: her complexion clear, her colour good. A few days later she fell ill of a tumour under her arm. The tumour turned purple and became an oozing abscess. In spite of the best – or worst – efforts of the doctors, the emetics in wine, the usual purgings and bleedings, the enervating clysters, the Queen became progressively sicker, and her pain increased proportionately.[36] To the amazement of her doctors, who understood the agonies she must be suffering, the Queen did not complain – but then she had seldom complained in her life.

As the situation rapidly worsened, the need for the Holy Sacrament to arrive from the chapel became acute. Normally the Sacrament was formally escorted by servants bearing

enormous flaming torches: it was the King who ordered the
ordinary candles on the altar to be taken because there was
no time to lose. He was right. The Queen was dying fast.
Did she murmur the words: 'Since I have been Queen, I
have had only one happy day'? And if so, which day was
it? No one knew. Her wedding day? Her wedding night,
when she was sure the King loved her? The day of the birth
of her first child, the son that everyone wanted? She did
not say. Marie-Thérèse, Infanta of Spain and Queen of
France, died towards the end of her forty-fifth year at three
in the afternoon on 30 July 1683. The King spoke his own
epitaph on this shy, unhappy, dull but ever dutiful woman
to whom he had been married for over twenty years: 'This
is the first trouble she has ever given me.'

Compared with the King's tender but solipsistic verdict,
the oration of Bossuet at Marie-Thérèse's state funeral was
predictably magnificent, as was Lully's Requiem, including
its solemn, plangent *Dies Irae*. Yet one could be forgiven for
thinking that Bossuet was actually lauding Louis XIV, not
burying Marie-Thérèse, so great was the emphasis on the
King and his works, above all his support of religion: 'Let
us not forget what made the Queen rejoice: Louis is the
bulwark of religion: it is religion which he has served with
his armies by land and sea.'

And in the prevailing tense political atmosphere, Marie-
Thérèse's Spanish birth and the claims of succession deriving
from it (now, of course, passed to her only child the
Dauphin) were given a special lengthy commendation. Only
as an afterthought did Bossuet throw in the fact that Marie-
Thérèse's virtues, as well as her high birth, had made her a
suitable bride for Louis XIV. With her Christian faith, her
love of Holy Communion and her dependence on its
efficacy: 'she now walks with the Lamb because she is
worthy of it.' To say however that Louis's love was as
steadfast as ever after twenty-three years was surely eco-

nomical with the truth. It was when Bossuet invoked the names of the two Queens, Anne and Marie-Thérèse, even closer in piety than in blood, that he struck a note with which everyone including the King could agree.

The funeral cortège was headed, by a splendid irony, by Madame de Montespan, since she had been Superintendent of the late Queen's Household (a job that had now vanished). According to the Grande Mademoiselle, Athénaïs, with her inborn sense of the grand style, was shocked by the levity of some of the younger members of the cortège. It remained to be seen in what direction the court would develop after the Queen's death: whether it would be dominated by the wayward spirit of the younger generation or whether the newly devout mood of the King, encouraged by Madame Now, would hold sway.

PART THREE

Autumn

CHAPTER 11

The King's Need

This is not the time to leave the King; he has need of you.

– Duc de La Rochefoucauld to Madame de Maintenon, August 1683

The death of Queen Marie-Thérèse at the end of July 1683 plunged Louis XIV into an inner crisis. It was generally assumed by his counsellors and courtiers that the King would marry again: his bride would be once more some great princess. That is what kings did, again and again if their wives persisted in dying, as happened to many European monarchs.

And why not? On the eve of his forty-fifth birthday Louis was still a vigorous man. The golden looks of his youth had faded: the beautiful hair that the Grande Mademoiselle had once admired had begun to recede in his thirties and by now he was in effect bald, relying on the massively full and curly wigs depicted in his state portraits. The King's mouth had begun to turn down from the Pan-like smile of his youth, his nose became more pronounced. The fine legs and feet, which like his hair had been so much admired as he danced heroic roles in the Court Ballet, were sometimes tortured with gout.

He was beginning to put on weight: which was hardly surprising considering his enormous appetite, the despair of those eating with him who were expected to match it with their own. Great piles of game birds were consumed, flagons of wine, starting early in the day and continuing to late-night suppers which would not have disgraced Rabelais's giant Gargantua; for night-time consumption, another fowl and more liquid refreshment were provided. Liselotte described how she had often seen the King devour a whole pheasant and a partridge after four plates of different kinds of soup, 'a large dish of salad, two great slices of ham, mutton served with gravy and garlic, a plate of sweet cakes and, on top of that, fruit and hard-boiled eggs'.[1]*

Yet if Louis no longer astonished onlookers with his godlike beauty, his sheer presence commanded them: 'that secret force of royal majesty'. And then there was his voice, the unmistakable voice of a King, seldom raised, expecting always to be obeyed. One veteran officer who was asking for a favour began to shake at the sound of his sovereign's voice and stammered out: 'Sire, I did not tremble like this in front of your enemies.'[2] As for Louis's gaze, the lively look of the mischievous boy had become the penetrating stare of the great King, with his slanting dark eyes which had something quasi-oriental about them.

Certainly there was still much about Louis XIV to make a princess content, to quote that wistful comment Françoise had made about Marie-Thérèse's choice of husband all those years ago at her official entry into Paris. His energies were undiminished. Despite his gout, the King still went shooting and hunting even if he sometimes used a convenient little carriage. His workload was as heavy as ever, and on the other side of the coin the fêtes at Versailles were still glorious. In 1684 Mansart would add the fabulous Hall of Mirrors to the state apartments. And besides all of this, the new bride of Louis XIV would be Queen of France.

Princesses of an appropriate age and status were not wanting: a Tuscan princess perhaps, in order to wield further

---

* After his death, it was discovered that his stomach and bowels in their size and capacity were double those of any ordinary man. No doubt this information consoled the surviving courtiers who had had to keep up with him.

influence in central Italy? Then there was the Infanta of Portugal: a Portuguese alliance always made good sense to balance the power of her mighty neighbour Spain on the Iberian peninsula. Liselotte's aunt Sophia Electress of Hanover nourished hopes that another German princess might join Liselotte herself and the Dauphine Marianne-Victoire at the French court: she had in mind her fifteen-year-old daughter Sophia-Charlotte, known as Figuelotte. Technically Figuelotte was a Protestant (as Liselotte had been), but Sophie delayed her daughter's Protestant Confirmation just in case another rapid conversion might be needed . . .[3]

As for Figuelotte, already a sensible girl, she was definitely up for the throne of France. There might be constraints to the position, but she would face constraints wherever she went; at least with Louis XIV 'it would be worth it'.* In spite of this sporting attitude on the part of the young Protestant Princess, the Catholic Portuguese Infanta remained the front runner – so far as the world knew. It was not until late November that the French Ambassador was told to let the Queen of Portugal down lightly:[4] there would be no marriage of the Sun King with the Portuguese Princess, thirty years his junior.

What no one outside a very small circle knew about in the high summer of 1683 was that crisis which the King first faced, and then resolved. A meeting of the Council held on 13 August decided, according to the report at supper, that second marriages were unfortunate.[5] The next year the sentiment (whether the Council's or the King's) was given emblematic significance. The Queen's apartments at Versailles were carved up, much of the space being taken

---

* The disappointed Figuelotte married another older man, the widowed Elector of Brandenburg, later first King of Prussia; her son was Frederick William I, the Soldier King, and her grandson Frederick the Great. Her possible progeny by Louis XIV – surely great warriors – are material for speculation.

by the King. In Versailles terms it was now quite obvious that there would be no Queen, since there were no Queen's apartments.

The ostensible reasons for the decision were twofold. First there was the present burgeoning royal family, coupled with the Dauphine's new, healthy pregnancy (she would deliver a second prince, the Duc d'Anjou, in December). Second, there was the awful example of past family squabbles. The rebellious behaviour of Louis's uncle Gaston d'Orléans had caused much pain, while the late Queen had disliked her stepmother, Philip's second wife, and felt nothing but hostility for her half-brother. A new young Queen of France would inevitably mean a new young family: Louis had after all begotten a child by Angélique de Fontanges only recently. These children would be half-siblings, possibly subversive half-siblings, to the Dauphin now in his twenties. Was that really welcome to a King who had grown up in the dreaded atmosphere of family dispute?

All this was true enough in dynastic terms. But one doubts whether Louis XIV would really have taken the unconventional step – by royal standards – of remaining a public widower if he had not had a strong private motive to do so. This motive concerned his salvation, that project which could at last be brought to a successful conclusion if he secretly married his best friend and now mistress, Françoise de Maintenon.

These secret unions, known as morganatic marriages, were in fact a feature of the period: they concerned the Church and not the state and were not registered. A marriage in a chapel, performed by the clergy with witnesses, sufficed, although the union brought with it no official position (that of Queen of France in this case). In 1665 for example George William Duke of Celle promised lifelong fidelity to his adored 'wife in the eyes of God', the lower-ranking

Eléanore d'Olbreuse.* Another way of describing such an alliance – except that an alliance in the diplomatic sense was exactly what it was not – was as a 'marriage of conscience'.[7] For of course both parties concerned would be in a state of grace for the future, where the Church was concerned, even if the lack of registration made the ceremony invalid in the civil sense. Children of morganatic unions were not able to inherit kingdoms or princedoms: but in the case of Françoise, now nearly forty-five, the question of children never seems to have featured at any point in her career.

The evidence of the rushed, hushed, anxious then ecstatic correspondence of Françoise at this point is that the King did not reach his decision in favour of the 'project of salvation' at once. This must mean that the Sun King took time to abandon the public values in which he had been raised, which would have made marriage to a woman of minor birth, a few years older than himself, widow of a dubious artist, an unthinkable proposition. He was for example declining to award the court the focal point of a new Queen; a role which he took extremely seriously, as we have seen, following the early example of his mother.

According to custom the King of France could not remain in the presence of death: following the demise of Marie-Thérèse, Louis went to Saint-Cloud. But Françoise stayed at Versailles. Madame Now, hitherto his constant companion for advice, solace and encouragement, quite apart from the lighter pleasures, was scrupulous enough in her conscience and careful enough of her reputation to know that her already equivocal position had been rendered still more precarious.

* Although morganatic marriages were principally used to enable a man of royal rank to marry a women of inferior status, it has been suggested that the Grande Mademoiselle married her suitor Lauzun in this manner when he was released from his long imprisonment, as many of their contemporaries believed.[6]

The idea that on her deathbed Marie-Thérèse passed a diamond ring as a token of her approval of Françoise as her successor is certainly apocryphal, being quite out of character for a great Spanish princess who was in any case dying in agonies.[8] What was true was that Marie-Thérèse had had a satisfyingly tranquil relationship with Madame Now during her lifetime, Françoise being careful to show the greatest respect at all times; the previous autumn Marie-Thérèse had bestowed her own portrait set in diamonds upon her, a traditional sign of exceptional royal favour. But Marie-Thérèse was gone, and with her the illusion of respectability.

It was at this moment that Louis's friend and contemporary, the Duc de La Rochefoucauld, son of the author, took a fateful decision. He had been Grand Master of the Royal Wardrobe (an intimate appointment) as well as Grand Hunter (a convivial one) for the last ten years. No one knew the King better in all his moods of melancholy and celebration, the former suppressed by his formidable self-control, the latter by his sense of his own dignity.

'This is not the time to leave the King,' said the Duc to Françoise, 'he has need of you.' So Madame de Maintenon travelled after Louis to Saint-Cloud. When he went on to Fontainebleau, she joined him there too. Perhaps this ancient and romantic château was the appropriate setting for the critical discussions which now passed between the couple. Fontainebleau was one of the few royal residences where Louis XIV had not so far cast his builder's eye, and remained much as he had inherited it. Grandly old-fashioned, not very large, quite dark with chimneys that smoked, it served as a kind of periodic retreat, especially for the hunting seasons with its convenient and beautiful forest. The transient nature of royal occupation was emphasised by the fact that when the court was away – most of the year – the children of the nearby villagers loved to bathe in the fountains of the château while their mothers did the laundry there, and their animals grazed on the terraces.[9]

In the forest where the young Louis had once ridden with Marie Mancini and Henriette-Anne, Françoise now took her walks in a state of constant agitation, accompanied by her long-time friend the Marquise de Montchevreuil, an unsmiling woman so devout that she was described as putting the most pious off religion. This frenzy on the part of Françoise, the violent uncertainty of her state – her thoughts, her fears, her hopes – was recalled later by Marguerite de Caylus, then twelve years old, whom Françoise had 'adopted' three years earlier.[10]

It is clear from her correspondence that Françoise at this point was still quite uncertain about the course the King would take: given their closeness, this makes it likely that Louis himself was uncertain too. On 18 August Françoise asked her friend Madame de Brinon to relate what people were saying on the subject (a reference to the Infanta of Portugal). On 22 August she hoped Madame de Brinon would go and see Madeleine de Scudéry, now at quite an advanced age but still at the centre of polite gossip, and 'send me all you hear that is good or bad'.

On 22 August Madame de Maintenon in her cautious way was still ridiculing all the gossip about the 'Louis and Françoise' affair. It was not until 19 September that Françoise wrote to her director of conscience: 'My perturbations are over. And I am in a state of peace, which I will take much more pleasure in telling you about than the troubles we used to discuss between ourselves. Don't forget me before God for I have a great need of strength to make good use of my happiness.'[11]

The crucial decision seems to have been taken by the King in the first week of September. A riding accident on 2 September, in which his shoulder was feared broken but was actually dislocated, may have played its part. This was not so much because it gave Françoise an opportunity to display womanly tenderness (Louis was surely convinced of that already, since it was the quality which had first attracted him about her in the ménage of the rue de Vaugirard) but because it anchored the King himself, kept him from returning to Versailles for a month, and thus enforced upon him a period of proper reflection. The King loved Françoise and he did not after all imagine that he would fall in love again. He was wrong about that, but in 1683 could hardly have imagined the circumstances of his last great passion. When the twentieth anniversary of his mother's death was solemnly celebrated in January 1686, Louis could feel that her tears and prayers for his salvation had not been in vain.[12]

So when did this marriage, which was never officially announced to the world and for which no direct documentary evidence exists, take place? For there can be little doubt that it did take place, although to the end of her life Françoise would never directly confirm it even to her most loyal acolytes.[13] The preponderance of historical opinion goes for the night of 9–10 October, with the old chapel at Versailles, subsequently rebuilt, as the most likely venue. It would have been held late at night, for the sake of discretion, and was probably performed by the Archbishop of Paris, Harlay de Champvallon, with the curé of Versailles as another possibility. If it is known, as one source suggests, that green vestments were used, that means that it must have taken place on a weekday between Pentecost and the First Sunday in Advent. The ever-discreet Bontemps would have arranged everything and may in addition have acted as a witness, along with Françoise's faithful attendant since her widowhood, Nanon Balbien. Other potential witnesses, of less intimate standing, were the King's new supreme minister since the death of Colbert in September, the Marquis de Louvois, and the Marquis de Montchevreuil, a decent if rather stupid fellow, husband of Françoise's tight-lipped friend.

Gossip spread across Europe on the subject of the marriage, and by 1686 a song was being sung contrasting the reputation of Françoise's old friend the courtesan Ninon de Lenclos with that of the virtuous Roman wife Lucrece: 'Whether she's wife or mistress / Whether Ninon or Lucrece / I couldn't care less.' As for the King who 'from lover has become husband / He does what one does at his age'. In 1687, according to Liselotte, few people at court doubted that the couple were married; though she personally found it hard to believe 'so long as there has been no official announcement'. Being Liselotte, she could not resist adding a swipe at the morals of the French court: 'If they were married their love would hardly be as strong as it is. But perhaps secrecy adds a spice not enjoyed by people in official wedlock.' The following year Liselotte, with her strong sense of rank, was still perplexed by the lack of official announcement (she should not have grumbled because it enabled her to continue to take precedence over 'the old woman'). But Madame had to admit that Louis had never felt 'such passion for any mistress as he does for this one'.[14]

Françoise had her own ideas of how her position should be handled. She refused for example to take the post of Dame d'Honneur to the Dauphine, the senior female appointment at court, when the Duchesse de Richelieu died, despite the pleas of Marianne-Victoire. (The latter had seen the light: when she arrived in France she had displayed hostility to Françoise, encouraged by her husband; now she realised her mistake.) This self-denial was said to be 'very generous and noble behaviour' on Françoise's part; but in truth she did not want to be seen to tread the path of Athénaïs, the mistress created Superintendent of the Queen's Household. On the other hand, by 1692 Françoise was enjoying the right to visit enclosed convents, theoretically exercised only by the Queens of France. She also had the crucial privilege of sitting down in royalty's presence – always a vital clue to status at Versailles.

The real proof of the marriage lay, however, in the attitude of the clergy, above all that of the Holy See. In order that Françoise should maintain her position as a woman of virtue, it was necessary that the Pope should be informed privately of the marriage. This had probably happened by 1685. Certainly the Papacy awarded her every respect, which would hardly have been the case if she had continued simply as the mistress or the so-called best friend of the King. A lapis lazuli crown for a statue of the Virgin and a gold medal were among the presents sent from Rome to Françoise.[15]

As the years passed, there were clues, slips of the pen or of etiquette, which would admit of no other solution than marriage between the two of them. The drunken reference of the dissolute Charles d'Aubigné to his royal 'brother-in-law' should not be counted as evidence, since Charles liked to embarrass when he could and certainly had no privileged information. But there was the letter of the Abbé Godet des Marais, Françoise's director of conscience following Gobelin, who referred to her as 'a woman occupied with the glory of *her husband*' (italics added). And there was the more ribald incident when Monsieur happened upon his brother alone with Françoise on a bed with the covers drawn back because of the heat (he was taking medicine rather than making love). The King merely laughed and said: 'In the condition in which you see me with Madame de Maintenon, you can imagine what she is to me.'[16]

One of the clear indications Louis XIV had given that there would be no new official Queen of France was his transformation of his late wife's living quarters. Now Madame de Maintenon's own apartments were adapted from time to time to suit her new status – whatever it was – and she was granted a proper reception room (and a better *garde-robe*) so that the King could enjoy the domesticity he wanted. Instructions for redecoration were mixed up with orders for the King's own apartments, and those of the Dauphin and Dauphine. But despite the heavy damask in the various rooms, red, green, crimson and gold, on seats, beds and tables as well as walls, they could never be mistaken for the apartments of a Queen. Only the bed in the alcove with its four bouquets of feathers waving above had something quasi-royal about it.[17]

The King gained no kudos from the match, which in the eyes of his subjects awarded him neither the prestige of a royal bride nor the virility signified by a glamorous mistress. A popular rhyme indicated this: 'I sinned many times with Montespan / I sinned with that good wench / And with this one here / I do my penance.'[18] What he gained was what he wanted to gain: a new puritanism at court. *O tempora! O mores!* There were gallants of both sexes at the court who must have reflected with Cicero upon the change of morals brought by time when at Easter 1684 the King criticised sternly those who had not performed their religious duties.

A certain gallant lady who must have looked quizzically upon the change was Athénaïs, still present at court, still receiving her ritual daily visits from the King. Her sumptuous New Year present to the King in 1685 was much admired: it consisted of a book inlaid with gold and miniatures depicting all the towns in Holland which Louis had captured in 1672; the text was partly supplied by Racine. The Marquis de Dangeau reported on its exquisite appearance and good taste in his *Journal*[19]* (though there was surely an element

---

* The *Journals* of the Marquis de Dangeau, from 1684 onwards, are an important source for the day-to-day routine, including the health, of Louis XIV.

of nostalgia in recalling those vanished campaign days – and nights). A triple outing for the hunt in the autumn of 1685 in a carriage containing Françoise, Athénaïs and the King also recalled the pairing of Louise and Athénaïs fifteen years earlier. But power had shifted for ever.

Already Athénaïs had been moved out of her gorgeous apartments to dwell solely in the Appartement des Bains on the ground floor. The inlaid marble floor had to be replaced with parquet to make it habitable in winter. In December it was Françoise to whom Athénaïs applied to get a position with the Dauphin for her son by her first marriage, the twenty-year-old Marquis, later Duc, d'Antin. (She had hardly seen him in childhood after her husband took him away, and her daughter Marie-Christine had died in her early teens.) At Françoise's instance, the King agreed. D'Antin, handsome and lively, with his mother's good looks and her wit, went on to have a distinguished career at court and in the army.

Françoise's power was however circumscribed both by her own inclination – she had her particular notion of what she should do – and by the King's disinclination to suffer feminine interference in what he saw as the male sphere. The Revocation of the Edict of Nantes in 1685 was a case in point. In 1598 a law promulgated by Henri IV had granted civil and religious liberties to his Huguenot subjects. Although Cardinal Richelieu had annulled its political clauses in 1629, it was Louis XIV's Revocation which put into effect forced conversions, with other Huguenots fleeing abroad. All this had everything to do with the direction of Louis XIV's ecclesiastical policy since the beginning of his reign, and nothing to do with Françoise.[20]

The only people who blamed her for it were the spiteful Liselotte, who tried to pretend that 'the old whore' and Father La Chaise together had imposed this penance on the

King for sleeping with the Montespan, and Saint-Simon, only nine years old at the time. Distasteful as the Revocation is to modern hearts and minds, still more so the horrifying sufferings of the Huguenots left in France which followed, the Revocation was popular among Louis's predominantly Catholic subjects."

Tolerance at this time was widely seen as leading to social disorder – Charles II had met with no success in attempting to establish 'freedom for tender consciences'. The principle first proposed in 1526 at the Diet of Speyer of *cujus regio ejus religio* (the religion of the territory was to be that of its ruler) was widely approved. The persecution of the 'pretended Reformers', that is the Protestants, was seen as adding to the King's glory rather than detracting from it. Louis was praised as extirpating the monster of heresy: 'this hydra that your hand has strangled'."

For reasons to do with her mixed Protestant–Catholic background, Françoise had a far more pragmatic attitude to religion than many of her contemporaries. She was not a persecutor by nature but a persuader. As a young woman, she had come to appreciate the truth of the Catholic religion in which she now profoundly believed. But she also had come to understand that in Catholicism, the state religion, lay the key to the better life, and she expected others to come to the same conclusion. As she wrote in 1681 to her cousin's wife, the Marquise de Villette, who was a Protestant: 'I hope that God who has given you so many good qualities will withdraw you from a state which makes you useless for this world and the next.'" One notes the order in which the two worlds are placed.

Starting in about 1684, Françoise kept a series of little leather-bound 'Secret Notebooks' in which she noted religious texts, biblical quotations and sayings of the Saints that appealed to her such as St Francis de Sales and St Augustine, along with her own annotations.[24]* The result is a holy rag-bag with some anodyne pious sentiments: 'Keep a rule and it will keep you,' for example, and the frequently repeated text from the New Testament: 'He who does not become as a little child will not enter the Kingdom of Heaven.' At the same time it does provide a clue as to how Françoise saw herself and her destiny. She must be as submissive towards the King as Sarah was towards Abraham (who were of course husband and wife). Nevertheless, Françoise resolves: 'that I may not keep from him anything of the things he needs to know from me and that nobody else has the courage to tell him'. Where kings in general are concerned, there is considerable emphasis, in the manner of Bossuet and Bourdaloue, on the reign of God: 'It is from me, God, that wisdom comes …', 'Kings reign thanks to me.' And there is a critical reference to the hedonistic court behaviour Françoise had witnessed from the outside: 'Jesus Christ is offended above all by the lovers of pleasure' (*amateurs de plaisirs*).

It was in her work for education, particularly the education of the sort of poor girl she had once been, that Françoise found her true vocation; for it could be argued that guiding the King was a vocation which had been thrust upon her by a combination of circumstances. For all her professed aversion to court life (an aversion which was expressed more strongly as the years passed) Françoise had not been able to resist the challenge and the triumph. But the education of the young was something she had always cared about, even before she was appointed governess to Maine and his siblings. By the means of two 'adoptions' Françoise honed her skills in this respect.

Marthe-Marguerite de Villette, known as Mademoiselle de

---

* The eight little volumes, $4\frac{1}{2}$ inches by $2\frac{1}{2}$ inches, are now preserved in the Bibliothèque Municipale de Versailles.

Mursay after the château, was the daughter of the first cousin Françoise had loved in youth, Philippe de Villette. Born in 1671, Marguerite was an intelligent and lively girl, but her relationship with the famous lady she always called her aunt was not to be without its ups and downs. Marguerite also had a rebellious streak. She did not at first appreciate being turned into a little Catholic, although it was to her worldly advantage, any more than Françoise herself had done. By her own account, 'at first I cried a good deal, but next day I thought the King's Mass was so beautiful that I agreed to become a Catholic, on condition that I could hear it every day – and that I would not be whipped!'[25]

Something in Marguerite seems to have irritated Françoise: why could she not accept her place in society and see how lucky she was to have been advanced so far? But not too far. Françoise found her lazy, despite her natural gifts at singing and dancing, and suspected her of frivolity when Marguerite came to prefer the amusing Mortemart-style circle of Madame la Duchesse (Louise-Françoise, the King's daughter by Athénaïs) to the severe circle of her 'aunt'. Early on, Marguerite, who was pretty enough in her own right to attract suitors, had a putative romance with a member of the King's guard. Madame de Maintenon seems to have taken a kind of grim pleasure in Marguerite's failure to capitalise on her chances, as she saw it. 'She won't do as well as she might have,' Françoise reported in September 1684, 'but she will always be better matched than she could have expected naturally.'

However, when it came to a question of Marguerite's marriage, Françoise actually turned down one suitor, the Duc de Boufflers, saying: 'My niece is not a good enough match for you.' Yet her eventual choice of the Comte de Caylus, to whom Marguerite was married off at fifteen, was disastrous. Despite his good court connections as a member of the Dauphin's household, despite his military talents,

Caylus turned out to be a drunk, who wanted to eat apart from his wife in order to indulge in alcohol unobserved.

Françoise's second 'adoption', that of her actual niece, Françoise-Charlotte d'Aubigné, went much better. Françoise-Charlotte, born on 5 May 1684, the year after the secret royal marriage, was the child of Charles d'Aubigné and Geneviève Piètre, the *bourgeoise* he had insisted on marrying to his sister's disgust. Against Françoise's persistent benevolence towards the ungrateful Charles should be weighed her equally persistent scorn for Geneviève. Here was a woman who not only ate butter and jam at the wrong time of day but also had a terrible accent 'as from Les Halles' (the Parisian market). In fact the best and worst of Françoise's character was displayed in her twin reactions to the d'Aubignés as a couple.

Almost immediately after the little girl's birth, Françoise decided that this child should be her heiress, that is, to the Maintenon estate. Her letter to her brother on the subject was brisk: she would 'marry [Françoise-Charlotte] according to my taste, since you gave her to me'. He must not expect too much. However, little Françoise-Charlotte turned out to be the most delightful child,* pretty and obedient, young enough to be the grandchild of the King and his secret wife, a foretaste of the pleasures of such a relationship, where sheer youth amuses an older man. However, the admirable Françoise-Charlotte did not escape her aunt's strictures altogether: at one point she was warned not to regard herself as 'a person of importance' since she was totally dependent on Madame de Maintenon for her prospects and might be fobbed off with 'some miserable country gentleman' if her aunt died.[26]

It was a piece of good fortune that Madame de Main-

---

* She is the wide-eyed, curly-haired little girl who features in the most famous portrait of Madame de Maintenon.

tenon's interest in the education of girls, especially girls like herself, of gentle birth but lacking a dowry, coincided with the King's increasing need to be amused by younger women (hence his indulgence to his illegitimate daughters). The result was the establishment known as the Foundation of Saint-Louis at Saint-Cyr in 1686: It was for the free education of daughters of the impoverished gentry. Only royal donations were permitted to support the Foundation; the teachers were to be known as the Dames and the girls as the Demoiselles of Saint-Louis. Twelve ladies were invited from the charitable school Saint-Maur to instruct the Dames how to do their work.[27]

This was a subject on which there was perfect unison between the King and his secret wife. Neither Françoise nor Louis wanted Saint-Cyr to be a convent. Françoise herself had resisted going into a convent; Louis had not totally appreciated those endless convent visits accompanying his mother as a young boy. Sentimentally interested in young women and their welfare, Louis gave his characteristic attention to detail to matters such as their bonnets. Where once the royal virility had been celebrated by the spectacle of his numerous mistresses, Louis XIV was happy now to be regarded in a patriarchal role: guardian of 'the pearls of the kingdom'. And he was particularly happy that the daughters of soldiers who had fallen in war – in royal service – should be looked after.

A satirical pamphlet printed in Holland referred to Saint-Cyr as 'a seraglio which the old Sultana prepared for the modern Ahasuerus' (Louis XIV).[28] This was true only in so far as Louis gloried in the all-female atmosphere of the charming children and girls, aged between seven and twenty, who came to fill the establishment. He loved their modesty: the way that they never permitted themselves to stare outright at the august figure of their sovereign, although they were obviously longing to do so. Louis paid frequent visits, sometimes on foot (Saint-Cyr was conveniently close to Versailles), and enjoyed the excellent music of the scholars. They were divided by age into the youngest Reds, early teenage Greens, Yellows and finally more or less adult Blues. At one point a Mademoiselle de Beaulieu, a Green, with a particularly lovely voice, decided to organise an impromptu song in the King's honour as he was departing on foot after Vespers. So the sweet sound came to him: 'Let him live and triumph for ever, our hero.' It was just what the King wanted; it was indeed what any celebrated older man might want.

Madame de Maintenon, for her part, found here the perfect opportunity to control and mould according to her own values. It should also be remarked in her favour that just as Françoise was ahead of her time in her genuine affection for children and their company, she was also modern in her belief in the need for female education to make society work properly (she had already tried one experiment at Noisy in the grounds of Versailles). Françoise spent a great deal of time at Saint-Cyr, sometimes arriving at six o'clock in the morning. On occasion events there produced that rather dry sense of humour which was another aspect of Françoise's character. There was the eager question from a Demoiselle: what should they look out for 'on entering the world'? Instead of a solemn admonition, Françoise replied lightly: 'Don't get dirty in the mud of the courtyard.' On another occasion she had spent a long time chatting in the kitchen when the need arose to attend some formal ceremony. 'But Madame,' cried one of those present, 'you smell just a little of cooking fat!' 'True,' replied Françoise, 'but no one will ever believe it's me.'[29]

No detail was too small for her to notice (acute attention to detail was something that Louis and Françoise had in common). Good teeth for example were a subject that obsessed her, and dentistry was provided for these provincial girls: the wilful Marguerite had been forced to have her inadequate teeth seen to. The girls were impressed that Françoise interested herself in details of their lingerie, and even more so when she ordained that the portions of food should not be too small, tasting the food herself to make sure of the quality.

The aim was to turn out good Christian women rather than nuns: in fact the emphasis was on the teaching which would enable them to take their place in the world as respectable and useful wives to gentlemen. Thus cheerfulness – always helpful in a wife – was a recommended virtue. French was to be spoken with a proper accent. Sacred writings were obvious materials for study, and some classical texts. It was notable that the theatre was considered a proper area of study where novels were not; but then Louis XIV was and remained a passionate lover of the theatre and the girls could hardly go wrong, could they, in pursuing an art which gave their 'hero' such pleasure. In January 1689 the King lent jewellery, some 'brilliant stones' from his collection, as well as suitably rich tapestries, for a performance of *Esther* by Racine with music by Jean-Baptiste Moreau, a disciple of Lully.

The playwright was by now a friend and ally of Françoise, and may even have helped her with her 'Secret Notebooks' as well as the Constitution of Saint-Cyr. He was also a frequent visitor to her château of Maintenon. He went there for example, together with his fellow writer and Royal Historiographer Nicolas Boileau, for rest and recreation in August 1687, when Racine found Madame de Maintenon 'full of wit and good sense'.

The simple and delightful dwelling of Maintenon was, as ever where the presence of Louis XIV was concerned, undergoing alterations and additions: these included two new wings designed by Mansart, cobblestones outside where his guards could strike their bayonets with a noise like thunder to greet their King, and a passage for him to reach a special *tribune* or gallery from which he could overlook the village church and partake in Mass, unseen. It was shortly after a royal visit that Louis granted his secret wife the Marquisate of Maintenon in June 1688: though ironically, Françoise's dream of a peaceful life there, never really fulfilled, was by now coming to an end altogether owing to the increasing demands of the King's militaristic ambitions.[30]*

Then there was the aqueduct which had been intended to reach the height of the cathedral of Notre-Dame, and which Charles d'Aubigné found 'grotesque'.† It was part of an ambitious plan on the part of the King to divert the waters of the river Eure to feed the fountains of Versailles. Soldiers toiled and workmen died of fever from the marshes; in the end the project was abandoned.

Where the themes of plays at Saint-Cyr were concerned, 'holy theatre' was the desired note. Almost immediately however Racine ran into a problem with *Esther*. His play was taken straight from the biblical story of the virtuous Israelite Esther preferred by King Ahasuerus over the 'arrogant' and contemptuous Vashti, who had 'reigned a long time over his offended soul'. It was hardly difficult for the gossipmongers to equate Esther with Françoise and Athénaïs with Vashti. The emphasis was all on the renewal of Ahasuerus's life, thanks to the serenity of Esther: 'The darkest shade of care she wafts away / And turns my gloomiest days to gleaming day,' and again: 'Everything in Esther breathes innocence and peace.' By the end of the play the chorus of Israelites was saluting Ahasuerus's own virtue: 'The roaring lion is a peaceful lamb,' and thanking

---

* It has been calculated that in the twenty-four years Françoise owned the property she spent between eight and ten months there, if all the visits are added up.[31]

† Now a charming ruin, resembling a picture by Hubert Robert.

God for the outcome: 'In Thy hand is the heart of Kings.' To avoid the embarrassment of the amusing parallel to the King's love life, Racine hurriedly wrote a Prologue making it clear that Ahasuerus was nothing but a stage King ... This Prologue was spoken by Piety, played by Marguerite, Françoise's protégée and the star performer at Saint-Cyr, who declaimed it by heart.[32]

The King adored *Esther* and saw it at least five times. It confirmed him in his opinion of Saint-Cyr as 'a dwelling inhabited by Grace', in the words put into the mouth of Piety by Racine.[33] He loved the sight and sound of the young girls playing the chorus of Israelites: 'A swarm of innocent beauties / What amiable modesty is painted on their faces.' The court too was only too happy to find an enjoyable entertainment of which their newly puritanical master actually approved. Madame de Sévigné had wondered how a young girl could encompass the part of Ahasuerus. A little later she was able to see for herself, sitting behind the row of superior duchesses at the front. Afterwards she had one of those banal dialogues with royalty which nevertheless give pleasure to the most intelligent of their subjects.

'Madame, I have been assured that you were pleased,' began the King. 'Sire, I was charmed,' gushed Madame de Sévigné, 'all that I experienced is beyond words.' 'Racine has plenty of intelligence,' observed the King. 'Sire, he does indeed,' she agreed, 'but to be honest, the young people were also very good; they attacked their roles as if they had never done anything else.' 'Ah, how true that is!' were the King's final satisfying words. And off he went, leaving Madame de Sévigné the object of general envy by the court for the gracious notice she had received.[34]

Sixteen eighty-six, which marked the agreeable establishment of the 'seraglio' at Saint-Cyr, was also the King's *annus* *horribilis* where his health was concerned. Some premonition must have caused him to anchor Françoise to his side, for he certainly needed a wife at this point, not a mistress. We know a great deal – at times perhaps more than we want – about the health of Louis XIV from the detailed journals of his doctors, as well as those of Dangeau.[35] He was purged routinely once a month, known as 'taking medicine' (doses of herbs), as well as being given *lavements* (enemas) with mixtures of water, milk, honey and almond oil.* But early in 1686 a boil on his thigh, combined with the painful gout in his right foot, meant that he could hardly walk, despite tinctures of myrrh and aloes, red wine and absinthe. The boil was eventually cauterised, but it was not until May that the King could once again walk in his beloved Orangery at Versailles. In the meantime he had been obliged to lie down for Council meetings and shoot from his little carriage. In August the introduction of quinine helped the gout. But worse was to follow.

In the autumn the King developed an anal fistula, an abnormal fissure in that area. Painful as this was, the treatment, which involved separating the tissues with a scalpel (in an age, of course, before anaesthetics), was even more agonising. The Grand Operation, as it was later known, took place at seven o'clock in the morning of 19 November. It was kept a close secret. The people who shared it were Françoise, Father La Chaise, the doctor Fagon and the surgeon Félix. (It was said that Félix's hand trembled for the rest of his life – after the event.) Louis, the master of self-control, displayed exemplary fortitude and bore it all with a single cry of 'My God' when the first incision was

---

* Le Roy Ladurie has argued that bleeding and especially purging fulfilled 'a ritual of royal purity, comparable to the constant washing and bathing incumbent on the highest Brahmin circles in the Indian caste system'. Enemas were regularly prescribed by seventeenth-century doctors to rid the patient's body of its noxious humours.[36]

made.[37] His silent sufferings resembled those of the tortured Titan in the Fountain of Enceladus at Versailles, whose shoulder is half-crushed by the rocks of Mount Olympus; his eyes are staring, but only the noise of the water coming out of his speechless mouth can be heard.

Almost as extraordinary as Louis's fortitude under the knife was the fact that he actually held a Council meeting that night. The next morning he also held his normal *lever* for the court, although the sheen of perspiration could be seen on his dead-white face. Messages were sent to the royal family after the event, but they were forbidden to rush to him. Despite this, the Dauphin arrived at a gallop, in floods of tears. Athénaïs, who was with her daughter Madame la Duchesse at Fontainebleau, also hurried to Versailles only to be told that there was no crisis and she should go back. By the time Louis saw the old Prince de Condé on 22 November he was able to observe with sangfroid: 'People who weren't here believe my illness to have been great, but the moment they see me, they realise that I have scarcely suffered.' (It was in fact the Grand Condé who died a few weeks later.) Unfortunately another smaller operation was needed to remedy the suppuration following the first one. The second cure worked: by the middle of March 1687 Louis was able to mount a horse again for the first time.

During his year of illness, Louis had not been able to attend the unveiling of his equestrian statue on 16 March in the Place des Victoires in Paris, laid out by Mansart the previous year; the Dauphin went in his place.* Now, in 1687, he was able to make one of his rare visits to Paris and inspect it for himself. Here the great King saw himself mounted aloft, above bas-reliefs on the pedestal of the Passage of the Rhine. The scale was magnificent and certainly

* The present statue is a nineteenth-century replacement of the original, which was destroyed at the time of the French Revolution.

in keeping with the contemporary notion of Louis le Grand: twenty men could and did dine inside the belly of the horse during its installation. The vogue for statues of the King was spreading through the provinces and far beyond: Quebec, the capital of New France since 1663, was graced with a bust of Louis XIV in its Place Royale. Louisiana, the area of North America conquered by Robert La Salle in 1682, went further and commemorated the King in its actual name.[38] These salutations kept pace with his own policy of *réunions* mentioned earlier, that is to say, acquiring territories that he considered to be properly French. Then there were other lands which he considered had been bestowed upon France by marriages to heiress-princesses. The Spanish Netherlands was a prominent example of this.

It was in 1685 that the death of Liselotte's childless brother the Elector Palatine induced in Louis a new rush of territorial adrenalin: he would claim for Liselotte certain lands not covered by Salic Law (which prohibited female inheritance); or rather he claimed them for Monsieur, since by French law, the wife's rights were subsumed into the husband's. The League of Augsburg of 1686, an alliance against France which included Austria, Spain and Bavaria, was aimed at French expansionism. It provided the excuse for a disingenuous Declaration by the King to the effect that he was now obliged to resort to arms against his own will.

By the autumn of 1688 it was decided by the Council that a quick preventative war would secure the desired German cities. On 10 September six thousand troops entered Bonn, and the Dauphin himself was dispatched to seize Philippsburg. By December, Louvois was drawing up plans according to 'the intentions of His Majesty ... to destroy the city and citadel of Mannheim and all its houses'.[39] In the meantime Louis had quarrelled with the Papacy over the nomination of the new Bishop of Cologne and had taken the opportunity to seize Avignon.

The misery of Liselotte herself throughout this autumn can hardly be exaggerated. In particular she was horrified at the plans to raze Mannheim to the ground, the city which her father had rebuilt with such care: 'My name is being used for the ruin of my homeland.' She told the Dauphin that she saw the destruction of Heidelberg and Mannheim in her nightmares. Unable to control her suffering in public, Liselotte incurred the strong disapproval of the King, both for her sentiments and the uncontrolled manner of their expression. A few years earlier she had been ticked off indirectly by Louis – his confessor spoke to hers – for a variety of failings. Her language was vulgar: she had for example told the Dauphin that even if she saw him bollock-naked from the soles of his feet up, she would not be tempted by him (nor anyone else). She had allowed her ladies to indulge in gallantries, and had merely laughed with the wayward Marie-Anne de Conti about her own behaviour instead of reprimanding her.[40]

Liselotte was privately furious. She was not 'a chambermaid', she told her aunt Sophia, to be treated like this, unlike the King's precious Maintenon 'who was born to it'. She was not the Princesse de Conti's governess either, to stop her having lovers if she wanted them. Her frank language – and with her talk of crapping and pissing it *was* frank – she blamed on the King: he had said a hundred times that in the family one could say anything. And as for her ladies' gallantries, 'such conduct was not without precedent' and in fact 'quite usual at any court'. (Liselotte certainly had a point there.) In general, Liselotte's slavish devotion to Louis was fading. When she pleaded for her father and he merely replied: '*Je verrai*' (I shall see) Liselotte wrote bitterly that this royal formula was worse than a straightforward refusal.*[41]

---

* *Je verrai* was unpopular with others besides Liselotte: a one-armed Gascon soldier exclaimed: 'If I had said "I shall see" to my general, ordering me into battle, I should still have my arm.'[41]

The truth was that neither Liselotte as Second Lady nor the Dauphine as acting First Lady of Versailles was fulfilling Louis's expectations; the latter had to be instructed to form a suitable circle with the curt words on the subject of royal duties: 'We are not individuals.'[42] it was here that the absence of a Queen-figure mattered to the whole harmony of the court: this was a need that Françoise could not fulfil.

The King's decision to attack Germany in September 1688 was however to have unexpected consequences in that respect. There soon would be a Queen at Versailles, if not a Queen of France. The German foray meant that Louis failed to support the besieged Catholic King of England, James II, whom his own Parliament was trying to oust after a disastrous reign of under four years. He calculated that James's Protestant son-in-law William of Orange would not dare to invade England in late autumn. He was wrong. In the absence of the French navy, which Louis directed elsewhere, William sailed triumphantly towards England, landing on 4 November at Brixham in Torbay in the West Country. Within weeks Queen Mary Beatrice and her infant son were fleeing for France. As Louis XIV received the pathetic refugee, he was welcoming, of course, not only an unhappy woman, but also a policy: it was a policy of support for the Jacobite cause, as that of the exiled King James would soon become known.

CHAPTER 12

Grandeurs of the World

You see what becomes of the grandeurs of the world, we shall come to that, you and I.

– Louis XIV to the Dauphin, 1690

Mary Beatrice, the fugitive Queen of England who flung herself upon the mercies of Louis XIV, was no longer the shy, sweet princess who had passed through France on her way to marriage fifteen years earlier. Then the tender King had described himself to the pretty teenager as her 'godfather'; she was after all the daughter of a Mazarinette, Laura Martinozzi, who had been matched by her Cardinal-uncle to the future Duke of Modena. But Mary Beatrice's marriage had been from the first extremely testing both privately and publicly, and she had changed.

In 1673, at the age of fifteen, she found herself matched to an ageing and not particularly prepossessing prince twenty-five years her senior. James, then Duke of York, had been a dashing soldier in his youth, but somehow the Stuarts (those that kept their heads) did not improve with age. He was also a notorious *roué* like his brother Charles, but without the charm that enabled the Merry Monarch to carry these things off: so ugly were his mistresses that Charles wittily suggested they had been imposed upon him by his confessors. The young Catholic Duchess of York had to tolerate her husband's bastards, as well as the two Protestant daughters by his first wife, Mary and Anne. James's marriage was from the first extremely unpopular in the country:

understandably so, since Charles II's intention in agreeing
to it was to curry favour with the French King rather than
the English Parliament.

The Protestants were cheered, and Mary Beatrice devastated, by the fact that she appeared to be unable to bear
children that survived beyond infancy. Isabella, who died in
1681, reached four and a half; the rest died at birth or very
young, and there were at least four miscarriages, the last in
May 1684. That meant that the Protestant Mary, since 1677
wife of William of Orange, would in the course of time
succeed; her equally Protestant sister Anne, wife of George
of Denmark, would follow her, should William and Mary
have no children. Perhaps the Protestants were foolhardy in
supposing that a woman still in her twenties who had
conceived nine times in ten years would not do so again.
At any rate in the autumn of 1687 Mary Beatrice found
herself pregnant once more. Possibly the therapeutic mineral
waters at Bath which she had visited in September were
responsible for her renewed fertility, or even a visit to the
miraculous St Winifred's Well in North Wales a few years
earlier.

A day of thanksgiving in England was decreed on 23
December in the hope that 'the Queen might be the
joyful mother of children'. The invocation of the Irish
Catholic poet Diarmaid MacCarthy that God might
vouchsafe a son and heir to James, whom he called 'that
bright shining star of bliss', was not however generally
shared; nor for that matter was his lyrical description of
James himself.[1] The trouble was that this child if male
would be heir to the throne – and Catholic. By the time
Mary Beatrice did give birth to a healthy boy on 1 June
1688 it was found necessary to invent such fantasies as
the baby having been smuggled into the Queen's chamber
in a warming-pan: this despite the usual presence of a
vast number of courtiers on the occasion, including

Protestants.* Yet this birth, so long awaited by Mary Beatrice and James, was undoubtedly the catalyst for the crisis which erupted in English politics in the high summer of 1688, resulting in the invitation to William of Orange by a group of Whig grandees.

Helpless before William of Orange's invasion, which was joined by many of his alleged supporters, King James was taken prisoner. Queen Mary Beatrice and the little Prince James Edward escaped with the aid of the Duc de Lauzun, the Grande Mademoiselle's erstwhile fiancé. He had been brought out of his long imprisonment by the generosity of Anne-Marie-Louise. By this successful action Lauzun did at last restore himself to favour. Mother and son arrived at Calais on 21 December, awaited news of James, and then moved on to meet the King.

The result of all these eventful years, culminating in the ordeal of the flight, had been to make of Mary Beatrice a strong, intelligent woman of much resolution concealed under a modest, graceful and extremely feminine exterior. At thirty she had lost none of her youthful brunette beauty: she had an extremely good figure, on the thin side, but that only enhanced the impression of willowy grace. Her hair was 'black as jet', she had a white skin, full red lips, beautiful teeth, dark eyebrows and soulful dark eyes, even if they were currently 'dim with weeping'.[2] All this made her not dissimilar to her aunt Marie Mancini, although Mary Beatrice's features, set in a perfect oval face, were far more classical. It was no wonder that she had been one of the favourite subjects of court artists such as Lely and Kneller, who painted her over and over again.

---

* The real fantasy was the Protestant belief that the Queen was unable to conceive: four years later, she did in fact give birth to another healthy child who survived to maturity, Princess Louisa Maria, known for good reasons as 'the Consoler'. James of course had had numerous illegitimate children by other women.

Furthermore, this Queen was cosmopolitan, speaking and writing excellent French as well as Italian and English, and enough Latin to read from the scriptures in that language daily.³ Above all, Mary Beatrice was naturally and sincerely devout. She had never wavered in the Catholicism in which she had been raised, despite the winds of change around her. For all these qualities, the whole French court, including the King and Madame de Maintenon, were from the first Mary Beatrice's respectful admirers.

Mary Beatrice was greeted on 6 January at Versailles by Louis XIV and given all honours. She was then escorted to Saint-Germain-en-Laye, her new home by kind permission of the King, who also endowed the household generously and provided a lavish pension. Four days later Madame de Sévigné was in ecstasy over the court's newest royal acquisition, hailing her for her 'distinguished bearing and her quick wit'. This, coupled with Mary Beatrice's beauty, meant that she had 'natural sovereign power', as Lord Peterborough had reported long ago, inspecting his future bride for James II. The refugee Queen certainly understood the manners of Versailles. When Louis XIV fondled the six-month-old Prince of Wales, the Queen remarked that hitherto she had envied her tiny son's good fortune in knowing nothing of the calamities that beset him, but now 'I pity him because he is also unaware of Your Majesty's caresses and kindnesses.'⁴

When King James did arrive it was thanks to a discreetly blind eye turned by William III. The new King, as he would shortly become at the instance of Parliament, joint sovereign with his wife Mary, had no wish to add to the embarrassment of the family usurpation by keeping his dispossessed father-in-law a prisoner. So James was allowed to slip away, joining his wife and baby son at Saint-Germain. Mary Beatrice raised her hands to heaven. 'How happy I am! How happy I am!' she cried. The French court was less ecstatic.⁵ James certainly did not receive the golden opinions garnered by

Mary Beatrice. It was probably a question of age: James was fifty-five and this was his second full exile in a lifetime (there had been other, shorter episodes). People noted that Mary Beatrice was by now the more ambitious of the two, not only because she was still in her prime, but because she had a young son to root for.

Very quickly the King and Queen of England, supported by Louis both financially and emotionally, were integrated into the court rituals of Versailles, once the difference between English and French rules of kissing had been sorted out: English duchesses, unlike French ones, did not expect to be kissed, but the French got their way after protests. Only the Dauphine Marianne-Victoire found something – as usual – to grumble about, since Louis insisted on Mary Beatrice being accorded the full precedence due to a Queen. This technically displaced the Dauphine, whose husband was a mere heir, not a King; she tried to avoid being visibly demoted by receiving Mary Beatrice in bed – a well-known ploy which left her precedence open to question. Marianne-Victoire could not stay there for ever. In the end she did get out of bed during Mary Beatrice's visit for fear of the King's displeasure. The situation was further complicated when Mary Beatrice gave birth to a daughter Louisa Maria, in June 1692: here was a princess who was a King's daughter even if the King concerned was over the water. There was no other such legitimate princess at court. There would be further ploys as Louisa Maria grew up, for her to establish her true precedence, for others to avoid it.

In all this Louis himself was gravely concerned to support the Queen, who from the first appealed to his sense of chivalry, while Madame de Maintenon quickly established a proper friendship with her; the two women, a quarter of a century apart in age, had much in common as regards their piety and good sense, besides which the beautiful and virtuous Mary Beatrice was a faithful if suffering wife, exactly the sort of friend Françoise wanted the King to have. There were after all some less suitable contenders, even if it *was* only a question of friendship these days. For example, there was the Anglo-Irish beauty married to a French aristocrat, Elizabeth Hamilton, Comtesse de Gramont. Once known for good reason as '*la belle Hamilton*', a former raffish member of the court of Charles II, Elizabeth was now ostentatiously pious, corresponding regularly with Bishop Fénelon. She remained however sharp and amusing even if her colourful past was behind her; in seeking and on occasion demanding her presence, the King chose to manifest a small measure of independence from his secret wife. Louis's addiction to her company was so great that Françoise once confided to a friend that if she died, Elizabeth would take her place.

Mary Beatrice, the unfortunate refugee, posed none of these problems to Françoise. There was certainly no glint of naughtiness in her dark eyes, whereas '*la belle Hamilton*' in her conversation at least retained something of the wit and sauciness which had enchanted the English. Marly, the King's new pleasure-house where he loved to retreat with designated courtiers (mostly ladies), was close enough to Saint-Germain for Louis to pay Mary Beatrice almost daily visits in 1689, as Dangeau's *Journal* records.[6]

As to Versailles, the first version of his famous book entitled *The Way to Present the Gardens of Versailles* was actually produced in July 1689 to coincide with her visit 'to view the waters'.[7] According to Dangeau, numerous refreshments were served during a tour which started at the Fountain of Neptune. All this was exactly as laid down by Louis, with his usual eye for detail including the refreshments: 'Go along the top end of the Latona, pause there, go to the Marais where there will be fruit and ices ... Go to the Trois-Fontaines along the top and be sure that there are ices there.'

Ices were good, but it was also considerate of someone

trailing round Versailles in the July heat (a testing experience had by myriads since) that *The Way* also instructed: 'Be sure that the carriages are waiting at the gate to the Trianon.' In any case there were by now at least fifteen 'wheeled chairs' at Versailles, upholstered in damask of different colours, for the weary or the middle-aged. To say nothing of boats and gondolas, which thronged the canals and artificial water: another leisurely, beguilingly effortless way of enjoying Versailles. One is reminded that the iron-willed Sun King could also understand the weakness of others. As he sauntered around his *potager* (vegetable garden) the courtiers who followed were told that they could pick the fruit and eat it. In general the great outdoors brought out the best in Louis XIV.

This was the light-hearted man who adored his hunting dogs – his Pistolet, his Silvie, his Mignonne, his Princesse – as much as Liselotte liked her domestic pets, and had a particular love of English setters. He carried biscuits for them 'made daily by the royal pastrycooks' in his pockets, and designated a special chamber near his own, the Cabinet des Chiens, where he fed his dogs by hand. These favourites had magnificent beds of their own in all Louis's palaces, made of veneered walnut and ebony marquetry lined with crimson velvet (like their human counterparts the mistresses, for Louis looked after his own). It was the King who cancelled a Council meeting in February 1685 because the weather was so good and he wanted to be outside, with a jaunty parody of an air from Quinault and Lully's *Atys*: 'As soon as he saw his dog, he left everything for her / Nothing can stop him / When the fine weather calls.'[8] (The actual text referred to Bellona, the Goddess of War: 'As soon as he saw her / He left everything for her' – rather more the popular image of Louis XIV.)

Encouraged by King Louis XIV, who provided a small force of French troops and French officers, King James

273

left for Ireland in the spring of 1689. His plan was to recover his English throne through the back door of Ireland. Louis's farewell to his cousin was a reversal of the salutation by which he had said goodbye to the young Marie-Louise d'Orléans of Spain: 'I hope, Monsieur, never to see you again. Nevertheless if fortune so wishes it that we meet again, you will find me the same as you have always found me.'[9] Mary Beatrice was left behind, her dignity and good sense admired more than ever as the English royal fortunes waned. King James's personal campaign ended with his defeat by his son-in-law William III at the Battle of the Boyne on 12 July (NS) 1690, and he returned to France. The joint French and Irish campaign went on until it suffered a final defeat at the Battle of Aughrim a year later.

Thenceforward the exiled King languished at Saint-Germain, receiving none of the plaudits from the French court which his wife continued to merit. They found him irresolute and self-pitying: thus charmless by the standards of Versailles. Occasional forays were planned to recover his lost kingdom. None were successful. The defeat of the French navy off Cap La Hogue in May 1692 prevented the army assembled at Cherbourg from sailing. Four years later another potential invasion was cancelled due to lack of 'Jacobite' response over the water.

There was an irony here. If Louis XIV had chosen to uphold James II by force against William III as early as the autumn of 1688, he would certainly have altered the course of William's invasion and might even have successfully quashed it. The support of an Irish campaign and the subsequent terser initiatives were too little, too late. Instead Louis involved France – and the whole of Europe – in a struggle that would last for nearly ten years, by his ill-considered and in many ways brutal invasion of Germany. The destruction of cities which had given Liselotte nightmares in advance, as she confided to the Dauphin, proved every bit as horrific as she had anticipated.

Wars are always expensive, and long wars bring further depredations for every population whether their leaders are winning or losing the battles. This was certainly true of the so-called War of the League of Augsburg. The imploring words of Lalande's great *De Profundis*, which was first heard in 1689 – 'Out of the depths have I cried unto Thee' – stood for the anguish of many. So the people of France started to suffer; in addition the weather began to fail the Sun King, the cruel cold of 1692 leading to bad harvests and so to famine conditions by the winter of 1693. John Evelyn in England, who had once admired the grave boy King, now wrote of an ambitious monarch intent on pursuing his conquests while France was in 'the utmost misery and poverty for want of corn and sustenance'. In their desperation the poor were eating cats, horseflesh from horses thrown on the dust heap, and drinking the blood running from slaughtered beef and cattle in the abattoirs. The number of the deprived made to 'languish' by 'famine and misery', according to an official of the Bishop of Beauvais, was infinite.[10]

More spectacular if less painful, the glistening silver furniture of Versailles and the fine silver holders for orange trees were sacrificed: an inventory drawn up in 1706 of all the silver melted down between 1689 and 1690 lists about twelve hundred objects including borders of mirrors, chandeliers, basins, urns, flagons, plates, salt-cellars, as well as 'some of the most sumptuous furniture that ever existed'. So the glamour of Versailles, the showplace of a King in the prime of his glory, began to seep away. Furthermore, the death of Louvois in 1691 meant that Louis's own industry in directing had to be redoubled: Dangeau thought he worked an extra three or four hours as a result. 'Having given his orders as a general ... he then worked as King on the affairs of state, of which he neglected nothing, not the slightest detail.'[11]

As for war itself, it was no longer quite so glorious as in those palmy days when the King progressed to Flanders with one Queen and two mistresses. Yet the ladies still went. Madame de Maintenon's account of it all in the early summer of 1692 is vivid enough, if depressing. Louis joined the army in May, in order to besiege Namur, on the Meuse; the town fell to the French at the end of June. Where Racine, the heroic writer, found himself 'so enchanted, so dazzled by the brilliance of the shining swords and muskets, so deafened by the sounds of the side-drums, swords and kettle-drums', Françoise the middle-aged woman struck a very different note. She described to a correspondent what it was like to travel with the King: the horror of the bad roads, the carriages lurching and falling, ladies hanging on for dear life. The water was bad, wine rough, the bakers were for some strange reason concentrating on the need of the army and the royal servants could not find bread. The town (Namur) was very muddy and the pavements ghastly, since the minor roads served as general privies. Besides, the whole town shook with the firing of the artillery. And the King had gout in both his feet. To another correspondent, a Dame at Saint-Cyr, Françoise struck a slightly lighter note: 'If one could conscientiously wish a nun to venture outside her convent, I would like you to experience for a short while the places of the war we have passed through. You would be delighted, Madame, to smell only tobacco, hear only the drum, eat only cheese ...' She herself, added Françoise, who was beginning to suffer badly from rheumatism, would willingly be back doing tapestry with 'our dear ladies'.[12]

Back at Versailles, three deaths, a wedding and a retirement began the inevitable rearrangement of an ageing court. The first and most tragic death was that of Marie-Louise, the ill-fated girl whom Louis had dispatched to be Queen of Spain, in March 1689. She was twenty-eight. Her death, after years of unhappiness, was rumoured to be caused by poison, and for once there may have been some substance in the story that she had been given arsenic. Or perhaps there had been drugs to remedy the sterility which the Spanish blamed on the unfortunate girl rather than their King: those might have proved poisonous. Marie-Louise was violently ill for two days with vomiting and gastro-enteritical pains before dying. On her deathbed she told the French Ambassador that she did not after all believe she had been poisoned, although that had once been her suspicion. (Nevertheless he relayed the rumours back to France.)[13]

Throughout her ten years as consort to the cretinous and cruel Carlos, Marie-Louise had tried hard to fulfil her role as France's envoy, fighting the influence of Austria in Spain. In the process she had made many enemies. Now the position of Queen of Spain was once more vacant, and this time the winner – in terms of material prospects but no other way – was a plain German princess, Maria Anna of Neuburg, in the Habsburg sphere of influence. She had nothing to commend her but a large bosom and a family reputation for fertility: Pope Alexander VIII coarsely remarked of the Neuburg princesses that they had only to hang their husbands' breeches at the end of the bed to get pregnant. Unfortunately neither Carlos II nor his breeches were able to have the desired effect, and it became increasingly certain that he would die childless, with enormous consequences for the whole European balance of power.

Louis XIV greeted the news of Marie-Louise's death, including the rumours of poisoning, with outward calm: court mourning was ordered and all balls and masquerades cancelled. He talked of the paternal affection he had felt for the dead young woman, 'and besides she could contribute much to peace between her husband and myself'. As for the rumours, any attempt to investigate them on behalf of

France would, he felt, produce 'neither usefulness nor satisfaction'. But Louis took pains to break the news of Marie-Louise's death personally to her father, when he woke at his usual hour of 11 a.m. The Comtesse de La Fayette reported that Monsieur was as sad about this 'as he could ever be about anything'.[14] It had indeed been 'Farewell. For ever,' as Louis had said so imperiously to Marie-Louise when she left, weeping, for Spain in 1679.

The second death had a more immediate effect on the court: that of the Dauphine Marianne-Victoire in the spring of 1690. She was in her thirtieth year. Her health had never been good, especially since the birth of her last child, although it was discovered later by autopsy that she actually died of lung disease. By degrees she spent more time lying in bed than engaged in the Dauphine-like social activities which the King thought appropriate. Nevertheless, unlike Marie-Louise, Marianne-Victoire had produced three healthy boys, three dukes with the titles of Bourgogne, Anjou and Berry, who were respectively seven, six and three at the time of her death on 20 April. Marianne-Victoire's deathbed was sufficiently protracted for her to give a blessing to each one of her sons, telling 'my poor little Berry' that she gave him it with a good heart, 'although you cost me dear'. Liselotte for her part wept to see colours of the House of Wittelsbach, which both German princesses shared, over the coffins. At the same time she took a secret oath to survive the hated 'old Rumpumpel' (Maintenon), who was after all nearly twenty years older.[15]

Louis XIV took the opportunity to counsel his son: 'You see what becomes of the grandeurs of the world, we shall come to that, you and I.' Marianne-Victoire was accorded the same honours in death as the late Queen Marie-Thérèse, although according to etiquette, the King did not wear mourning. This was because Marianne-Victoire ranked as Louis's daughter (although in fact his daughter-in-law), and the King of France did not wear mourning for his children. There was another tricky point of etiquette when the body of the late Dauphine was ceremonially laid out, with her face exposed. The ladies who did not have the right to be seated in the Dauphine's presence in her lifetime were taking the opportunity to sit down during their watch, now she was dead. It had to be explained that an uncovered face still counted as being in the presence of the Dauphine, and so standing must be maintained.[16]

The third death was that of the Grande Mademoiselle, at the age of sixty-six, on 5 April 1693. Her vast inheritance, which had dominated her life and prospects, finally for the worse not the better, passed to Monsieur, the beginning of the great fortune of the Orléans family which would begin to rival in monetary terms that of the senior Bourbon branch. Lauzun, who had been her heir, forfeited at last the great love she had borne for him, by his infidelities and his ingratitude for the payments she had made to free him from prison. She refused to see him on her deathbed. (He subsequently married a girl of fifteen.)

The Grande Mademoiselle had spent many of her last months writing a commentary on *The Imitation of Christ* in which the salient message ran as follows: 'Greatness of birth and the advantages bestowed by wealth and by nature should provide all the elements of a happy life ... yet there are many people who have had all these things and are not happy. The events of my own past would give me enough proof of this without looking for examples everywhere.'[17] It was a sad but accurate judgement on an existence which neither in public nor in private had fulfilled its promise. And as a judgement it also had something in common with the melancholy message of Louis XIV to his son on the death of the Dauphine.

The retirement was that of Athénaïs, and the marriage that of her younger surviving daughter, Françoise-Marie, one of the two children who were the fruits of her reconciliation with the King. But there was no connection between the two events. Indeed, it was a sign of the times, this distancing of Athénaïs, representative of the King's seamy past, from her offspring, that the mother was not even invited to the daughter's wedding.

It has been seen that shortly after the King's secret marriage, Athénaïs was removed from her palatial suite of apartments, similar to a Queen's, and installed in her Appartement des Bains on the ground floor, once the scene of such luxurious dissipation with the King. In 1691 she made the mistake, in a fit of temper, of announcing via Bishop Bossuet her departure 'for ever' from the court and headed for Paris. Swiftly – after all Louis knew his Athénaïs – the King gave the Appartement des Bains to Athénaïs's son, the Duc du Maine.* It was said that the young man was in such a hurry to take advantage of the King's offer that he had his mother's furniture thrown out of the window 'by orders of the Duc du Maine'.[18] Unfilial as such conduct might be, one has to bear in mind that Françoise, not Athénaïs, was the true mother-figure in Maine's life, plagued by his physical disability: 'the limping boy', as Liselotte crudely called him.

The rest of Athénaïs's life was devoted to good works, much as that of her pious mother had been, whose example she followed at long last. One notes that both Louis and Athénaïs, whose mothers had been friends, reverted to the path of virtue, as though the maternal pull was too great – that, or the influence of their mothers in Heaven, as contemporaries would have believed. Athénaïs's once-

* Today at Versailles only the original shutters remain in place in the former Appartement des Bains of Athénaïs: dolphins spouting water, shells and seaweed can be discerned (the marble bath, as already noted, is now in the Orangery, having had an exciting period when it was given to Madame de Pompadour).

An engraving of the visit of Louis XIV to Saint-Cyr in 1704, the superior establishment for the education of poor but well-born girls founded by Madame de Maintenon; the King took a great interest in Saint-Cyr, enjoying music and theatricals there.

The Château de Maintenon bought by Madame de Maintenon with money given by the King; later donated to her niece Françoise-Charlotte on her marriage to the Duc de Noailles; as ever the King was interested in making improvements to it. *Above*, the aquaduct which was abandoned; *right*, Madame de Maintenon's bedroom as it is today.

PARTE II. LIBRO X.   43

(*left*) Marie-Jeanne d'Aumale acted as Madame de Maintenon's secretary, and is an important source for her later life; the King enjoyed her lively company.

(*centre*) The Dauphin and Dauphine: the Dauphin was a good-natured man who lived only for hunting; Marianne-Victoire of Bavaria was intelligent and cultured but lacked any kind of beauty. They are shown here with their three sons the Ducs de Bourgogne (right), Anjou (centre) and Berry (on his mother's lap).

(*bottom*) The betrothal of 'Monsieur', the King's only brother, to his first cousin Henriette-Anne d'Orléans, 1661; from a fan.

Henriette-Anne of England, first wife of Monsieur, Duc d'Orléans, with her favourite spaniel Mimi, given to her by her brother Charles II; Henriette-Anne loved the dog so much that she even danced holding her in the Court Ballet.

The royal family of France painted by Jean Nocret in 1670, at the request of Monsieur, in the guise of gods and goddesses. On the left Monsieur (seated) has his own family grouped round him including his first wife Henriette-Anne (standing). Louis XIV has his wife Marie-Thérèse of Spain (seated lower, on his right) patting the Dauphin's head and his cousin the Grande Mademoiselle (standing, right) at the edge of the picture.

Henriette-Anne, Duchesse d'Orléans, with a medallion of her husband Monsieur; his appearance shows the dark 'Medici' strain which many of the descendants of Henri IV and Marie de Medicis shared.

Henriette-Anne with her spaniel Mimi on a stool and a musician playing; the toilette of a great lady (held in her bedroom) was a social occasion; from a fan.

Monsieur holding a portrait of his favourite daughter, Marie-Louise d'Orléans.

(*below left*) Liselotte, the German princess who became Monsieur's second wife, known as 'Madame', and wrote amusing, often bawdy letters home describing the French court.

(*below right*) Liselotte, Duchesse d'Orléans, in later life; she herself mocked her vast figure and weather-beaten face, due to hunting for long hours without wearing a mask as was customary for ladies.

Marie-Louise d'Orléans, niece of Louis XIV and the highest-ranking young woman at the French court, since he had no legitimate daughters; she was married off to the grotesque King Carlos II of Spain for reasons of state; her beauty is a darker version of her mother, Henriette-Anne.

Marie-Anne, Princesse de Conti, daughter of Louis XIV by Louise de La Vallière, was generally rated the most beautiful of his daughters and he spoiled her; having been widowed childless very young, she declined to marry again but lived a life of happy dissipation at court.

The two surviving daughters of Louis XIV by Athénaïs de Montespan: Françoise-Marie who married the heir to the Duc d'Orléans and Louise-Françoise who married the Duc de Bourbon and was known as Madame la Duchesse; both scandalised the court with their wayward and often louche behaviour.

Bénédicte Duchesse du Maine, wife of the King's illegitimate son; tiny, described by Liselotte as 'the little toad', Bénédicte was extremely intelligent with a real interest in the arts which she patronised in her salon at Sceaux.

Louise Benedicte de Bourbon Duchesse du Maine; c̸
une Mademoiselle de Charôlois fille de henry jules, de Bourbon, Prince de Condé, et d'Ch
tine de Bauierre Naquit le 8. de Novembre 1676. Elle a Espouse Louis Auguste Bourb
e du Maine, dans la Chapelle du Chasteau Royal de Versailles le 19. Mars 1692. en
rence du Roy. de Monseig.r le D'auphin, des Princes et Princesses.

Mary Beatrice d'Este, daughter of the Duke of Modena, the Catholic second wife of James Duke of York, later James II; her combination of virtue, dignity and beauty impressed Louis XIV and Madame de Maintenon.

Queen Mary Beatrice.

The English royal family in exile at Saint-Germain-en-Laye, as guests of Louis XIV in 1694: (*left to right*) James Edward Prince of Wales whose birth as a Catholic heir helped to bring about the crisis of 1688 and led to his parents' ejection; Queen Mary Beatrice; Princess Louisa Maria, born in exile, aged two; James II who was twenty-five years older than his second wife and died in 1701.

A hunting-party at Saint-Germain-en-Laye, given by Louis XIV 'to alleviate the misfortunes' of James II and Mary Beatrice, depicted on a Sèvres vase.

Letter from Adelaide, Duchesse de Bourgogne to her 'dear grandmother' Madame Royale of Savoy when she was fifteen; Adelaide apologises for the fact that the entertainments of carnival have prevented her replying sooner; she is happy to hear that her grandmother has had good reports of her, wishing to please her in everything and preserve the friendship her grandmother has always had for her. From the State Archives of Turin.

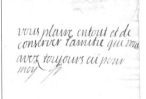

ce 20 mars 1700

Il ny a point de temps ou je ne
retour vos lettre avec plaisir ma
chere grand maman mais il
est vray le carnaval ma bien
occupé et que les bals ont des
suittes qui prenois tout mon
temps cest ce qui ma empeché
de vous ecrire je suis ravie
de ce que les relations quin
a faittes de moy vous ont
esté agreable desirant de

Madame la Duchesse
de Bourgogne   1700 20. Mars

vous plaire en tout et de
conserver l'amitie que vous
avez toujours eü pour
moy

Adelaide Duchesse de Bourgogne.

Adelaide Duchesse de Bourgogne in hunting-costume (red was a favourite colour) in front of the Grand Canal at Fontainebleau; her slim figure is well displayed.

The marriage of Adelaide of Savoy and Louis Duc de Bourgogne, grandson of Louis XIV, on 7 December 1697, the day after her twelfth birthday, in the Royal Chapel at Versailles; note the dominating figure of the King compared to the tiny bride and groom. By Antoine Dieu.

Perspective view of the Château de Versailles in 1668 before it had become the King's official seat.

(*centre*) Construction of the Château de Versailles in about 1679; although the King moved there officially in 1682, when he was in his forties, building works continued for most of the reign, causing much discomfort to court ladies, with the noise, the dirt and the smell of wet plaster.

The Basin at Versailles containing the mute agonised figure of the giant Enceladus with water spouting from his mouth; Louis XIV showed the same fortitude during the ordeal of his operation for a fistula.

At a court function at Fontainebleau in September 1714, the Duchesse de Berry (born Marie-Élisabeth d'Orléans) can be seen in her black and white widow's weeds following the death of her husband earlier in the year (fourth from right).

The Orangerie at Versailles which can still be seen; Louis XIV took much pleasure in his orange trees which he acquired from many sources and also gave as presents to his favourites.

Louis XIV adored his sporting dogs: Bonne, Nonne and Ponne are here shown; he fed them himself in the luxurious closet known as the Cabinet des Chiens with biscuits specially made by the royal chef.

Interlaced double L is taken from the wood-carving round the windows of the King's chamber at Versailles.

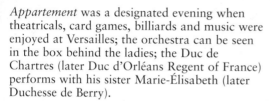

Appartement was a designated evening when theatricals, card games, billiards and music were enjoyed at Versailles; the orchestra can be seen in the box behind the ladies; the Duc de Chartres (later Duc d'Orléans Regent of France) performs with his sister Marie-Élisabeth (later Duchesse de Berry).

Tobacco was a taste enjoyed by women as well as men, including the illegitimate daughters of Louis XIV, although it scandalised their elders that ladies should smoke pipes 'like sailors'.

The cascade at Marly, the pleasure-house of Louis XIV, where formalities were minimal and invitations were coveted.

The most famous image of Louis XIV in later years by Hyacinthe Rigaud in
1701; the heroic beauty of his youth has vanished while leaving an air of
impregnable majesty tinged with melancholy.

famous beauty had vanished. Ten years after her retirement, when Athénaïs was sixty, Liselotte was able to crow over the terrifying sight that the former favourite represented: the skin that looked like paper 'which children have folded over and over', the whole texture a mass of tiny lines, the beautiful blonde hair entirely white.[19] (Was Liselotte, grossly fat by her own admission, with her big red face at which no one had ever swooned, or ever would, quite the right person to rejoice?)

It is true that Athénaïs did occasionally haunt Versailles. There she was compared poetically by Marguerite de Caylus to 'those unhappy souls who return to the places where they lived to expiate their faults'.[20] At the same time there is no reason to suppose that she was all that melancholy, with the satisfaction of atonement through good works to support her (any more than Louise de La Vallière, busy with her own expiation, was unhappy). A later confessor, Father Pierre François de La Tour, even persuaded Athénaïs to apologise to her husband. With her practical streak, Athénaïs was happy enough mending shirts for the poor, dining frugally, and dressing in crude fabrics at the orders of the clergy, as once she had been feasting (a little too much) and dressing in diamonds to divert the King.

The next generation, however, did not present that interesting mixture of sexuality reined in by religious fervour which their parents had exhibited. Françoise-Marie, for whom the glorious fate of marriage to Monsieur's only son, Philippe Duc de Chartres, was proposed, had no such inhibitions. This was a yet higher step for a (legitimised) bastard: Françoise-Marie's sister and half-sister had married Princes of the Blood, the Duc de Bourbon and the Prince de Conti respectively, but Philippe was a Grandson of France, and in direct line to the throne, after his three cousins, the young dukes. This meant that Françoise-Marie, younger than Madame la Duchesse and Marie-Anne de

Conti by five and twelve years respectively, now took precedence over them, and they were obliged to call her 'Madame'. In vain the angry sisters tried to get away with cries of 'Darling' and 'Sweetheart': the King had to utter a rebuke at this dereliction of etiquette.

For Liselotte, the horrified mother of the bridegroom, it was a step altogether too far. She cried all night before submitting because she had no choice. The King's will was law. She responded, however, to the King's request with the briefest of curtseys, according to Saint-Simon, a mere *pirouette* in ballet terms, before turning on her heel. Louis, for his part, swept such a deep bow or *révérence* that by the time he straightened himself all he could see was the retreating back of his sister-in-law. In the public language of Versailles, this was the nearest she could come to expressing her disgust.

Liselotte was bitter on two counts. First, there was her rooted objection to the stain of bastardy as such, which for her could never be wiped away by legitimisation (at least Athénaïs had been officially separated from Montespan at the time of Françoise-Marie's birth). Then she suspected Monsieur's favourites of persuading him to agree, in return for the King's help in other ways; and of course 'the old trollop' was at the back of the whole thing. Liselotte outdid herself in venom on the subject of her future daughter-in-law: 'the most disagreeable person in the world, with her crooked figure and her ugly face, although she considers herself a raving beauty and is forever fussing about her appearance and covering herself with beauty spots'. Madame behaved, wrote Saint-Simon, like Ceres whose daughter Proserpine had been taken down to the underworld by Pluto – except she was bewailing a son, not a daughter.[21]

In truth Françoise-Marie was more than adequately pretty in youth, as her pictures show: not unlike her catlike sister Madame la Duchesse, if not quite as ravishing as Marie-

Anne. She does seem to have had some curvature of the spine, but her figure was none the less 'stately', with a fine bosom. She had remarkable eyes and good if long teeth. Her hair grew 'prettily' even if it was not particularly thick and she had long eyelashes, although her eyebrows were scanty. It was her character that grated, and her upbringing or rather lack of it. She had been born to a couple no longer passionately in love, and she had not been raised by Madame de Maintenon (even though she was born at her château). The result was a wilful child who had been spoilt and indulged with sporadic but ineffective correction. There was something touching – but significant – about the scene in which her august destiny was broken to Françoise-Marie. She was dressed up magnificently, like a fashion-doll used by dressmakers to display their wares, but she actually imagined she was going to be scolded until Madame de Maintenon took her on to her lap.[22]

Unfortunately Françoise-Marie had the violent urges of both her parents but none of the style and charisma which made them, even at their worst, magnificent. She neither pretended to love her husband nor expected him to love her. 'All that matters is that he should marry me,' the future Duchesse de Chartres, lording it over her sisters, was reputed to have said. It was true that she had the Mortemart wit, that languishing tone of voice in which impossible things could be said, and it was through Françoise-Marie and her descendants that the 'wit' would be perpetuated into the eighteenth century long after the death of its most famous exemplar. But as a teenager she already drank heavily, and within a few years as Duchesse de Chartres, she was 'drunk as drunk' three or four times a week. A love of food combined with the Mortemart tendency to plumpness meant that her fine figure degenerated: besides, Françoise-Marie, with her mother's high fertility, gave birth to seven healthy children, and repeated pregnancies did not help. Her pride was inordinate: it was said that even on her *chaise percée* (commode) she remembered she was a Daughter of France, and her husband wryly nicknamed her Madame Lucifer.[23]

As for Liselotte, she might be compelled to bow to the will of the monarch, but when her quaking son came to break the news that he had agreed to the match (what could poor Philippe do against the King and his father?) she slapped him in the face. It was a slap which echoed throughout Versailles – but with a hollow sound. Whatever Liselotte's values, Françoise-Marie, Duchesse de Chartres, illegitimate at birth, was now the Second Lady at Versailles after her disgruntled mother-in-law.

Saint-Cyr and its virtuous charming seraglio was at least a pure pleasure for the King and Madame de Maintenon, guaranteed salubrious entertainment. This was in contrast to a Versailles which offered endless gambling and a thrice-weekly social evening known simply as *Appartement*. Gambling in itself was not seen as wrong: both Anne of Austria and the late Queen had been great gamblers, as had Mazarin; the King had had to pay Marie-Thérèse's debts after her death. A courtier was expected 'to play like a man of honour', according to the Chevalier de Méré, 'ready to win or lose without showing whether one has won or lost in one's expression or behaviour'. It could be a form of social advancement: the Marquis de Dangeau for example, he of the *Journals*, was admired for his gambling skills: 'Nothing distracts him, he neglects nothing, he profits by everything.'[24]*

The games concerned sound simple enough, but so do most gambling games to those who are not wagering on them. *Bassette* for example came from Venice, and included

---

* Apart from his gambling skills, Dangeau was a licensed jester, able to impersonate Louis XIV, to whom he bore a strong physical resemblance.

a banker, with players betting on the draw of their cards; Louis got so angered by the excessive losses of this game that he forbade it in 1679. *Reversi*, from Spain, a particular favourite of Louis himself according to Liselotte, was introduced by him during the court's expedition to Strasbourg to give Marie-Thérèse something to do; the winner scored the lowest points and made the least tricks. *Tric-trac* was a game of dice to advance pawns across a board. *Lansquenet*, which dethroned the popular *Reversi*, was a card game introduced into France by German mercenary soldiers (*Landsknechts*). By 1695 it was 'all the rage': even simpler than *Reversi*, it consisted once again of betting on the draw. For some reason, *Lansquenet* aroused particularly foul language in its frustrated players; the King ordered an end to the swearing but he could not successfully forbid *Lansquenet*. There were many others, including the long-established Lottery, passing or enduring fashions: *Portique*, where little ivory balls were rolled through arches, and another somewhat similar 'game of skill' invented by Louis himself in 1689, a form of hoop-la.[25]

As money got tighter, the gambling became more frenzied. Louis would have to pay enormous gambling debts on behalf of his son the Dauphin, his daughter Madame la Duchesse, and in time for his grandson the Duc de Bourgogne. No wonder the stern Father Bourdaloue lashed out in one of his sermons in the chapel of Versailles: 'Gambling without measure is not a diversion for you [the court] but an occupation, a profession, a traffic, a passion, a rage, a fury. It causes you to forget your duties, it deranges your households, it dissipates your revenues.'[26] And yet the King could not control it, this instinct for amusement, any amusement, diversion, any diversion, where the younger members of court were no longer engaged by the solemn rituals and found going to the King's pleasure-house at Marly frankly dull.

Informality was deliberate at Marly and the wearing of full court dress was abolished. A charming custom arose whereby courtiers found all they needed overnight including *robes de chambres* and toiletries already laid out in their rooms (as in some modern luxury hotel). This demonstrated Louis's thoroughness as a host – or perhaps his passion for controlling every detail of life around him. Work had begun in 1679 and the first fête was held in July 1684; for the rest of the reign, annual visits were paid in increasing numbers. Those who were frequently present were known as *'les Marlys'*. With time informality was demonstrated even by the methods of dining: there was a sideboard piled with plates, glasses, wine and water, and a mechanical table *à la clochette* (summoned by a bell from below) so that the meal was virtually servant-free. Even the method of invitation was informal – or intended to be (it was in fact extremely testing). Would-be guests had to step forward and propose themselves: 'Sire, Marly?' Afterwards an emissary either confirmed or denied the visit. In spite of all this, Marly was still not a riot of fun, and due to the presence of water, Liselotte at least came to complain about mosquitoes. There was also a great deal of tea- and coffee-drinking, even if the British Ambassador would have preferred a good Burgundy to 'all these stupid drinks from the Indies'.[27]*

Compared to all this, Saint-Cyr seemed to offer not only an agreeable alternative but a solution to the King's equal need for diversion. It was therefore an enormous disappointment in the early 1690s when King Louis's troubles with his own Catholic Church, spilling out from his troubles

---

* Marly today is a place of extraordinary natural beauty, still sign-posted as *Demeure champêtre du Roi* (the King's Rustic Retreat), although the buildings were destroyed at the time of the French Revolution. The verdant site is on a gentle slope looking down towards Paris and up to where there were once cascades; the surviving reservoir is a reminder of the centrality of water in the vision of Louis XIV.

with the Holy See, complicated the simple establishment of Saint-Cyr. There was a warning shot in January 1691 when Racine proposed another edifying tragedy, *Athalie*, to be performed by the young ladies, in succession to the enormously successful (and edifying) *Esther*. Athalie herself, another powerful female like Vashti in the earlier play, was declared to be against the natural order as a ruler on the grounds of her sex: a reference perhaps to the situation in Britain where Mary, ungrateful daughter of James II, was co-ruling with her husband William. Here was Athalie, an 'impious stranger / Seated, alas, on the throne of kings', and again: 'This haughty woman with her head held high / Intruded in a court reserved for men.'[28]

Trouble was made however by Madame de Maintenon's confessor the Abbé Godet des Marais over the performance of this piece by young girls. Godet des Marais had just succeeded Gobelin because the latter now felt himself too humble to counsel such an exalted lady. Godet des Marais on the other hand was professionally forthright. *Athalie* was unsuitable for the Demoiselles but it was not unsuitable in itself. After all, the emphasis of the text was all on the vanquishing of the unnatural Athalie, followed by the triumphant coronation of the rightful ruler-by-blood the young boy Joas. Here were more contemporary allusions: either to the future restoration of James II, or to Louis's ultimate heir, the eight-year-old Duc de Bourgogne, France's 'dearest delight' and, it was to be hoped, France's future Joas.[29]

In the end the piece was performed by the girls in ordinary clothes, a sort of concert performance. When King James and Queen Mary Beatrice asked to see *Athalie* in February, Madame de Maintenon agreed, but once again there were to be no costumes. This time Father La Chaise and the theologian the Abbé François Fénelon, tutor to Bourgogne since 1691, did attend, but still Françoise's confessor declined.

The Abbé Godet des Marais, ten years younger than Madame de Maintenon, was prominent among those who encouraged her in her feelings of destiny, the one chosen by God where the King was concerned. But he also preached a distaste for the theatre, as opposed to good works, which Madame de Maintenon did not share (still less Louis XIV). It was all about the threat to innocence: Marguerite de Caylus, the best actress of them all, was demoted from her part because she was felt to be unbecomingly adept at the art. The ecclesiastical hold tightened in 1692 when it was deemed unacceptable for Saint-Cyr to remain outside the structure of the Church. Henceforward the lives of the girls, and the ladies who taught them, would be much more conventionally those of nuns and aspirant nuns.

Louis XIV had been involved in a bitter struggle with the Papacy over ecclesiastical revenues, the so-called 'regalian rights', for some years. The Saint-Cyr foundation became involved in the controversy when he tried to use the revenues of the Abbey of Saint-Denis to fund it. The Holy See complained vociferously about a foundation partaking of religious revenues where the women concerned had taken no vows. Madame de Maintenon's position in all this was sensitive, since whatever private assurances the Papacy had received about her status, in the eyes of the world she had none – or worse still, that of mistress.

So Saint-Cyr was changed, the uniform was changed, although Louis XIV, with his eye for detail and his dislike of the morbid, suggested that at least the young ladies should not be stripped of their charming *bronzé* leather gloves. These were a fashion item much in demand, also as love tokens. (Samuel Pepys laid out ten shillings on such, 'very pretty and all the mode'.) No wonder the King, a sentimental admirer of young women, protested: 'Would you take from them their cloaks, their gold crosses and the gloves?' he enquired plaintively. The gloves at least were restored. Madame de Maintenon's authority as supreme head of Saint-Cyr was however not touched. As her girls sang to her in 1695: 'You are our faithful foundress ...'[30]

The death of Marianne-Victoire in 1690 had left the Dauphin, still not yet thirty, in theory the most eligible bachelor in Europe – if you accepted the fact that his father was otherwise engaged. But the Dauphin, like Louis XIV before him, chose domestic bliss over duty, on the grounds that by providing three sons, he had already done more than enough. He settled down at Meudon with his mistress Marie-Émilie Jolie de Choin, who had originally been a lady-in-waiting to his favourite half-sister Marie-Anne de Conti. No beauty – with her short legs and round face she looked 'like a bull terrier' – she was intelligent and very sympathetic. She provided him with the security that his over-severe childhood had stolen from him; this comfort was symbolised by a pair of 'monstrously large breasts' which were said to 'charm' him because he could beat on them 'as if they were kettle-drums'.[31] It seems likely that in the course of time this couple too went through some form of morganatic marriage for which after all nothing was needed except a priest and two witnesses.

No French Queen (and no prospect of one) and no Dauphine meant that Liselotte was now the First Lady of Versailles. At least she did not have to pay the despised 'old woman' the respect due to the King's wife; offering her the chemise at her *lever* for example as senior royal lady. It seemed unlikely that Liselotte would be ousted from the '*métier*' which made her groan – but which she also treasured – until the marriage of France's 'dearest delight' in the shape of Louis's grandson the Duc de Bourgogne.

In view of the wartime situation, that was certainly a match which would be dictated by strong diplomatic considerations. The League of Augsburg had been transformed into the Grand Alliance by the adherence of England and Holland. In 1693 Louis failed to capture Liège (he never joined his troops in the field again). Two years later William III took back Namur for the Alliance. Flanders was not the only sphere of action: in the south France invaded Spain.

The sufferings of France itself (never mind the other countries) were beginning to be denounced by those quite close to royal circles. Prominent among these was the Abbé Fénelon, Bourgogne's own preceptor, who had managed to establish a tender, quasi-paternal relationship with the boy. 'I will leave the Duc de Bourgogne behind the door,' he said, 'and with you I will be no more than little Louis.' Fénelon, now in his early forties, had been a disciple of Bossuet. Tall and ascetic-looking, he had famously burning eyes and preached 'like a torrent', according to Saint-Simon. But Fénelon had sweetness too, and a genuine love of the young: he wrote a treatise on girls' education for Louis XIV's devout friends the Duc and Duchesse de Beauvillier who, having nine daughters, certainly stood in need of it.[32]

Fénelon was fearless, as Bossuet and Bourdaloue had been before him. He had denounced the Revocation of the Edict of Nantes in a strong letter to Madame de Maintenon. Now he wrote the 'Anonymous Letter to Louis XIV' of 1694, which, via Beauvillier, may even have reached the King himself; certainly Françoise knew of it. He referred to the putative 2 million dead in the recent famine. As for the King: 'You live as though with a fatal blindfold over your eyes.' And again: 'The whole of France is nothing but a huge desolate hospital.'[33]

Appropriately enough, Louis now sought to use Bourgogne's marriage to a Savoyard princess as part of a package which would bring about peace between France and Savoy. It would also hopefully control the mercurial and wily Duke of Savoy, Victor Amadeus, who with his numerous changing allegiances coupled with his advantageous geographical position, was showing form as the gadfly of Europe. Fortunately Victor Amadeus did have a daughter, still very young, but of an appropriate age to wed Bourgogne one day. Her mother was the French princess Anne-Marie d'Orléans, like the unhappy Marie-Louise a daughter of Monsieur by his first marriage to Henriette-Anne.

The name of the child was Adelaide. She was three and a half years younger than her proposed bridegroom Bourgogne. Since Victor Amadeus specialised in tantalising his would-be allies with the other possibilities before him, he was also considering an Austrian Habsburg prince for his little daughter, maybe the Archduke Charles. Time would reveal whether Adelaide was to be yet another unhappy cipher at a foreign court, where the 'grandeurs of the world' very often led to acute unhappiness on the part of the imported bride, as witness Liselotte and Marianne-Victoire in France. Or perhaps this particular princess would have inherited something of the special grace of her grandmother Henriette-Anne which would enable her to survive and flourish ...

CHAPTER 13

Becoming a Child Again

Everyone at court is becoming a child again.

– Liselotte, Duchesse d'Orléans, November 1696

The betrothal of Marie Adelaide, Princess of Savoy, and Louis, Duc de Bourgogne, was announced in June 1696. This union of two young people – ten and a half and just under fourteen respectively – personified the Treaty of Turin by which the opportunist Duke of Savoy abandoned the Grand Alliance for the winning force of Louis XIV. It was a Treaty which marked an important step in the direction of general European pacification.

The hostilities which had cost France (and others) so much in men and money in the War of the League of Augsburg were not finally ended until the Treaty of Ryswick of 1697. Nevertheless in 1696 it was already possible to regard the little Savoyard bride as a harbinger of peace – as the Spanish Marie-Thérèse had once been. 'Is she a princess? Is she an angel?' ran one welcoming poem. 'Don't you see the vital difference? / The angel simply announces peace. / She herself gives it to us.'[1] Furthermore, it was part of the deal that the peace-bringing princess should be educated in France. She was young enough, it was felt, to be moulded into the ways of Versailles even before the actual wedding took place. So Adelaide set out for her glorious destiny in the autumn of 1696, her tiny person conveyed by a huge carriage draped in purple velvet (royal mourning for a deceased cousin of Louis XIV).

The circumstances of Adelaide's childhood conspired to prepare her for what she would find at Versailles. First of all, her mother, Anne-Marie d'Orléans, had taught her of the superior nature of all things French, like many another expatriate French princess before her. Adelaide spoke French well, and with a proper accent (although she could adopt an exaggerated Italian accent when she wanted to tease); in any case the court of Savoy has been described as 'polyglot', German as well as Italian competing with French.[2]

Quite apart from her upbringing, much of Adelaide's blood was actually French. She had two great-grandmothers who were French princesses, daughters of Henri IV: Henrietta Maria and Christine de France, Duchess of Savoy. Her grandfather, Monsieur, was French and her grandmother Henriette-Anne was half French. Her father's mother (a strong influence upon her), Jeanne-Baptiste de Savoie-Nemours, known as Madame Royale, was partly French; she had been born in Paris and descended from Henri IV via one of his bastards, César, Duc de Vendôme.

Duchess Anne-Marie had left the court at which she was raised twelve years earlier but had forgotten none of the details. As a result Louis XIV himself would comment much later that Adelaide had been taught in advance 'the only way she could be happy with us'. For example there was to be no foolish snobbery about Madame de Maintenon such as the late Dauphine had once evinced, since her influence was already palpable when Anne-Marie left for Savoy. In a brilliant move, little Adelaide would address her by the honorific title of aunt; 'Tante' was respectful and intimate but also delightfully vague. In Adelaide's attitude towards Françoise, obedient and very affectionate, the hand of her powerful grandmother Madame Royale, once Regent of Savoy, can be detected: 'I have carried out what you ordered me to do,' she wrote to Madame Royale on one occasion in the course of their continuing correspondence.[3]

In quite a different way Adelaide was prepared for life at Versailles by her early experiences. For example, her father Victor Amadeus, known – to her anyway – as *le Grand*, was the strong male figure who was the centre of her world; he was also blatantly unfaithful to her mother. Adelaide grew up understanding that men had mistresses and that mistresses bore them children (Victor Amadeus's *maîtresse en titre* the Comtesse de Verrue had two that he acknowledged).[4] Then, much of her childhood had been spent in the country, the Vigna di Madama, a favourite haunt of Duchess Anne-Marie, having something of the French style. Here Adelaide made cheese and milked cows; here she learned to love flowers, gardening and animals – all the things in short that Louis XIV loved.[5]

It was not however a childhood that had been totally without trauma. Victor Amadeus's earlier rupture with France, which he deserted for the League of Augsburg, had led to depredations by French invaders and the destruction of Savoyard buildings: although that experience carried with it the connotation of France's immense strength as a power. Then the winter of 1693, shortly after Adelaide's eighth birthday on 6 December, had been no better in Savoy than in France, with vineyards and orchards destroyed, and starvation threatening the poor.

By nature Adelaide was kind, exceptionally so, hating to cause pain to anyone in the world, and she was gentle. Her manners were superb. Her greeting of the exiled Queen Mary Beatrice, for example, was perfectly judged, the young woman on the verge of a great destiny showing the greatest respect and tenderness for one whose fortunes were so markedly in decline. In other ways Adelaide was shrewd as the children of troubled marriages are shrewd – for such her own parents' marriage certainly was, give or take Victor Amadeus's sporadic sleeping with his wife in the hopes of begetting a male heir. (A healthy prince had however not yet arrived before Adelaide's departure for France, only another daughter known as Louison, born in 1688.)

Ill-educated as she might be by the standards of Saint-Cyr, Adelaide was naturally intelligent, quick, amusing and very, very lively. In fact she might have been specially designed to divert the ageing Louis XIV – Adelaide arrived at Versailles when Louis was in his fifty-ninth year – a man with a pious older governess of a wife, troublesome daughters both spoilt and dissipated, and the cares of Europe (as he saw it) on his shoulders. This was the man who had gloomily warned his son that 'the grandeurs of the world' would all turn to dust, King, Dauphin not excluded. Six years later this sweet little monkey of a girl took Versailles by storm and in the process captured the heart of Louis XIV.

The King seems to have had some premonition of the emotional importance Adelaide would have in his life. He insisted from the first – that is, before her marriage – that she should have proper precedence as the First Lady of Versailles. This gave her parity with Queen Mary Beatrice, whose rank Louis had hitherto jealously guarded. Since it was not planned for Adelaide and Bourgogne to marry yet awhile, the King ordained that she should be known simply as 'the Princess' – a single title, like all the grandest titles in Versailles. The proud sisters Françoise-Marie and Madame la Duchesse were indignant: a mere 'Princess of Savoy' to step ahead of them![6]

Liselotte, however, demoted from the position she had occupied for the last six years, did not particularly mind. She was more concerned to have a swipe at Madame de Maintenon: at least she would not have to hold the chemise for 'the old whore' if she was officially acknowledged as Queen (a familiar obsession): that would be for Adelaide as senior royal lady. Liselotte was in a particularly grumpy mood towards Françoise these days over the marriage prospects of her only daughter, the hoydenish and rather plain Élisabeth-Charlotte d'Orléans, born in 1676. Liselotte blamed Françoise for denying her daughter the position of the Dauphin's second wife out of 'spite'; Liselotte had also thought of Élisabeth-Charlotte for Bourgogne, despite her six years' seniority.[7]

At least Liselotte was spared the horror of another bastard polluting her pure family when the Duc du Maine was married off to a member of the Bourbon-Condé family, Bénédicte, the midget sister of Louise-Françoise's husband Monsieur le Duc. Known to Liselotte as 'the little toad', Bénédicte was however quite proud enough for Liselotte's liking: although she accepted Maine, she had originally twitted his sisters on their illegitimate birth when they tried to mock her diminutive appearance 'like a ten-year-old child'. As for Athénaïs's second royal son, the Comte de Toulouse, 'We have given the little stinker the slip,' Liselotte reported proudly.[8] In the end Élisabeth-Charlotte had to make do with Duke Leopold Joseph of Lorraine: a legitimate princeling and occupying a geographically debatable area on the fringes of France. It was not the great marriage Liselotte had envisaged. (She was also annoyed that Élisabeth-Charlotte's half-sisters, Henriette-Anne's daughters, had made superior matches to the King of Spain and Duke of Savoy respectively.)

The King's premonition about 'the Princess' took a further form when he insisted on riding to greet her at Montargis, twenty-odd miles south of Fontainebleau, instead of waiting there with the whole court. There he stood on a balcony, watching the road like the King in a fairy story for the dust of the Princess's cortège to signal her approach. There had been considerable fuss about the arrangements for her arrival the French Ambassador reporting tersely: 'We want the Princess naked,' that is to say, there were to be no inferior Savoyard clothes ... only her shoes were allowed to come from Turin. Otherwise Adelaide's trousseau was modest indeed, a few chemises and gowns, some lace lingerie, while she awaited the full panoply of French fashion which would be bestowed upon her on arrival. Her 'body', that is to say a corselet built around her actual shape, had been sent to France before her, including a ribbon to indicate her minute waist. Nor for that matter were there to be presumptuous Savoyard servants to encourage homesickness.

Victor Amadeus minded less about the clothes – which after all were saving him expense – than he did about the servants. It was understood that a great Princess should have a great household chosen from the great ladies of her adopted country. In fact the French had been squabbling over these appointments since the betrothal was announced: there had not after all been such a prominent royal household since the death of the Dauphine in 1690. The winners, including the Duchesse de Lude as Dame d'Honneur, owed much to the influence of Françoise and Nanon, her famous confidential servant. A genuine feeling of pity for his little daughter seems to have gripped Victor Amadeus. Was not this mere child to have a familiar servant looking after her chamber-pot, for example? The Duke worried that Adelaide might forget herself unless 'some intimate woman' was present to calm her 'in her moments of weakness'. In the end there was a mild effort at compromise on the part of France: Adelaide was allowed to bring one woman with her, Madame Marquet, on condition she returned to Savoy at once although in reality Madame Marquet managed to stay for two years. Fortunately Adelaide's First Equerry was the Comte de Tessé, who had acted as Ambassador Extra-ordinary to Savoy during the negotiations for the marriage, a middle-aged man she trusted and who acted as a kind of father figure.

France's ruthless attitude – that of the King, who as usual supervised every detail – was based on the principle of being cruel to be kind. Louis wanted all her tears to be shed before Adelaide reached her new country (he was of course being kind to himself rather than the child). So it was that the Handover took place, a symbolic event whenever a foreign princess left her own country for a glorious marriage. In this case the Princess was installed in her carriage on a hump-backed bridge which joined the two countries, back wheels in Savoy, horse and front wheels in France. She got into the carriage in one country and out in another.

Certainly all tears had been shed before the momentous meeting between King and Princess at Montargis at six o'clock on 4 November 1696. (She had spent the previous three days at La Charité-sur-Loire for the Feast of All Saints.) Adelaide, like the star she was, rose superbly to the occasion, despite her tender age. Understandably she showed signs of nerves when the King held a flambeau to her face. But when he declared: 'Madame, I have been waiting impatiently to greet you,' Adelaide replied: 'This, Sire, is the greatest moment of my life.'[9] Whoever coached her in these words – Madame Royale? – had taught her well. And as she tried to kneel before the King he lifted her up 'like a feather'. Then Adelaide put her hand in his. But there was – there had to be – one moment of kerfuffle over a matter of etiquette, when Monsieur, her biological grandfather, bustled forward to greet the Princess only to find that the Dauphin, as her future father-in-law, took precedence.

What did the King see? Fortunately his letter back to Madame de Maintenon, waiting with the rest of the royal family (including the fiancé Bourgogne) at Fontainebleau, has survived. The new Princess, he reported, had 'the greatest charm and the prettiest little figure I have ever seen ... the more I see her, the more I am satisfied'. She was in fact doll-sized, and when the King first appeared with her, the impression was given, wrote Saint-Simon in a memorable phrase, that he actually had her in his pocket. Louis's description was of course written to the woman who was going to take charge of this little doll, and he therefore dwelled on her faults. She had 'very irregular teeth' (and teeth generally would always be a problem for Adelaide). Her lips were very red but also rather thick. On the other hand her pink-and-white complexion was superb. Despite a natural grace Adelaide curtsied badly 'in the Italian manner' – never a term of praise in France – and altogether there was 'something slightly Italian' about her appearance. Yet Françoise would be enchanted, as he had been, by her modesty.[10]

Adelaide's 'Italianate' look was partly due to that Médicis strain which her tragic aunt Marie-Louise of Spain, for example, had shared. Her eyes were huge and black, her notably long eyelashes also very black. But it was partly due to the fact that her hair seems to have been sprayed darker for the meeting, to make her skin look whiter. Liselotte described her as having 'pretty blonde' hair, while taking the opportunity to sneer at Adelaide's 'real Austrian mouth and chin'.[11] From the portraits the answer seems to be that Adelaide's hair was a kind of bright chestnut which darkened later – she was after all only ten years old at this point. Certainly everyone agreed that her hair was wonderfully thick and lustrous.

What the King did not mention in his letter to Françoise was the measure of his enchantment with this little 'doll or plaything' – the term often used by observers – but a walking, talking doll with the prettiest ways imaginable and a plaything who had been educated to respect his wishes in every single matter. No wonder Françoise told Adelaide's mother that the little girl had 'all the graces of eleven years and all the perfections of a more advanced age'. For when Françoise tried to 'deny the caresses' Adelaide gave her, saying she was too old, the girl replied charmingly: 'Not at all too old.' (Although it is true that Françoise was ageing well; at sixty-one she had hardly a grey hair; her eyes were still 'very fine', as an English visitor wrote, and there was about 'her whole person' an indefinable charm which old age could not destroy.) After this bit of childish blarney, Adelaide sat on Françoise's lap and uttered the perfect expression of her training: 'Teach me well, I beg you, what I have to do to please the King.'[12]

It is plausible to argue that Louis XIV loved Adelaide of Savoy more than he loved anyone in his life, with the possible exception of the strong love he felt for his mother. It is more difficult to get at Adelaide's feelings for this kindly, all-powerful grandfather-figure. Marguerite de Caylus, who observed the scene, did not doubt that she genuinely loved him, but added the rider that Adelaide was by nature 'coquettish' and easily influenced by those around her.[13] What is remarkable about Adelaide's correspondence with her father, mother and grandmother is the prominence it gives to Louis XIV and the scarcity of mentions of the Duc de Bourgogne. She reiterates her love for the King, his kindness to her – but of Bourgogne there is hardly a trace.

Perhaps this was hardly surprising, since the two young fiancés were being carefully kept apart, with meetings not only strictly chaperoned but rationed to one a fortnight (his brothers, Anjou and Berry, could meet Adelaide once a month). Bourgogne himself was hardly a glamorous figure. His misanthropic temperament had led to the nickname of 'Alceste', and with strong religious convictions he would probably have been happier as a younger son who could have become a Cardinal Prince of the Church, as in bygone days. His pious austerities were notorious as when he refused to attend a ball at Marly because it was the Feast of the Epiphany. Even the holy Fénelon had to reason with him that 'a great Prince should not serve God in the same way as a recluse'. The counterpoint to this piety was a violent temper which Bourgogne was unable to control: he was, wrote Saint-Simon, 'born furious'. A favourite method of relief was smashing clocks.[14]

Nor was his physical appearance prepossessing. Bourgogne was quite short, with a raised shoulder that gradually turned to a hump. His face was dominated by a beaklike nose, which together with his receding chin and pronounced upper jaw made him look positively odd. As against that, Bourgogne enjoyed music, the opera and the theatre. He was insecure but he was not mean-spirited. And of course, like his grandfather, he fell madly in love with Adelaide, despite the strict prohibitions which would not let him kiss so much as the tips of her fingers.

The general enchantment of the population, King downwards, by 'the Princess' had a curious effect on what had become a somewhat stultified society. Of course she was an object of intense interest from the start, not only in terms of lucrative appointments to her household. There was such a crush on her first arrival at court that there was a danger of the whole company collapsing 'like a pack of cards' as grand ladies such as the Duchesse de Nemours and the Maréchale de La Motte pushed their way relentlessly to the front; according to Liselotte, Maintenon herself would have been felled if she had not personally held 'the old woman's' arms upright.[15] Quite apart from Bourgogne, there was trouble about who might and who might not kiss 'the Princess', with the Duchesse de Lude like an eagle of etiquette, ever on the watch against an unlawful buss.

Saint-Simon wrote of Adelaide that her youth and high spirits enlivened the whole court. Liselotte, describing how she had joined in a jolly game of blind man's bluff, which she had to admit she had much enjoyed, commented that everyone was busy 'becoming a child again'.[16] When Adelaide admitted that she missed the Savoyard dolls which had not been allowed to accompany her, special dolls were sent for from Paris, more gorgeous than anything mere Savoy could imagine. Games of spillikins were also pronounced beneficial by Madame de Maintenon because they promoted 'dexterity'.

There is a vignette of the little Princess 'sledging', that is to say, being whirled down the polished corridors of Versailles, which is curiously touching when one thinks of the awe in which this establishment was held by the whole of Europe. An English visitor about this time, Dr Martin Lister, gaped at what he saw: 'it were endless to tell all the furniture of these gardens, of marble statues, and vases of brass and marble, the multitude of fountains, and those wide canals like seas running in a straight line from the bottom of the gardens as far as the eye can reach. In a word, these gardens are a country ...' To Adelaide however, frolicsome to a fault, skipping, chattering, 'rumpling' the King and Tante Maintenon, these gardens were her playground.[17]

Louis might now be a man in late middle age plagued by gout, who wore unromantic *galoches** when the weather was wet: reflected in the child's eyes he saw himself in quite a different light. As Marguerite de Caylus reported, the King was so 'completely bewitched' by Adelaide that he could not bear to be parted from her for a single moment and even took her to council meetings. As for Adelaide, Dangeau reported significantly that the little girl 'never had a cold' when it was a question of going out with the King.[18]

It was true, as has been mentioned, that Adelaide was not well educated: but how convenient that she could be enrolled in Tante's nearby Saint-Cyr three times a week! (Even if she had to be in a class of those below her own age.) Here she formed a friendship with Françoise's niece Françoise-Charlotte d'Aubigné, and she also acted a 'little Israelite', part of the young chorus, in a production of *Esther*; subsequently she played Joas's bride Josabit in *Athalie*,

---

* A form of clog with a wooden sole and leather upper from which the modern word 'galosh' derives.

although there was some heart-searching about her participation in this controversial play.[19] Her handwriting remained childish – at the age of thirteen she was still vowing to improve it – but at least Saint-Cyr gave her some opportunities for youthful society in an otherwise highly ceremonious life.

All this innocent fun made such a pleasant change from the louche young royals of the court with their drinking, their endless shrieking and above all their gambling. It was hardly to be expected that these attractive, spoilt princesses, mated – one has to use the word – at an early age for reasons of state, would ignore the opportunities for gallantry around them. Marie-Anne de Conti, the eldest, had led the way; Madame la Duchesse eventually settled into a long affair with the Marquis de Lassay; Françoise-Marie's 'discretion' in handling her affairs was, for once, praised by her mother-in-law Liselotte.[20]

Liselotte's real gripe was less against the morals than the sheer laziness of the princesses. They were such layabouts and so debauched that they could hardly be bothered to dance any more. (This critic was the Liselotte who had thoroughly enjoyed an impromptu farting competition within her family circle, won by Philippe, who could make 'a noise like a flute'.) Worst of all, at any rate for those around them, was their daring use of tobacco. Although tobacco was used as a curative in certain cases of great pain – Catherine de Médicis administered it to the young François II for migraine – that was a case of taking the tobacco in powder form as a drug. Rakish gentlemen might indulge themselves by handing it round in elegant boxes (Don Juan's valet Sganarelle opens Molière's play by reflecting that 'there's nothing like tobacco'). But it was regarded as a disgusting habit for a lady to smoke tobacco in a pipe as sailors did. On the other hand inhaling tobacco caused 'dirty noses', in the words of Liselotte, as if the ladies had rubbed their fingers in the gutter, or rummaged in a man's tobacco pouch. Nevertheless the princesses did it, for all the complaints.[21]

Madame de Maintenon's take on tobacco was similarly disapproving – although to the Demoiselles of Saint-Cyr who had to make their way in the world and could not risk giving offence, she advocated more pragmatic behaviour: avoid tobacco altogether, unless it was offered by 'a person of importance', in which case a girl should take a little and let it drop 'imperceptibly' to the ground. Further measures against what would now be called date-rape were the avoidance of wine, and the wearing of a corset at all times.[22]

The marriage of Adelaide and Bourgogne was ordained to take place on her twelfth birthday, 6 December 1697, roughly a year after her arrival. Adelaide did not allow her coming grandeur to go to her head: when the aged Bishop Bossuet, appointed her Almoner, knelt before her, she protested strongly. 'Oh, Monseigneur, I am ashamed to see you thus.' The King however was in an extravagant mood, although he had recently dressed very simply, curtailing expenditure due to the demands of the War of the League of Augsburg just concluded. He ordered 'some fine clothes' for the occasion and he indicated in addition that his courtiers would please him with a certain deployment of splendour. Sure enough the Duc and Duchesse de Saint-Simon between them spent twenty thousand livres on their outfits (nearly seventy thousand pounds in today's money).[23]

Having decreed splendour, the King should not have been too surprised when the usual chicaneries of Versailles society, based on rivalry, took place. Louis himself chose the embroideries for Adelaide's costume but stipulated that the embroiderer should not immediately abandon all his other clients for the royal commission. Madame la Duchesse, with no such scruples, kidnapped the tailors of the Duchesse de Rohan to work on her own robes exclusively but was obliged to give them back. At the ceremony itself Bourgogne wore black velvet lined with rose-coloured satin and Adelaide wore silver, dotted all over with so many rubies and diamonds that the total weight, together with that of her bejewelled coiffure, was said to be more than her own. The heavy cloak flowing from her shoulders was blue velvet strewn with the golden fleur-de-lys of France.

The wedding night which followed was a purely formal occasion according to the dictate of the King. James II and Mary Beatrice, as the senior royals present, handed the young couple their chemises. There was some chat by the Dauphin and after that the ceremony was over. Bourgogne did daringly kiss his bride, despite the deep disapproval of the Duchesse de Lude, and that was all. But it was the Duchesse who had correctly interpreted the King's instructions: he was furious at the news since he had expressly forbidden contact. Only 'that naughty little rogue' Berry, ten years old and already livelier than his brothers, said that he would have attempted far more ...

The next stage – the consummation of the marriage – did not come for nearly two years. In the meantime the young Bourgognes were carefully introduced to a limited and asexual married life. It included visits to the theatre. In October 1698 for example a trip to see *Le Bourgeois Gentilhomme* produced uproarious laughter from both Duc and Duchesse. There was a ballet to celebrate Adelaide's birthday in 1698 at which Bourgogne danced Apollo and Adelaide danced a Muse. Perhaps there were courtiers present who recalled the grace of Adelaide's grandmother Henriette-Anne dancing the same kind of role forty years earlier (although few would care to have compared poor bent Bourgogne to the magnificent young Louis XIV).

Adelaide also learned the routine of attending military occasions: where Françoise, with no taste for glory, had not liked these outings and still did not, Adelaide had an enjoyable time. 'I am a good Frenchwoman,' she told her grandmother when she expressed joy over a French success.[24] Of course Savoy was at this point on the side of France and the sorrows of a princess hearing the 'good news' of her native country's destruction, such as had torn Liselotte apart, had not yet come the youthful Adelaide's way ... Yet in spite of this, in spite of Bourgogne insisting on nightly visits to his wife in November, after an original stipulation of every other night, Adelaide did not for the time being get pregnant.

The ascendancy of Adelaide over both Louis and Françoise had the happy effect of consolidating a relationship which had recently come as near as it ever did to foundering. How strange that trouble developed over the matter of religion, the very subject which had welded Louis and Françoise so closely together! The temporary cloud and its vanishing demonstrate how little, if at all, the King was prepared to compromise in anything in order to please his secret wife, and how irresolute, even timid, Françoise herself became when there was any kind of clash. The central Catholic Church in France was threatened – as it believed – by any doctrine which assailed the conventional view of the Church as the essential mediator between individuals on earth and God. One of these doctrines was so-called Quietism, a mystical practice of the Catholic religion somewhat akin to modern meditation, in which prayer, even repetitive prayer, was everything.

Françoise did not exactly dabble in Quietism but she did become a friend of the brilliant, charismatic Jeanne-Marie Guyon, a widow with four children, and allowed her to have contact with Saint-Cyr. Madame Guyon's book on 'short and simple Orisons' which could be practised daily, printed in 1687, got her arrested the next year; Madame de Maintenon managed to secure her release. But Madame

Guyon's second arrest, her incarceration in the fortress of Vincennes and her interrogation by La Reynie found Françoise either unable or unwilling to help.

The influence of the Abbé Godet des Marais was important, because he urged Françoise strongly to side with the orthodox and severe Bossuet on the subject of Quietism: something Bossuet condemned in a sermon at Lent 1696. Along the way Fénelon became a victim too. Now Françoise abandoned the man who had been her friend and sat by, helpless, while Fénelon was forbidden contact with Bourgogne and all the Quietists were purged from the young Duc's household. Françoise's abandonment of her former friends was seen as cowardice – although she would probably have justified it as part of her essentially pragmatic attitude to religion. In any case Louis became subtly cold towards Françoise, suggesting that Fénelon had been 'a bad shepherd' who had been wrongly appointed to tend his grandchildren. As for poor Bourgogne, he was heartbroken, pleading in vain to be allowed at least to write to Fénelon: there was to be no further contact between Fénelon and his 'little Louis' till 1701.[25]

The whole protracted episode caused a degeneration in Françoise's health which may have been at least in part psychosomatic. It was significant that her reconciliation with the King occurred when he came and stood beside her bedside with the words, which had something of love but also much of impatience about them: 'Well, Madame, are you going to die of this then?' And so the way was prepared for an apotheosis. At a military review at Compiègne in September 1698 the King leaned ostentatiously on the open window of Madame de Maintenon's sedan-chair. He took off his hat and left it on top of the chair in order to describe the proceedings to her in full view of troops and courtiers alike. Louis hardly spoke to anyone else, and even Adelaide found it difficult to get him to answer her questions. It was as open a declaration as he ever made on the subject of her status, and left a profound impression on all present, including Saint-Simon.[26]

It was however an apotheosis which had only occurred at a certain cost. Although Françoise had busied herself using her influence to secure bishoprics for her friends – Godet des Marais was made Bishop of Chartres and her ally Antoine de Noailles Archbishop of Paris – she now discovered that the price of influence was orthodoxy plus submission to the King's will, should she happen to cross it. As Madame de Maintenon confessed to the Archbishop when she had failed to bring about a particular Church appointment: 'I see that the King was not as docile as I thought.'[27] She was very far from being the strong-willed manipulator of Liselotte's and Saint-Simon's depiction: more the pliant 'Thaw' of the Sévigné nickname. In the upbringing of Adelaide, however, Françoise clearly had her role, which was not that of Queen precisely, so much as grandmother-cum-governess. Adelaide needed Françoise and Louis needed Adelaide: order was restored. So the unacknowledged but painful rift was healed.

Did Maintenon hanker after the full role of Queen in public? Naturally her enemies said she did, but there is no evidence of it beyond their prejudices. Equally there is no evidence that Louis XIV ever seriously contemplated giving it to her: dynasty was sacred to him, royalty too, as had been impressed upon him from his earliest years by Anne of Austria, a mighty Princess. While he had chosen a discreet and virtuous private life with Françoise, it was not within his imaginative range to see her sitting on the throne once occupied by his mother (and by Marie-Thérèse, another mighty Princess). What would have been the point? With the increasing selfishness of the ageing, particularly in a man trained from the start to be self-centred as a form of duty, the King knew that he had what he wanted.

It did not occur to him to question seriously whether

Françoise was equally content ... He treated her at all times with scrupulous politeness. Although Françoise burned the King's letters after his death, a few little notes do survive about daily arrangements, in which the language is formal and above all considerate, with the reiteration of phrases like 'if you approve' and 'I shall conform to your wishes'. There is certainly no hint of command. 'If you would like to take a promenade with me at three or four o'clock,' wrote the King on one occasion, 'come to the Basin of Apollo, where I shall be with a chair for you'; but 'please don't feel obliged to do this'. And probably in most ways Françoise *was* content, reflecting passively on 'the enigma' of her destiny in the words of her confessor Godet des Marais: God had put 'the salvation of a great king' in her hands ... 'You are his refuge, remember that your room is the domestic Church where the King retires.'[28]

So long as her reputation was secure, Françoise was satisfied (as she had said of herself), and *pace* Liselotte nobody really thought of her in the 1690s as an 'old whore' – old, yes, since she was in her sixties, but whore seemed very wide of the mark. It is true that the scurrilous pamphlets got going on her as they did on everyone of note. Despite the restrictions of censorship (which could be overcome by printing in Holland), mockery was widespread and lewd: no one was spared.

For example, it is to this period that a satirical pamphlet suggesting that the true father of Louis XIV was actually the Comte de Rantzau belongs. Rantzau, a Maréchal de France originally from Holstein, died in 1650; there was of course no contemporary evidence for this wild surmise.[29] If the King's past was smirched, so was his present. A medal of 1693 showed Louis being tugged away from the front line by four women, with a legend on the subject of unsuccessful invasion that was a rude adaptation of Caesar's famous aphorism: *Venit, vidit sed non vincit* (He came, he saw but he did not conquer). Eight years after its erection, the equestrian statue of 1686 in the Place des Victoires was adapted for a scurrilous engraving showing a new pedestal with the King in chains to four mistresses, Louise, Angélique, Athénaïs and Françoise, in place of his military triumphs. The printer, bookseller and his boy assistant were all hanged for their efforts.[30] But the satires did not cease.

Françoise therefore could hardly expect to be spared. She was said to have been seduced long before she met Scarron, 'the breach already made' by the Marquis de Montchevreuil, featured inaccurately as the Duc de Montchevreuil. There was a ridiculous rumour that while still very young she had given birth to an illegitimate child called Babbé. Despite the tone of these attacks on 'the old she-monkey', in which age was a prominent feature, the worst accusation was that which had her doing a deal with the Jesuits: her own secret marriage to the King in exchange for the Revocation of the Edict of Nantes.[31] None of this was true.

It was Louis XIV however whose feelings constituted the real enigma to the outside world. There was a celebrated moment when Pierre Mignard was about to paint Madame de Maintenon in the role of St Frances of Rome; the King's permission was sought to drape her in ermine robes, the style of a Queen. (Something that was incidentally done in other portraits of great ladies, other than queens.) 'Certainly St Frances deserves ermine!' replied the King laughingly, leaving no one much the wiser as to his precise meaning. But he did love the picture: a miniature based on it was something he carried with him in his waistcoat pocket till the day of his death.*

The Treaty of Ryswick, signed in September 1697, which brought to an end the nine-year War of the League of

---

* Now preserved, appropriately enough, at the Château de Maintenon.

Augsburg, was hailed by a loyal courtier like the Marquis de Dangeau in glowing terms: 'The King gave peace to Europe upon conditions which he wished to impose. He was the master ....'[32] It is true that if he lost Lorraine, 'the master' retained French Hainault and Lower Alsace including Strasbourg; in the West Indies, Santo Domingo (since the 1790s Haiti) was an important acquisition for the future. Yet there was much he had also acquired – at enormous cost in casualties – which Louis did not retain. The French armies which in the popular imagination had succeeded the Spanish armies of his youth as Europe's invincible warriors were no longer to be seen in quite that light. William III, once merely the modest Prince of Orange, was Europe's foremost martial leader.

By implication, the Treaty also acknowledged William for the first time as King of England. Here Louis XIV did act with some spirit: he refused to banish the former King James II and Queen Mary Beatrice, with their children, from France. Furthermore he showed his sensitivity to the ordeal which the Treaty represented for these unhappy exiles by ordering that there should be no triumphant music and celebrations in their presence. Since the finalisation of the Treaty coincided with their traditional autumn visit to Fontainebleau, foreign news was not to be brought to him unless he was alone. And Louis pressed William for the payment of Mary Beatrice's jointure of fifty thousand a year, settled upon her by Parliament.

Part of this support for the exiles was due to Louis's genuine reverence for Mary Beatrice, in every way the dominant character of the pair these days, as ex-King James's conversation, never scintillating at the best of times, centred more and more upon his impending death. But neither he nor any other European could be unaware that the question of the eventual English succession remained unsolved. William and Mary (who died in 1694) had no children. Her sister Anne seemed to be unable to raise a healthy child, the only survivor from infancy of her huge brood, the young Duke of Gloucester, a virtual invalid with a hugely swollen head, was to die at the age of nine in July 1700. Under these circumstances, it would need the certainty of hindsight to rule out the chances of ten-year-old James Edward succeeding. Still styled the Prince of Wales, Mary Beatrice's son was a happy, healthy child, and lived under the protection of France.

Not the English but the Spanish succession now threatened this lull of European peace. On 1 November 1700 Carlos II of Spain, that monarch whose demise had been predicted since his birth, did actually die at the age of thirty-nine, and of course he died childless. In a bold gesture of contempt for the various rulers who had been notionally sawing up his empire over the years, Carlos left his entire dominions to his half-sister's grandson on condition that they were kept together: this was none other than the Duc d'Anjou, second son of the Dauphin of France. It was perfectly possible to argue that Anjou was Carlos's nearest heir (Anjou's elder brother Bourgogne, like the Dauphin himself, was ruled out as being a future King of France). Equally the descendants of Carlos's full sister Margarita Teresa, who had married the Emperor, could mount a claim: her grandson Joseph Ferdinand of Bavaria, a prince but not a threateningly powerful one, was a suitable choice: unfortunately he died in 1699. The next imperial choice was more openly Habsburg: the Emperor's younger son the Archduke Charles (he who had once been proposed as a bridegroom for Adelaide).

In assessing Louis XIV's decision to accept the throne on behalf of his grandson, once again, as with the fate of James Edward Stuart, one must avoid hindsight. It was not in Louis XIV to reject such a great dynastic prize for *his* dynasty – and of course deprive the Habsburgs of it at the same time. He did not need the urging of Madame de Maintenon (who in any case did no such thing as urge but merely sided politely with the favourably inclined Dauphin).[33] The man who placed the need for glory at the centre of his youthful ambitions was not going to reject it on behalf of Anjou now, even if common sense must have told him that the crown would not be surrendered by the Austrian party without a struggle. Where Louis failed was in not seeing further into the anxieties of Austria: he should, at the same time as accepting on behalf of Anjou, have made it clear that Anjou would never succeed to the French throne himself. (The Bourgognes at this point had no children, so that this was within the bounds of possibility.)

Who knows? Perhaps secret imperial dreams also excited Louis, and the thought of the two crowns of France and Spain united was not totally inimical to him. As it was, he broke the news of his decision to his grandson as Anjou was playing cards. The boy stood up respectfully, took the news with 'the gravity and coolness of a king of eighty years' and then sat down at once as though weighed back into his seat by the cares of a heavy crown.[34]

'I hope Your Majesty will sleep well tonight,' said Louis XIV. Anjou, who was not quite seventeen, was a sober, intelligent lad without the tiresome piety of Bourgone or the mischievous nature of fourteen-year-old Berry. Whether Anjou, now transformed into Philip V, did sleep is not related. Liselotte as usual had something livelier to say. Out hunting with the new monarch, she ostentatiously let him pass: 'After you, great King,' she said. The Duc de Berry 'almost died laughing'.[35]

But the accession of the French candidate to the throne of Spain was to prove no laughing matter. The War of the Spanish Succession which followed would be described by Winston Churchill in his life of Marlborough as 'the first

world war' because it involved other continents as well as
Europe. In the course of it, every kind of ruin would
encompass France.

PART FOUR

Winter

CHAPTER 14

Gaiety Begins to Go

Even my gaiety is a little bit diminished.

– Adelaide Duchesse de Bourgogne, 1700

'I am no longer a child,' wrote Adelaide the married woman to her grandmother in Savoy, on 16 November 1700.[1] Adelaide was in fact on the brink of her fifteenth birthday. She was not yet a mother: an inspirational Holy Water stoup containing a carved white coral baby sent to her from Savoy by the Princesse de Vaudémont had not yet done its work – or the austere Bourgogne had not yet done his, despite his passionate love for his wife. Or perhaps they were both just too young.

The Comte de Tessé had accompanied the coral baby with an admonitory letter: 'I devoutly believe that she sent it so that the coral baby may reawaken you, every evening and morning, to the thought that you owe one to us, and that no other thought, not of your lovely figure, nor of anything else compared with that is of the slightest importance.' He ended: 'I am your old servant whom you sometimes deign to call old fool.'[2] For all the mock-modest salutation, Tessé's message was quite clear: this was Adelaide's prime purpose. At all events she did conceive her first child towards the end of 1702, but suffered a miscarriage. Another miscarriage followed a year later. Her first living child – a son, to the general ecstasy of King and court – was born in July 1704 when Adelaide was eighteen. Instantly

317

created Duc de Bretagne by Louis XIV, this important great-grandson lived only till the following April, when he died very suddenly. Liselotte as usual blamed the doctors. Adelaide on the other hand wrote a correct letter to her mother on the workings of the Divine Will: 'If we did not receive all the sorrows of this life from God, I do not know what would become of us. I think He [God] wants to draw me to Him.'[3]

So Adelaide was still without a family when she reached her twentieth birthday on 6 December 1705. For this and other reasons, she began to show increasing signs of melancholy and tension – 'even my gaiety is a little bit diminished' – interspersed by bouts of hectic celebration and constant movement. She would parade on her donkey, drive her little cart round the gardens of Versailles, or clamber like a cat over the rocks at Fontainebleau. Adelaide adored riding: a delightful portrait of her in a red riding-dress (a favourite colour) shows off her tiny waist and shapely if slender figure. Like her grandmother Henriette-Anne, Adelaide never seemed to sleep and loved to roam about at night, which she described as 'one of her greatest joys'. At the same time she had to preserve the ingenuous quality which charmed the King. That was part of the trouble. Adelaide felt that her girlhood was passing – 'I am no longer young,' she bewailed once again in 1702 in what was becoming a familiar theme – but her childhood was not.[4] The King would not let it go.

On the one hand she struggled to fulfil her most important womanly role and add to the dynasty as was expected. On the other hand she had to maintain that mischievous sweetness which had entranced Louis XIV in the ten-year-old child and captured his heart. She was also capable of feeling jealousy for another sweet little girl (of much less august birth) who teased and entertained the King. Jeannette Pincré was the youngest of eight children who entered the Maintenon household when her widowed mother flung herself on Françoise's charity; the King insisted that Jeannette stay there.

Of course Adelaide, no fool, did make her childishness work for her. It was not entirely done to please the ageing King. Her inquisitiveness was proverbial at the court (and caused much disgust in observers such as Liselotte). The King's papers, to say nothing of those of Madame de Maintenon, were deemed to be fair game, and a good deal of playful rummaging took place: Adelaide could be a naughty squirrel as well as a mischievous monkey. In this manner she chanced upon a list of men who were about to be created Maréchaux de France by the King, and was shocked to find that her favourite, the Comte de Tessé, hitherto only a Maréchal de Camp, had been omitted. She ran to her 'grandfather' in floods of tears. This flagrant nosiness and interference was almost too much for the King – almost but not quite. To prevent his little sweetheart being upset, he decided that he would make no marshals at all on that occasion. (Tessé was made a Maréchal de France in 1703.)

The sudden death, from a stroke, of Monsieur, Adelaide's biological grandfather, in June 1701 brought her further sadness; it was after all Monsieur not the King who was the connection to her absent mother. Poor Monsieur! It was bizarre that his dramatic end should follow a blazing row with the King over the conduct of his son Philippe. It was true that Philippe at twenty-five was a byword for debauchery, spending all night with the whores of Paris, impregnating his wife Françoise-Marie but also producing children by his mistress at roughly the same time. According to Liselotte, Monsieur's favourites acted as Philippe's pimps. But when the shocked Louis remonstrated, Monsieur chose (unpardonably from Louis's point of view) to remind his brother of bygone days when the King had run Louise and Athénaïs in tandem ...

The great King's reaction to Monsieur's death was that of any human being robbed of a sibling, the irreplaceable connection to distant childhood. 'I don't know how to accept the fact that I shall never see my brother again.' Liselotte's attitude to her husband's death on the other hand was resolutely unsentimental. She protested strongly at the idea that she might have to retire to a nunnery according to her wedding contract. 'No! No convent for me!' she was heard to cry in a loud voice. And so she was spared to continue her life at Versailles. Then, in the process of burning Monsieur's numerous love letters from his favourites, she declared herself nauseated by their perfume ...⁵ Liselotte also sneaked into theatrical performances incognito, although conventional mourning dictated a two-year abstinence.

In the course of the arrangements for Liselotte's widow-hood, Françoise was able to taste a sweet revenge. Not all of Liselotte's highly uncomplimentary letters about 'the old strumpet' and her relationship with the King had escaped attention in an age when international correspondence was routinely intercepted. The King passed the letters to Françoise and asked her to deal with the situation. This she did by accosting Liselotte in her apartments. Rashly the widow complained of the King's recent coolness only to have Françoise blandly display the correspondence. A humiliated Liselotte, in floods of tears, could only apologise profusely. It was Françoise who promised to intervene with the King.

Thereafter Louis, in his accustomed mode of forgiveness, was graciousness itself. He even laughed when Liselotte, in her own words to her aunt Sophia, 'artlessly' explained the whole thing as follows: 'If I hadn't loved you, I shouldn't have hated Madame de Maintenon when I thought she was depriving me of your kindness.'⁶ (Which was probably the truth.)

He also showed benevolence towards the dissipated Philippe, now Duc d'Orléans in succession to his father, when his first son by Françoise-Marie, after a string of daughters, was born on 4 August 1703. Philippe asked for the title of Duc de Chartres, which had previously been his, for the baby.* Louis asked if that was all he wanted. Philippe admitted that his household had urged him to press for more 'but it would be tactless in these hard times'. 'Then I myself will anticipate your request,' replied the King genially, 'and grant your son the pension of the first Prince of the Blood.'

The death of Monsieur and the substitution of Philippe, with a seemingly flourishing house of Orléans around him, was a matter for the rearrangement of the court. It also marked the emergence of a new problem, due to the longevity of the present monarch – by 1703 Louis had reigned longer than any previous French King. There was one surviving Child of France, the Dauphin. Then there were Grandchildren of France, in the shape of his three sons, also Philippe Duc d'Orléans and his sister, now Duchess of Lorraine. In each case the use of the word 'France' signified direct descent from a ruling monarch. Might there now be a new rank of Great-Grandchild of France? In which case that would apply to the infant Duc de Chartres.

The claims and counterclaims for precedence, the squabbles between dukes, Princes of the Blood and royal princes, would only grow fiercer as the years passed. For example Françoise-Marie was naturally zealous in support of her large brood of daughters who, like their brother Chartres, should surely enjoy the rank of Great-Grandchild of France, and she was anxious that her eldest daughter Marie-Élisabeth should be granted the simple honorific title of 'Mademoiselle'

* This male birth was important in the Bourbon dynasty: with Adelaide still childless, the infant Duc de Chartres ensured the continuation of the Orléans branch of the dynasty. The baby was of course Louis's great-nephew, but also his grandchild, via his legitimised daughter Françoise-Marie.

instead of 'Mademoiselle d'Orléans'. This was after all a society in which, however farcical to outsiders, the vital distinction between '*Madame*, Duchesse d'Orléans' and 'Madame *la* Duchesse d'Orléans' was seen as quite crucial: whereas the former was married to a Child of France, the omission of the comma, the addition of the article, indicated that the latter was married more remotely to a mere Grand-child.[7]

The long-anticipated death of the former King of England, James II, from cancer took place three months later on 16 September.* Every article in the royal apartments at Saint-Germain was removed, to be replaced with violet mourning for James Edward, as the new King, grey for Mary Beatrice and Louisa Maria. Furnishings apart, the event had immediate and serious political consequences. In 1697 Louis XIV had tacitly agreed that William III was the *de facto* King of England, even though he refused to banish James, Mary Beatrice and their children. Unfortunately for the military destinies of France, if fortunately perhaps for Louis's moral character, he now proceeded to acknowledge James Edward as King James III. In England, however, James Edward was 'the pretended Prince of Wales' or merely 'the Pretender', guilty of high treason by an act of Parliament of 1702. Under the circumstances, Louis's decision to ignore this was, as Saint-Simon noted, a policy 'more worthy of the generosity of a Louis XIII and a François I than his [Louis XIV's] wisdom'.[8]

It was a question of a deathbed promise given to James himself: the exiled English King could die happy since his son would be acknowledged as his successor. At the time

---

* The fine memorial to James II displaying the royal arms of England, still to be seen in the church at Saint-Germain, was erected in 1824 by George IV, who had a sentimental attitude to his Stuart relations, now beyond claiming the throne. The text, in French and English, describes James as 'welcomed to France by Louis/Lewis XIV'.

the dying James gave hardly a flicker of recognition of what had just been communicated to him. The real point of the French King's noble gesture was achieved later when he told Queen Mary Beatrice what he had done. After the French naval defeat at La Hogue in 1692 Louis had refused to accept the disastrous consequences for the cause of James II. On the contrary, he had boasted to Mary Beatrice that he would be the one to give her 'the last embrace' before she boarded the ship which took her back at last to England. Justice and 'your piety' would ensure Heaven's blessing on the enterprise. Heaven might have been laggard in its blessing, but nine years later the King of France did not waver in his support for the English Queen. Subsequently he announced his decision to the court at Marly and all applauded him (although many shared Saint-Simon's practical doubts).[9]

Undoubtedly Louis's tender admiration for Mary Beatrice, and Françoise's similar affection, transformed into a close friendship, was the major factor in this 'Jacobite' decision. How much simpler from the point of view of French foreign policy to have let the subject rest! Once again, when William died in 1702, Louis could have by default acknowledged James Edward's Protestant half-sister Anne Stuart as Queen: the little girl who had once spent happy times in France with her first cousin Marie Louise d'Orléans. As it was, Louis refused to allow court mourning for the death of William, even for those who were related to him – including Liselotte, who had wanted to marry him.

It was the pleading of Mary Beatrice which had brought this about: if James Edward was not acknowledged in France, his lack of any proper status would remind the world once more of the malicious slurs concerning his birth in 1688, those ludicrous warming-pan stories so prejudicial (and comical) to Whig ears, so painful to her own. Thus Mary Beatrice continued to enjoy her privileged if fundamentally sad situation at the French court. To Françoise she was 'this great Queen whose state is so worthy of pity that I can hardly express it'. Celtic poets sang of 'Mary, the languid-eyed / The beautiful branch of the pure palm of Modena / ... The alms-giving Queen / Religious and charitable, prudent and sensible'.[10] Her intelligence was much respected. The King among others commented on her shrewd judgement, and her dignity in difficult circumstances was equally admired.

Naturally the satirists sniped at her moral character (Mary Beatrice was still a very beautiful woman in her forties): she was portrayed as Messalina and accused of lovers including the Papal Nuncio the Archbishop of Paris, any passing page and of course Louis XIV himself.[11] Most of this list was obviously ridiculous, but the King might have been another matter. However, even Liselotte had to admit that Mary Beatrice's friendship with Françoise made the tempting notion impossible. Indeed, Françoise's support of Mary Beatrice's wishes regarding her son was the most direct example of her political influence so far.

So the little court-in-exile at Saint-Germain survived and Mary Beatrice formed an important part of Louis and Françoise's intimate circle. James Edward played with Adelaide, three years his senior, and she in turn made friends with the young Princess Louisa Maria. Perhaps the girl might even make a bride for Bourgogne's brother, Berry, currently the most eligible *parti* at the French court. Queen Mary Beatrice, with a survivor's quality that her appearance belied, even overcame a bout of cancer in 1705. As for James Edward, he was allowed to fight with the French armies, although 1708 brought yet another failed expedition in pursuit of 'his' throne. With time he adopted the convenient appellation of Chevalier de Saint-George, which called for no particular commitment of loyalty while making his identity clear.

*

It was Victor Amadeus of Savoy who had supplied the French-born Philip V with his wife, none other than Adelaide's sister Louison, now transformed into Queen Maria Luisa of Spain. Louis XIV had approved the choice for his grandson of this girl who was 'past her twelfth birthday' and supposed to have a body as beautiful as Adelaide's: 'important for a woman and for the children one expects'. Two daughters who were or would be on two great thrones were however not enough to keep the mercurial Victor Amadeus on board the French (and Bourbon-Spanish) ship. First he allied in secret with his cousin Prince Eugene of Savoy, the brilliant general in the employ of Austria, in early 1702. His treachery was suspected at Versailles where, as Tessé put it, everyone was aware of Victor Amadeus's characteristic desire to have 'a foot in both boots'. But it was not known for sure.[12] In 1703 however Victor Amadeus announced publicly that he had joined the (new) Grand Alliance which consisted of England, Holland and the Austrian Empire. His motive was palpably opportunistic: he did not believe any longer that the War of the Spanish Succession would lead to a quick French victory.

Now it was Adelaide's turn to endure the agonies of a foreign-born princess caught on the wrong side of the hostilities – 'my unhappy destiny' – much as Liselotte had done.[13] In Adelaide's case she suffered not only for her father but for the future of her mother and the two young brothers born to her after Adelaide's departure, as also for her grandmother. Unlike those of Liselotte, however, Adelaide's sensibilities were treated with great tenderness by Louis XIV. The subject of her father was not discussed between them, this bland disdain for the situation being symbolised when the King went ahead with the full carnival festivals of February 1704, with Adelaide the central attraction, as though the war with Savoy was simply not taking place.

It was Madame de Maintenon who had to deal with Adelaide's increasing misery. Françoise had become involved – encouraged by the King – in a correspondence with a remarkable lady known in France as the Princesse des Ursins (from the Italian Orsini, the princely name of her second husband). This imposing, brilliant woman, born into the French Frondeur aristocracy, had been put in charge of Adelaide's sister, the young Queen of Spain. As *camerera-major*, in the Spanish phrase, or senior lady, the Princesse des Ursins performed every known function for Maria Luisa and Philip V, down to holding candles, chamber-pots, and even on occasion the King's breeches when he wished to resume them.

Maintenon and Ursins were now dealing with 'two incomparable princesses', the daughters of the renegade Victor Amadeus; but their correspondence also provided Louis XIV with an important private link to Spain. A visit to France from the Princesse in 1705 cemented the friendship. Louis had taken the opportunity of Philip's marriage to give one of his little sermons on the need to avoid any feminine influence, as he had done to his son the Dauphin: 'the dishonour that such feebleness brings ... One does not pardon it in individuals. Kings, exposed to the public view, are even more scorned.'[14] But it is noticeable that he was quite prepared to use an alliance of two intelligent and discreet women to his advantage, and even to foment it, as he had once employed Henriette-Anne over the Treaty of Dover in 1670.

To the Princesse des Ursins, Madame de Maintenon confided the tumultuous feelings that were tearing at Adelaide: above all it was the unhappiness of her beloved grandfather which tormented her. Her very seriousness on this subject upset Françoise, although in other ways the ever-present governess in her had been trying to school Adelaide away from frivolity.

Every now and then her high jinks went too far. A crude practical joke played on the aged Princesse d'Harcourt, whose skirts and sleeves were fastened to her stool before a page put a firework under it, still raised a smile from the King. However, when Adelaide amused herself making faces behind the back of a peculiarly ugly musketeer she got a sharp reproof from Louis. Personally, he said, he found the man one of the best-looking in his kingdom because he was one of the bravest. To counteract this tendency, Françoise suggested to the Marquis de Dangeau that Adelaide should be presented with a picture of some historic princess as a role model: modest and delicate in character for preference. Simply to give her a history book, which might have seemed the obvious solution, was thought to be 'a risk'.[15] (What was feared? The life of Joan of Arc? Catherine de Médicis?)

Perhaps it was inevitable that this child-woman, the centre of the indulgent attention of the whole court – almost the whole court – should be tempted by the grown-up world of gallantry. She was not in love with Bourgogne, who was in any case dispatched by his grandfather campaigning according to the practice by which royal princes were supposed to prove their leadership qualities in war (supported by more experienced generals). The ambiguity inherent in the whole subject of gallantry has already been noted: the word covered anything from platonic friendship, via mild flirtation to a full-blooded physical affair. The names of three men, very different in character, were linked with Adelaide's at this period. That is, they were linked with her name by Saint-Simon, writing at a safe distance of forty years; Liselotte, writing at the time, remained silent on the subject, which is one cogent reason for doubting the depth of Adelaide's involvement, since Liselotte did not love the King's little favourite. While Marguerite de Caylus, Madame de Maintenon's relation and confidante, thought it was unlikely that there was much in it.[16] Adelaide's turning to these three men seems in fact to tell us more about her own feelings of melancholy and frustration at Versailles than about her sexual nature.

The Marquis de Nangis, born the same year as Bourgogne, had 'a pleasant enough countenance' and carried himself well, but physically he was nothing out of the ordinary. It was his special gift of intimacy which appealed; he was said to have learned the knack of pleasing the ladies from his mother and grandmother, famous intriguers both, and 'past mistresses' in the arts of love. As it happened, Nangis had a mistress of his own, the Marquise de La Vrillière, but he certainly seems to have found time to enjoy a delightful flirtation with Adelaide, especially when he returned to court from campaigning as a wounded man, a subject therefore for both pity and admiration.

The Marquis de Maulévrier was a much more dangerous prospect: coarser than the easygoing Nangis but also cleverer. Ten years older than Adelaide, a nephew of Colbert, he was married to one of the daughters of Tessé, the former Ambassador to Savoy. Maulévrier seems to have been stung to envy by Nangis's ease of access to the Duchesse, and contrived to 'lose' his voice, thus enabling him to whisper sweet but hoarse nothings in Adelaide's ear. It all ended in tragedy: Maulévrier, an unbalanced character, became violently jealous of Nangis, whom he abused. Angered by rejection, he threatened to tell everything to the King and Madame de Maintenon. In the end he committed suicide at Easter 1706.

So far Adelaide had had a little crush on Nangis (who was in any case committed emotionally to another woman) and a foolish involvement with Maulévrier which went wrong. The third man in her life, the Abbé Melchior de Polignac, at forty-five was a sophisticated older man with an interest in the sciences and religion. It was notable that Bourgogne liked his company for this reason. He also knew how to be utterly charming to all the world. Famous for his egregious flattery, he was the author of the immortal remark to Louis XIV on the subject of the rain at Marly, when the King feared that the courtier's fine clothes were being drenched: 'Sire, the rain of Marly does not wet.' It could not last. Polignac was dispatched to Rome, out of harm's way (and Adelaide's); similarly it was discovered that Nangis's wounds were healed, and it was time for the court gallant to become a gallant soldier again. Adelaide wept all day at the departure of Polignac: but she wept on Tante Maintenon's bosom, rather than alone.

The ever-watchful presence of Françoise, to say nothing of the numerous ladies-in-waiting and at another level the Swiss Guards roaming the King's palaces, is the real reason why Adelaide cannot plausibly be accused of adultery or anything near it: 'She was too well guarded,' in the words of Marguerite de Caylus.[17] Françoise would simply not have given her the opportunity. She understood exactly how to handle Adelaide: for example, she took advantage of the young woman's proverbial nosiness to teach her a lesson. Riffling through Françoise's papers, Adelaide was horrified and embarrassed to discover a letter from a certain Madame d'Espernay relating a great deal about her 'intrigue and imprudence' with Nangis. This discovery can hardly have been the result of pure chance. Certainly it had a salutary effect. As part of the subsequent ticking-off that Adelaide received from Tante, she was told that she must never betray what she had read in the presence of Madame d'Espernay herself.

As it turned out, it was the lamentable progress of the war, already so grievous a subject for Adelaide, not the lectures of Tante, which brought her to long-delayed adulthood and, in the most painful way, aroused in her proper protective loyalties towards her husband. Such changes, of course, could not help threatening the artificial but effective nature of her relationship with Louis XIV, on whose lap Adelaide was still expected to sit in her mid-twenties.

A litany of terrible French defeats, with high casualties and vast numbers of wounded, marked this progress. On 13 August 1704 the daring English commander Marlborough snatched a brilliant victory at Blenheim, a Bavarian village on the Danube. He had the assistance of Prince Eugene who, as the son of Olympe Mancini, was regarded at Versailles as some kind of spiritual traitor even if, as a Savoyard, he was not technically one: 'I hate Prince Eugene in the most Christian way I can,' observed Madame de Maintenon some years later.[18] The surviving French were decisively pushed back and Bavaria was out of the war. The next catastrophic defeat was on 23 May 1706 at Ramillies in the Spanish Netherlands, when Marlborough smashed the fifty-thousand-strong French army under Maréchal de Villeroi; the latter was subsequently replaced by the Duc de Vendôme, who had been campaigning against Victor Amadeus in the south. For while nearly all Flanders was now outside French control, things had gone better in Piedmont.

The French siege of Turin naturally brought agony to Adelaide, although it is noticeable that never at any point did she show sympathy for the Savoyard cause. As she wrote to Duchess Anne-Marie: 'I confess the truth, my dearest mother, that it would be the greatest pleasure in this life if I could see my father brought back to reason.' To Victor Amadeus himself, she managed more restraint: 'I own that affection may be somewhat wounded at seeing you arrayed against both your daughters ...'[19] When the Duchess and her two young sons had to flee from the French threat of invasion, Adelaide suffered for them – but she suffered as a loving daughter who had nevertheless totally identified herself with the French cause.*

Then Vendôme was ordered to Flanders. On 7 September 1706 the siege of Turin was raised with the help of Prince Eugene and the French were driven out of Italy, leaving Victor Amadeus himself to invade France the following year when he besieged Toulon. Matters were hardly better in Spain, where the English general Lord Peterborough marched on Madrid, so that Philip V and Maria Luisa had to flee to Burgos. There would be a five-year period when the rivals for the Spanish throne, Philip V and the Habsburg Archduke hailed as Charles III by his supporters, contended inconclusively for the throne, with periodic advances and retreats as in some solemn dance.

Adelaide was by now pregnant once more. In November 1706 she announced the care she was taking in frank terms: 'I have no wish to lose the fruit of all my pains.' Her child, mercifully another boy, was born on 8 January 1707; the King seems to have had no hesitation in instantly granting him the same title as his dead brother: Duc de Bretagne. But there were to be no lavish celebrations for the successful birth of this great-grandson, as there had been in 1704. The hardship of the times did not permit it, nor did the atmosphere at court, where the rising casualty list meant that family members were beginning to vanish; others returned wounded, often visibly mutilated.

It would be pleasant to believe that Adelaide found in the intimacy of motherhood some kind of solace for the restrictions and frustrations of her life. Unfortunately, where a great Princess was concerned there was very little possibility

---

* It is important to note Adelaide's 'French' patriotism, displayed throughout her correspondence, and her total lack of political support for Victor Amadeus, in view of the French historian Michelet's hostility to her in the nineteenth century, including accusations of treachery for which there is absolutely no evidence.

of this kind of relationship: a household and a host of servants stood between the Duchesse de Bourgogne and the Duc de Bretagne. Adelaide's letters to her grandmother did dutifully report on the appearance of teeth and so forth, and she boasted of having 'the most beautiful baby in the world'; but she also criticised the royal governess the Duchesse de Ventadour for spoiling the little boy and making him unnecessarily peevish and ill-behaved. Very rarely did royal mothers in this period break through the apparently unassailable cordon of etiquette which held mother and child apart; Anne of Austria had been one of the few, but Marie-Thérèse and the late Dauphine had definitely not been. A sad letter from Adelaide to Madame Royale made the point: 'I only go and see my son very rarely in order not to be too attached to him.'[20]

Madame de Maintenon, for all her criticisms of Adelaide's behaviour – her gambling, her secret addiction to the bad company of Madame la Duchesse with her drinking and tobacco-smoking – continued to adore her. Increasingly the secret wife depended on female company to sustain her in her own arduous existence as the consoler and supporter of the King. As she told Madame de Glapion, she, Françoise, was the one who had to succour him: 'When the King returns from hunting, he comes to my room; the door is shut and nobody is allowed to enter.' Alone with Louis, Françoise 'listened to all his cares and woes' and staunched the tears he sometimes could not control.[21]

It was to her confessor however that Françoise confided that another aspect of her duties had not ceased: the King still made sexual demands upon her; she described these occasions as 'pénibles' (burdensome). Perhaps she hoped that the confessor would sympathise with this problem of a woman in her seventies; instead, he told her quite sharply that this was still part of her chosen destiny: 'It is at the same time an act of patience, of submission, of justice and of charity.' As it was, Françoise was Louis XIV's 'Madame Solidity': 'Kings have majesty,' said Louis, 'and Popes have sanctity but you have solidity.' He sometimes addressed her as such in the presence of his ministers, meeting in her room, when he enquired what 'Your Solidity' might think on a certain topic.[22]

To the country at large, particularly the soldiers in the French armies, Madame de Maintenon was increasingly regarded as a possible source of help. For example, the soldiers at the new French fortress of Fuenterrabia on the borders of Spain wrote to her in December 1705 under the grandiose title of 'Protectress of the Realm': they wanted pay and also clothing, jackets and shirts – 'our sergeants, Madame, are no happier than us', and in general implored her 'glorious protection'.[23]

In all this Madame de Maintenon herself suffered increasingly bad health. Rheumatism beset her, cold increased it (but the King could see nothing wrong with having all the windows open), and her chamber was often so crowded with men on official business that she could hardly retire to bed. She sat in her 'niche', a covered chair, to ward off draughts. By November 1704 she was describing herself as 'sick and old'; the following May things were worse: 'The life we live here kills me, I am no longer made for this world.'

The flood of petitioners who sought her patronage also caused her pain, as she confided to Marguerite de Caylus. If the King honoured her wishes, he would have less to dispose of elsewhere. If he refused, 'he will upset me. If he upsets me, he has too much feeling for me not to be annoyed, so I become a sadness in his life. Do you think this was God's plan in bringing me close to him?' Françoise told Madame de Glapion that she felt like someone backstage at the theatre where 'the enchanted palace' was revealed as mere canvas: in short, 'I see the world in all its ugliness.'

She would even return to America (that is, the West Indies where she was raised) if she was not told that God wanted her to stay.[24]

Did it ever occur to Françoise, weary and often racked with pain, that Athénaïs had had the better deal out of life? The Marquise de Montespan had begun with supreme beauty, given and received much sensual pleasure and ended with a life full of good works. At Oiron, a magnificent Renaissance building Athénaïs bought with money given to her by the King, she created a hospice in 1703 for 100 poor men and women. She died in May 1707 at the spa at Bourbon which she had once visited at the height of her powers as *maîtresse en titre*, with every royal governor trying to greet her on her way. Athénaïs was sixty-seven. Her will testified to her deep and practical interest in charities; the possessions she left included two pictures of herself as Magdalen, plenty of pious books, some miniatures of the King – and thirty pairs of corsets. Before her death, the King had reduced her pension among his other economies: Athénaïs accepted the deprivation with equanimity on the grounds that all her money went to the poor anyway.

Montespan, that saturnine and tortured man, had rejected her request for pardon, which had been inspired by Athénaïs's Jansenist-inclined confessor. (Father de La Tour did rather better in persuading her that it was her Christian duty to eat less.) Yet when he died in 1701, from whatever motives, last-minute possessiveness or generosity, he made her executrix of his will. Her own death was, according to d'Antin, her son by Montespan, the only one of her children present, 'the most firm and Christian death one could witness'. The funeral was delayed by rows between various local clergy and did not take place until July; then Athénaïs was interred in the church of the Cordeliers at Bourbon with a simple square stone plaque in the wall engraved as follows: 'Here lies the body of Françoise-Athénaïs de Rochechouart, marquise de Montespan.'[25]

At least d'Antin had not suffered from the maternal deprivation of his childhood (to say nothing of his disagreeable father Montespan). He was a popular and successful courtier, a Maréchal de Camp, made Governor of Orléans in 1707. He had inherited something of his mother's taste for grand gestures. This was the year in which he entertained Louis XIV on his estate at Petit-Bourg, choosing to remove an entire chestnut avenue overnight because it obstructed the view from the King's bedroom; in the morning nothing was to be seen, not even cart-ruts, 'as if a fairy had waved her wand'. Now Louis was told the news of Athénaïs's death in a letter from d'Antin as he was about to go hunting. He did not cancel the expedition but on return adjourned to his own room, indicating that he wished to be alone. The courtiers heard him pacing late into the night. But when the bold Adelaide asked him whether there was to be no outward show of grief, the King merely replied that the Marquise de Montespan had been dead to him ever since she had left Versailles.[26]

Louise de La Vallière – Sister Louise de la Miséricorde – lasted another three years. She was not quite sixty-six when she died in June 1710, and had spent over half her life as a Carmelite nun. On hearing this news, Louis repeated virtually the same words with which he had greeted the death of Athénaïs: from the moment she found God, Louise had been dead to him. He did however have a long talk with his confessor and take Communion the next day.

Like many women whose allure owed much to youthful freshness, Louise had long since lost her early prettiness. The extreme penances she imposed upon herself did not help and she was positively emaciated by the time of her death. By 1701 Liselotte wrote that 'not a soul' would now recognise the former Duchesse de La Vallière. Louise was buried, according to the custom of the Carmelite Order, under a simple mound of earth, a small stone indicating her name in religion and the date of her death.[27]

In contrast to the illegitimate children of Athénaïs, who were largely indifferent to their mother, Marie-Anne de Conti had been faithful in her visits to Louise. There was therefore some justified satisfaction for Marie-Anne in the fact that she alone was allowed to wear mourning for her mother: the miasma of the Double Adultery still hung about Françoise-Marie and Madame la Duchesse; to their annoyance, mourning was forbidden to them.

Madame de Maintenon, while complaining (quite a lot) of her daily round, found increasing comfort in the company of the young. Her love of the company of small children was no affectation while, unfashionably for the period, she had no time for pets. When the Marquis de Villette offered her some rare birds, she replied that she much preferred children. So a human pet, a little Moor named Angola, was substituted for the birds. Angola was educated and also converted to Catholicism: he died young, blessing, we are told, the name of his protectress. A young Irishwoman who was also a protégée proved luckier: she went back to her native country and, blessing Maintenon equally, married a rich man.[28]

A typical lament from Françoise of 1709 – 'One has either to die or be alone on earth for I have scarcely any new friends' – ignored the reality of her cosy circle. There were the sympathetic women of the next generation to her own such as Sophie de Dangeau, who was forty in 1704. Sophie had begun life at court as a maid-of-honour to the Bavarian Dauphine, being herself descended from the Bavarian royal family by a morganatic marriage. She married the journal-keeping, high-rolling Dangeau as his second wife. Family feeling from Marianne-Victoire went just so far: she threw a hysterical fit when she heard of the signature 'Sophie de Bavière' at the wedding and the more plebeian 'Sophie de Lowenstein' had to be substituted. It was, wrote Madame de Sévigné, a 'brilliant and ridiculous scene'.[29]

Poverty, noble birth and the blonde looks of 'the angels' all made Sophie utterly suitable from Françoise's point of view and also the King's. In fact Sophie rather resembled the late Angélique de Fontanges, except that she was modest, spiritual and virtuous; all this and a graceful dancer too. One has glimpses of the kind of female intimacy in which the King was wrapped in the notes exchanged between Françoise and Sophie. For example, Françoise told Sophie that the King wanted her to come to dine with them tomorrow and play *brelan*, a game of cards. This was an advance warning so that Sophie should not take the famous incapacitating medicine for a purge that day. 'And pip, pip our stomachs!' scrawled Sophie on the note in return. 'I shall come, I shall find health and money, two great miracles.'[30]

Then there was Marie-Jeanne d'Aumale, who was roughly Adelaide's age and acted as Françoise's confidential secretary from 1705 onwards.[31] Coming from an ancient family of Picardy, Marie-Jeanne lacked looks but was clever, well read and industrious. She was also a lively correspondent: witness her description of the royal doctor Fagon, whose wig fell so far over his face when campaigning that if his nose had not been so big 'no one would have known which was the front and which was the back of his head'. Then there were her droll farming reports about 'the pearl of cows' who gave four and a half pints of milk a day, or the duck who met an unfortunate end and had to be replaced by three others to avoid the displeasure of 'Madame'. The merits of liveliness in entertaining not so much Madame de Maintenon but the ever-present Louis should never be underestimated.

Meanwhile Marguerite de Caylus, her marriage a disaster and her husband now dead, had been languishing in Paris receiving strict advice from Françoise on her conduct. This was the tenor of her remarks: 'Bring up your children, look after your affairs, do my commissions and above all satisfy your parish priest [of Saint-Sulpice].'[32] Doing Françoise's commissions was a work in itself, since the former governess was fond of a bargain, especially if Marguerite was there to hunt it out. Marguerite was advised to establish a relationship with some good second-hand clothes dealers: she should look out for bargains in skirts, petticoats and gloves because Françoise had heard that things in Paris were cheap: a grey-brown damask sample was wanted, not too thick so that it would not be too expensive. The tone is also sometimes sanctimonious, and there was indeed that side to Françoise: 'A costume can never be correct if it might lead to sin,' for example. Yet the femininity of her youth creeps in too: 'If we take Barcelona I'll wear green and pink if the Archduke Charles [the rival candidate for the Spanish throne] falls into our hands.'[33] (Neither thing happened.) In 1708 Marguerite returned to Versailles and occupied an apartment above Françoise, so that she could be summoned to her side via a convenient shared chimney.

Françoise-Charlotte d'Aubigné, transformed into the Duchesse de Noailles by the excellent worldly marriage arranged by her aunt, was also part of the support group: Maintenon, no longer part of the elder Françoise's way of life, was donated to her niece two weeks before her wedding on 30 March 1698. Françoise-Charlotte's aristocratic future made up for the lifelong disappointment afforded by Charles d'Aubigné. He died in 1703 having been finally confined to a rest-home for elderly gentlemen of good family. Charles's *bourgeoise* wife Geneviève, so much disliked by Françoise, was – more or less against her will – confined to a similar establishment for ladies. There were the *maréchaux* of the army too, with most of whom Maintenon was on excellent terms, and with whom she corresponded, discussing the King's wishes.

This satisfactory network of alliances was unfortunately matched by the Cabal, as it became known, at Meudon, home of the Dauphin. Here Madame la Duchesse, Marie-Anne de Conti and others including Athénaïs's son the Duc d'Antin told malicious stories about Tante – and looked to the time when the Dauphin would become King. It was hardly surprising that they should do so: Louis XIV would celebrate his seventieth birthday on 5 September 1708, and at such times, as Saint-Simon duly noted: 'the thoughts of everyone are turning towards the future.'[34] The viciousness of the Cabal would be seen at its height in the events of 1708, and the chief victim would be the Dauphin's son Bourgogne.

The year began well enough with celebrations at which the sixteen-year-old English Princess Louisa Maria in yellow velvet and diamonds was among the beauties. She opened the ball with her brother in a gallery lit by two thousand candles.[35] An incident in February was however a presage of disaster: Adelaide miscarried while at Marly. She was in the early stages of a new pregnancy (little Bretagne was just over a year old) and it seems that her ladies had not wanted her to make the journey, given her difficult gynaecological history. The King's will was however absolute, and he wanted her with him. Then, as he was feeding the carp in his fish pond after Mass, awaiting Adelaide in order to go on to Fontainebleau, a message was whispered in his ear: the Duchesse de Bourgogne was 'injured' (the contemporary euphemism for a miscarriage). After a short pause, the King made a brief announcement as to what had happened. Then a group of gentlemen with more temerity than tact made noises to the effect that this was 'the greatest misfortune in the world', since the Duchesse had already experienced such difficulty in bearing children and might now not be able to have any more.

The King exploded. 'What do I care about who succeeds me? Even if the Duchesse de Bourgogne never has another child, the Duc de Berry is of an age to have children. As to the miscarriage, since it was going to happen, thank God it is over! I shall no longer be nagged by doctors and old women. I shall come and go at my pleasure and be left in peace.' An appalled silence fell; in modern terms the courtiers were gob-smacked. Saint-Simon put it more elegantly: 'You could hear an ant walking ...'[36] After a while the King leaned over the balustrade and made some remark about the fish.

This episode does of course primarily illustrate the frightful selfishness of Louis XIV these days where his own routine was concerned; it is thus on a par with the icy fresh air from open windows which tortured rheumatic Françoise, or the hideous journeys court ladies were obliged to make, compulsory eating and drinking throughout, with no comfort stops provided since the King majestically never needed them. (In one notorious episode, the wretched Duchesse de Chevreuse scarcely endured the journey, such was her agonising need for relief; on arrival she rushed to the chapel and made speedy use of the font.) But there is also something in it of his frustration where Adelaide was concerned: why could she not be the perfect little girl of the past, at his beck and call with no womanly duties to distract her? The little girl who never had a cold when it was a question of going out with the King ... As well as somehow providing healthy heirs on the side ... Why did she gamble so recklessly with unwise gentlemen who risked Louis's disfavour? Why did she hunt, go to parties ...?

In the early summer of 1708 the King took a step which at the time seemed to offer Bourgogne, his shy and austere grandson, an opportunity to shine in the conventional manner for a royal prince, that is in the field of battle. Louis told Adelaide of his intention in a special courtesy visit after stag-hunting, and then announced it to the court on 14 May. Saint-Simon noted rather gloomily that the day marked the anniversary of the death of Louis XIII and the assassination of Henri IV; but that was after the event. At the time the real problem lay not in the coincidence of unfortunate anniversaries but in the tricky problem of royal princes' authority versus that of commanders in the field. Bourgogne was being sent to Flanders, where Vendôme was now in charge. It was not a match made in heaven, nor was it likely to work on the battlefield. Bourgogne was young, untried except for a brief venture to war a few years earlier, and, as has been noted, lacked confidence. Nevertheless he greeted the news with delight; he would no longer 'have to stay idle at Versailles, Marly and Fontainebleau'.[37]

Vendôme, now in his fifties, was seasoned and successful, in fact the most successful living French general.* He was immensely popular with the army, while at court he leaned towards the Dauphin and Meudon set. He was also exceptionally debauched (some found Sodom a convenient rhyme for Vendôme), and in the past had needed a cure for syphilis.

It can never be known for sure – since much obfuscation ensued – whether the third colossal French defeat at Oudenarde on 11 July was the responsibility of Bourgogne, of Vendôme, or of some innate problem of communication between the two of them. With what the Princesse des Ursins once described to Madame de Maintenon as '*l'audace de Milord Marlbouroug*' (*sic*), the English commander had moved his forces from Brussels with such enormous speed

---

* His grandfather was César Duc de Vendôme, Henri IV's bastard, who had been legitimised; Vendôme was thus the first cousin once removed of Louis XIV.

that he took the French by surprise.[38] Vendôme launched straight into battle on the right wing. But Bourgogne, whether owing to cautious advisers or to ignorance of Vendôme's intentions, failed to support him on the left. He stayed entrenched. Six thousand French were killed or wounded, seven thousand taken prisoner. Afterwards Vendôme, smarting with military humiliation, and forced to order a retreat to Ghent, accused Bourgogne of cowardice in failing to follow his commands.

The news of the defeat itself reached Versailles on 14 July. Previous rejoicings over the taking of Ghent died away. Madame de Maintenon told the Princesse des Ursins in Spain that the King was enduring this latest mischance 'with full submission to the will of God', displaying his usual calm courage.[39] The recriminations between Vendôme and Bourgogne were much more difficult to endure. Vendôme's point of view, which was quickly expounded in a plethora of highly combative correspondence, backed by the Cabal at Meudon, was dogmatic: had Bourgogne advanced to support him, as he had the right to expect, a great French victory must have followed. Thus Bourgogne was delineated as a coward and also as a failure. He suffered in particular from his grandfather's lack of faith in him, believing that Louis XIV was taking Vendôme's version of events for granted with all too much ease.

Adelaide was the one who sprang to Bourgogne's defence. Their relative characters can be judged by the fact that Bourgogne wondered whether it was not 'un-Christian' for her to do so. She might have gone 'a little too far' in certain speeches. Maybe Madame de Maintenon should rein her in? At the same time he was charmed by her 'affection and trust'; Adelaide was not a troublemaker by nature; she lacked what Bourgogne called a mischievous 'woman's spirit'; she had on the contrary 'a solid mind' – masculine, presumably – 'much good sense and an excellent and very noble heart'.[40]

Certainly Adelaide was forthright in her opposition to Vendôme. And she refused to be reined in: Vendôme was 'a man for whom she would always feel the greatest loathing and contempt'. Adelaide the frivolous, who had loved nothing so much as to gamble, now spent hours in vigils in the chapel when she was supposed to be asleep. In the meantime Lille fell to Marlborough on 23 October, increasing the dismay at court. When Bourgogne himself returned to Versailles it was to the sound of ribald verses from Madame la Duchesse with lines like this: 'For he's a coward / And a bigot too …' As Françoise commented to the Princesse des Ursins: 'He [Bourgogne] will need all his religious faith to sustain the unjust attacks of the world.'[41] Moreover, Vendôme was back too, but he was the centre of a very different kind of attention.

The lauding of Vendôme, both by the King and at Meudon, was a source of terrible anguish to Adelaide. She wept in Françoise's arms: 'Oh, my dear Tante, my heart is breaking.' Finally she prevailed over Vendôme, but not before the King had criticised his darling sharply for not showing the usual relentless gaiety which was demanded as of right at Versailles. Depression in public was not an option: 'The King was irritated and more than once harshly reprimanded her for displaying ill-humour and chagrin.' Nevertheless Adelaide continued to earn the plaudits of Saint-Simon (who was an admirer of Bourgogne) for being 'indefatigable' and 'full of strength'.[42]

It was at Marly that Adelaide got her revenge. Invited to make up a table for the game of *brelan* in which Vendôme was taking part, she pleaded to be excused: Vendôme's presence at Marly was sufficiently distressing already, she explained, without playing cards with him too. In the end, with the aid of Madame de Maintenon, a deal was brokered by which Vendôme was allowed to Marly one more time, but then understood himself to be excluded. Presently

Adelaide also managed to eject him from Meudon, too, on the grounds of her distress (the Dauphin was after all the humiliated Bourgogne's father). As Saint-Simon wrote in admiration: 'One saw that huge monster blown over by the breath of a brave young princess.' It was Liselotte who commented that the years after 1708 saw at last Adelaide truly in love with her husband.[43] The protective instinct turned out to be the strongest one in her nature – she who had been protected, often artificially so, most of her life.

Adelaide began, in the nicest possible way, to dominate the unassuming Bourgogne. He nicknamed her 'Draco' after the famously severe Athenian legislator with his 'Draconian' code, but gallantly saluted his subordination: 'Draco, how sweet it is to be your slave ...'[44] When it was decided – not before time – to give Bourgogne a proper military education, Adelaide was included in the lessons: there is a vignette of the two of them poring over maps. All this was a good omen for the time in the distant future when Bourgogne, a good weak man, would be King of France: but he would have his Draco beside him as a far more redoubtable Queen than anyone had supposed. It was unfortunate that Bourgogne never actually received his new command: the need for economy meant that it was out of the question to pay for the expensive trappings needed when a Child of France went to war.

In the meantime a sudden spell of bitter cold, its severity 'beyond living memory', gripped the country at Twelfth Night 1709 and lasted for two months. Adelaide told her grandmother that it was 102 years since there had been such devastating weather in France. Every river was frozen, and what no one had ever seen before, the sea itself froze hard enough 'to bear transport all along the coasts'. Worse than the original frost was the sudden complete thaw, followed by another big freeze which, if not quite so long as the first, kept the vegetables, the fruit-trees and the crops totally ice-bound. Indoors, even the bottles of eau de cologne froze in the cupboards and the ink froze on Liselotte's pen as she wrote. Outdoors, as she reported, 'as soon as you leave the house, you are followed by the poor, black with hunger.'[45]*

There was a bleak parallel here with the fortunes of France and her King. A further defeat at Malplaquet in September 1709 saw nearly five thousand Frenchmen killed and eight thousand wounded. All the ladies at court were weeping on behalf of husbands and sons. Adelaide was among those whose 'huge eyes' frequently filled with tears. The court prayed the whole day of the battle: alas, their prayers were not heard. Marie-Jeanne d'Aumale's brother was wounded with 'everything to be feared'. Also wounded, hanging 'between life and death', was Philippe Marquis de Courcillon, son of the Marquis de Dangeau and Sophie.[46]

Although the King might choose to go hunting, leaving the lists of casualties to be read only on his return (gross insensitivity or magnificent aplomb according to taste), he could not avoid the sight of the Dangeau son and his like on their eventual return. While there began to be a noted contrast in the complexions of the courtiers: 'black and red' indicated those who had fought, while skins 'too white' were frowned upon as betokening lack of service. Unfortunately all too many of the noble 'black and red' brigade were visibly mutilated.[47]

'Princes never want to envisage anything sad,' wrote Maintenon bitterly to the Princesse des Ursins. The selfishness of men, especially royal men, was a persistent theme in her correspondence by this time: since she could not let go in front of the King, she took refuge in her letters for a continuous kind of moan. Courcillon however stood for the many members of the court who had been mutilated: at the age of twenty-two, following two operations, he returned

* It has been estimated that 800,000 people died of cold and famine.

without a leg. Courcillon's irrepressible high spirits saved him: he made little *pantalonnades* (farces) with his wooden leg. But he had to be pardoned the omission of his sword and hat at court, since he could not manage them.[48] And there were many other Courcillons in what Maintenon described as 'this tragic year'.

CHAPTER 15

We Must Submit

'Lalande, we must submit.'

– Louis XIV to the composer, pointing to the sky, 1711

S ophie de Dangeau consoled herself for the grievous wounding of her son at Malplaquet with thought of the King, and 'that it was for him that my son risked himself'. Others were not so loyal or so resigned. The Dangeaus had been among the first to give up their silver vessels for the war effort: now the courtiers who had done likewise began to complain about the intolerable 'dirtiness' of using mere pewter and earthenware.[1]

There was no doubt that by the end of 1709, as Adelaide told her grandmother, the War of the Spanish Succession had lasted so long that there was no one who did not wish it was over, while Françoise told the Princesse des Ursins: 'Our woes augment every day.' Françoise herself had a naturally pacifist temperament and was far from encouraging the King in his pursuit of war. Her own feeling for the sufferings of the poverty-stricken country was so strong that she tried (in vain) to dissuade the King from building himself a magnificent new chapel at Versailles. Marie-Jeanne d'Aumale reported that Françoise 'more than doubled' her charities. Far from avoiding the ragged crowd of dirty, half-naked child beggars, she increasingly disliked Marly because it was cut off from them: there was no one to whom she could give money.[2]

Where once Louis had been satirised (and more than half admired) for his priapic adventures, now he was attacked for his failures in battle and the economic state of the country. Even his previous reputation for virility was used against him: 'The French King's Wedding' of 1708 described him as impotent nowadays – at war and in bed. 'The Plagues of War and Wife consent / To send the King a packing. / You cannot give your spouse content ...' Another satirical rhyme ran: 'Our father that art in Versailles / Thy name is no longer hallowed / Thy Kingdom is no longer so great / Thy will is no longer done either on earth or sea / Give us our daily bread which we can no longer obtain / Forgive our enemies who have beaten us ..."[3] The fact that France now had a King in his early seventies whose immediate heir, the Dauphin, was, as immediate heirs of senior parents tend to do, beginning to eye the throne, did not increase contentment.

It was against the background of 'these recent and unhappy years', in Françoise's phrase to Maréchal de Villeroi, that the battle of the marriage of the Duc de Berry, youngest son of the Dauphin, was fought. Adelaide managed to give birth to another healthy boy on 10 February 1710 shortly after the third birthday of Bretagne; he was created Duc d'Anjou, the traditional title of the second son, which Philip V had enjoyed before his accession to the Spanish throne. Her labour was long and intense, her sufferings so great that those males present by tradition retreated from the room. However, high infant mortality meant that the succession was not necessarily secure with two knaves in the hand; Berry's future, bringing hope of more children, was also important.

The King had announced that there was to be no question of a match with a foreign princess, given the international situation, and the economic realities of the time. The Stuart princess, Louisa Maria, was Madame de Maintenon's candidate, as being the daughter of her adored Mary Beatrice, but nobody else thought that was a solution. Taking into account the real possibilities at Versailles, it was Adelaide who took a prominent part in advocating the candidature of Philippe and Françoise-Marie's daughter Marie-(Louise)-Élisabeth. Her motives for this, a campaign which would lead in the end to disaster all round, were not of the finest. Her chief aim was to keep out the daughter of Madame la Duchesse, known as Mademoiselle de Bourbon. Both these girls were granddaughters of Louis XIV, via their legitimised mothers. But their characters were very different.

Marie-Élisabeth was fifteen. She was her father's favourite out of his numerous daughters.[*] Unpleasant gossip gathered around their too-intimate relationship; certainly she consoled him for the loveless marriage he had been forced to make. Marie-Élisabeth had also been brought up by her father to despise her mother for 'the defilement of her adulterous birth', an act of revenge on his part. The girl was from the start highly unstable, with a violent temper whenever her will was crossed; no one had ever tried to control her – not her notoriously lazy mother and certainly not her doting father, whom she treated 'like a negro slave' and ruled much as Françoise ruled the King according to Saint-Simon. Vivacity was Marie-Élisabeth's strong suit, that, and a certain wit, reminding courtiers that she was Athénaïs's granddaughter.

Physically however she allowed her appetites to hold sway: Marie-Élisabeth became grossly fat quite young, so that the King shuddered with distaste. Once upon a time when she had been a little girl, Marie-Élisabeth had charmed him, like other little girls; at the age of twelve after hunting

* Françoise-Marie had displayed the same high fertility as her mother Athénaïs. By 1710, the Duc and Duchesse d'Orléans already had four daughters of whom Marie-Élisabeth was the eldest; two more would follow. Chartres remained their only son.

she had been invited to dine with him, an unusual honour for a person of her rank. Now he suggested that she was so fat that she might be infertile. Liselotte's pen portrait of her granddaughter was not flattering: pale blue eyes with pink rims, a short body with long arms, a clumsy walk and in general lacking any grace in anything that she did; only her neck, arms and hands were flawlessly white. Nevertheless the tyrannical Marie-Élisabeth must have had something: Liselotte had to admit that her son Philippe was convinced 'Helen was never so beautiful'.[5]

Adelaide's refusal to back the far more suitable Mademoiselle de Bourbon, aged seventeen in 1710, was partly based on her strong dislike of her mother. Madame la Duchesse had scorned the little Princess of Savoy from the start, the pretty child who had displaced her as the young star of the court; and then there was Madame la Duchesse's unforgivable behaviour over Bourgogne's military troubles. But as Adelaide headed towards thirty – the age at which she had decided to give up dancing – she also feared that Mademoiselle de Bourbon, with her charming teasing ways, would replace her in the old King's affections. She certainly employed her own apparent naïvety in the cause of Marie-Élisabeth. Adelaide observed innocently out loud on one occasion what a lovely bride the Orléans princess would make for the Duc de Berry, and then stopped as though aghast at her own temerity: 'Tante, what have I just said? Did I say something wrong?'[6]

As Adelaide supported Marie-Élisabeth (who went on a special diet, eating only when she was walking to improve her chances), the two mothers in question, Françoise-Marie and Madame la Duchesse, were also locked in a poisonous struggle. Old sibling rivalries came into it – Madame la Duchesse's humiliation at having to yield precedence to her younger sister for example. And then the Dauphin, as father of the bridegroom, had some say in it all, even if the King gave the ultimate verdict.

The matter was concluded when Philippe was persuaded by Saint-Simon to write a letter to the King proposing Marie-Élisabeth as a bride for Berry, with Saint-Simon advising on its contents. A moment was chosen to present this letter when the King was reported by one of his doctors to be in a good mood; he took it away unopened. The next day Louis announced that he agreed in principle, but needed some time to talk round the Dauphin, which he proceeded to do 'in the tone of a father, mixed with that of King and master'. This was a different approach from the one he had recently taken over the sons of Maine and Bénédicte: then 'that most severe and tyrannical of parents' had humbled himself to the Dauphin and Bourgogne in order to establish that the boys should have the same rank as their father.[7] The whole matter of the bastards, their descendants and their degree was a delicate one, as time would show. But Louis was on surer ground when it came to the marriage of a (legitimate) grandson.

Up till now, no one had thought to ask the opinion of Berry himself. Aged nearly twenty-four, he had grown up from his mischievous boyhood into being a mild-mannered and good-natured young man who was especially devoted to his brother Bourgogne (and to Adelaide, whom he had known since childhood). He certainly displayed no jealousy of his two elder brothers' superior destinies. When Philip was made King of Spain, Berry sensibly announced: 'I will have less trouble and more fun than you,' and gave as an example that he would now be able to hunt the wolf 'all the way from Versailles to Madrid'. Somehow his education had been neglected, perhaps because the Dauphine's death had left 'my little Berry' motherless at the age of three and a half. He was certainly not as intelligent as Bourgogne or Philip V, and tended to be inarticulate in public as well as terrified of his grandfather (just as the Dauphin had been). Nevertheless, with his fine head of fair hair and his fresh complexion, Berry was positively handsome by the standards of a Bourbon prince; quite apart from his rank, Marie-Élisabeth could be pleased with her catch. As for his own feelings, Berry, told by his grandfather that Marie-Élisabeth was the highest-ranking princess in France, was uneasily non-committal.

So the betrothal was announced on 5 July 1710. The event led to glacial exchanges between the sisters. It was even suggested to Madame la Duchesse by Françoise-Marie – surely a gratuitous act of triumph – that another Orléans daughter might marry a Bourbon-Condé son. Madame la Duchesse merely replied that her son would not be of an age to be married for a long time and besides he had only a small fortune. But worse lay ahead for her. At the formal ceremony, Mademoiselle de Bourbon, the slighted fiancée, was next in rank and thus by etiquette had to carry the train of Marie-Élisabeth. This was intolerable!

The King, who believed in etiquette but was also kind-hearted where these matters were concerned, suggested that Marie-Élisabeth's younger sisters should be hauled back from their convent to perform the task (their rank being higher than that of Mademoiselle de Bourbon). At least that pleased the two little girls in question, known respectively as Mademoiselle de Chartres and Mademoiselle de Valois, who at eleven and nine had bewailed their incarceration. The decision to put them in a convent was generally ascribed to Françoise-Marie's laziness over her maternal duties, and the girls were so upset passing through Paris, that the curtains of their coach had to be drawn. Although the times did not 'permit much entertainment', the wedding was described by Adelaide to her grandmother as being 'as magnificent as policy permitted'.[8]

Unfortunately this brilliant marriage – in worldly terms –

had the effect of encouraging Marie-Élisabeth in her vile behaviour, and Berry had no resources to cope with it. At first he was quite mesmerised by his bride, according to Liselotte, although the passion wore off thanks to her behaviour. The rest of the court was more horrified than mesmerised. 'Terrifyingly bold ... wildly proud, vulgar beyond the bounds of decency': these were some of the descriptions she merited from Saint-Simon. She gorged prodigiously in public (gone were the days of the diet) and scarcely ever failed to drink herself unconscious, 'rendering in all directions the wine she had swallowed'. Having no religion herself – she proclaimed she did not believe in God – she mocked those like her husband who did. At one particular supper-party given by Adelaide at Saint-Cloud, Marie-Élisabeth became so 'sottish' that the effects, 'both above and below', were embarrassing to all present. Her father was also drunk on the same occasion – but the daughter was the drunker of the two.[9]

Liselotte tried to take a hand in the education of her wayward granddaughter, calling her 'my pupil'. It is true that Marie-Élisabeth showed a rare graciousness in her reluctance to take precedence over her grandmother (which as the wife of the Duc de Berry she was now entitled to do): 'Push me forward, Madame, so as to propel me in front of you. I need time to grow accustomed to that honour ...' But when it came to a question of a beautiful necklace of pearls and yellow diamonds which had belonged to Anne of Austria, which she coveted for a court ball, Marie-Élisabeth's behaviour to her mother was the reverse of gracious. When her mother refused to hand it over, Marie-Élisabeth insolently pointed out that the necklace belonged to her father by descent from Monsieur and he would certainly let her have it.

Sure enough, in a moment of weakness Philippe did. But the matter did not rest there. Françoise-Marie complained bitterly and Liselotte took a hand, going to the King herself. Louis hated this kind of trouble among women and was furious. In the end Marie-Élisabeth was induced to apologise to her mother and the matter was smoothed over. The whole unpleasant incident, so trivial and yet so important by the values of Versailles, made it clear that Marie-Élisabeth was more than unruly: she was quite out of control, and even the King found it difficult to check her.

Furthermore, there was no large, consoling brood of royal children to make it all seem worthwhile in dynastic terms. A year after her marriage, the Duchesse de Berry miscarried: because 'it had been female', wrote Saint-Simon, 'everyone was soon consoled'.[10] All the same, it was to be well over a year before Marie-Élisabeth conceived again, and by then the balance of power at court had been radically altered.

Sudden death is 'the ruffian on the stair' where hereditary monarchy is concerned.[11] Nobody would have predicted in the spring of 1711 that the Dauphin, a healthy, well-set-up man in his fiftieth year, would fall victim to smallpox, although it was the universal and egalitarian killer of the time. He is supposed to have caught the infection by kneeling at the wayside when a priest was passing carrying the sacred host. The Dauphin was unaware that the priest in question had just visited a victim of smallpox.

The people of Paris, with whom he was by far the most popular member of the royal family due to his bluff cheerfulness (and visible self-indulgence), sent a deputation of market-women promising him a Te Deum to celebrate his recovery. 'Not yet, wait till I am well again,' was the message from the Prince. But by midnight he was all too obviously at death's door. The Dauphin, Louis de France, died on 11 April. Bourgogne and Adelaide were both completely dazed and 'pale as death'. Berry lay on the floor sobbing loudly. Upstairs Mademoiselle de Choin, his long-term mistress and (probably) morganatic wife, was condemned, by the harsh rules of Versailles, to lurk unseen in an attic room. No one brought the news of the Dauphin's death and she only realised what had happened 'when she heard the sounds of lamentations'. Two friends bundled her into a hired coach and took the unacknowledged widow away to Paris. It was the King who continued to act with patient dignity even though his eyes kept filling with tears. Liselotte even went so far as to admit that Louis needed Françoise at this time for consolation, although she was currently laid low by one of her bouts of illness.[12]

Saint-Simon excoriated on the subject of the late Dauphin: he had been 'without vice, virtue, knowledge or understanding' and was quite incapable of acquiring any such qualities: 'Nature fashioned him as a ball to be rolled hither and thither.'[13] Fortunately Father François Massillon, a great orator in the tradition of Bossuet and Bourdaloue (both now dead), did rather better at his funeral. But perhaps the kindest verdict was the fact that both Mademoiselle de Choin and the people of Paris truly mourned him.

In the end it was Louis himself who found the right words. Michel-Richard de Lalande, composer and church organist, had become an increasingly important figure in the rituals of court music. He was able to produce a stream of the kind of grand motets on which the court of Louis XIV flourished; he had overseen the musical education of Louis's illegitimate daughters. One critic, Le Cerf de la Viéville, had heard one of his motets at a Mass and commented with enthusiasm: 'It seems to me that the King is served in music as well as he ought to be ... in sum, better than in any other place in his kingdom.' Two of the composer's daughters died about the time of the death of the Dauphin. Lalande did not like to mention their deaths, and thought it presumptuous to commiserate with his sovereign. It was Louis who brought up the subject: 'We must submit, Lalande,' he said, pointing towards the sky.[14]

At a stroke the map of the court at Versailles was altered for ever. The Duc de Bourgogne, aged twenty-eight, was now the direct heir to the throne, the Dauphin with his two sons following him.* (But the special title of 'Monseigneur', created for his father, was not to be used for him: it was felt to be too painful.)[15] Louis XIV in his grief solaced himself by indicating that Adelaide, now 'Madame la Dauphine', was to have all the rights due to a queen, including control of her own household. Her royal escort was doubled to twenty-four, and there were two Swiss guards outside her door, hitherto a privilege reserved for the monarch. Not for nearly thirty years – since the death of Marie-Thérèse – had there been such a female position of power. And of course at a stroke, too, the wasps of the Cabal in the nest at Meudon lost their power to sting. At least poor Mademoiselle de Choin was treated decently by Louis XIV: she received a pension and a house in Paris.

The great loser – in her own opinion – was the Duchesse de Berry. Her position and that of Adelaide had not been so different in the lifetime of the Dauphin. As the *Second* Lady at Versailles she was now according to etiquette compelled to hand the chemise to Adelaide at her ritual dressing.[16] Marie-Élisabeth, with her usual lack of control, went over the top in complaining about this 'valetage', which had after all been routinely performed at Versailles in the past by ladies as great as if not greater than herself, including her grandmother (who had only made a fuss at the phantasmagorical prospect of handing the chemise to Françoise ...). When Marie-Élisabeth was at last obliged to give in, she performed the ceremonial functions extremely

---

* Here he will continue to be referred to as Bourgogne, to avoid confusion with his late father.

slowly and with an ill grace. Adelaide kept her cool, pretending not to notice the delay which had left her virtually
naked. In her great desire to have 'a happy relationship'
with her sister-in-law, she was willing to overlook 'this latest
prank', according to Saint-Simon.

Adelaide, as Dauphine, did not lose sight of all her own
monkey tricks, the ways which had so entranced the King.
Perhaps one of her little games was not quite so entrancing:
Adelaide loved to get the confidential servant Nanon to give
her a *lavement* (enema) before a theatrical performance; she
then spent the whole performance in a state of wicked glee
at the thought of her secret condition before Nanon attended
to her relief.* More beguiling was her treatment of Madame
la Duchesse and Marie-Anne de Conti when they were
rolling their eyes at her childish conduct on one occasion at
Fontainebleau. Adelaide had been 'diverting' the King by
pretending to chatter in a dozen different languages and
other such nonsense while the two princesses eyed each
other and scornfully shrugged their shoulders. As soon as
Louis had gone into his special cabinet to feed his dogs,
Adelaide grabbed the hands of Saint-Simon's wife and
another lady; pointing at the scornful princesses she said:
'Did you see them? I know as well as they do that I behave
absurdly and must seem very silly, but he [the King] needs
to have a bustle about him and that kind of thing amuses
him."[18]

Adelaide went further than that. Swinging on the arms of
the two ladies, in the words of Saint-Simon 'she began to
laugh and sing: "Ha-Ha! I can laugh at them because I will
be their queen. I need not mind them now or ever, but they
will have to reckon with me, for I shall be their queen,"

* In the general obsession with health-giving *lavements*, Adelaide was not alone
in this practice; the Duc de Richelieu for example took senna every evening
followed by a *lavement* even when attending the Parlement. Under the circumstances Saint-Simon strongly disliked the idea of sitting next to him.[17]

and she shouted and sang and hopped and laughed as high as loud as she dared.' When the two ladies tried to hush her, in case the princesses heard, 'she only skipped and sang the more: "What do I care for them? I'm going to be their queen."' Yet who was to say that Adelaide would not one day make an excellent caring queen? The chattering girl was beginning to have serious reflections on the nature of royal duty: 'France is in such a pitiable state ... we must try by our charity to help the poor.' They are after all 'our brothers and sisters, exactly like ourselves', but since it is to us God has given riches, 'so we are all the more obliged to help others'.[19]

Louis XIV continued to think of Adelaide as more or less perfect with one exception – a sloppiness in her dress and a frank indifference to the subject which irritated him even more now that she was Dauphine. Adelaide's lack of interest in matters such as bonnets, muffs, gloves and even jewellery is engaging at a distance in contrast to the avidity of most ladies at that time. But it struck at Louis's sense of order, still so strong. In vain Adelaide made it clear that she preferred lounging about in casual clothes, as they would now be called, when she was pregnant; Bourgogne backed her choice not to wear her corset for comfort's sake. Tante's reaction was that such a style was not becoming to the new Dauphine – nor to her rank. She gave Adelaide one of her reprimands: 'Your untidiness displeases the King."[20] As to wearing jewellery, the gems would draw proper attention to her beautiful complexion and neat figure. Adelaide shrugged her pretty shoulders and compromised by storing her prodigious collection of jewellery in Tante's room, so that they could be assumed before her visits to the King and discarded afterwards.

Adelaide personally was not entirely at fault in this. Her Mistress of the Wardrobe, the Comtesse de Mailly, another Maintenon protégée who had begun life as a poor and virtuous girl, was at best 'indolent' and at worst was mis-appropriating the large funds set aside to dress her employer. Thus when the King decided to make Adelaide 'absolute mistress of her own Household' one of Adelaide's first moves was to replace the Comtesse de Mailly with the altogether more satisfactory Madame Quentin.

In late 1711 there were general 'appearances' of peace, as Adelaide wrote to her grandmother in Turin, which she hoped were well founded. Although it would take a couple of years to achieve, no one much doubted that in the end peace would break out. The death of the Emperor Joseph I on 11 April 1711 had led to the accession of the Archduke Charles, hitherto the rival candidate for the Spanish throne, in his place. If the new Emperor Charles VI also acquired Spain, he would join Vienna to Madrid – quite as unpopular a prospect for his allies as the union of France and Spain. The possibility of peace with Queen Anne of England led to another of Adelaide's artless aphorisms after which she pretended to be taken aback by what she had just said. 'Tante, it cannot be denied that England is better governed under a queen than under a king,' she said, 'and do you know why? Because under a king, a country is really ruled by women, and under a queen by men.'[21] Adelaide did not know that the public nostalgia for Queen Elizabeth in England which grew in the later years of Charles II was based on exactly the same premise.

In the meantime the advent of a Tory government in place of the Whigs in England meant that the solid support for the audacious general 'Milord Marlboroug' had vanished, just as Sarah Duchess of Marlborough had been displaced in the affections of Queen Anne. Englishmen, like French-men, were tired of the war. In the so-called Preliminaries of London of September 1711, the possibilities of a settlement, including an Anglo-French commercial treaty, were explored.

In the meantime, in her private correspondence Adelaide

began to make glancing references to toothaches. Her teeth had been one of her imperfections on her arrival, and thereafter Adelaide, who had no false pride, admitted that they were frankly black. Now she was plagued with pains in her mouth. In late January 1712 the problem flared up once more, and her face was so swollen when she reached Marly that she had to play cards with the King with her face enveloped in a hood. From evidence later, it seems that Adelaide was also in the very early stages of pregnancy. At all events, her constitution, weakened by much child-bearing and child-losing over the last ten years, to say nothing of the perpetual draining caused by rotten teeth, was already frail when Adelaide fell ill with a fever on 5 February. At the time an Italian-style stew that she loved was blamed (once again 'Italian' was a term of abuse). Then there was a kind of cheesecake full of sugar and spice which she had been making at her Menagerie as she loved to do, with memories of her childhood at the Vigna di Madama; had Adelaide eaten too much of it?

If only greed had been the culprit! By Sunday 7 February Adelaide was again ill, although she tried valiantly to go to Mass.[22] A piercing pain, worse than anything she had ever endured, then laid her low and continued for twenty-four hours despite the best (or worst) efforts of the doctors, their usual bleedings, both from arm and foot, and the emetics which made hideous so many sickbeds of the time. She was given opium to relieve the pain and even allowed to inhale the dreaded tobacco, which was regarded as a satisfactory prophylactic, if hateful social practice. Nothing worked. The fever and the opiates meant that she was often quite confused when the King visited her.

At last some spots emerged and measles was announced; hope was felt that she would recover when the rash had broken completely. It did not happen. On the morning of Wednesday 10 February the distraught King found his

Princess sufficiently lucid to hear some of the details of the peace-making process which had started at Utrecht. 'I have an idea that peace will come,' said Adelaide sadly, 'and I shall not be there to see it'; it was a pathetic testimony to how much the fraught situation between France and her native Savoy had weighed upon her. That night Adelaide was visibly worse to the watchers at her bedside. Madame de Maintenon was there all the time, except when the King was visiting, and Bourgogne most of the time despite his own growing feverishness – but they put that down to exhaustion.

On Thursday 11 February the King felt desperate enough to ask publicly for the aid of St Geneviève, patron saint of Paris (she who had been so prominent in the appeals over his own birth so long ago). The coffer containing the saint's remains was to be uncovered at daybreak for the faithful to implore her protection. It was an action which, intended for times of national emergency, could only be taken with the consent of Parlement, but the assembly eagerly endorsed it. Alas, by daybreak on Friday 12 February the Princess was *in extremis*.

The night before it had been judged time to bring in the last sacraments and the matter of her last confession was raised. By her silence Adelaide politely rejected the offer of the Jesuit Father de La Rue, although they had always been on excellent terms. In fact Adelaide had never really wanted a Jesuit confessor in the first place, but had accepted the Jesuit because he was the King's choice – her usual obedient stance. Now she felt she had a right to her own way. Father de La Rue dealt with the situation with calm understanding and established that she preferred Father Bailly, a parish priest of Versailles with Jansenist tendencies, favoured by the more devout ladies of the court. (Adelaide had probably always leaned in that direction.) When Father Bailly proved to be away – and Father de la Rue had to tell her there was no time to lose – Adelaide settled for a Franciscan Father Nöel. At the time nothing was seen as particularly odd about this, it was the privilege of a dying woman: in fact Adelaide's sister, Queen Maria Luisa of Spain, who died two years later, also asked for a change of priest.

Adelaide's confession, which she made alone, took some time. Afterwards, when Madame de Maintenon returned, Adelaide told her: 'Tante, I feel quite different, as though I were entirely changed.' 'That is because you have come close to God,' said Françoise.

Later, when Adelaide asked for the prayers for the dying, she was told the time had not yet come. Meanwhile Louis and Françoise desperately convened a conference of doctors, seven of them altogether, including some brought down from Paris. The verdict as ever was more bleeding, and a further emetic if the bleeding had no effect, beyond of course weakening the patient. Poor Adelaide now began to worry obsessionally about her gambling debts: 'Tante, I have one big anxiety …' She really wanted to see her husband and explain, but when this was banned on the grounds of infection, Adelaide asked for her writing-case, managed to open it, and tried to leaf through her papers. The task was beyond her (what a sad parody of the lively Adelaide who had burrowed through the King's and Madame de Maintenon's papers with such energy!). Maintenon continued to assure her on the matter of the debts: Bourgogne would take care of them 'out of his love for you'.

It was pathetic how, even in her agonies, Adelaide's childhood training in trying at all times to please the King still held up. When asked why she did not speak to Louis, she replied that she was afraid of crying: as though anything now could upset the King further. At various points Adelaide recognised the Duchesse de Guiche – 'My beautiful Duchesse, I am dying' – and then murmured some words, unbearably sad to her listeners: 'Princess today, tomorrow nothing, and in two days forgotten.'

In spite of the doctors – who bled the poor dying Princess for the fifth time from the foot, so that she actually fainted under their care – in spite of the prayers, in spite of the penance, Adelaïde's fever continued to rise. By now she was virtually unconscious, violent emetics simply weakening her still further without bringing her to her senses. Françoise went to the chapel to pray. The King refused to leave Adelaïde's bedside. Some kind of strong powder produced by a gentleman-in-waiting was tried as a desperate measure; Adelaïde did manage to comment how bitter it was. Hearing that the Dauphine was conscious, Madame de Maintenon came back. And it was she who gently acknowledged to the girl that the end was coming. 'Madame, you go to God,' she said. 'Yes, Tante,' repeated Adelaïde obedient to the last. 'I go to God.' A few moments later Adelaïde, Princess of Savoy, Duchesse de Bourgogne and Dauphine of France, was dead.

Louis XIV had left the dying girl's chamber a few minutes earlier according to the tradition by which a monarch was never in the presence of death (except his own). 'We must submit,' he had told Lalande over the death of his son, pointing to the sky. But he could not have imagined how much more submission was going to be required of him. Adelaïde had once mocked her husband's excessive piety: she told her ladies that she would like to die first and then he could marry a nun. But poor broken-hearted Bourgogne survived a mere six days after the death of his wife, his Draco to whom he had been a willing slave. He had been fatally infected by the measles which killed her in his early devoted and dogged visits to her bedside. In this atmosphere of tragedy, sometimes the tiny things were the most poignant. Liselotte was reduced to tears by the sight of Bourgogne's little dog searching for him in the chapel because he had last seen him kneeling there: 'The poor beast sadly looked at everyone as though to ask where his master had gone.'[23]

And still the need for submission was not past: the little Duc de Bretagne, five years old, was also fatally infected, and died on 8 March while the doctors were in the act of bleeding him from the arm. He had lived just long enough to be appointed Dauphin in his father's place, according to the King's wish.[24] Louis XIV had now lost his son, grandson, great-grandson – three Dauphins – and, worst of all, his beloved granddaughter-in-law in a span of eleven months. Adelaide's surviving young son, Louis Duc d'Anjou, was saved only by the revolutionary and defiant action of the governess of the Children of France, the Duchesse de Ventadour. The doctors wanted to bleed him also. But this splendid woman, who could see what no one dared acknowledge, that the doctors were killing their enfeebled patients with their ministrations more effectively than any disease, simply barricaded herself and the two-year-old Prince into her apartments and would not allow the doctors access.*

So Louis XIV was left with a tiny great-grandson, still in leading-strings, who would presumably in the course of time succeed him, and a grandson in the shape of the Duc de Berry, next heir if little Anjou died (as so many children had died). After that came Philippe Duc d'Orléans. It was part of the nastiness as well as the grief of the times that it was actually suggested Philippe had poisoned the princes. It has been seen that most sudden deaths of prominent people were accompanied by these lamentable charges. Not only did Liselotte strongly rebut them, saying she would put her

---

* Charlotte Duchesse de Ventadour, who died in 1744 at the age of ninety-three, continued to act as governess to the Children of France for the next twenty years; King Louis XV, as the little Duc d'Anjou became, never forgot that she was the woman who had saved his life.

hand in the fire to prove Philippe's innocence – a natural defence of her son, perhaps – but Madame de Maintenon, who detested Philippe, thought there was nothing in it either. Nor did Louis XIV show any signs of believing these charges. There was in fact no need to look for the lurid explanation of poison to explain these deaths: there was a virulent plague of measles at the time, and as many as five hundred died in Paris and Versailles alone; but they were not royal.

While some fingers pointed at Philippe (just because he had moved up two places in the succession), others took a more vengeful line. The deaths of the royal family, said Frederick I of Prussia, were 'God's judgement' on Louis XIV for sacking Heidelberg fifteen years earlier, when so many deceased Palatine Electors and Electresses had been 'dragged from their tombs'.[25] The judgement of heaven was harder for Louis to rebut: for the rest of his life he had to submit to it.

As Louis XIV had surely loved Adelaide more than anyone in his life, so her death caused him the greatest sorrow. Saint-Simon for one thought it was 'the only real grief he ever experienced'.[26] Liselotte was equally convinced of the personal tragedy for Louis. Adelaide's loss was irreparable, as 'she had been brought up entirely to his liking'. She was 'his comfort and joy, and had such gay spirits that she could always find something to cheer him up'. Liselotte also quoted the usual horoscope predicting the event which is always cited (as with Henriette-Anne) when someone dies young – ignoring all the other horoscopes which did not predict it. Adelaide was supposed to have been told in Turin that she would die in her twenty-seventh year and cried out: 'I must enjoy myself because it won't be for long ...!'[27] This however is contradicted by her saucy admonitions to her aunts: 'I'm to be Queen ...' which one must believe was the true Adelaide.

The bereaved King and Françoise did attempt to fill the enormous gap as far as was humanly possible, by concentrating on the girl who, at seventeen, was now the First Lady of Versailles: Marie-Élisabeth Duchesse de Berry. As Louis had embraced his surviving grandson Berry with the words 'I have no one but you', so there was a real effort to mould Marie-Élisabeth into suitable material for an august position close to the throne, and an intimate one close to their hearts. But how very different the two young women were! Marie-Élisabeth's raucous behaviour and her proverbial drunkenness have already been noted; she now began to torture her husband with a flagrant affair with a member of her household, one La Haye. Perhaps infidelity could be overlooked if it was stylish infidelity: after all, it was not exactly unknown at Versailles in times gone by ... Unforgivable was her dismissive attitude to self-presentation. *Mouches* (literally flies) or beauty-spots were becoming fashionable. Marie-Élisabeth splattered her face with them, up to twelve at one time. You look like an actress, not the First Lady of Versailles, groaned Liselotte.[28] Worst of all, Marie-Élisabeth had failed to conceal her glee at the death of Adelaide, because it led to her own elevation.

The impossibility of making something – anything – of the new First Lady was, surely, partly responsible for a kind of bitterness which swept over Françoise at the death of Adelaide. 'I shall weep for her all my life,' she told her nephew-by-marriage the Duc de Noailles, 'but I am learning things every day which make me think she would have caused me a great deal of trouble. God took her from us out of pity.'[29] In practical terms it is of course possible that Françoise found incriminating matter concerning Nangis, for example, or that courtiers badmouthed Adelaide (no longer able to respond) on the same subject. But the predominant cause of this bitterness was the betrayal that the old feel when the young die first. Her comments that

Adelaide would not after all have turned out so well belong to this category. In February 1712 Louis was seventy-three and Françoise seventy-six. Adelaide, nearly fifty years younger, had somehow broken the contract by which *she* would divert and care for the old couple at the head of the court until *their* deaths ...

The *canards* of her treachery on the other hand belong to the middle of the eighteenth century, and certainly do not hold water according to the evidence of her own correspondence (nor psychologically according to her character). Burrow as she might in the King's papers, Adelaide was never in a position to discover war plans and pass them back to Savoy. That was in any case not her game: a typical letter to her mother in 1711 expressed the wish that she could bring Victor Amadeus 'back to reason' – that is, back to support for France.

There was an alleged remark of Louis XIV to Madame de Maintenon, when they were alone, reported in the *Historiography of France* of 1745. It was the work of Charles Pinot Duclos, who would have been eight years old at the time of Adelaide's death. 'The *coquine* [little rascal],' the King was supposed to have said of Adelaide, 'she betrayed us.' As has been pointed out by historians, this was not the language of Louis XIV, nor is it clear how a conversation between two individuals on their own ever got reported.[30] Duclos had an entertaining career as a colourful, sometimes scabrous novelist, and it is surely to his talent for fiction rather than fact that this remark belongs. Adelaide's loyalties had so clearly passed to France from the moment she arrived, just as Louis XIV had planned when he deprived the child of her familiar ladies-in-waiting. Adelaide still loved Victor Amadeus in theory, but her letters to him were highly critical, with those lamentations that he was fighting the countries of both his daughters. Latterly her new devotion to her husband's interests aroused even Liselotte's admiration.[31]

The awesome double funeral of the Dauphin and Dauphine of France was something no one ever forgot. Voltaire, writing a generation later, said that even during the next reign, any mention of the deaths of 1712 produced involuntary tears from courtiers. Their hearts were taken to Val-de-Grâce according to royal custom; their bodies lay in state and were then buried at Saint-Denis. 'I don't think that the world has ever seen what we are about to see now,' wrote Liselotte, 'a man and his wife being taken together to Saint-Denis.' She added rather touchingly: 'I almost think that all of us here will die, one after another,' as though up till now they had all been immortal. Saint-Simon met his father-in-law the Duc de Beauvillier on his return from the solemn ceremonies at Saint-Denis and embraced him with the words 'You have just buried France!'[32]

The body and soul of Louis XIV lingered on, but it is difficult to believe that much was left of his heart. As Saint-Simon wrote of Adelaide years later: 'Mourning for her has never ceased, a secret involuntary sadness remains, a terrible void which nothing can fill.'[33]

CHAPTER 16

Going on a Journey

He [Louis XIV] gives all his orders as though he were only
going on a journey.

– Liselotte Duchesse d'Orléans, 27 August 1715

The peace that Adelaide, true to her dying prophecy, did
not see came about in the year after her death. The
Treaty of Utrecht of 11 April 1713 led to a general European
and North American settlement between France, Spain,
England and Holland. Lille and Béthune were restored to
France, while Luxembourg, Namur and Charleroi were given
to the Elector of Bavaria. Nice (then a Savoyard possession)
was restored to Victor Amadeus and Sicily promised to him.
Philip V was at last recognised as King of Spain by
the Habsburgs, although Philip and his successors had to
renounce their rights to the French throne, and the southern
Netherlands, scene of so many blood-drenched battles, went
to the Empire. An important part of the settlement was the
full recognition of Queen Anne as the rightful monarch of
Great Britain. This meant that the man known there as 'the
Pretender', James Edward, had to be asked to leave France.
He went to Bar-le-Duc in Lorraine.

Already for Queen Mary Beatrice it was a time of terrible
sorrow. Her daughter Princess Louisa Maria, the girl on
whom she doted, had died suddenly of smallpox in April
1712 at the age of twenty, two months after Adelaide, who
had been her friend. It was yet another blow to the Jacobite
cause: some of its supporters had harboured dreams of this

delightful girl, whose countenance 'mixed the noble features of the Stuarts and the d'Estes', marrying, say, a Hanoverian prince and thus reconciling the two religious sides of the family. Madame de Maintenon told Louis XIV that Louisa Maria had been Mary Beatrice's 'companion and chief comfort'. Now King and deposed Queen met in a visit of condolence. The two of them wept to see that 'they, the old, were left, and that death had taken the young'.[1]

And the toll of deaths in the French royal family was not over. Marie-Élisabeth, the unsatisfactory Duchesse de Berry, failed to redeem herself in dynastic terms by producing a healthy son. The baby boy born in June 1713, created Duc d'Alençon, died after a few days. Apart from that, Marie-Élisabeth, like many self-centred people, did not have a talent to amuse. In vain Louis XIV showered jewels upon her, all the jewels of the crown, so that she could bedizen herself regally in just the way that Adelaide had failed to do. Marie-Élisabeth's extravagant hair-styles were also in contrast to the simple arrangements which Adelaide had adopted towards the end of her life. Her crazy drunken antics – it is kindest to regard Marie-Élisabeth as verging on madness if not actually mad – were not the sort to appeal to the fastidious Louis XIV.

Marie-Élisabeth was pregnant again in the spring of 1714 when Berry himself died at the age of twenty-eight, as a result of a riding accident out hunting at Marly in which the pommel of his saddle pierced a vein in his stomach. His life with Marie-Élisabeth had been more and more wretched as a result of what Saint-Simon called her 'sudden, swift and immoderate' love affairs. There was one frightful incident at Rambouillet when, provoked beyond endurance, he actually kicked her backside in public.[2] But the rules of Versailles did not permit Berry to be released from his bondage.

Berry's posthumous child – a premature daughter – died on 13 June 1714. Perhaps it was just as well, again from a dynastic point of view, since Marie-Élisabeth's notorious train of lovers, chosen as though on purpose to affront her husband, caused the satirists to make merry on the subject of the baby's true paternity with a list of possible candidates. After that the widowed Duchesse de Berry no longer offered the possibility of a further royal heir to supplement the single life of the little Duc d'Anjou. Yet Louis remained remarkably tolerant towards her: even when she reviewed a regiment dressed in a soldier's costume and made her ladies do likewise, the sad old King only issued a mild protest. He himself had spoken the truest word on his own martyrdom: 'I shall suffer less in the next world,' said Louis XIV, since God was punishing him for his sins in this one, and 'I have merited it.'[3]

An ageing monarch and a tiny child as his heir meant that barring an accident – such as the death of the child in question – a Regency was inevitable. Philippe Duc d'Orléans, the King's forty-year-old nephew, was the obvious candidate because he was next in line of succession after Anjou. Regencies were of course hardly unknown during the sixteenth and seventeenth centuries, with a series of child-kings succeeding in France, including Louis himself, but the Regent in question had been the Queen Mother. Indeed, Anjou's mother Adelaide might have made a great Regent if she had survived Bourgogne – but the truth of that would never be known. Philippe however was on bad terms with Madame de Maintenon, who strongly disliked his openly debauched way of life: it was therefore as some kind of warning to him not to exceed his powers, that the idea of entering the legitimised bastards into the royal succession came into play. Madame de Maintenon's influence in this was surely crucial: her love of Maine, her dislike of Philippe, all added up to an alteration in the rules which Louis would not have countenanced in his prime: it went against every principle of order and legitimacy which he had always maintained.

For all the groans of Liselotte, the moans of Saint-Simon about 'the golden age of bastards', these princes and princesses had their role to play. The 'mouse-droppings' in Liselotte's crude phrase might fill a rigidly pious man like the late Duc de Bourgogne with horror, but in fact Charles II's bastards were regularly received at the French court. For example, Barbara Villiers' son, the Duke of Grafton, went swimming with the Dauphin, and her daughter the Countess of Sussex attended *Appartement* at Versailles. James II's son the Duke of Berwick was a brilliant soldier, so that even Saint-Simon had to admit that his genius cancelled out his dubious birth. The position of the Duc de Vendôme, descendant of Henri IV, has already been mentioned. Civilised behaviour was one thing: the Russian Ambassador to Versailles, A. A. Matveev, in his account of French court life, suggested Louis XIV, in his treatment of the Duc du Maine, as a role model for Tsar Peter the Great, who had his own bastards at home.[4] But there was a vast difference between the rank Louis had begged for Maine's sons in March 1710, and the potential accession of Maine or his brother Toulouse to the throne – both born when their mother was married to another man.*

Maine's marriage to Liselotte's 'little toad', Bénédicte de Bourbon-Condé, had turned out surprisingly well (although her size did not increase, justifying Françoise's early worry that the weight of her jewels would stop her growing). With her sparkling wit and tireless energy, the tiny Duchesse created quite a different world at Sceaux: it was a place both high-spirited and intellectual, where Plutarch, Homer and Terence were the gods. There was much emphasis on the theatre, the plays of Molière for example being revived. In

* Although Athénaïs had been legally separated from Montespan before the birth of Toulouse in 1678.

short it resembled the early court of Louis XIV in the 1660s, if the scale was not quite so grand.

The Duchesse even had her own literary society, the Order of the Fly in Honey, which consisted of forty chevaliers, both male and female; a medal was struck for it in 1703 with the motto: 'I may be small but beware my sting.' Gradually it became accepted that fun was to be had at Sceaux, but it was innocent and imaginative fun, not debauchery, and thus tolerated by Madame de Maintenon. Even Liselotte brought herself to admire the wonderful new fountains – water was always a status symbol at that time – as once upon a time everyone had gaped at those of Versailles. 'Her court was charming,' wrote Marguerite de Caylus of the Duchesse du Maine. 'One was as much amused there as one was bored at Versailles.' As for Bénédicte's extravagant way of life, 'she could not have ruined her husband with more gaiety.'[5]

Naturally the Duchesse du Maine was delighted at the prospect of her husband's elevation.[6] Although her Bourbon-Condé nephews were in the line of succession as Princes of the Blood, as were the Bourbon-Contis, Maine had not been. Now he leaped to eighth place, with his two sons acknowledged as Grandsons of France at nine and ten.* Was it quite out of the question for Bénédicte, born a Princess of the Blood, to become Queen of France? Only in her dreams, perhaps, was it a real prospect. And yet she was living in an age when three ranking members of the royal family had been wiped out within eleven months; in England the second cousin of the late Queen Anne, son of Liselotte's recently deceased aunt, Sophia of Hanover, had just succeeded to her throne as George I; that was something

---

* The order of the first seven ran as follows: the little Duc d'Anjou; Philippe Duc d'Orléans and his son the Duc de Chartres; three Bourbon-Condé princes, sons of Monsieur le Duc du Bourbon; the Prince de Conti.

which would never have been envisaged at the birth of George of Hanover.

The decree which carried all this out was promulgated in July 1714. 'If in the course of time all the legitimate princes of our august house of Bourbon die out, so that there does not remain a single one to inherit the crown,' the legitimised bastards could succeed.[7] The following May Maine and Toulouse were given the rank of Princes of the Blood, with precedence over the other princes of sovereign houses. More crucial to the present, however, was the testament the King made giving charge of the future child King's 'person and education' to Maine and not to Philippe. Once again it was the need to please Françoise which prevailed over the need to placate Philippe (who remained inescapably the future Regent). Such a testamentary condition was a clear slap in the face for the Duc d'Orléans.

In the early summer of 1715 English bookmakers began taking bets on the date of the French King's death. On 16 May the Maréchal de Villeroy wrote to Françoise about his concern over his master's health: he looked ghastly and could hardly walk.[8] Louis XIV was visibly fading. He had put on weight in his fifties: now he seemed quite wizened as his flesh began to fall away in the manner of very old people. There was little trace here of the young Apollo, or even the handsome, virile King whose wife Françoise Scarron had once lightly envied. But then who now remembered Apollo? And you would have to be over eighty to remember plausibly the accession to the throne of the child Louis in 1643. The King spent much of his time among women: Françoise's secretary Marie-Jeanne d'Aumale continued to amuse him with her wit and zest for life. And his love of music remained to the last: Louis would be taken to Françoise's room to hear chamber music. The King's final visit to Marly was in June. After that no courtier stepped forward to enquire anxiously: 'Sire, Marly?'

The last act of the drama took place at Versailles, the palace that Louis XIV had created,* dazzling with mirrors, set around with the fountains and the statues and the orange trees he loved, their silver pots long ago sacrificed to the needs of war.[10] On 12 August Louis complained of pains in his thigh. The specific cause of his degeneration was the condition of his leg, which became gangrenous. Dr Fagon did not dare order an amputation, which might have saved the King – although surely not for very long since he was suffering from gout, gravel, and hardening of the arteries. From 17 August onwards, the King no longer left his room, and Fagon slept there too. Throughout the long ordeal of his deathbed, however, Louis maintained all the standards of heroic dignity which he had set himself for so long.

The great national Feast of St Louis on 25 August, for example, had to be celebrated as ever, with drums and fife bands underneath his windows and twenty-four fiddlers in the antechamber before dinner. Yet the farewells were already starting to take place. In an important interview on the same day with Philippe and Maine, Louis confirmed their relative positions as Regent and effective governor of 'the future King' (courtiers blenched when their master used these words). In principle the King decided to die as he had lived – in public: 'I have lived among the people of my court, I want to die among them. They have followed the whole course of my life; it is right that they should witness the end of it.' And he chided those so much younger than himself for their laments: 'Did you believe me to be immortal?' asked the King. 'For myself, I never believed it.'

There was an elegiac quality to these last days which had

---

* And is for ever associated with his name, despite the many internal alterations during the eighteenth century, due in part to the fact that Louis XV had a large family of *legitimate* children, needing suitable accommodation.[9]

been singularly missing from the recent unhappy years of military defeat and personal bereavements. The Marquis de Dangeau wrote on 25 August: 'I have come away from the greatest, the most touching and the most heroic spectacle that men have ever seen.' Liselotte called it in similar terms 'the saddest and most poignant spectacle that one could witness in this life'.[11] (Both of them instinctively used the language of the theatre.)

Louis's control remained awesome despite his agonies. Liselotte praised his serenity: 'He gives all his orders as though he were only going on a journey,' she wrote, these orders including the demand for unity among the sparring princesses at court. The Duc d'Anjou, a handsome little boy of five and a half who strongly resembled his mother, with her 'large pitch-black eyes' and long black eyelashes, was brought in to see his great-grandfather. '*Mignon*,' said the King, 'soon you are going to be a great king.' But he also told Anjou, in a memorable phrase: 'Try to remain at peace with your neighbours: I have loved war too much ...'

Louis made altogether three farewells to Madame de Maintenon as his life still lingered on, causing her to return from Saint-Cyr. His *alter ego*, the giant Enceladus, the silent Titan in the fountain of Versailles, with tormented staring eyes, had still some way to go before his release. The first took place on the day after the discovery of gangrene was confirmed. This exchange was more realistic than gallant and referred to her three years' seniority: considering her age, they would soon be reunited, said the King. Françoise then took refuge at Saint-Cyr.

The second time he apologised to her for not making her happy; lastly he worried about her future: 'You have nothing, Madame.' It was true: Françoise had never taken any steps to build up a fortune, and exulted in giving away most of her money in charities; she also took pride in the fact that she cost the King very little compared to his other mistresses, as she frequently told Marie-Jeanne d'Aumale: they received more in three months than she got in a year, and anyway she gave it all to the poor ... 'I am nothing,' she now replied, 'and I only think of God.' All the same Louis did speak to the future Regent on the subject, a crucial conversation given the ill feeling between Philippe and Françoise. 'She only gave me good advice,' said Louis XIV regarding Madame de Maintenon. 'She was useful in every way, but above all for my salvation.'

Françoise departed for the last time on 30 August, when she was assured by her confessor: 'You can go, you are no longer necessary to him.' She was not there at the end and did not plan to be. Later Madame de Maintenon was criticised for this, by the standards of another century. The tradition of the time of Louis XIV was different: a deathbed was more for the clergy than the courtier. As Louis had exclaimed over his dying mother half a century earlier: 'we have no more time for flattery.'

The memoirs of Marie-Jeanne d'Aumale, who was present, are an important source for these last days.[12] When Louis reached into the little pouch where he kept his private possessions it was to Marie-Jeanne he gave a little tortoiseshell sweet-box. To Françoise, however, he gave a rosary from the same pouch 'as a souvenir not a relic'. In keeping with Saint-Évremond's maxim – 'when we grow old, it reanimates us to have a number of living creatures about us' – the dogs were ever present.[13] For a long time Louis continued to feed tit-bits to a favourite little dog, and when he could no longer do so, he told Marie-Jeanne: 'Do it yourself.' It was Marie-Jeanne who with Françoise helped the King destroy his papers and recorded him laughing at the emergence of a guest-list for Marly: 'You can certainly burn that.'

On the subject of her departure Françoise told

Marie-Jeanne that on the one hand she dreaded not being able to control her sorrow in the presence of the King; on the other hand she lived in genuine dread of Philippe's behaviour towards her once he had assumed power. And there was a question of public insult to her carriage on the road to Saint-Cyr: Françoise, an old woman still concerned by her reputation, feared that too.[14]

By 31 August the King was unconscious, and he died at eight o'clock in the morning of Sunday 1 September 1715. His last spoken words were: 'O my God! help me, hasten to succour me.' Louis XIV was four days away from his seventy-seventh birthday and had reigned over France for seventy-two years. 'He died,' wrote Dangeau, 'without any effort, like a candle going out.'* The very next day Louis Blouin, who had succeeded Bontemps as the King's chief *valet de chambre* and served him altogether for thirty-seven years, sold his position for fifty thousand livres. Blouin's wish was to indicate publicly that he could never serve anyone else in place of the incomparable Sun King. But it was in keeping with the other spirit of Versailles, the materialistic one, that Blouin, who had already built a fine country house on the proceeds of his job, now profited from the end of it.[15]

The funeral of Louis XIV took place at Saint-Denis on 28 October. Lalande's beautiful and sombre *De Profundis*, first heard in 1689, was transformed with extended solos such as *De Iniquitatis* – 'If Thou, O Lord, did keep account of our sins, who would survive?' It ended on the awesome *Requiem Aeternum*, a pinnacle of French baroque music: 'Grant eternal rest to them, O Lord, and let perpetual light shine on them.' The ceremony was deeply spiritual, although

---

* Long reigns produce such simple but effective analogies. Queen Elizabeth I was described as dropping like a ripe apple from a tree and Queen Victoria was compared to a great liner going out to sea.

demonstrations of hostility at the funeral procession as it passed indicated how far the esteem for the old King had sunk in the popular imagination.

Father François Massillon, the eloquent priest who had spoken at the death of the Dauphin, gave a resounding oration which began with the words: 'God alone is great, my brothers, and in these last moments above all where he presides over the death of kings.' Louis XIV was saluted for his acknowledgement of the truth: 'This king, the terror of his neighbours, the wonder of the universe, the father of kings, greater than all his ancestors, more magnificent than Solomon in all his glory, has recognised himself that all is vanity.'[16]

Nor was the sermon one of unadulterated praise. The Catholic Church had not entirely forgotten those early battles to save the King from 'the fire of Voluptuousness'. There was an allusion to the time of his youth as 'a perilous season when the passions begin to enjoy the same authority as the sovereign and mount the very throne with him'.

But Louis was praised for his generosity to James II and 'a pious Queen' (Mary Beatrice). And the royal deaths were mentioned, including that of Adelaide, 'who relaxed Louis from the cares of monarchy'. Most touching of all was the invocation: 'Go to rejoin Marie-Thérèse, Louis [his son the Dauphin] and Adelaide who are waiting for you. Together with them for all eternity, dry the tears that you have shed over their deaths.' It is a pleasant thought that Adelaide was waiting on the other side, for ever young, to greet the King.

Despite the King's deathbed expectation, Madame de Maintenon lived on for several years after him. She spent her time in seclusion at Saint-Cyr, where she was known simply as 'Madame'. It was here that Marie-Jeanne d'Aumale came to her on 1 September and told her that everyone at Saint-Cyr had gone to the chapel to pray; from this delicate intimation, Françoise understood that Louis was dead. Marie-Jeanne, in her memoirs, described the sobbing procession of Demoiselles who now passed in front of Madame de Maintenon on this, 'the saddest day in the world'. Françoise also wept, she told Madame de Glapion proudly: 'It is a fine thing, dear girl, to weep for a king.' This was a man she had seen die 'like a Saint and a Hero'. Five days later her worries about her future were allayed when the Regent Philippe paid her a visit of courtesy and assured her of a lifelong pension of forty-eight thousand livres (nearly two hundred thousand pounds in today's money). When Madame de Maintenon tried to thank him, Philippe replied that he was 'only doing his duty' – which was true enough.[17]

The new Regent certainly had nothing to fear from the 'old woman'. The will of Louis XIV concerning Maine's position was quickly set aside and his functions towards the young King Louis XV much diminished. (There was a precedent for this cavalier ignoring of the late King's wishes: the will of Louis XIII had also been set aside, and it has been suggested that the ageing Louis XIV, helpless but not stupid, may even have anticipated this.)[18] The bastards, by a second edict, were removed from the royal succession: if the reigning house died out 'it is for the nation itself that the right goes to repair the danger by the wisdom of its choice'. That demotion made Saint-Simon, for one, an extremely happy duke.

After the death of the King, Madame de Maintenon received letters of condolence from foreign dignitaries which might have been sent to a queen.[19] For example Marie Casimir, the Queen of Poland, referred to her 'extreme affliction' and 'great loss': she hoped that God would give Madame de Maintenon the fortitude she needed to support it. The great and good at the French court wrote to her – cardinals, bishops and duchesses – generally addressing their letters to Marie-Jeanne d'Aumale for fear of disturbing her mistress in her 'sorrow and retreat'. All mentioned Madame de Maintenon's 'special loss' following the death of 'the greatest and best of the Louis who were kings'. The Archbishop of Strasbourg dispatched one of the late King's rosaries: 'it could not be in better hands'; he sacrificed it so that she should remember him in her prayers. Chamillart, one of Louis's ministers, quoted St John Chrysostom on the subject of an affliction which 'gives us a new glory'.

In future, memorial services for the late King would be held not only all over the French dominions but also in the Spanish empire, including Mexico, where a sermon was preached in the cathedral: Louis was after all the grandfather of Philip V. Once again, as at Saint-Denis, Louis's help to James II and Mary Beatrice was stressed as part of his 'apostolic' work for the true Faith, carried out 'with enthusiasm and with spending worthy of his royal magnificence'. He had maintained the exiled Stuarts in the same grand style as they used to live in London: doing what could be done to re-establish them in the peaceful possession of their crown so that the Catholic religion could flourish in that realm.[20]

As for Françoise, she had after all been the visible companion of Louis XIV for twenty-two years – from that moment after the death of Marie-Thérèse when the Duc de La Rochefoucauld urged her to go to the King because he needed her. There can have been few who doubted at the time that some discreet ceremony of marriage, acceptable to the Catholic Church, had taken place. Françoise herself however remained resolute in her refusal either to confirm or deny the fact. 'She didn't want us to speak about that,' wrote Marie-Jeanne d'Aumale. If 'a child or simple person' questioned her on the subject, her reply was merely: 'Who told you that?' When Marie-Jeanne read to her from her own Secret Notebooks, she was stopped before she reached any passage which might concern the King. Much later came the real moment when Madame de Maintenon was 'treated like a queen', in the words of her great-nephew the Duc de Noailles: her ashes were disinterred at the French Revolution as a protest against the *Ancien Régime*, just like those of the official royals in Saint-Denis.[21]*

To the court of France however the woman that Saint-Simon called 'that eighty-year-old witch' was 'forgotten and already as good as dead'. Living quietly at Saint-Cyr and wearing the plainest clothes, Françoise herself put it more elegantly: 'I have left the world I did not like.' Yet she retained her agreeable appearance until the end. Ironically, this was true of Françoise, who had never depended on her beauty to make her fortune, rather than the gorgeous Athénaïs, who had lost her looks entirely by middle age. Even Liselotte admitted in 1711 when Françoise was in her mid-seventies that her enemy 'didn't look her age in the slightest'; to the last she had little if any white hair, according to her relatives.[23]

It took an intrepid character like the Russian Tsar Peter the Great to penetrate the seclusion. On a visit to France in the summer of 1717, he announced his firm intention of seeing this celebrated relic of the previous reign. According to one account, he first flung open the window, and then pulled back the bed curtains in order to peer in at the old lady lurking within. 'Are you ill?' the Tsar was said to have asked, and when she said she was, 'What's wrong?' 'A great age,' replied Madame de Maintenon. It is a bizarre scene, not made less so by the fact that their dialogue had to be conveyed through an interpreter, the Tsar's minister Kourakin.[24]

Apart from calls from her beloved Maine, Françoise was

---

* Since 1969 the mortal remains of Madame de Maintenon have been placed in the chapel of Saint-Cyr, now the Lycée Militaire, after some journeyings in times of revolution and war.[22]

solaced by the continuing friendship with Mary Beatrice, which was important to them both. In 1715 James Edward launched another fruitless effort to gain the British throne: the Regent Philippe took care that the French did not support it. The former English Queen was left to pay a weekly visit to Saint-Cyr. Here the two women, sitting in similar armchairs, were served by the young ladies, with a handbell at Françoise's side to speed things along. After coffee, the Demoiselles withdrew. Françoise and Mary Beatrice, the Queen that never was and the Queen that was once, communed alone for two or three hours.

Mary Beatrice had become the heroine of the Jacobite cause: a heroine who was also a saint. She died in 1718 at the age of sixty, her battle with cancer finally lost. Poets saluted her in Gaelic as well as English. Sometimes the language was so hagiographic as to suggest another grieving mother, the Virgin Mary. An Irish lament for 'the wife of James II' was entitled 'The Grievous Occasion of My Tears'. It began: 'The Gaels are left in gloom' at the loss of 'A woman generous with alms / A beauty, pious, generous and just ...' and went on: 'This was the greatest Mary / That has yet to come ... This was the never-lying Mary / Who died for my life."[25]

By the early spring of 1719 Françoise was clearly failing: on 13 March she told a Demoiselle: 'It's all over, dear girl, I'm on my way.' She died on 15 April 1719. She was in her eighty-fourth year. The court paid little attention, but at least Liselotte had achieved her long-held ambition of surviving the woman she resented so much. When she learned the news, Liselotte reacted with characteristic zest: 'I just learned that old Maintenon croaked last night,' she wrote triumphantly (*die alte Schump ist verreckt* – a word usually used for the miserable death of an animal). 'If only it had happened thirty years earlier!' In the next world, she suggested, Françoise would have to choose between Paul

Scarron and Louis XIV. Nor did Liselotte let herself down when her turn came to die in 1722: 'You may kiss me properly,' she said to an attendant. 'I am going to the land where all are equal.'[26]

The princesses of the next generation, Marie-Anne Princesse de Conti, Louise-Françoise Madame la Duchesse and Françoise-Marie Duchesse d'Orléans, all lived until their seventies, dying in 1739, 1743 and 1749 respectively.* Bénédicte, Duchesse du Maine, with her agreeable and sophisticated lifestyle at Sceaux, outlived all three sisters-in-law whose bastard birth she had been wont to compare unfavourably with her own: she died in 1753 at the age of seventy-seven. Her imperturbable royal self-confidence caused Madame de Staël to write that the Duchesse du Maine 'believed in herself in the same way as she believed in God and Descartes, without explanation or discussion'. It was a confidence which extended towards her own acting abilities: none of the professionals who acted with her dared mention the fact that the tiny Duchesse was a remarkably bad if enthusiastic actress. Voltaire wrote his first poetry during his five years at Sceaux as a young man and paid a second visit towards the end of the Duchesse's long life, from 1746 to 1750. He hailed Bénédicte as the 'Spirit of the Grand Condé' (her grandfather the great soldier) and saw in her with admiration a true representative of the *grand siècle*. Yet since Voltaire considered that a fine piece of theatre would do the dying Duchesse more good than Extreme Unction, it is obvious that Bénédicte was in fact far closer to the secular spirit of the Enlightenment.[27]

There was an exception to these long lives. The widowed Marie-Élisabeth Duchesse de Berry continued her rackety

* Marie-Anne's monument in Paris in the church of Saint-Roch, rue Saint-Honoré, refers to her as the daughter of Louis XIV, and her birth at Vincennes in 1666 is recorded; but there is no mention of her mother Louise de La Vallière.

existence, at once immoderate and immoral, into the next reign, to the despair of her father the Regent. She gave birth to a still-born daughter in the spring of 1719 by her lover Rions. Her health, already weakened by excess, never fully recovered; Marie-Élisabeth died in July on the eve of her twenty-fourth birthday.

Louise de La Vallière's descendants died childless; Madame de Maintenon left none. It was the fertile marriage of Françoise-Marie and Philippe d'Orléans – six daughters and one son – which spread the blood of Louis XIV and Athénaïs into all the Catholic royal families of Europe. The legitimate blood of Louis XIV, in the direct male French line from his marriage to Marie-Thérèse, died out in 1883 with the Comte de Chambord (although there were and are Spanish Bourbons). But his descendants by Athénaïs flourished, a tribute to the vigour of her stock. They included the so-called Philippe Égalité, Duc d'Orléans in the French Revolutionary era, and – a little more to the Grand Monarch's taste one must suppose – Louis Philippe the King of the French. Thus the present claimant to the French throne, the Comte de Paris, descends from Louis XIV and Athénaïs: a victory of a sort for the supreme mistress.

CHAPTER 17

Never Forget

Never forget that kings have a severe judge placed over them in heaven.

— Joad the High Priest, *Athalie*

Louis XIV was lucky in love. His tumultuous private life even added to his personal glory, the concept that was so important to him, in the eyes of the world, at any rate when he was in his prime. It certainly makes for a more congenial spectacle than that other major part of his concept of glory, his lust for military conquest. Fénelon wrote in his didactic story of 1695 *Télémaque* that 'great conquerors' are like 'overflowing rivers', which destroy the very countryside they are supposed to be watering. At home things were different. 'There never was a court which was so gallant as that of Louis le Grand,' wrote Bussy-Rabutin with undoubted admiration. 'As he was of an amorous complexion, everyone found it a pleasure to follow that prince.'¹

His mother's advanced age when the 'Godgiven' Louis was born, the years of miscarriage followed by barrenness she had endured, her difficult relationship with Louis XIII, all these things went to make Louis the great love of Anne of Austria's life – and she can at least bid to be the most important woman in his. These fierce maternal feelings, favouring Louis ostentatiously over his younger brother Monsieur, were justified by Queen Anne in terms of her sons' relative positions: Louis was the Dauphin and then quite rapidly the King, the little boy of four and a half before whom she knelt in homage in 1643. Monsieur, two years his junior, was merely the heir presumptive, before the birth of the Dauphin in 1661. But of course from the point of view of Louis's and Monsieur's shared childhood, what mattered was not so much *why* Louis was the adored one, as the fact that from the first he could have utter confidence in his mother's love and support.

Meanwhile Anne of Austria herself gave Louis XIV an ideal of a woman who besides being a Queen was also virtuous, dignified, intelligent and strong. It would take the King until his early forties to achieve this kind of helpmeet in the former Françoise d'Aubigné: when the 'perilous season' of passions, as Father Massillon put it in his funeral oration, was over. But in choosing this modest if wise woman a few years older than himself, Louis was undoubtedly influenced by the maternal example set to him so many years ago. The tears of Anne of Austria, shed for so long over the question of his promiscuity and his 'salvation', were never quite forgotten; it was significant that when Louis XIV was dying and wished to commend Madame de Maintenon to the Regent, he praised her for the good advice she had given to him, her usefulness above all on the subject of this salvation.

In this story there have after all been remarkably few accounts of happy marriages: Liselotte spoke for many when she described marriages as 'like death ... you can't escape'. But it is possible to argue that Louis XIV was happily married twice – once to a young woman who brought him the international stature he desired then and who gave him no trouble, as he said, except by dying, and once to the saviour of his soul.

In the meantime Louis was certainly lucky during the 'perilous season' itself. Handsome and godlike as all contemporary observers agreed, and with the aura of royalty to act as an aphrodisiac, there was never any question that Louis would enjoy the favours of the ladies if he wished. It was hardly a disagreeable fate to be seduced by the young Louis XIV, but in any case the evidence is that the ladies met him more than halfway, enjoying the pleasure and also the material rewards. With Louis there are no stories of crude abductions, violations, unwilling maidens: this was for Athénaïs's husband, Montespan, not her lover the King.

This view does not, of course, take into account the strictures of the Catholic Church on adultery. Sex outside marriage put a person in a state of sin. The immense popularity at court of the plain-speaking preacher Bourdaloue (much admired by Louis XIV), the aristocratic crowds who flocked to hear him, demonstrate the seriousness with which the issue was taken. Fortunately all the mistresses of Louis XIV, like the King himself, managed to die as so many penitents in a state of grace.

Certainly, with one or two possible exceptions, the women in the life of Louis XIV were not victims and did not see themselves as such. And there was a point in the King's favour which even the critical Saint-Simon admitted: he was kind and generous to his former mistresses.* It is true that the court was not always an 'enchanted palace'. The women from time to time may have witnessed the canvas and cardboard scenery, the ropes and pulleys backstage, in Françoise's evocative phrase. But there was another equally potent side to court life as described by Madame de Sévigné: 'the hunt, the lanterns, the moonlight, the drive, the meal in a place carpeted by jonquils ...' The women were there too.

It may be cynical to suggest that there were many worse options in the life of a seventeenth-century woman of a certain class than to be the mistress of Louis XIV, but it is

---

* This was no Henry VIII, the fate of whose six wives is traditionally recorded as 'Divorced, beheaded, died, divorced, beheaded, survived.' With Louis XIV there were no divorces and certainly no decapitations: the mistresses who abandoned the court were not compelled to do so.

also realistic. Primi Visconti, observer of Louis's court, believed that 'ladies are born with the ambition to become the King's favourite' and there was certainly something in what he said. The alternative for the vast majority of women was to accept the robust advice of St Jeanne de Chantal: 'Put yourself in God's hands and then your bridegroom's.' Others, lacking a bridegroom, simply put themselves in God's hands in a convent, but it was a life which did not suit everyone who ended up there, and educational initiatives for girls were otherwise in their infancy, as Madame de Maintenon understood.

The number of Louis's minor flings cannot be computed with any certainty, particularly during the period when he was indulging in what are now called one-night stands (in his case one-afternoon stands). We do not know how often he enjoyed himself *chez les dames*, as the contemporary phrase had it, but materially at least no one suffered from the experience. The known number of his children is also fluid: there were at least eighteen of them including his six legitimate children by Marie-Thérèse He thus had roughly the same number of bastards as Charles II, although the latter had no legitimate children. Another first cousin, Charles Emmanuel of Savoy, also enjoyed an energetic sex life, with at least five bastards: given Monsieur's talent for procreation, whatever his tastes, it seems right to salute the philoprogenitive blood of their shared grandfather Henri IV.

Despite that proverb to the effect that a man could beget as long as he could lift a sheaf of straw, Louis sired no known bastards after the son of Angélique who died. Thanks to Madame de Maintenon, he was still able to enjoy the pleasures of family life, including the cosy atmosphere of Saint-Cyr. Françoise's love of children was that particular emotion, with much of the teacher in it, common to certain women who have none of their own. Thus Louis was able to admire Françoise's tender maternal qualities without the inconvenience of her pregnancy.

One possible exception to this lack of victimhood might be Marie Mancini, promised so much by the eighteen-year-old Louis, but abandoned by him in the line of duty: a sacrifice which has become celebrated in Racine's line: 'You weep and yet you are the King.' Yet it is difficult to criticise Louis's decision, which was in any case heavily supported by Cardinal Mazarin, no fan of his erratic niece. The marriage of a great king was an important element in any foreign policy, particularly a marriage which could bring 'peace' along with 'the Infanta' to a war-torn country. Marie's subsequent unhappy wandering career deserves sympathy. She ended back in Italy after the death of her tyrannical husband Prince Colonna, and died in the same year as Louis: her son Cardinal Colonna erected a monument with the epitaph she had chosen herself: 'Ashes and Dust.'² At the same time Cardinal Mazarin, that wily man of affairs, was right to perceive in his niece something sadly self-destructive.

Louise de La Vallière is the sole plausible exception to the general rule that women did quite as well out of Louis XIV as he did out of them. Not for nothing did women passing through the King's bedroom when it was empty, according to etiquette, curtsy to the royal bed ... On the whole the King did not press his attentions on young girls – a few boisterous adventures trying to reach the maids-of-honour do not count – but Louise was different. Unquestionably a virgin, she also had a strongly religious temperament; falling insanely in love with the Sun King at the age of sixteen meant that she transferred for a period her religious emotions intended for God Almighty on to Louis, her personal Apollo.

This was the great romantic affair of Louis's life: as with any seduction of an innocent religious girl in literature it was more or less bound to end in betrayal – and the shedding of rivers of tears.* Louise's subsequent long years of penance, which even precluded her mourning the death of her son because of the circumstances in which he had been conceived, attest to the sincerity of the religious side of her nature. Surely there was something self-punishing in her role as godmother to the daughter of Louis and Athénaïs, named Louise-Françoise apparently after her – but actually after the King and her supplanter. Thus Louise did truly incarnate the penitence of Magdalen, her favourite saint.

While La Vallière attempted to fulfil one Christian ideal, it has to be noted that Louis for a period enjoyed a feature in theory more familiar to oriental rulers than Christian ones: the harem. For it is difficult to see the period of 'the three Queens' Marie-Thérèse, Louise and Athénaïs, in their war-going coach, in any other light. It is true that the King needed Louise as a cover for his new affair with a married woman (who had a troublesome husband). Nevertheless this was the harem as described in *Bajazet* by Racine, who demanded in the Preface: 'Indeed, is there a court in the world where jealousy and love can be better known than in a place [the harem] where so many rivals are shut in together?' This situation was the moral responsibility of Louis XIV. As Racine added, 'the men there very probably do not love with the same refinement.'[4]

The trouble was that after the first thrill of desire, Louis discovered that he had a further need which the vulnerable 'hidden violet' Louise could not fulfil – nor for that matter could his wife Marie-Thérèse. He had discovered something of that need and its satisfaction in his *amitié amoureuse* with

* It was appropriate that in the mid-nineteenth century Flaubert had Madame Bovary turn to La Vallière for inspiration when she attempted to recover her faith after being abandoned by her lover: 'in the pride of her godliness, Emma compared herself with the great ladies of old, they whose glory she had dreamed of over a portrait of La Vallière, those who . . . shed at the feet of Christ the tears of a heart wounded by the world.'[5]

his sister-in-law Henriette-Anne as they danced together in the wonderful Court Ballets of the early part of the reign. As he developed the notion of the Sun King, the monarch who dazzled the whole of Europe and made the French court the envy of the world (including Louis's young opponent William III), Louis reached out for a woman who was worthy to take her place beside him, even if it was an illegitimate place.

Here he was lucky to find – or be found by – Athénaïs Marquise de Montespan, an unhappily married woman in her mid-twenties, who combined a voluptuous nature with lavish beauty, a taste for the arts with a royal instinct for patronage. For the long years in which Athénaïs exercised her role as *maîtresse en titre* were not entirely about the sexual hold she had over the King, although that was obviously part of the allure; he was not for example sexually faithful to her, and during her frequent pregnancies Athénaïs does not seem to have expected it of him: her maid the Demoiselle des Oeillets and possibly her own sister offered diversions. It was the presence and style of Athénaïs which provided the Sun King with exactly what he wanted over so many years of the 'perilous season'.

What was remarkable, however, about this season was that the unrelenting campaign of the Catholic Church to secure Louis's salvation – in other words his connubial fidelity – was waged throughout. It was all very well for a court lady like Madame de Meilleraye (as reported by Saint-Simon) to give her 'considered opinion that where a man of birth is concerned, God would think twice before damning him'. This was not the official message of the Catholic Church towards kings, who as God's regents on earth were expected to behave better, rather than worse, than their subjects. Although many people secretly agreed with the Marquise de Polignac that, while it might be very necessary to die in a state of grace, it was very boring to live in it,

Bossuet thundered forth on the subject on a very different note: 'How great the wrong if kings seek pleasures which God forbids' and 'Suffer not the noise of men surrounding you to deaden the Voice of the Son of God speaking within you.'⁵ Liselotte's very protestations about her lack of Catholic faith showed how out of joint with the times she felt.

One of Racine's plays that Louis much admired was *Athalie*. The last lines by the high priest Joad make the message clear: 'Never forget that kings have a severe judge placed above them in heaven.'⁶ Individual confessors such as the Jesuits, with the wisdom of the world, believed that a young King should be allowed latitude, on the grounds that he would repent in time (Father La Chaise was right: that was exactly what happened). But this complaisant line was not taken by the great preachers of the era. Both Bossuet and Bourdaloue made comparisons to King David the adulterer in court sermons. This was strong stuff: but it never stopped. Nor did Louis throughout his life ever quite forget the severe judge.

Louise fled to a convent on the first occasion for fear of a Lenten sermon; Athénaïs was actually made to give up the King when a humble parish priest refused her Communion at Easter. The fact that this separation ended when the King's rampant physical feelings in her presence overwhelmed him does not negate the fact that it took place. There is no evidence that King Charles II, another lover of women but an altogether more cynical fellow, underwent crises of conscience on the subject: he believed on the contrary that God would never damn a fellow for a little pleasure. Louis XIV was different. 'We must submit,' said the King over the death of his son, pointing to the skies. In the end, spiritually at least, he did submit to the dictates of heaven as interpreted by the Catholic Church.

The unfortunate affair of Angélique de Fontanges, twenty years younger than the King, beautiful as her angelic name indicated but rather stupid, may be regarded as Louis's last fling before he settled for the virtuous domestic existence preached to him for so long. Angélique, although a virgin, was not a victim, except to her own tragic gynaecological history: with a taste for grandeur, she was eager to fill the place of the *maîtresse en titre* for which no one, and finally not Louis himself, thought her suitable.

Certainly nobody could call Françoise a victim, except possibly she herself in her later years with the King, when bad health induced a slightly wearisome series of complaints made to her correspondents. It was true that Louis was lucky to find her, a remarkable woman by any standards, and one who was prepared to carry out the famous work of salvation, seeing in it her divinely appointed mission. By his secret marriage he gave up the prospect of another grand bride, say the Infanta of Portugal, with the prestige and alliance that might bring; and there would be no official queen in France for over forty years, despite the perceived importance of the position.

Through her early life among the *Précieuses*, in the intellectual salons which would remain unknown to Louis XIV personally, Françoise had been able to acquire the new female art of conversation, something in which sympathy certainly played a part and gallantry was merely an option. Madame de Sévigné was quick to point to her ability in this direction when she perceived Françoise's influence rising: here was someone with whom you could have a conversation. There were four types of women according to Baudeau de Somaize in his *Grand Dictionary of the Historic Précieuses of 1661*; they ranged from the completely ignorant, via those of natural gifts if no great education and those who tried to lift themselves up, to the *femmes illustres*.[7] Françoise was a mixture of the second and third types: she had natural gifts and she also tried to improve her lot. The Benedictine rule adapted for women and widely quoted in the middle of the seventeenth century described 'your sex' as 'weak, fragile and inconstant if the reins are let loose': none of this applied to Françoise d'Aubigné. Her self-control was admirable, and the control of others which she sought was mainly for the good.

Nevertheless Françoise's denunciations of court life cannot altogether obliterate the fact that she did in some way seek out her destiny. The displacement of Athénaïs, however religiously motivated, was definitely to the advantage of Françoise. This is not to say that Françoise bore any resemblance to the old whore, strumpet, garbage or ordure of Liselotte's vulgar terminology. It was a long journey from little Bignette chasing the turkeys to the Marquise de Maintenon, 'glorious ... Protectress of the Realm', as the soldiers addressed her in 1705. No one achieves such a remarkable position as Françoise did, holding it for over twenty years, without some streak of ambition – even if the ambition was only to save the King's soul.

How amusing to find the lovely, amoral Madame de Pompadour in the reign of Louis XV, whose hold over the King was definitely no aid to his salvation, deciding to emulate the pious Madame de Maintenon! 'If the Queen were to disappear,' the King would want 'to buy peace for his conscience' like his great-grandfather, wrote the Austrian Ambassador: 'the plan of the marquise is formed on the example of Madame de Maintenon.' The Pompadour proceeded to order a lot of religious paintings from the sensuous Boucher in order to bolster her claims to be a holy 'secret wife'.[8] So much for human plans: in the event it was not Queen Maria Leczinska but the Pompadour who died ...

Now Françoise, as the King's secret wife, was left with the problem of amusing him. The coming of little Adelaide of Savoy into the life of Louis XIV, solving the problem at a stroke with her cute childish ways, was therefore the greatest piece of luck for both Louis and Françoise.

Henceforward all the King's hopes and affections were utterly focused on this small, sprightly creature; and since she was the future Queen of France, he could feel it was his absolute duty to do so.

Louis's generosity and courtesy to women, his enjoyment of their company outside the bedroom, have been stressed throughout this book. He loved his daughters and spoilt them; he loved his granddaughters too. But there was also a ruthless side to his nature where women were concerned – royal women. Liselotte was condemned to witness the destruction of her homeland: her own royal rights were invoked to press the claims of France, and she found it infinitely distressing. Yet Louis reacted to her grief with irritation; such feelings of chagrin were not permitted at Versailles. Marie-Louise d'Orléans was sent briskly off to Spain to marry the appalling Carlos II in spite of her tearful pleas. 'Farewell. For ever,' was the reaction of Louis XIV. It was a fate which subsequently caused Liselotte to exclaim that being a queen was hard anywhere, 'but to be the Queen in Spain is surely worse than anywhere else'.[9] Even the beloved Adelaide incurred her grandfather's resentment when she displayed something less than her usual gaiety at the denigrations of her husband. Yet these experiences, for better or for worse, were part of the lives of royalty at the time, not only for women: arguably Berry was just as badly treated in not being allowed to separate from the incontinent Marie-Élisabeth. And one should balance Louis XIV's tenderness towards the deposed Queen Mary Beatrice – not always to the advantage of France – against his ruthlessness towards Marie-Louise.

This sense of order makes Louis's firm choice of Madame de Maintenon as his second, if secret, spouse all the more remarkable. She shone no glory on him; rather to the contrary, her early association with Scarron was considered disreputable. Not only Liselotte but the satirists lamented that she was a nobody in hierarchical terms, and older than the King. But the King chose her and kept to her. In his forties, thanks to the lucky – in these terms – death of Marie-Thérèse, he selected the kind of woman, in nature if not rank, that his mother had been, and he stuck to her. Good women – in the moral sense – were always fascinating to Louis XIV, and for all his (justified) reputation for promiscuity in youth and the establishment of his 'harem' as he reached thirty, one notes that he spent at least half of his seventy-seven-odd years in their company.

'Greatness of birth and the advantages bestowed by wealth and by nature should provide all the elements of a happy life,' wrote Louis's first cousin the Grande Mademoiselle in her final months. 'But experience should have taught us that there are many people who have had all these things who are not happy.' She added: the good moments arrive but they do not last. Louis XIV certainly had a happier life in emotional terms than the Grande Mademoiselle whose ill-conceived but valiant efforts to make a late marriage to Lauzun he had quashed (another example of his ruthless determination where dynastic matters were concerned). It would be fair to say that most of the happiest moments of his life were associated with women, whether enjoying Anne of Austria's marble bath in the Louvre, riding romantically with Marie Mancini or Louise when he was young, throwing away the sword that dared to hurt Marie's hand, lending his own hat to put on Louise's golden curls, amusing himself at summer nights of revelry with Henriette-Anne or travelling with her granddaughter Adelaide round the gardens of Versailles in a little pony cart when he was old.

For the latter attachment he paid a terrible price: the Sun King who would not let there be clouds in his presence, forbidding mourning as a matter of principle, was brought to acknowledge his own impotence in the face of heaven's decrees and 'submit'. In the dignity of this grief and the stoicism of his death, Louis XIV was entitled to call himself an *honnête homme*, a civilised man, that ultimate term of seventeenth-century praise.

We must also remember that in the century when Louis XIV chose the sun as his symbol – 'the most vigorous and the most splendid image of a great monarch' – one of the declared attributes of the sun was 'the light which it shines on those other stars which surround it like a court'. And those stars in their turn, the women in his life, lit up the court of the Sun King.

NOTES

Full bibliographical details of the works cited in short form will be found in the list of Sources.

CHAPTER I *Gift from Heaven*

1 Motteville, I, p. 33.
2 *Gazette de France*, 28 April 1638.
3 Kleinman, p. 137.
4 Sackville-West, p. 49.
5 Spanheim, p. 32.
6 Dulong, *Femmes*, p. 74; *Dictionary of Saints*, St Leonard.
7 Motteville, I, p. 22; Bluche, *Vie quotidienne*, p. 131.
8 Bluche, *Louis*, p. 11.
9 Motteville, I, pp. 14–15; Kleinman, p. 65.
10 Saint-Simon (1856), I, p. 36.
11 La Porte, p. 36.
12 Kleinman, p. 17.
13 La Porte, p. 93.
14 Bouyer, p. 35.
15 Levi, pp. 14, 19, makes a case for Mazarin's paternity throughout his biography of Louis XIV based on the evidence of a document which has vanished; he does not tackle the question of Monsieur's birth two years later. Historians generally accept that Louis XIII was the father of Louis XIV.
16 Petitfils, *Louis*, pp. 24ff.
17 Teissier, pp. 35ff; Goubert, p. 17.
18 Teissier, pp. 57ff.
19 Dulong, *Anne*, p. 142, accepts the storm story; Bertière, I, p. 306, is sceptical.
20 Petitfils, *Louis*, p. 25.
21 Muhlstein, p. 206.
22 *Journal de la Santé*, p. 386.
23 Decker, p. 58; Duchêne, *Femme*, p. 211; Henriette-Anne d'Orléans in 1662, Norrington, p. 54.
24 Wolf, p. 4 & note 2, p. 623; Dunlop, p. 2.
25 Horoscope by Liz Greene, *Equinox*.
26 Pitts, p. 124.
27 La Porte, p. 133; Louis, *Mémoires*, I, p. 120.
28 Mademoiselle Andrieu, quoted in Kleinman,

pp. 112–13 & note 54,
p. 303.
29 Motteville, I, pp. 170ff.
30 Bonneville, pp. 82–3;
Petitfils, *Louis*, p. 117;
Muhlstein, p. 236; La Porte,
p. 135.
31 Motteville, I, p. xxvii.
32 Corneille, *Le Cid*, Act III,
scene 6.
33 Wolf, p. 11, calls it
'improbable … perhaps the
story is one of those that
should have happened even
if it did not'.
34 *Ormesson*, I, p. 43; Miller,
Bourbon, p. 85.
35 Motteville, I, p. 102.
36 Dunlop, p. 27.

CHAPTER 2 *Vigour of the Princess*
1 See especially Wolf, pp. 46,
85, & 626, note 4 to ch. 8,
who suggests 'a secret
marriage'; but Kleinman,
p. 226, refers to the 'lack of
solid evidence' for it.
2 Madeleine Laurain-
Portemer, see Kleinman ref.
63, p. 322.
3 Visconti, p. 6; Ziegler,
p. 193.
4 Dulong, *Amoureuses*, p. 26;
Dulong, *Mazarin*, p. 137.
5 Clairambault MSS, 1144,
fols 90–100.
6 Muhlstein, p. 193; Leroy &

Loyau, *Sagesse*, p. 780.
7 *Maximes d'Éducation*, *passim*;
Leroy & Loyau, *Sagesse*,
p. 33.
8 Cornette, 'Éducation',
p. 217; Pitts, p. 16; La
Rochefoucauld, p. 121.
9 Muhlstein, p. 398; *Maximes
d'Éducation*.
10 Motteville, I, p. 236.
11 *Halifax*, p. 55.
12 Motteville, II, pp. 282ff.
13 Motteville, II, p. 341.
14 Pitts, pp. 5, 231.
15 Déon, p. 284.
16 Louis, *Mémoires*, I, p. 120.
17 Evelyn, I, pp. 268–9.
18 For the Court Ballet, see
especially Christout (1967);
Christout (1987); Guest,
p. 12; also Hilton, *Dance*;
Quirey.
19 Christout (1987), p. 153.
20 Wolf, p. 115.
21 Petitfils, *Louis*, p. 171,
describes his short stature as
'a myth'; see Bertière, I,
p. 490 & note.
22 *Verney*, III, pp. 65–6.
23 Beaussant, *Louis*, pp. 14ff.
24 See Oresko, 'Marriages',
passim.
25 Doscot, p. 33; Egerton MS
23, fol. 32, 91.
26 Mallet-Joris, pp. 9ff.
27 Although Bertière, I, p. 23,
correctly describes this

story as an 'unverifiable tradition', it has been generally accepted; see also Carré, *Vallière*, p. 18; Decker, *Louis*, p. 120.

28 Saint Simon (1856), I, p. 34.

29 Motteville, IV, p. 158.

CHAPTER 3 *Peace and the Infanta*

1 Oresko, 'Marriages', *passim*, for the careers of the seven Mazarin nieces and their interaction with the politics of Savoy.

2 Buckley, pp. 238, 296.

3 Pitts, p. 160.

4 Motteville, IV, p. 85.

5 La Fayette, *Secret History*, p. 16.

6 Corneille, *Le Cid*, Act V, scene 3.

7 Loyau, *Correspondance 1709*, p. 51; Davis, *Society*, p. 124.

8 Davis, 'Women in Politics', p. 178; Craveri, p. 358; Duchêne, *Sévigné*, p. 72.

9 Scudéry, *Sapho*, pp. 45, 58.

10 Doscot, p. 107.

11 Doscot, p. 215, note 2; Doscot points out that even if Saint-Bremond edited them, he used Marie's own Italian text; and see Wolf, p. 627, note 3: 'If … not written by Marie Mancini

herself, it was obviously written by someone who knew her and her career very, very well.'

12 Beaussant, *Louis*, p. 35.

13 Motteville, IV, p. 118.

14 Buckley, p. 308.

15 Dunlop, p. 43; Motteville, IV, p. 110.

16 *Journal de la Santé*, note 2, 'Maladie du Roi à Calais', pp. 372–8; Meyer, *Éducation*, p. 151.

17 *Journal de la Santé*, note 2, 'Maladie du Roi à Calais', pp. 372–8.

18 Bouyer, p. 147.

19 Dunlop, p. 49.

20 Doscot, p. 109.

21 Wolf, p. 105 & note 5, p. 627.

22 Motteville, IV, p. 144.

23 Voltaire, p. 283.

24 Motteville, IV, pp. 147, 156.

25 Racine, *Bérénice*, Act IV, scene 5; Act V, scene 6; La Rochefoucauld, p. 29; La Fayette, *Mémoires*, p. 12.

26 Motteville, IV, p. 133.

27 *Caylus* (1908), p. 41.

28 Bertière, II, pp. 43ff.

29 Cortequisse, p. 32.

30 Pitts, p. 151.

31 Cortequisse, pp. 33ff.

32 Motteville, IV, pp. 165ff.

33 Bluche, *Louis*, p. 90.

CHAPTER 4 *Our Court's Laughing Face*

1 Geffroy, *Maintenon*, I, p. 70.
2 Brandi, p. 488; Wolf, p. 124.
3 Motteville, IV, p. 322.
4 Cortequisse, p. 87.
5 For the composition of the *Mémoires*, see Déon, pp. 55ff; Petitfils, *Louis*, p. 217.
6 Oresko, 'Marriages', p. 145.
7 La Fayette, *Mémoires*, p. 30.
8 Loret, IX, p. 29; Motteville, IV, p. 256.
9 Saint-André, pp. 96ff.
10 Bussy-Rabutin, p. 250.
11 Saint-André, p. 34.
12 Hamilton, p. 91; Cowen, p. 6; Burke, p. 2; Dunlop, p. 142.
13 The title of Nicolas Poussin's allegorical picture *A Dance to the Music of Time*, painted about twenty years earlier; La Fayette, *Mémoires*, p. 35.
14 La Fayette, *Mémoires*, p. 32.
15 Déon, p. 301.
16 Loret, p. 129; Bottineau, p. 728.
17 Decker, *Louis*, p. 51.
18 La Fayette, *Mémoires*, pp. 31ff.
19 Motteville, IV, pp. 260ff.
20 Saint-Simon (1967), II, p. 790.
21 Lair, p. 61, note 4.
22 Sonnet, p. 151; Loyau,

Correspondance *1709*, p. 65, note 1; Duchêne, *Femme*, p. 75.
23 Petitfils, *Vallière*, pp. 34ff.
24 Bertière, II, p. 93.
25 Carré, *Vallière*, p. 45.
26 Lair, pp. 52ff.
27 Bussy-Rabutin, *Mémoires*, II, p. 111.
28 Dunlop, p. 87.
29 Loret, XI, p. 173; Decker, *Louis*, p. 63.
30 Loret, XI, p. 173.
31 Déon, p. 162.
32 Petitfils, *Masque de Fer*, p. 58.
33 For Jansenism see Doyle, p. 29 and *passim*; Couton, pp. 61ff & note 9.
34 Lear, pp. 75, 107; J. P. Landry, 'Bossuet', *DGS*, I, pp. 215–17; Minois, *passim*.
35 Carré, *Vallière*, p. 36; Lair, p. 75.
36 Couton, p. 31; Bajou, p. 28.

CHAPTER 5 *Sweet Violence*

1 Petitfils, *Vallière*, p. 106; Couton, p. 43; Bardon, p. 302 & notes 107 & 111.
2 Hamelin, p. 8.
3 Haskins, pp. 15ff.
4 Jardine, p. 245; Norton, *Sun King*, p. 29.
5 Molière, *Dom Juan*, trans. Frame, Act I, scene 2.
6 See Gaimster *et al.* 'Dudley Castle condoms'.

7 Le Roy Ladurie, *Saint-Simon*, p. 113; Dulong, *Vie quotidienne*, pp. 90ff.

8 Pitts, pp. 174–5; Hufton, *Prospect*, p. 182.

9 Carré, *Vallière*, p. 80.

10 Castro, p. 28; *Ormesson*, p. 496, note 2.

11 Saint-Maurice, II, p. 60.

12 Bussy-Rabutin, II, p. 151; Christout (1967), pp. 111ff.

13 See Solnon, *Versailles, passim*; Norton, *Sun King*, p. 44; Grasse, p. 29.

14 Farmer, p. 100.

15 Mitford, p. 20.

16 Bluche, *Louis*, p. 180.

17 Beaussant, *Lully*, p. 800.

18 Solnon, *Cour*, p. 256; pp. 274ff.

19 Mallet-Joris, p. 39.

20 Solnon, *Cour*, p. 260; Duchêne, *Molière*, pp. 381ff.

21 Pitts, p. 250, note 30; Molière, *Tartuffe*, Act V, scene 7.

22 Motteville, IV, pp. 344ff.

23 Motteville, IV, p. 357.

24 Kleinman, pp. 283ff.

25 Motteville, IV, p. 392.

26 Georges Matoré, 'Galant, Galanterie', *DGS*, I, pp. 632–3; Scudéry, *Galant*, p. 21; Scudéry, *Clélie*, I, pp. 178ff.

27 Sarti, p. 134.

28 Saint-Simon (1967), III, p. 463; Hilton, p. 157; Pitts, pp. 177–8.

29 Motteville, IV, pp. 339ff.

30 Louis, *Mémoires*, I, p. 117.

31 Motteville, IV, pp. 437ff.

32 Pitts, pp. 174–5.

33 Sévigné (1955), p. 169.

34 Motteville, IV, p. 447; Dulong, *Amoureuses*, p. 11.

35 Racine, *Bajazet*, Act I, scene 1, trans. Hollinghurst.

CHAPTER 6 *The Rise of Another*

1 Decker, *Louis*, p. 82; Saint-Maurice, pp. 105, 130; Couton, p. 84.

2 Carré, *Vallière*, p. 127; Genlis, p. 112.

3 Bertière, II, p. 197.

4 Decker, *Montespan*, p. 45.

5 Hilton, p. 18; Saint-Simon (1967), II, p. 131.

6 Scudéry, *Galant*, p. 112.

7 Petitfils, *Montespan*, pp. 1ff.

8 Hilton, pp. 119ff.

9 Couton, p. 98.

10 Scudéry, *Sapho*, p. 43; Duchêne, *Femme*, p. 268.

11 Backer, pp. 91–2.

12 Decker, *Montespan*, p. 29.

13 La Rochefoucauld, p. 38.

14 Saint-Simon (1856), I, p. 251; Burke, p. 5; Leroy & Loyau, *Sagesse*, p. 145; Petitfils, *Louis*, p. 322.

15 Lebrun, p. 50; Gady, p. 59; Sabatier, pp. 361–6.
16 Davis, 'Women', p. 168, Saint-Maurice, pp. 71ff.
17 Lair, pp. 170–1.
18 Furetière, *Dictionnaire*, 'Légitimer'.
19 Louis, *Mémoires*, II, p. 313; Lair, pp. 176–80.
20 *Letters of a Portuguese Nun*, p. 18.
21 Kay *et al.*, p. 167.
22 Hilton, p. 55.
23 Castro, p. 56.
24 Saint-Maurice, pp. 204ff.
25 Duchêne, *Molière*, pp. 511–12.
26 Castari, p. 478; Mainardi, p. 7; Couton, p. 135.
27 Norrington, p. 153.
28 Bertière, II, Annexe 1, p. 490, 'a girl?'; Hilton, p. 71, 'most likely a girl' (Louise-Françoise).
29 Saint-Maurice, p. 527.
30 Flandrin, pp. 114–29; Grieco, p. 70; Duchêne, *Femme*, p. 223.
31 Duchêne, *Sévigné*, p. 132; Goreau, p. 107; Barker, p. 213.

CHAPTER 7 *Marriages Like Death*
1 Christout (1967), p. 118.
2 Christout (1967), p. 133,

note 179; Saint-Simon (1856), II, p. 60.
3 Pepys, IX, p. 352; Fraser, p. 235.
4 Cowen, p. 181.
5 Dunlop, p. 173.
6 Bertière, II, p. 142; Norrington, p. 194.
7 Norrington, p. 195; Saint-Maurice, p. 402.
8 *Visages du Grand Siècle*, p. 232.
9 Fraser, pp. 273ff.
10 Hartmann, p. 314.
11 La Fayette, *Mémoires*, pp. 76ff; Hartmann, pp. 326ff.
12 Dr Jean Fabre, *Sur la Vie et Principalement la Mort de Madame*; see Hartmann p. 333; Bertière, II, p. 152: 'no symptoms of poisons ... Everything points to natural death'; Barker, pp. 113ff.
13 Erlanger, p. 135.
14 Lear, pp. 157ff; Couton, pp. 103–4.
15 Lear, p. 107.
16 *Sévigné* (1955), p. 43; La Fayette, *Mémoires*, p. 9.
17 Pitts, pp. 186ff; Bouyer, pp. 206ff.
18 *Berwick*, I, pp. 75–6; Bertière, II, p. 171.
19 Wolf, p. 312.
20 Hilton, p. 92.

21 Kroll, p. 46; Liselotte Briefe, p. 51; Forster, pp. 5, xxviii.

22 Kroll, pp. 106, 14; Forster, p. 10.

23 Saint-Simon (1967), II, p. 448, Kroll, p. 18.

24 Kroll, p. 27.

25 Cruysse, p. 121.

26 Cruysse, pp. 193ff.

27 Louis, *Mémoires*, II, p. 570.

28 Bertière, II, p. 319.

29 Kroll, p. 27; Bertière, II, p. 319.

CHAPTER 8 *A Singular Position*

1 Haldane, p. 75.

2 Carré, *Vallière*, p. 183.

3 Hilton, p. 117.

4 Norton, *Sun King*, pp. 67ff.

5 Fumaroli, p. 373; Couton, p. 138; Visconti, p. 70.

6 Fumaroli, p. 370.

7 Bluche, *Louis*, p. 196; Cowen, p. 92.

8 Molière, *Tartuffe*, Act IV, scene 3.

9 Mallet-Joris, pp. 211ff; p. 217, note 1.

10 Doscot, p. 172.

11 Saint-Évremond, p. 269.

12 Bertière, II, pp. 185ff.

13 Desprat, p. 19.

14 Castelot, p. 50; Desprat, p. 236; Bandenier, p. 52.

15 Cordelier, pp. 8–9; Chandernagor, 'Maintenon', pp. 936–7.

16 *Guide Bleu: Les Antilles*, pp. 284–5.

17 Le Roy Ladurie, p. 101.

18 Leroy & Loyau, *Sagesse*, p. 41.

19 Leroy & Loyau, *Estime*, p. 28.

20 Bremond, p. 150.

21 Leroy & Loyau, *Sagesse*, pp. 37, 125.

22 Leroy & Loyau, *Sagesse*, p. 38.

23 Bray, p. 245; Mesnard, pp. 193ff.

24 Geffroy, *Maintenon*, p. 4.

25 Some kind of consummation – '*mariage gris*' as opposed to '*blanc*' – is a common verdict of historians: see Castelot, p. 43; Bertière, II, p. 226; Leroy & Loyau, *Sagesse*, p. 107.

26 *Caylus* (1908), pp. 62–3; Leroy & Loyau, *Sagesse*, p. 288; Geffroy, *Maintenon*, II, p. 328; Scudéry, *Sapho*, p. 22.

27 Saint-Simon (1967), I, pp. 94–5.

28 Castelot, p. 60 & 2 note 1.

29 Haldane, p. 42; La Rochefoucauld, p. 46.

30 Norton, *First Lady*, p. 3, note 1.

31 Bremond, p. 146; Milhiet, p. 15.

32 This seems the most certain link; see *Demoiselles*, p. 19,

which mentions the Allée but refers to the great house itself as having 'disappeared'; Petitfils, *Montespan*, p. 295.

33 See Bryant (2001), pp. 15–16, for 'subtle alterations to the original communications' and 'invented new letters'; Leroy & Loyau, *Sagesse*, p. 31; Desprat, p. 437.

34 Castelot, p. 79; Petitfils, *Montespan*, p. 117.

35 Geffroy, *Maintenon*, pp. 39, 57; see Chandernagor & Poisson, *passim*.

CHAPTER 9 *Throwing Off a Passion*

1 Petitfils, *Montespan*, p. 123.

2 Burke, p. 23; J.-P. Landry, 'Bourdaloue', *DGS*, I, p. 225.

3 Daeschler, p. 225; *Bourdaloue*, Preface; Saint-Simon (1967), I, p. 57, note 2.

4 *Bourdaloue Sermons*, p. 41; Couton, p. 123; Daeschler, pp. 284ff.

5 Wolf, p. 319.

6 Hilton, p. 139.

7 Minois, p. 303.

8 *Réflexions sur la Miséricorde*, no. 1, p. 17.

9 Minois, pp. 302ff.

10 *Sévigné* (1955), p. 97.

11 Couton, p. 141; Decker,

Montespan, pp. 132–3.

12 Decker, *Montespan*, p. 152.

13 Beaussant, *Lully*, pp. 579–92.

14 Fumaroli, p. 416.

15 *Caylus* (1986), p. 44.

16 Visconti, p. 117.

17 Solnon, *Versailles*, p. 107; Kroll, p. 91.

18 Bussy-Rabutin, II, pp. 167–9.

19 Norton, *Sun King*, p. 90; Wolf, pp. 321ff.

20 Fumaroli, p. 425; La Rochefoucauld, p. 73; Saint-Évremond, p. 21.

21 Dangeau, I, p. 34; see Bassenne, *passim*.

22 Mallet-Joris, p. 272.

23 Norton, *Sun King*, p. 91.

24 Bertière, II, p. 217.

25 Petitfils, *Vallière*, p. 293; Hilton, pp. 176ff.

26 Desprat, p. 192.

27 Chandernagor & Poisson, p. 66.

28 Dangeau, I, p. 220; Bertière, II, pp. 342ff.

29 Desprat, 1674 then not until 1679; Bertière II, end of December 1679 (when Dame d'Atour); Dulong, *Amoureuses*, 1680; Cordelier, 1680; Hilton, *c*.1680; Petitfils, *Montespan*, 'doubtless in 1680, perhaps a little earlier, perhaps a little later'.

30 Geffroy, *Maintenon*, II,
   p. 527.
31 Duprat, p. 261.
32 Desprat, p. 187.
33 *Sévigné* (1955), p. 253.

CHAPTER 10 *Madame Now*
 1 *Sévigné* (1959), p. 104.
 2 See also Mongrédien (1953);
   Mossiker (1972).
 3 Hilton, p. 187.
 4 Bluche, *Louis*, p. 275.
 5 *Sévigné* (1959), p. 120.
 6 Hilton, p. 49.
 7 Decker, *Montespan*, pp. 157ff.
 8 Mossiker, p. 223.
 9 Whittaker, pp. 104–5.
10 Saint-Simon (1967), I,
   p. 146; Bluche, *Vie
   quotidienne*, p. 41; Solnon,
   Cour, p. 360.
11 Bonneville, pp. 40ff;
   Vigarello, pp. 22ff;
   Somerset, p. 64; Saint-
   Simon (1967), I, p. 69; see
   Da Vinha, *passim*.
12 Somerset, pp. 287–8.
13 Bluche, *Louis*, p. 280.
14 Beaussant, *Lully*, p. 617, *et
   seq*.
15 Petitfils, *Montespan*, p. 246.
16 Lear, pp. 220–1; Saint-
   Simon (1856), I, p. 241;
   Brême, p. 99; Norton, *First
   Lady*, p. 75.
17 Beaussant, *Lully*, p. 617;
   Visconti, p. 155.

18 *Réflexions sur la Miséricorde*,
   no. V, p. 30.
19 Visconti, p. 155.
20 Kroll, p. 43.
21 *Journal de la Santé*, p. 387;
   Norton, *First Lady*, p. 77.
22 Kroll, pp. 37ff.
23 Kroll, p. 113.
24 See Liselotte Briefe, *passim*.
25 Spanheim, p. 45; Visconti,
   pp. 296–7.
26 Solnon, *Versailles*, pp. 119ff.
27 See Himmelfarb, pp. 307ff.
28 Chandernagor & Poisson,
   p. 50.
29 *Aumale*, p. 81.
30 Petitfils, *Montespan*, p. 232;
   Desprat, p. 212.
31 Haldane, p. 264.
32 Levron, p. 36.
33 See Solnon, *Versailles, passim*.
34 Saint-Simon (1967), I, p. 15,
   note 3.
35 Dunlop, p. 211; see Solnon,
   Versailles, p. 369, Annexe
   no. 2: 'La Cour de
   Versailles'.
36 Cortequisse, pp. 153ff.
37 See Cortequisse, Annexe,
   pp. 165–89.

CHAPTER 11 *The King's Need*
 1 Saint-Simon (1967), II,
   p. 470 & note 1; Kroll,
   p. 47.
 2 Voltaire, p. 296.
 3 Kroll, *Sophie*, pp. 178–9.

4 Chandernagor & Poisson, p. 50.

5 Wolf, p. 332.

6 Bouyer, p. 252; Pitts, p. 208.

7 Duchêne, *Femme*, p. 151; Kroll, *Sophie*, p. 120.

8 KROLL, P. 41.

9 SOLNON, *Cour*, p. 190; Bottineau, p. 290.

10 *Caylus* (1908), pp. 154ff; Desprat, pp. 215ff.

11 Desprat, pp. 216–17.

12 Dangeau, I, p. 92.

13 The following recent writers are among those who propose October 1683: Bertière, Chandernagor, Desprat, also Sarmant, AHG, to the author; but see Bryant for January 1684.

14 Chandernagor & Poisson, p. 38; Kroll, pp. 47, 49.

15 Langlois, 'Saint-Siège', pp. 33–72; Bryant, 'Maintenon', p. 33; Neveu, 'Institut', p. 141.

16 Chandernagor & Poisson, p. 47; *Aumale*, p. 81.

17 See Himmelfarb, *passim*; Sarmant, p. 344.

18 Wolf, pp. 423–4; p. 648, note 30.

19 Dangeau, I, p. 81.

20 Recent historians accept that her role has been exaggerated; see Petitfils, *Louis*, p. 478, for the effect of La Baumelle's forgeries; Goubert, p. 118; Garrison, *passim*.

21 Kroll, p. 46; Molière, *Dom Juan*, Act I, scene 1; *Vie des Français*, p. 51.

22 Burke, p. 102; Petitfils, *Louis*, p. 459.

23 Leroy & Loyau, *Estime*, p. 38.

24 *Les Petits Cahiers Secrets de Madame de Maintenon*, BMV, Registre 28; Langlois, 'Petits livres secrets', *passim*.

25 Leroy & Loyau, *Estime*, pp. 36ff.

26 Leroy & Loyau, *Estime*, p. 40; Leroy & Loyau, *Sagesse*, p. 261.

27 See *Demoiselles de Saint-Cyr*, *passim*.

28 Desprat, p. 270.

29 Leroy & Loyau, *Estime*, p. 39; *Aumale*, p. 81.

30 Milhiet, pp. 19ff; Chandernagor & Poisson, pp. 10ff.

31 Chandernagor & Poisson, pp. 33, 153.

32 Beaussant, *Artiste*, p. 245; Blanc, pp. 330ff.

33 Dubu, *Racine*, p. 117; Racine, *Esther*, Prologue.

34 Duchêne, *Sévigné*, pp. 492ff.

35 See *Journal de la Santé*, *passim*; Beaussant, *Roi-Soleil*, p. 50.

36 Forster, p. xxvi.

37 Bluche, *Louis*, pp. 468–9.

38 Wolf, pp. 443–4; Burke, p. 16.
39 Kroll, pp. 6off.
40 Visconti, p. 151.
41 Beaussant, *Roi-Soleil*, p. 115.
42 Bertière, II, p. 354.

CHAPTER 12 *Grandeurs of the World*
1 MacCarthy, 'A Hundred Thanks to God', p. 99.
2 *Sévigné* (1955), p. 313.
3 Oman, pp. 18–19.
4 Strickland, pp. 301ff; *Sévigné* (1959), p. 313.
5 Dangeau, III, p. 166.
6 Corp, 'Elizabeth Hamilton'; Saint-Simon (1967), I, pp. 216–17; Dangeau IV, *passim*.
7 Louis, *Gardens*, pp. 10ff.
8 MacDonogh, p. 139; Saint-Simon (1967), III, p. 115, note 2; Dangeau, II, p. 105.
9 Dangeau, III, p. 216.
10 Evelyn, II, p. 232; Goubert, pp. 166ff.
11 Dangeau, V, p. 180, 'Annexe sur l'Argenterie du Royaume'; pp. 261–2.
12 Bluche, *Louis*, p. 444, Leroy & Loyau, *Estime*, pp 73–5.
13 Bassenne, pp. 11ff; p. 310.
14 La Fayette, p. 159.
15 Dangeau, IV, p. 228; Kroll, p. 62.
16 Dangeau, IV, p. 230.

17 Pitts, p. 231; Bouyer, p. 231.
18 Dangeau, V, pp. 175, 198.
19 Kroll, p. 104.
20 *Caylus* (1986), p. 98.
21 Saint-Simon (1856), I, pp. 15–16.
22 Saint-Simon (1967), II, p. 442; Kroll, pp. 72ff.
23 Saint-Simon (1967), II, pp. 442–3.
24 Kroll, p. 40; Wolf, p. 284; Ariès, *Childhood*, pp. 79–80; Farmer, pp. 366ff.
25 Bluche, *Vie quotidienne*, pp. 65ff; Farmer, p. 366.
26 Farmer, p. 370.
27 See Maroteaux, *passim*; Dangeau II, pp. 90, 112; Strong, pp. 62–3; Oresko, 'Banquets', p. 75; Kroll, p. 108.
28 Racine, *Athalie*, Act II, scene 2, Barthes, p. 128.
29 Dubu, pp. 121ff.
30 Neveu, 'Institut', pp. 143ff; Pepys, IV, p. 100.
31 Kroll, pp. 64, 144 note 1, 149.
32 Melchior-Bonnet, p. 34.
33 Cornette, 'Bossuet', p. 466.

CHAPTER 13 *Becoming a Child Again*
1 Melchior-Bonnet, p. 91.
2 Oresko, 'Sabaudian Court', p. 231.
3 AST, fol. 170 (1698 nd);

Saint-Simon (1967), II,
p. 219.
4 Melchior-Bonnet, p. 76.
5 Norton, *First Lady*,
pp. 15–16; Elliott, p. 50.
6 Norton, *First Lady*, p. 60.
7 Kroll, p. 68.
8 Forster, p. 54; Gourdin,
pp. 31ff; Kroll, p. 80.
9 Carré, *Bourgogne*, p. 20;
Melchior-Bonnet, p. 81.
10 Norton, *First Lady*, pp. 64–5.
11 Forster, p. 95.
12 Norton, *First Lady*,
pp. 117–18; pp. 101ff.
13 Haussonville & Hanotaux,
I, pp. 225–6.
14 Melchior-Bonnet, pp. 34ff;
Saint-Simon (1967), II,
pp. 53, 227.
15 Kroll, p. 74.
16 Saint-Simon (1967), I,
p. 163; Forster, p. 95.
17 Maxwell, p. 46.
18 Haussonville & Hanotaux,
I, p. 225; Norton, *First Lady*,
p. 115.
19 Dubu, 'Racine the Courtier',
p. 127.
20 Bernot, p. 128; Kroll, p. 158.
21 Forster, p. 80; Bluche, *Vie
quotidienne*, p. 71.
22 Leroy & Loyau, *Sagesse*,
p. 137.
23 Lear, p. 525; Saint-Simon
(1967), I, pp. 96–8.
24 AST, fol. 170 (1698 nd).

25 Desprat, pp. 311ff; Bryant,
'Maintenon', pp. 8–9.
26 Desprat, p. 326; Saint-Simon
(1967), II, pp. 112–14.
27 Bryant, 'Maintenon', p. 8.
28 Haussonville & Hanoteaux,
I, pp. 88, 112–14.
29 Saint-Simon (1908), XX,
p. 254 & note 5; Sweetser,
pp. 107–8; Leibacher-
Ouvrard, *passim*.
30 Burke, p. 137; Duprat,
pp. 294–5; *Livres Défendus*,
FF, 21 743.
31 Leibacher-Ouvrard, p. 110.
32 Bluche, *Louis*, p. 441.
33 Desprat, p. 366.
34 Wolf, p. 509; Kroll, p. 93.
35 Saule, pp. 104–5; Forster,
p. 125.

CHAPTER 14 *Gaiety Begins to
Go*
1 AST, fol. 170 (16 Nov.
1700).
2 Norton, *First Lady*, p. 177.
3 Prescott-Wormeley, p. 202.
4 AST, fol. 170 (16 June
1698 & 22 Jan. 1702).
5 Erlanger, p. 244; Saint-
Simon (1967), I, pp. 158ff.
6 Cruysse, pp. 411ff.
7 Le Roy Ladurie, p. 52.
8 Nordmann, p. 91; Corp,
'Jacobite Court', pp. 245–8;
Saint-Simon (1967), II,
p. 316.

9 Oman, p. 195; Bryant, 'Maintenon', pp. 85–6; Blet, p. 174 (reference courtesy of Prof. Edward Corp).

10 Add. MSS, 20, 919, fol. 275; MacCarthy, 'A Hundred Thanks to God', p. 101; Sévigné (1955), p. 315.

11 Southorn, p. 7.

12 Wolf, p. 109; Norton, First Lady, p. 566.

13 AST, fol. 11 (31 Dec. 1708).

14 Add. MS 20918 fol. 31; Wolf, p. 524.

15 Carré, Bourgogne, pp. 162–3; Norton, First Lady, p. 116.

16 She did not cross 'the Rubicon', Melchior-Bonnet, pp. 155, 257; Caylus (2003), pp. 128–9.

17 Caylus (2003), p. 128.

18 Niderst, p. 278.

19 AST, fol. 11 (3 May nd).

20 Marie-Adelaide, p. 29; AST, fol. 170 (14 Mar. 1707).

21 Leroy & Loyau, Sagesse, p. 65.

22 Bertière, II, p. 413; Aumale, p. 94.

23 AHG, A1 189 fol. 249.

24 Leroy & Loyau, Estime, pp. 85, 97, 94.

25 Le Roy Ladurie, pp. 107, 210; Petitfils, Montespan, pp. 262–7, 273; Hilton, p. 297; La Liborlière, p. 171.

26 Saint-Simon (1967), I, p. 337; Hilton, p. 297.

27 Kroll, p. 104; Lair, pp. 350–1.

28 Haussonville & Hanoteaux, I, pp. 106–7.

29 Leroy & Loyau, Estime, p. 58.

30 Leroy & Loyau, Estime, p. 58.

31 See Aumale, passim; Milhiet, p. 64 & note 233, p. 218 & note 260.

32 Leroy & Loyau, Estime, pp. 19–20, 66.

33 Leroy & Loyau, Estime, p. 72.

34 Saint-Simon (1967), I, p. 353.

35 Southorn, p. 7.

36 Norton, First Lady, pp. 253–4.

37 Saint-Simon (1967), I, p. 362; Norton, First Lady, p. 253.

38 Add. MSS, 20, 918 fol. 24.

39 Loyau, Ursins Correspondance, pp. 63, 67.

40 Prescott-Wormeley, p. 206.

41 Loyau, Ursins Correspondance, p. 63.

42 Marie-Adelaide, p. 16; Saint-Simon (1967), I, p. 390.

43 Melchior-Bonnet, pp. 237ff.

44 Elliott, p. 378.

45 Saint-Simon (1967), I, p. 403; AST, fol. 98 (4 Feb. 1709 & 23 Feb. 1709); Cruysse, pp. 457–8.

46 Loyau, *Ursins Correspondance*, p. 289; Egerton MS 23, p. 133.

47 Leroy & Loyau, *Estime*, p. 278.

48 Loyau, *Ursins Correspondance*, pp. 143ff; Leroy & Loyau, *Estime*, pp. 231–3.

CHAPTER 15 *We Must Submit*

1 Leroy & Loyau, *Estime*, p. 233; Saint-Simon (1967), I, pp. 440–1.

2 AST, fol. 98 (9 Dec. 1709); Add. MS 20, 919 fol. 270; *Aumale*, p. 185; Bryant (2001), pp. 27–8; Bluche, *Louis*, p. 574; see Chandernagor, 'Maintenon', in *DGS*, II, pp. 936–7; Burke, pp. 137ff.

3 Burke, p. 137; Haldane, p. 224.

4 Barthélemy, I, pp. 29ff; Niderst, p. 271; Saint-Simon (1967) II, pp. 180ff.

5 Saint-Simon (1967), II, p. 65 & note; Kroll, p. 150.

6 Elliott, p. 406.

7 Saint-Simon (1967), II, p. 46.

8 Barthélemy, I, p. 41; AST, fol. 98 (23 June 1710 & 10 July 1710).

9 Saint-Simon (1967), II, pp. 332, 446ff; Le Roy Ladurie, p. 153.

10 Saint-Simon (1967), II, p. 185.

11 Madam Life's a piece in bloom
Death goes dogging everywhere;
She's the tenant of the room,
He's the ruffian on the stair.
  – W. E. Henley (1849–1903)

12 Kroll, pp. 146ff; Saint-Simon (1967), II, p. 143.

13 Saint-Simon (1967), II, p. 144.

14 Beaussant, *Artiste*, p. 271.

15 Kroll, p. 148.

16 Elliott, pp. 430ff.

17 Saint-Simon (1967), II, p. 297.

18 Saint-Simon (1967), II, pp. 221–2.

19 Marie-Adelaide, pp. 49–50.

20 Melchior-Bonnet, p. 266.

21 AST, fol. 98 (7 Dec. 1711); Elliott, p. 205.

22 Saint-Simon (1967), II, pp. 217–19; III, p. 321, Elliott, pp. 440ff; Melchior-Bonnet, pp. 284ff; Norton, *First Lady*, pp. 366ff.

23 Kroll, pp. 155–6; Carré, *Bourgogne*, p. 124.

24 Saint-Simon (1967), II, p. 234.

25 Kroll, *Sophie*, p. 271.

26 Saint-Simon (1967), II, p. 223.

27 Carré, *Bourgogne*, p. 219.

28 Bluche, *Vie quotidienne*, p 74.

29 Melchior-Bonnet, p. 294.

30 Adelaide is not believed to be a traitor by those who have studied her in detail; she was on the contrary 'ardent for all that concerned the honour of her husband', Geffroy, *Maintenon*, II, pp. 307–8; Norton, *First Lady*, p. 234; Prescott-Wormeley, p. 182; Elliott, p. 321.

31 Melchior-Bonnet, pp. 21, 194ff.

32 Kroll, p. 340; Voltaire, p. 340.

33 Saint-Simon (1967), II, p. 223.

CHAPTER 16 *Going on a Journey*

1 Cole, pp. 16–18.

2 Barthélemy, I, pp. 131ff.

3 Pevitt, p. 248; Wolf, p. 612.

4 Dangeau, III, p. 26; I, p. 35; Dupont-Logié, p. 51.

5 Dupont-Logié, pp. 41ff; Béguin, p. 24ff; Cessac & Couvreur, p. 9.

6 Gourdin, pp. 153ff.

7 Gourdin, p. 147.

8 Loyau, 'Double Mort', p. 295.

9 Hatton, 'Louis', p. 233.

10 For the death of Louis XIV, see Saint-Simon (1967), II, pp. 467ff; *Aumale*, pp. 198ff;

Déon, pp. 333ff; Bluche, *Louis*, p. 99.

11 Leroy & Loyau, *Estime*, p. 254; Kroll, p. 168.

12 *Aumale*, pp. 198ff.

13 Saint-Pierremond, p. 10.

14 See Loyau, 'Double Mort', *passim*.

15 Levron, pp. 52ff; Saint-Simon (1967), II, p. 501.

16 Sawkins, p. 3, Duprat, p. 12, see Massillon, *passim*.

17 Add. MSS, III, fol. 332; *Aumale*, pp. 205, 85.

18 Hatton, 'Louis', p. 260; Lebrun, 'Derniers jours', p. 50.

19 'Lettres adressées à Madame de Maintenon ...', G. 328 BMV.

20 See Tovar de Teresa for *Justo sentimento de la Santa Iglesia*, trans. Hugh Thomas.

21 *Aumale*, p. 86 & note 1; Leibacher-Ouvrard, p. 122; Langlois, 'Petits livres secrets', p. 367.

22 Milhiet, pp. 85ff.

23 Add. MSS, III, fol. 332; Saint-Simon (1967), III, p. 108; Kroll, pp. 150–1; Chandernagor & Poisson, p. 52.

24 Haldane, p. 268; Kroll, p. 187.

25 Ó Neachtain, trans. Niall

Mackenzie; for Irish see Ó Neachtain pp. 20–4.

26 *Aumale*, p. 234; Kroll, p. 245.

27 Gourdin, p. 337; Cessac & Couvreur, p. 10; Mortier, pp. 15, 20; Dupont-Logié, p. 201.

CHAPTER 17 *Never Forget*

1 Cornette, 'Bossuet', p. 467; Bussy-Rabutin, *Histoire amoureuse*, II, p. 49.

2 Doscot, p. 26; Combescot, p. 420.

3 Flaubert, p. 199, trans. Wall.

4 Racine, *Bajazet*, 2nd Preface, trans. Hollingshurst.

5 Saint-Simon (1967), I, p. 32; Erlanger, p. 53; Lear, p. 75.

6 Racine, *Athalie*, Act V, scene 8.

7 Backer, p. 16.

8 Hedley, p. 120.

9 Kroll, p. 102.

SOURCES

Place of publication of French editions is Paris and of English editions is London unless otherwise noted. Translations from French editions are my own if the name of a translator is not given; the translator's name is supplied for German, Italian and Spanish material.

ABBREVIATIONS
AHG   Archives Historiques de la Guerre, Vincennes
AN   Archives Nationales, Paris
AST   Archivio di Stato di Torino, Corte, Real Casa, Letteri principi diversi, mazzo 26, Turin
BL   British Library MSS, London
BMV   Bibliothèque Municipale, Versailles
BN   Bibliothèque Nationale MSS, rue de Richelieu, Paris

Adamson, John, ed., *The Princely Courts of Europe. Ritual Politics and Culture Under the Ancien Regime, 1500–1750*, 1999
Adamson, John, 'The Making of the Ancien-Regime Court 1500–1700', in Adamson, *Courts*
Adamson, John, 'The Tudor and Stuart Courts 1509–1717', in Adamson, *Courts*
Additional MSS, BL
Ariès, Philippe, *Centuries of Childhood*, trans. R. Baldick, pbk, 1979
Ariès, Philippe, & Bégin, André, *Western Sexuality. Practice and precept in past and present times*, trans. Anthony Forster, Oxford, pbk, 1985
[*Cahiers d'Aubigné*] 'Autour de Françoise d'Aubigné, Marquise de Maintenon', 2 vols, *Albineana*, 10 & 11, Niort, 1999
[*Aumale*] *Mémoire et lettres inédites de Mlle d'Aumale*, in Haussonville & Hanoteaux, II

Backer, Dorothy Anne, *Precious Women*, New York, 1974

Bajou, Thierry, *Paintings at Versailles. XVIIth Century*, Paris, 1998

Bandenier, Gilles, 'Onze lettres inédites de Benjamin de Vallois à Nathan d'Aubigné', in *Cahiers d'Aubigné*, I

Bardon, Françoise, 'La Thème de la Madeleine pénitente au XVIIème siècle en France', *Journal of the Warburg & Courtauld Institutes*, vol. 31, 1968

Barker, Nancy Nichols, *Brother to the Sun King. Philippe, Duke of Orléans*, Baltimore, 1989

Barthélemy, Edouard de, *Les Filles du Régent*, 2 vols, 1874

Barthes, Roland, *Sur Racine*, 1966

Bassenne, M., *La Vie tragique d'une Reine d'Espagne. Marie-Louise de Bourbon-Orléans, nièce de Louis XIV*, 1939

Beaussant, Philippe, *Louis XIV artiste*, 1999

Beaussant, Philippe, *Lully ou Le Musicien du Soleil*, 1992

Beaussant, Philippe, *Le Roi-Soleil se lève aussi*, 2000

Béguin, Katia, 'Les enjeux et les manifestations du mécénat aristocratique à l'aube du XVIIIe siècle', in Preyat, *Duchesse*

Bély, Lucien, 'Les maisons souveraines, acteurs ou instruments de l'action politique', in *La Présence des Bourbons en Europe XVI–XXIe siècle*, ed. Lucien Bély, 2005

Bernot, Jacques, *Mademoiselle de Nantes. Fille préférée de Louis XIV*, Paris, 2004

Bertière, Simone [II], *Les Femmes du Roi-Soleil. Les Reines de France au temps des Bourbons*, 1998

Bertière, Simone [I], *Les Deux Régentes. Les Reines de France au temps des Bourbons*, 1996

[*Berwick*] *Memoirs of Marshal the Duke of Berwick*, written by himself, 2 vols, 1779

Blanc, André, *Racine. Trois siècles de théâtre*, 2003

Blanning, T. C. W., *The Culture of Power and the Power of Culture. Old Regime Europe 1660–1789*, Oxford, pbk, 2003

Blet, Pierre, *Les nonces du Pape à la cour de Louis XIV*, 2002

Bluche, François, *Louis XIV*, trans. Mark Greengrass, Oxford, 1990

Bluche, François, *La Vie quotidienne au temps de Louis XIV*, 1984

Bonneville, Françoise, *Histoire du bain*, 2001

Bottineau, Yves, 'La Cour de Louis XIV à Fontainebleau', *XVIIe siècle*, vol. 24, 1954

Bourdaloue, Sermons du Père Bourdaloue, Compagnie de Jésus, T.I., Lyon, 1707

Bouyer, Christian, *La Grande Mademoiselle. La tumultueuse cousine de Louis XIV*, 2001

Brandi, Karl, *Charles V*, trans. C. V. Wedgwood, 1939

Bray, Benard, 'Madame de Maintenon épistolière: l'image des manuels éducatifs', in *Cahiers d'Aubigné*, I

Brême, Dominique, 'Portrait historié et morale du Grand Siècle', in *Visages du Grand Siècle*

Bremond, Henri, 'Madame de Maintenon et ses Directeurs', in *Divertissements devant l'arche*, 1930

Bresc-Bautier, Geneviève, ed., *The Apollo Gallery in the Louvre*, Musée du Louvre, 2004

[Bryant, 'Maintenon'] Bryant, Mark, 'Partner, Matriarch and Minister: Madame de Maintenon of France, clandestine consort, 1690–1715', in Campbell Orr, *Queenship*

[Bryant 2001] Bryant, Mark, 'Françoise d'Aubigné, Marquise de Maintenon: Religion, Power and Politics. A Study in Circles of Influence during the Later Reign of Louis XIV, 1684–1784', D. Phil. thesis, University of London, 2001

Buckley, Veronica, *Christina Queen of Sweden. The restless life of a European eccentric*, 2004

Burke, Peter, *The Fabrication of Louis XIV*, New Haven, US, pbk, 1994

Bussy-Rabutin, Comte de, *Mémoires*, 2 vols, 1857

Bussy-Rabutin, Comte de, *Histoire amoureuse des Gaules suivie de La France galante*, edn nouvelle, 2 vols, 1857

Campbell Orr, Clarissa, ed., *Queenship in Europe 1660–1815. The Role of Consort*, Cambridge, 2004

Carré, Lt. Col. Henri, *Mademoiselle de La Vallière*, 1938

Carré, Lt. Col. Henri, *La Duchesse de Bourgogne. Une princesse de Savoie à la cour de Louis XIV 1685–1712*, 1934

Castari, Nicole, 'Criminals', in Davis & Farge

Castellucio, Stéphane, 'Marly: un instrument de pouvoir enchanteur', *XVIIe siècle*, vol. 192, 1996

Castelot, André, *Madame de Maintenon. La reine secrète*, 1996

Castro, Eve de, *Les Bâtards du Soleil*, 1987

[*Caylus* 1908] *Souvenirs de Madame de Caylus*, ed. Lionel Péraux, 1908

[*Caylus* 1986] *Souvenirs de Madame de Caylus*, ed. & notes Bernard Noël, 1965 & 1986

[*Caylus* 2003] Caylus, Comtesse de, *Souvenirs sur Madame de Maintenon*, ed. Clémence Muller, 2003

Cessac, Catherine, & Couvreur, Manuel, 'Introduction', in Preyat, *Duchesse*

Chaline, Oliver, 'The Valois and Bourbon Courts *c*.1515–1750', in Adamson, *Courts*

Chandernagor, Françoise, 'Madame de Maintenon', in Chandernagor & Poisson

Chandernagor, Françoise, 'Maintenon', in *DGS*, II, pp. 936–7

[Chandernagor & Poisson] Chandernagor, Françoise, & Poisson, Georges, *Maintenon*, 2001

[Christout I] Christout, Marie-Françoise, *Le Ballet de Cour de Louis XIV 1643–1672. Mises en scène*, 1967

[Christout II] Christout, Marie-Françoise, *Le Ballet de Cour au 17e siècle. Iconographie musicale*, Geneva, 1987

Clairambault MSS, BN

Cole, Susan, 'Princess over the Water: Memoir of Louise Marie Stuart 1692–1712', Royal Stuart Society, XVIII, 1981

Combescot, Pierre, *Les petites Mazarines*, 1999

Cordelier, Jean, *Madame de Maintenon*, Préface, Gilbert Sigaux, 1970

Corneille, Pierre, *Théâtre complet, 1 & 2*, introd. & notes Jacques Maurens, 1968 & 1980

Cornette, Joël, 'L'éducation des rois à la guerre', in Cornette, *France*

Cornette, Joël, ed., *La France de la monarchie absolue. 1610–1715*, 1997

Cornette, Joël, 'La querelle Bossuet-Fénelon', in Cornette, *France*

Cornette, Joël, 'Versailles: le cérémonial de la Cour', in Cornette, *France*

Corp, Edward, 'Elizabeth Hamilton', in *DNB*

Corp, Edward, 'The Jacobite Court at Saint-Germain-en-Laye: Etiquette and the use of the Royal Apartments', in Cruickshanks

Corp, Edward, *The King over the Water. Portraits of the Stuarts in Exile after 1689*, Scottish National Portrait Gallery, Edinburgh, 2001

Cortequisse, Bruno, *Madame Louis XIV. Marie-Thérèse d'Autriche*, 1992

Couton, Georges, *La chair et l'âme. Louis XIV entre ses maîtresses et Bossuet*, Grenoble, 1995

Couvreur, Manuel, 'Voltaire chez la duchesse ou le goût à l'épreuve', in Preyat, *Duchesse*

Cowen, Pamela, *A Fanfare for the Sun King. Unfolding fans for Louis XIV*, Greenwich, 2003

Craveri, Benedetta, *L'âge de la conversation*, trans. (from Italian) Éliane Deschamps-Pria, 2002

Cruickshanks, Eveline, ed., *The Stuart Courts*, Foreword by David Starkey, Stroud, Glos., 2000

Cruysse, Dirk Van der, *Madame Palatine, Princesse Européenne*, 1988

Daeschler, R., *Bourdaloue*, 1929

Dangeau, Marquis de, *Journals*, vols I–X, 2002–5

Davis, Natalie Zemon, 'Women in Politics', in Davis & Farge

Davis, Natalie Zemon, *Society and Culture in Early Modern France. Eight Essays*, Oxford, 1987

[Davis & Farge] Davis, Natalie Zemon & Farge, Arlette, ed., *A History of Women in the West, III, Renaissance and Enlightenment Paradoxes*, Cambridge, Mass., 1993

Decker, Michel de, *Louis XIV, le bon plaisir du Roi*, 2002

Decker, Michel de, *Madame de Montespan. La grande sultane*, 1985

[*Demoiselles*] *Les Demoiselles de Saint-Cyr. Maison Royale de l'Éducation. 1686–1793*, Archives départementales des Yvelines, 1999

Déon, Michel, introd., *Louis XIV par lui-même. Morceaux choisis du roi avec introduction et commentaires*, 1991

Desaire, Jean-Paul, 'The Ambiguities of Literature', in Davis & Farge

Desprat, Jean-Paul, *Madame de Maintenon (1635–1719) ou le prix de la réputation*, 2003

[*DGS*] *Dictionnaire du Grand Siècle*, sous la direction de François Bluche, 2 vols, 1990

Dictionary of Saints, A, ed. Donald Attwater, pbk, 1979

[*DNB*] *Dictionary of National Biography*, Oxford, 2004

Doscot, Gérard, ed. & introd., *Mémoires d'Hortense et de Marie Mancini*, 1987

Doyle, William, *Jansenism*, Basingstoke, 2000

Dubu, Jean, 'Madame de Maintenon et Racine', in *Demoiselles*

Dubu, Jean, 'Racine the Courtier', *The Court Historian*, vol. 7, 2002

Duchêne, Roger, *Être femme au temps de Louis XIV*, 2004

Duchêne, Roger, *Madame de La Fayette. La romancière aux cent bras*, 1988

Duchêne, Roger, *Madame de Sévigné ou la chance d'être femme*, 2002

Duchêne, Roger, *Molière*, 1998

Dulong, Claude, *Amoureuses du Grand Siècle*, 1996

Dulong, Claude, *Anne d'Autriche*, 1980

Dulong, Claude, *Mazarin*, 1999

Dulong, Claude, *La Vie quotidienne des femmes du Grand Siècle*, 1984

Dunlop, Ian, *Louis XIV*, 1999

Dupont-Logié, Cécile, ed., 'Une journée à la cour de la Duchesse du Maine', *Musée de l'Île-de-France*. Domaine des Sceaux, 2003

Duprat, Annie, *Les rois de papier. La caricature de Henri III à Louis XIV*, 2002

Duron, Jean, Notes, *Atys, de M. de Lully, Les Arts Florissants*, Harmonia Mundi s.a., Arles, 1987

Egerton MSS, BL

Elias, Norbert, *The Civilising Process. The History of Manners*, trans. Edmund Jephcott, Oxford, 1978

Elliott, Charles, *Princesse of Versailles, The Life of Marie Adelaide of Savoy*, New York, 1992

Erlanger, Philippe, *Monsieur, Frère de Louis XIV*, 1953

Evelyn, John, F.R.S., *Diary and Correspondence ...*, new edn, 4 vols, 1850

Farmer, James Eugene, *Versailles and the Court under Louis XIV*, 1921

Flandrin, Jean-Louis, 'Sex in married life in the early Middle Ages: the Church's teaching and behavioural reality', in Ariès & Béguin

Flaubert, Gustave, *Madame Bovary*, trans. Geoffrey Wall, pbk, 2003

Forster, Elborg, trans. & introd., *A Woman's Life in the Court of the Sun King. Letters of Liselotte von der Pfalz, 1652–1722*, Baltimore, 1984

Fraser, Antonia, *King Charles II*, 1979

Fumaroli, Marc, *Le Poète et le Roi. Jean de La Fontaine en son siècle*, 1997

Furetière, Antoine, *Dictionnaire Universel, contenant tous les Mots Français ...*, 3 vols, Hague & Rotterdam, 1701

Gady, Bénédicte, 'The Reign of the Sun. Conception, Construction and Interpretation of the Apollo Gallery', trans. Michael Gibson, in Bresc-Bautier

Gaimster, David, Boland, Peter, Linnane, Steve, & Cartwright, Caroline, 'The archaeology of private life: the Dudley Castle condoms', *Post-Mediaeval Archaeology* 30 (1996), pp. 129–42

Garopon, Jean, 'Madame de Maintenon, d'après les souvenirs de Madame de Caylus', in *Cahiers d'Aubigné*, I

Garrisson, Janine, 'La révocation de l'édit de Nantes', in Cornette, *France*

Gazette de France, La

Geffroy, A., *Madame de Maintenon d'après sa correspondance authentique. Choix de ses lettres et entretiens*, 2 vols, 1887

Geffroy, A., ed. & notes, *Lettres inédites de la Princesses des Ursins*, 1859

Genlis, Madame de, *La duchesse de la Vallière, suivi de deux lettres de Mademoiselle de la Vallière*, avant-propos de Gabriel Balin, 1983

Girard, Françoise H., 'Le Système éducatif à Saint-Cyr', in *Demoiselles*

Goreau, Angeline, 'Two English women in the seventeenth century: notes for an anatomy of feminine desire', in Ariès & Béguin

Goubert, Pierre, *Louis XIV et vingt millions de Français*, 1966

Gourdin, Jean-Luc, *La Duchesse du Maine. Louise-Bénédicte de Bourbon, Princesse de Condé*, 1999

Grande Mademoiselle, La, *Mémoires*, ed. Chantal Thomas, 2001

Grasse, Marie-Christine, *Jasmine*, Grasse, 1996

Grieco, Sara F. Matthews, 'The Body, Appearance and Sexuality', in Davis & Farge

Guest, Ivor, *Le Ballet de l'Opéra de Paris. Trois siècles d'histoire et de tradition*, revised edn, 2001

Guide Bleu: Les Antilles, 1964

Guitton, Georges, 'Un conflit de direction spirituelle. Madame de Maintenon et le Père de la Chaize', *XVIIe*, no. 29, 1955

Haldane, Charlotte, *Madame de Maintenon. Uncrowned Queen of France*, 1970

Halifax: Complete Works, ed. with an introduction by J. P. Kenyon, 1969

Hamelin, Jean-Yves, Notes, *Charpentier. Salve Regina. Motets à voix seules et à deux voix*, Harmonia Mundi, Arles, 2000

Hamilton, Anthony, *Memoirs of the Comte de Gramont*, trans. Peter Quennell, introd. Cyril Hughes Hartmann, 1930

Hartmann, Cyril Hughes, *The King My Brother*, 1954

Haskins, Susan, *Mary Magdalen, Myth and Metaphor*, 1993

Hatton, R. M., 'Louis XIV and his fellow Monarchs', in Hatton, *Europe*

Hatton, Ragnhild, ed., *Louis XIV and Europe*, 1976

Hatton, Ragnhild, 'At the court of the Sun King', in A. G. Dickens, ed., *The Courts of Europe. Politics, Patronage and Royalty 1400–1800*, 1977

Haussonville, Cte d', & Hanoteaux, G., eds, *Souvenirs sur Madame de Maintenon. Madame de Maintenon à Saint-Cyr. Dernières lettres à Madame de Caylus*. [I] *Mémoire et lettres inédites de Mademoiselle d'Aumale [Aumale]*, 2 vols, n.d.

Hedley, Jo, *Seductive Visions*, Boucher Exhibition 2004

[Hilton] Hilton, Lisa, *Athénaïs. The Life of Louis XIV's Mistress, the Real Queen of France*, New York, 2002

[Hilton, *Dance*] Hilton, Wendy, *Dance at Court & Threatre. French Noble Style. 1690–1725*, 1981

Himmelfarb, Hélène, 'Les logements Versaillais de Madame de Maintenon: essai d'interprétation', in *Cahiers d'Aubigné*, II

Hufton, Olwen, *The Prospect before Her. A History of Women in Western Europe. 1500–1800*, pbk, New York, 1998

Hufton, Olwen, 'Women, Work and Family', in Davis & Farge

Jardine, Lisa, *Christopher Wren*, 2002
Journal de la Santé du Roi Louis XIV de l'année 1647 à l'année 1711, écrit par Vallot, d'Aquin et Fagon, introd. & ed. J. A. Le Roi, 1862

Kay, Sarah, Cave, Terence, & Bourne, Malcolm, *A Short History of French Literature*, Oxford, 2003
Kessel, Elisja Schutte van, 'Virgins and Mothers between Heaven and Earth', in Davis & Farge
Kleinman, Ruth, *Anne of Austria. Queen of France*, Columbus, Ohio, 1985
[Kroll] Kroll, Maria, trans. & ed., *Letters from Liselotte. Elisabeth Charlotte Princess Palatine and Duchess of Orléans*, 1970
[Kroll, *Sophie*] Kroll, Maria, *Sophie, Electress of Hanover. A personal portrait*, pbk, 1975

La Fayette, Madame de, *Mémoires sur le règne de Louis XIV. Histoire d'Henriette d'Angleterre. Mémoires de la Cour pour les années 1688 et 1689*, 2003
La Fayette, Madame de, *The Princesse de Clèves*, trans. Nancy Mitford, revised edn Leonard Tancock, pbk, 1978
La Fayette, Madame de, *The Secret History of Henrietta Princess of England ... Memoirs of the Court of France 1688–1689*, trans. J. M. Shelmerdine, 1929
Lair, J., *Louise de La Vallière et la jeunesse de Louis XIV*, 1902
La Liborlière, M. de, 'Remarques sur la novelle édition de l'Histoire du Poitou, par Thibandeau', *Bulletin de la Société des Antiquaires de l'Ouest*, 1842
Landry, J. P., 'Bossuet', *DGS* I, pp. 215–17
Langlois, (Abbé) Marcel, 'Madame de Maintenon et le Saint-Siège', *Revue de l'Histoire Ecclésiastique*, vol. 25, Louvain, 1929
Langlois, (Abbé) Marcel, 'Les petits livres secrets de Madame de Maintenon', *Revue d'histoire littéraire*, 1928
La Porte, Pierre de, Premier valet de Chambre de Louis XIV,

Mémoires contenant plusieurs particularités sur les règnes de Louis XIII et Louis XIV. 1624–1666, 2003

La Rochefoucauld, *Maxims*, trans. Leonard Tancock, pbk, 1959

Lear, H. L., *Bossuet and His Contemporaries*, 1874

Lebrun, François, 'Les derniers jours de Louis XIV', in Cornette, *France*

Lebrun, François, 'Marie Du Bois, témoin du Grand Siècle', in Cornette, *France*

Leibacher-Ouvrard, Lise, 'Sacrifice et politique satyrique: Mme de Maintenon dans les libelles diffamatoires', in *Cahiers d'Aubigné*, I

Leroy, Pierre E., & Loyau, Marcel, *L'estime et la tendresse, Mme de Maintenon, Mme de Caylus et Mme de Dangeau*, 1998

Leroy, Pierre E., & Loyau, Marcel, eds, *Madame de Maintenon: 'Comment la sagesse vient aux filles', propos d'éducation*, 1998

Le Roy Ladurie, Emmanuel, *Saint-Simon and the Court of Louis XIV*, with the collaboration of Jean-François Pitou, trans. Arthur Goldhammer, Chicago, 2001

Letters of a Portuguese Nun, trans. Lucy Norton, 1956

Levi, Anthony, *Louis XIV*, 2004

Levron, Jacques, *Les Inconnus de Versailles. Les coulisses de la Cour*, 2003

[Liselotte Briefe] Die Briefe der Liselotte von der Pfalz, Herzogin von Orléans vom Hofe des Sonnenkönigs: *Das war mein Leben*, Munich, 1951

Livres Défendus. Catalogue des livres dont la suppression a esté ordonnée par Monsieur le lieutenant général de police, Fonds Français, 21 743, BN

Loret, Jean, *La Muze Historique ou recueil des lettres en vers*, Livres IX–XI, 1658

Louis XIV, *Mémoires pour l'instruction du Dauphin* ... Notes by Charles Dreyss, 2 vols, 1860

Louis XIV, *The Way to Present the Gardens of Versailles*, trans. J. F. Stewart, Paris, 1992

Loyau, Marcel, 'Madame de Maintenon et la double mort de Louis XIV', in *Cahiers d'Aubigné*, II

Loyau, Marcel, ed., *Madame de Maintenon et la Princesse des Ursins. Correspondance 1709. Une année tragique*, 2002

MacCarthy, Diarmaid, 'A Hundred Thanks to God', included in *The Poems of David Ó Bruadair*, ed. John C. MacErlean, 3 vols, 1910–1917

MacDonogh, Katharine, *Reigning Cats and Dogs*, 1999

McNamara, Jo Ann Kay, *Sisters in Arms. Catholic Nuns through Two Millennia*, Cambridge, Mass., 1996

Mainardi, Patricia, *Husbands, Wives and Lovers. Marriage and Its Discontents in Nineteenth Century France*, New Haven, 2003

[Maintenon] *Les Petits Cahiers Secrets de Mme de Maintenon*, 8 vols, BMV

[Maintenon] *Madame de Maintenon à Saint-Cyr*, in Haussonville & Hanoteaux, I

[Maintenon] 'Lettres adressées à Madame de Maintenon à la suite de la mort de Louis XIV', G. 328, BMV

Mallet-Joris, Françoise, *Marie Mancini. Le premier amour de Louis XIV*, 1998

Marie-Adelaide de Savoie, Duchesse de Bourgogne, *Lettres inédites. Précédées d'une notice sur sa vie*, 1850

Maroteaux, Vincent, *Marly. L'autre Palais du Soleil*, Geneva, 2002

Massillon, François, *Oraison funèbre de Louis XIV*, ed. Paul Aizpurua, Grenoble, 2004

Matoré, Georges, 'Amour (Vocabulaire d'); Galant, Galanterie', in *DGS*, I, pp. 72–3; pp. 632–3

Maximes d'Éducation et Direction Puerile. Des devotions, meurs, actions, occupations, divertissemens, Jeux et petit Estude de Monseigneur le Daufin. Jusgue a laage de sept ans, Fonds Français, 19043, BN

Maxwell, Constantia, *The English Traveller in France 1698–1815*, 1932

Melchior-Bonnet, Sabine, *Louis et Marie-Adelaide de Bourgogne. La vertu et la grâce*, 2002

Mesnard, Jean, 'Françoise d'Aubigné et le Chevalier de Méré', in *Cahiers d'Aubigné*, I

Meyer, Jean, *L'éducation des princes du XVe au XIXe siècle*, 2004

Meyer, Jean, *Bossuet*, 1993

Milhiet, Jean-Joseph, 'Historique de la maison royale de Saint-Louis', in *Demoiselles*

Miller, John, *Bourbon and Stuart. Kings and Kingship in France and England in the Seventeenth Century*, 1987

Minois, Georges, *Bossuet. Entre Dieu et le Soleil*, 2003

Mitford, Nancy, *The Sun King*, 1966

Molière, *Le Bourgeois Gentilhomme*, Préface et Notes, Jacques Morel, 1985, 1999

Molière, *Don Juan*, trans. Neil Bartlett, 2004

Molière, *Les Précieuses ridicules*, introd. & notes, Claude Bourqui, 1999

Molière, *Tartuffe and other plays*, trans. Donald M. Frame, New York, 1967

Mongrédien, Georges, *Madame de Montespan et l'Affaire des Poisons*, 1953

Mortier, Roland, 'La Gurte de Sceaux, les écrivains de la duchesse du Maine', see Preyat, *Duchesse*

Mossiker, Frances, *The Affair of the Poisons*, 1972

Motteville, Madame de, *Mémoires sur Anne d'Autriche et sa Cour*, nouvelle edn, 4 vols, 1855

Muhlstein, *Reines éphémères, mères perpétuelles. Catherine de Médicis, Marie de Médicis, Anne d'Autriche*, 2001

Nahoum-Grappe, Véronique, 'The Beautiful Woman', in Davis & Farge

Neveu, Bruno, 'Du culte de Saint-Louis à la glorification de Louis XIV: la maison royale de Saint-Cyr', *Journal des Savants*, July–Dec., 1988

Neveu, Bruno, 'Institut religieux, fondation royale et mémorial dynastique', in *Demoiselles*

Niderst, Alain, 'Madame de Maintenon et la guerre de Succession d'Espagne', in *Cahiers d'Aubigné*, II

Nordmann, Claude, 'Louis XIV and the Jacobites', in Hatton, *Europe*

Norrington, Ruth, ed. & commentary, *My dearest Minette. Letters between Charles II and his sister, the Duchesse d'Orléans*, 1996

Norton, Lucy, *First Lady of Versailles. Marie Adelaide of Savoy. Dauphine of France*, 1978

Norton, Lucy, *The Sun King and His Loves*, The Folio Society, 1982

Oman, Carola, *Mary of Modena*, 1962

Ó Neachtain, Seán, 'The Grievous Occasion of my Tears (A Lament for the wife of King James II)', *The Poetry of Seán Ó Neachtain (Pt I)*, Dublin, 1911

Oresko, Robert, 'Banquets princiers à la cour de Turin, sous le règne de Victor-Amédée II, 1675–1730', in *Tables Royales et Festins de Cour en Europe 1661–1789*, ed. Catherine Arminjon & Béatrix Saule, 2004

Oresko, Robert, 'Maria Giovanna Battista of Savoy-Nemours (1644–1724): daughter, consort and Regent of Savoy', in Campbell Orr, *Queenship*

Oresko, Robert, 'The Marriages of the Nieces of Cardinal Mazarin. Public Policy and Private Strategy in Seventeenth-century Europe', *Frankreich im Europäisches Staatensystem der Frühen Neuzeit*, Deutsches Historisches Institut, Paris, 1995

Oresko, Robert, 'The Sabaudian Court 1563–1750', *see* Adamson, *Courts*

[Ormesson] *Journal d'Olivier Lefèvre d'Ormesson*, ed. M. Chéruel, 2 vols, 1850

Pepys, Samuel, *Diaries*, vols. IV & IX, 1668–1669, ed. Robert Latham & William Matthews, 1971, 1976

Petitfils, Jean-Christian, *Louis XIV*, introd. Pierre Goubert, 1997

Petitfils, Jean-Christian, *Louise de La Vallière*, 1990

Petitfils, Jean-Christain, *Madame de Montespan*, 1988

Petitfils, Jean-Christian, *Le Masque de Fer. Entre histoire et légende*, 2003

Pevitt, Christine, *The Man Who Would Be King. The Life of Philippe d'Orléans Regent of France. 1674–1723*, 1997

Piéjus, Annie, 'La Musique des Demoiselles', in *Demoiselles*

Pitts, Vincent J., *La Grande Mademoiselle at the Court of France 1627–1688*, Baltimore, 2000

Poisson, Georges, 'Le château de Maintenon, sept siècles d'histoire', in Chandernagor & Poisson

Prescott-Wormeley, Katharine, ed., *The Correspondence of Madame Princess Palatine, Marie-Adelaide de Savoie, and of Madame de Maintenon*, introd. C.-A. Sainte-Beuve, 1899

Preyat, Fabrice, ed., *La Duchesse du Maine (1676–1753). Une mécène à la croisée des arts et des siècles*. Études sur le XVIIIe siècle, Brussels, 2003

Quirey, Belinda, *May I Have the Pleasure? The Story of Popular Dancing*, reprint, 1987

Racine, Jean, *Bajazet*, trans. Alan Hollinghurst, 1991

Racine, Jean, *Complete Plays*, trans. Samuel Solomon, 2 vols, New York, 1967

Racine, Jean, *Théâtre complet*, ed. Jean-Pierre Collinet, 2 vols, 1983

Réflexions sur La Miséricorde de Dieu par Soeur Louise de la Miséricorde, Religieuse Carmelite, nommée dans le monde Duchesse de La Vallière, Brussels, 1712

Rohou, Jean, *Jean Racine. Entre sa carrière, son oeuvre et son Dieu*, 1992

Sabatier, Gérard, 'Charles Le Brun, peintre officiel', in Cornette, *France*

Sackville-West, V., *Daughter of France. The life of Anne Marie Louise d'Orléans, duchesse de Montpensier, 1627–1693. La Grande Mademoiselle*, 1959

Saint-André, Claude, *Henriette d'Angleterre et la Cour de Louis XIV*, 1931

[Saint-Évremonde] *The Letters of Saint-Évremonde. Charles Marguetel de Saint-Denis, Seigneur de Saint-Évremond*, ed. & introd. John Hayward, 1930

Saint-Maurice, Marquis de, *Lettres sur la Cour de Louis XIV 1667–1670*, ed. Jean Lemoine, 2 vols, 1910

[Saint-Simon 1856] *Mémoires complets et authentiques du Duc de Saint-Simon ... collationné sur le manuscrit original par M. Chéruel et précédés d'une notice par M. Sainte-Beuve ...*, 13 vols, 1856

[Saint-Simon 1908] *Mémoires de Saint-Simon*, ed. A. de Boislisle, 20 vols, 1908

[Saint-Simon 1967] Saint-Simon, Duc de, *Historical Memoirs*, 3 vols, ed. & trans. Lucy Norton, 1967–72

Sarmant, Thierry, *Les Demeures du Soleil: Louis XIV, Louvois et le surintendance des Bâtiments du roi*, 2003

Sarti, Rafaella, *Europe at Home. Family and Material Culture. 1500–1800*, New Haven, 2002

Saule, Béatrix, *La Journée de Louis XIV. 16 novembre 1700*, 1996

Sawkins, Lionel, 'Music in France 1680–1770', *Les Délices d'un Roi. Music for Versailles*, 2004

Scudéry, Madeleine de, *The Story of Sapho*, trans. & introd. Karen Newman, Chicago, 2003

Scudéry, Madeleine de, *Clélie, histoire romaine*, 3 pts, ed. Chantal Morlet-Chantalat, 2001–3

Scudéry, Madeleine de, *De l'air galant et autre Conversations (1653–1684)*, ed. Dephine Denis, 1998

[Sévigné 1955] *Letters from Madame de Sévigné*, trans. Violet Hammersley, 1955

[Sévigné 1959] *Selected Letters of Madame de Sévigné*, trans. & ed. H. T. Barnwell, 1959

Solnon, Jean-François, *La Cour de France*, 1987

Solnon, Jean-François, *Histoire de Versailles*, pbk, 2003

Somerset, Anne, *The Affair of the Poisons. Murder, Infanticide & Satanism at the Court of Louis XIV*, 2003

Sonnet, Martine, 'A Daughter to Educate', in Davis & Farge

Southorn, Janet, 'Mary of Modena, Queen Consort of James II and VII', Royal Stuart Papers, XL, 1992

Spanheim, Ézéchiel, *Relation de la Cour de France en 1690*, ed. Émile Bourgeois & Michel Richard, 1973

Strickland, Agnes, *Lives of the Queens of England*, VI, reprint Bath, 1972

Strong, Roy, *Feasts. A History of Grand Eating*, 2002

Tannahill, Reay, *Sex in History*, pbk, 1989

Teissier, Octave, *Histoire de la Commune de Cotignac*, Marseille 1860, 1979 reprint

Tovar de Teresa, Guillermo, ed., *Bibliografica Novohispana de Arte*, Segunda Parte, Mexico, 1980, for *Justo sentimento de la Santa*

Iglesia Cathedral de Valladollid en Las Indias, Reyno de Mechoacau ... Luis XIV el Grande

Verney, Margaret M., *Memoirs of the Verney Family*, vols III & IV, 1894 & 1899
Vie des Français au temps du Roi-Soleil, L'Histoire au Quotidien, ed. François Trassard, 2002
Vigarello, Georges, *Concepts of Cleanliness. Changing attitudes in France since the Middle Ages*, trans. Jean Birrell, Cambridge, UK, 1988
Vinha, Mathieu da, *Le valets de chambre de Louis XIV*, 2004
Visages du Grand Siècle: Le portrait français sous le règne de Louis XIV. 1660–1715, Musée des Beaux Arts de Nantes, Nantes, 1997
[Visconti] *Mémoires de Primi Visconti sur la cour de Louis XIV 1673–1681*, introd. & notes Jean-François Solnon, 1988
Voltaire, *Le Siècle de Louis XIV*, 1910

Whittaker, Katie, *Mad Madge. Margaret Cavendish, Duchess of Newcastle, Royalist, Writer and Romantic*, 2003
Wolf, John B., *Louis XIV*, 1968

Ziegler, Gilette, *The Court of Versailles in the Reign of Louis XIV*, trans. Simon Watson Taylor, 1966

INDEX

also available from
THE ORION PUBLISHING GROUP

———————

☐ **Love and Louis XIV** £9.99
ANTONIA FRASER
978-0-7538-2293-7

☐ **Marie Antoinette** £9.99
ANTONIA FRASER
978-0-7538-1305-8

☐ **King Charles II** £9.99
ANTONIA FRASER
978-0-7538-1403-1

☐ **Mary Queen of Scots** £9.99
ANTONIA FRASER
978-1-8421-2634-9

☐ **The Six Wives of Henry VIII**
£9.99
ANTONIA FRASER
978-1-8421-2633-2

☐ **The Weaker Vessel** £9.99
ANTONIA FRASER
978-1-8421-2635-6

☐ **The Warrior Queens** £8.99
ANTONIA FRASER
978-1-8421-2636-3

☐ **The Gunpowder Plot** £9.99
ANTONIA FRASER
978-0-7538-1401-7

☐ **Cromwell** £10.99
ANTONIA FRASER
978-0-7538-1331-7

All Orion/Phoenix titles are available at your local bookshop or from the following address:

Mail Order Department
Littlehampton Book Services
FREEPOST BR535
Worthing, West Sussex, BN13 3BR
telephone 01903 828503, *facsimile* 01903 828802
e-mail MailOrders@lbsltd.co.uk
(Please ensure that you include full postal address details)

Payment can be made either by credit/debit card (Visa, Mastercard, Access and Switch accepted) or by sending a £ Sterling cheque or postal order made payable to *Littlehampton Book Services*.
DO NOT SEND CASH OR CURRENCY.

Please add the following to cover postage and packing

UK and BFPO:
£1.50 for the first book, and 50p for each additional book to a maximum of £3.50

Overseas and Eire:
£2.50 for the first book plus £1.00 for the second book and 50p for each additional book ordered

---

BLOCK CAPITALS PLEASE

name of cardholder ....

delivery address
(if different from cardholder)

address of cardholder ....

....

....

....

postcode ....

postcode ....

☐ I enclose my remittance for £...............................

☐ please debit my Mastercard/Visa/Access/Switch (delete as appropriate)

card number ☐☐☐☐☐☐☐☐☐☐☐☐☐☐☐☐☐☐

expiry date ☐☐☐☐   Switch issue no. ☐☐

signature ....

prices and availability are subject to change without notice